W9-CHV-195

Boys Over Flowers
Hana Yori Dango
Vol. #11
Shôjo Edition

**Story and Art by
Yoko Kamio**

**English Adaptation by
Gerard Jones**

Translation/JN Productions
Touch-up Art & Lettering/Stephen Dutro
Cover & Interior Design/Yuki Ameda
Editor/Ian Robertson

Managing Editor/Annette Roman
Director of Production/Noboru Watanabe
Editorial Director/Alvin Lu
Sr. Director of Acquisitions/Rika Inouyé
Vice President of Sales & Marketing/Liza Coppola
Executive Vice President/Hyoe Narita
Publisher/Seiji Horibuchi

HANA-YORI DANGO ©1992 by YOKO KAMIO
All rights reserved. First published in Japan in 1992 by
SHUEISHA Inc., Tokyo. English translation rights in the
United States of America and Canada arranged by
SHUEISHA Inc. through CLOVERWAY INC. The stories,
characters and incidents mentioned in this publication are
entirely fictional.

Printed in Canada.

Published by VIZ, LLC
P.O. Box 77010
San Francisco, CA 94107

10 9 8 7 6 5 4 3 2 1
First printing, March 2005

PARENTAL ADVISORY
BOYS OVER FLOWERS is rated T for Teen.
May contain sexual themes.
Recommended for ages 13 and up.

VIZ

store.viz.com

www.viz.com

Story thus far

Tsukasa flies back to Japan after discovering the true identity of Tsukushi's Kinsan. At first, Tsukushi refuses to believe him, but she is forced to accept that Kinsan is actually the son of a powerful Dietman in the Japanese Parliament. He had tried, several times, to correct her mistaken impression of him, but was unable to because she had cut him off each time.

Kinsan invites Tsukushi to a party that his father is holding for him. His father intends to introduce him to the public and the press as his heir, but Kinsan intends to use that opportunity to make it clear to everyone that he has no intention of following in his father's footsteps. Since Tsukushi can't convince her friend Yuki to go with her she ends up going with Rui Hanazawa.

The party is a grand affair, and whom should she meet there, but Tsukasa! When Kinsan's father finally introduces his son, we learn for the first time that his real name is Seinosuke Amakusa. Seinosuke takes the mic and makes his shocking disclosure. He then goes on to say that he will introduce the girl he would like to marry one day. When he heads directly for Tsukushi, Tsukasa jumps in to beat him up. The media have a field day, and Tsukushi ends up in the headlines and on the TV news the next morning.

Tsukasa can neither declare himself to Tsukushi, nor give her up. He decides that she is not a good match for him because she comes from such a poor family, but she could overcome that if she had some sort of "title" which would make people see that she was "right" for him. When she comes to him to borrow a million yen to pay off her father's debt, he gets an idea. He'll lend her the money if she will enter a beauty contest held on Christmas Eve. She can pay off her debt by winning the contest and giving him the prize of a million yen!

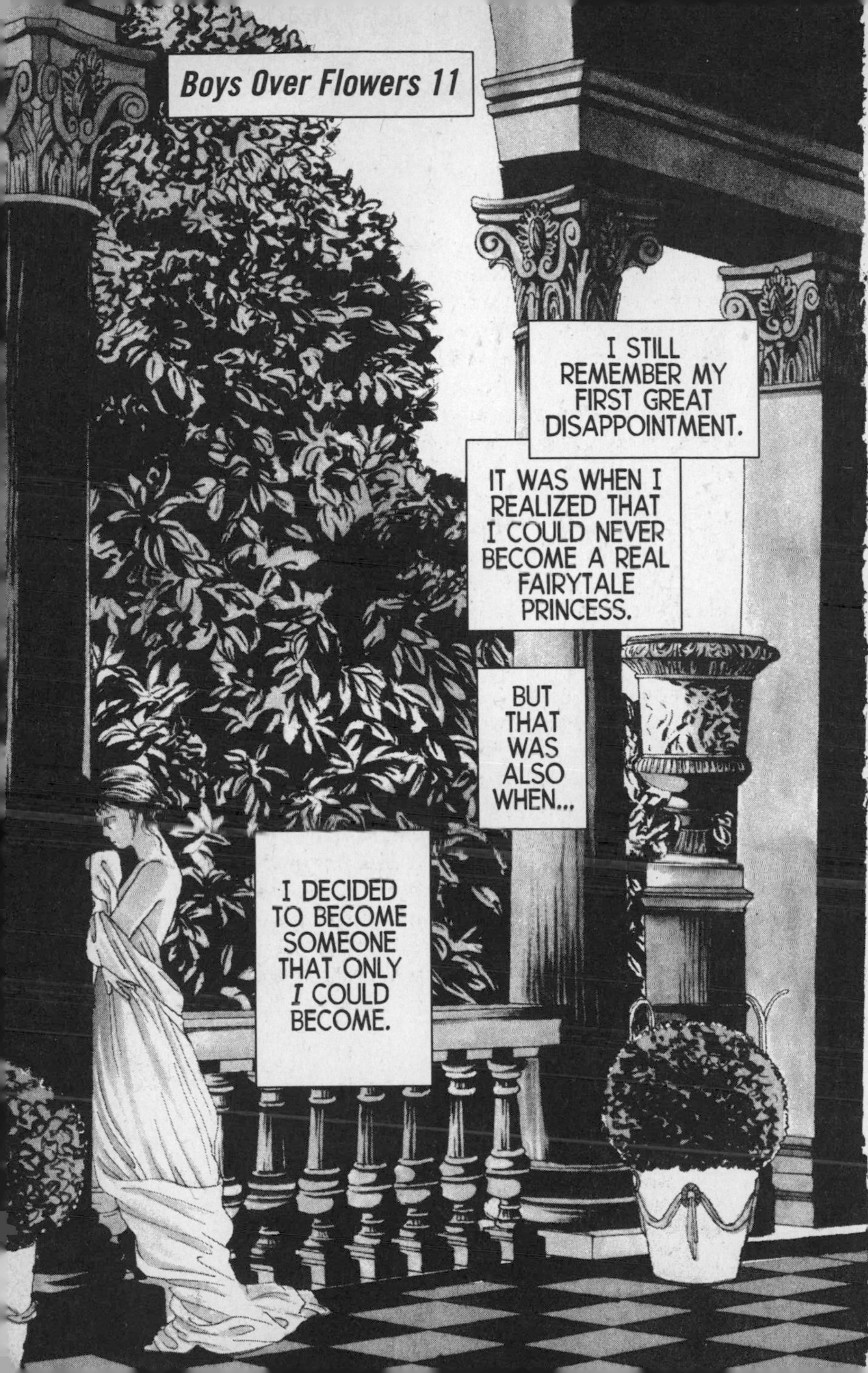
Boys Over Flowers 11
I STILL REMEMBER MY FIRST GREAT DISAPPOINTMENT.
IT WAS WHEN I REALIZED THAT I COULD NEVER BECOME A REAL FAIRYTALE PRINCESS.
BUT THAT WAS ALSO WHEN...
I DECIDED TO BECOME SOMEONE THAT ONLY *I* COULD BECOME.

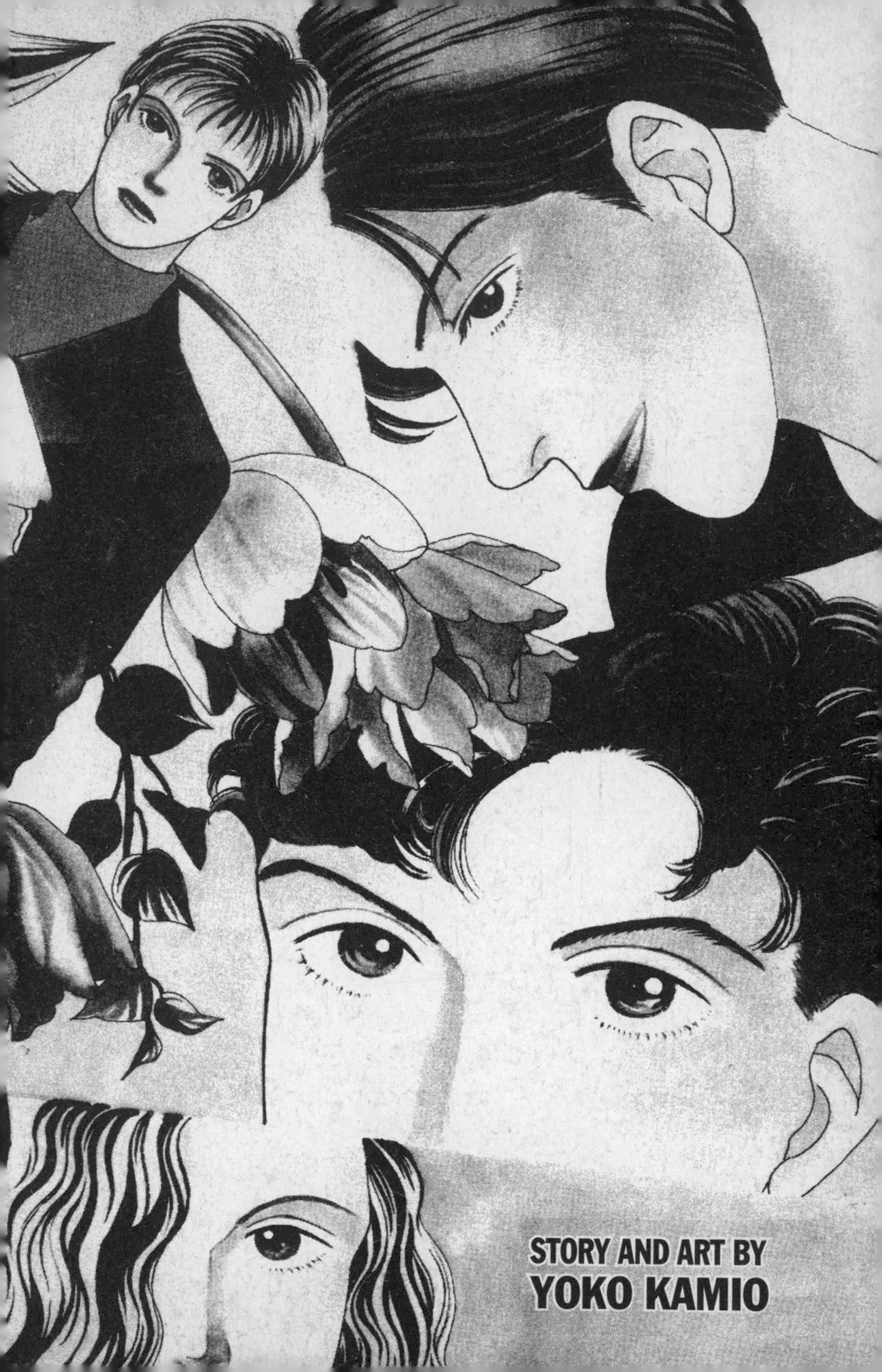
STORY AND ART BY
YOKO KAMIO

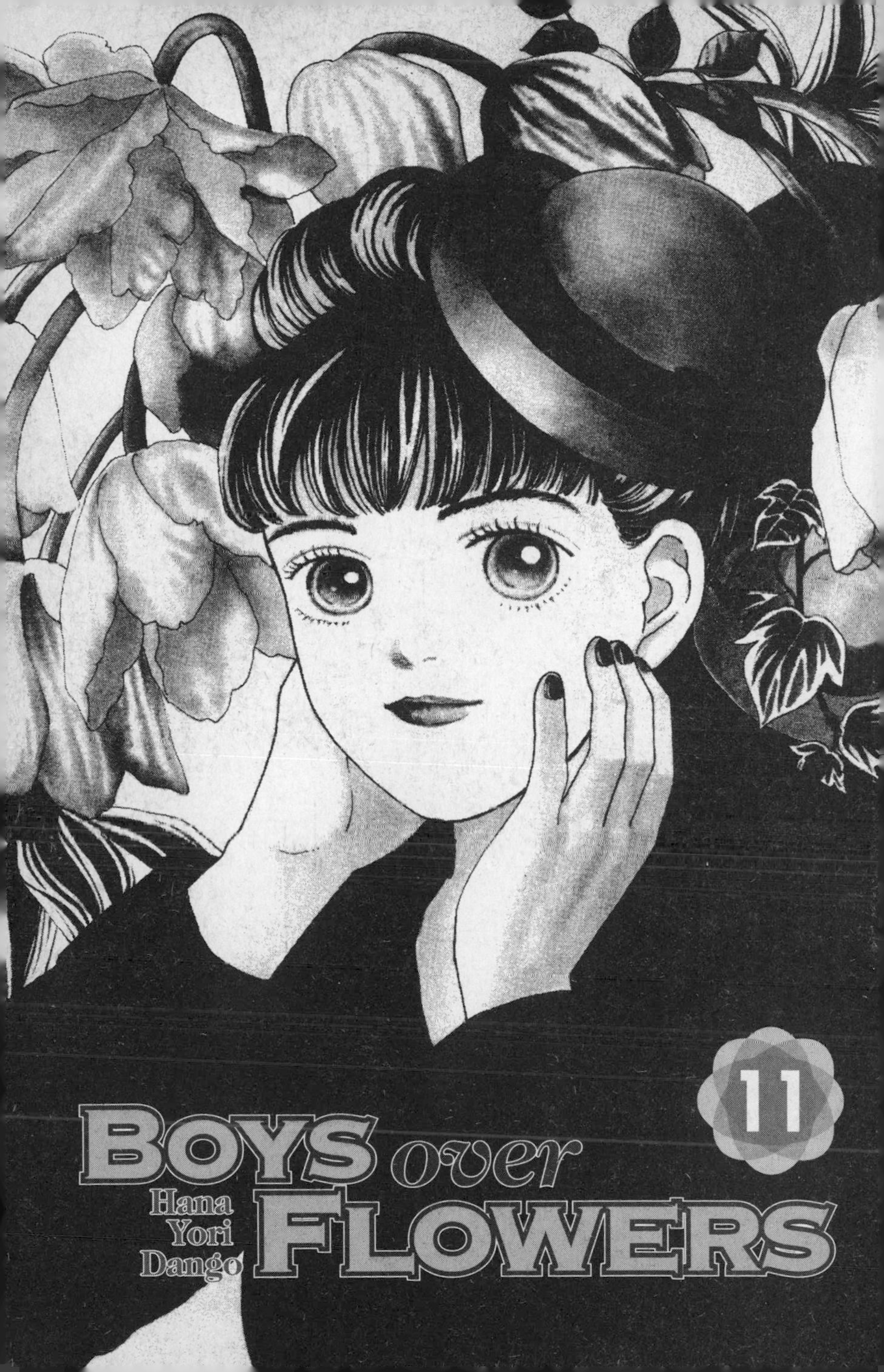
11
BOYS over FLOWERS
Hana Yori Dango

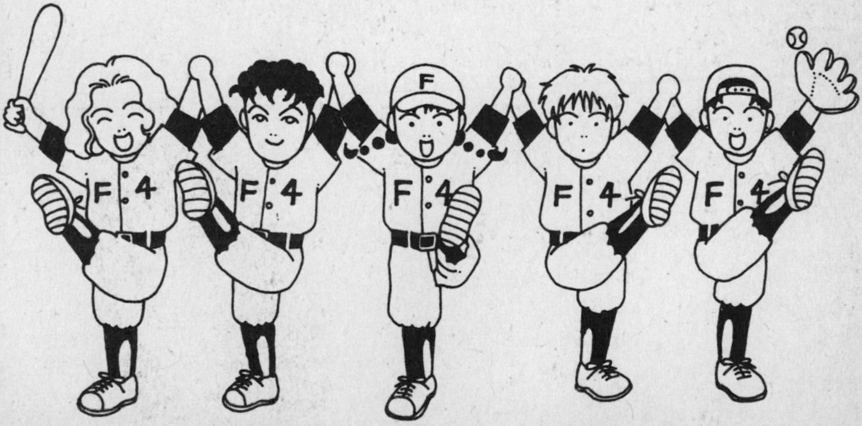
F
F 4
F 4
F 4
F 4
F 4

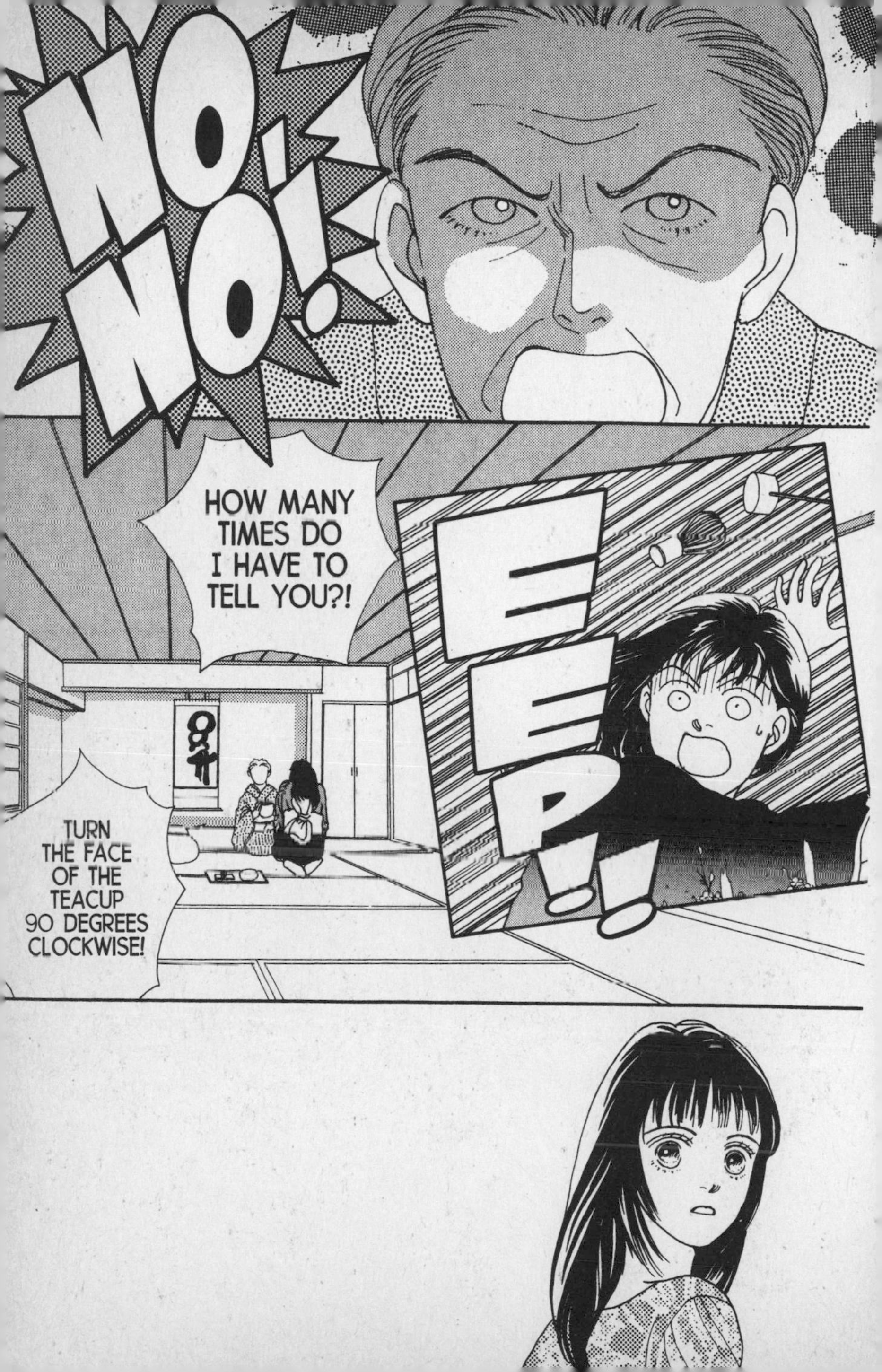
NO! NO!
HOW MANY TIMES DO I HAVE TO TELL YOU?!
EEEP!
TURN THE FACE OF THE TEACUP 90 DEGREES CLOCKWISE!

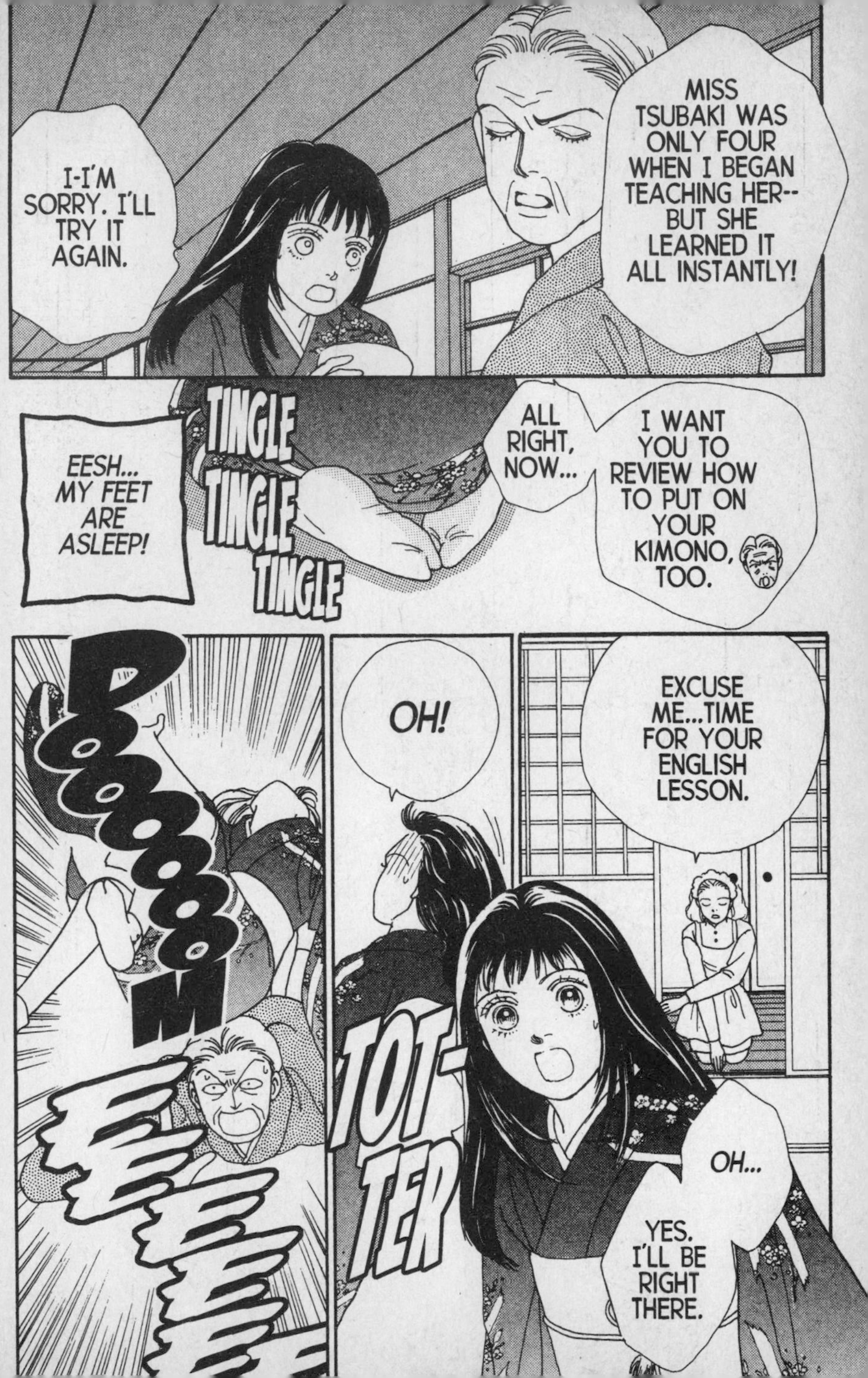
MISS TSUBAKI WAS ONLY FOUR WHEN I BEGAN TEACHING HER-- BUT SHE LEARNED IT ALL INSTANTLY!
I-I'M SORRY. I'LL TRY IT AGAIN.
ALL RIGHT, NOW...
I WANT YOU TO REVIEW HOW TO PUT ON YOUR KIMONO, TOO.
TINGLE TINGLE TINGLE
EESH... MY FEET ARE ASLEEP!
EXCUSE ME...TIME FOR YOUR ENGLISH LESSON.
OH...
YES. I'LL BE RIGHT THERE.
OH!
TOT-TER

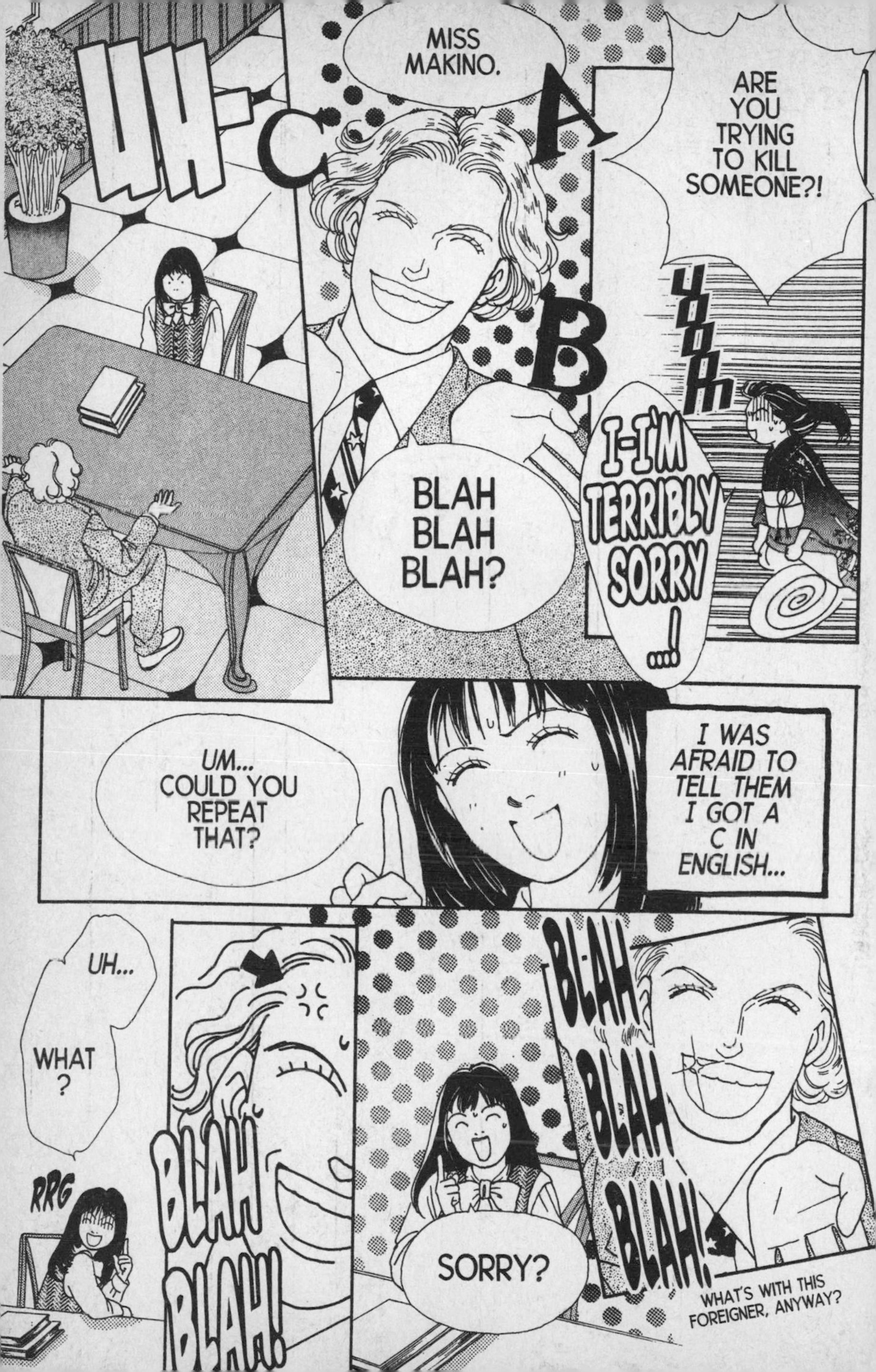
ARE YOU TRYING TO KILL SOMEONE?!
I-I'M TERRIBLY SORRY ...!
MISS MAKINO.
A
B
BLAH BLAH BLAH?
C
UH-
I WAS AFRAID TO TELL THEM I GOT A C IN ENGLISH...
UM... COULD YOU REPEAT THAT?
BLAH BLAH BLAH!
SORRY?
WHAT'S WITH THIS FOREIGNER, ANYWAY?
BLAH BLAH!
UH...
WHAT?
RRG

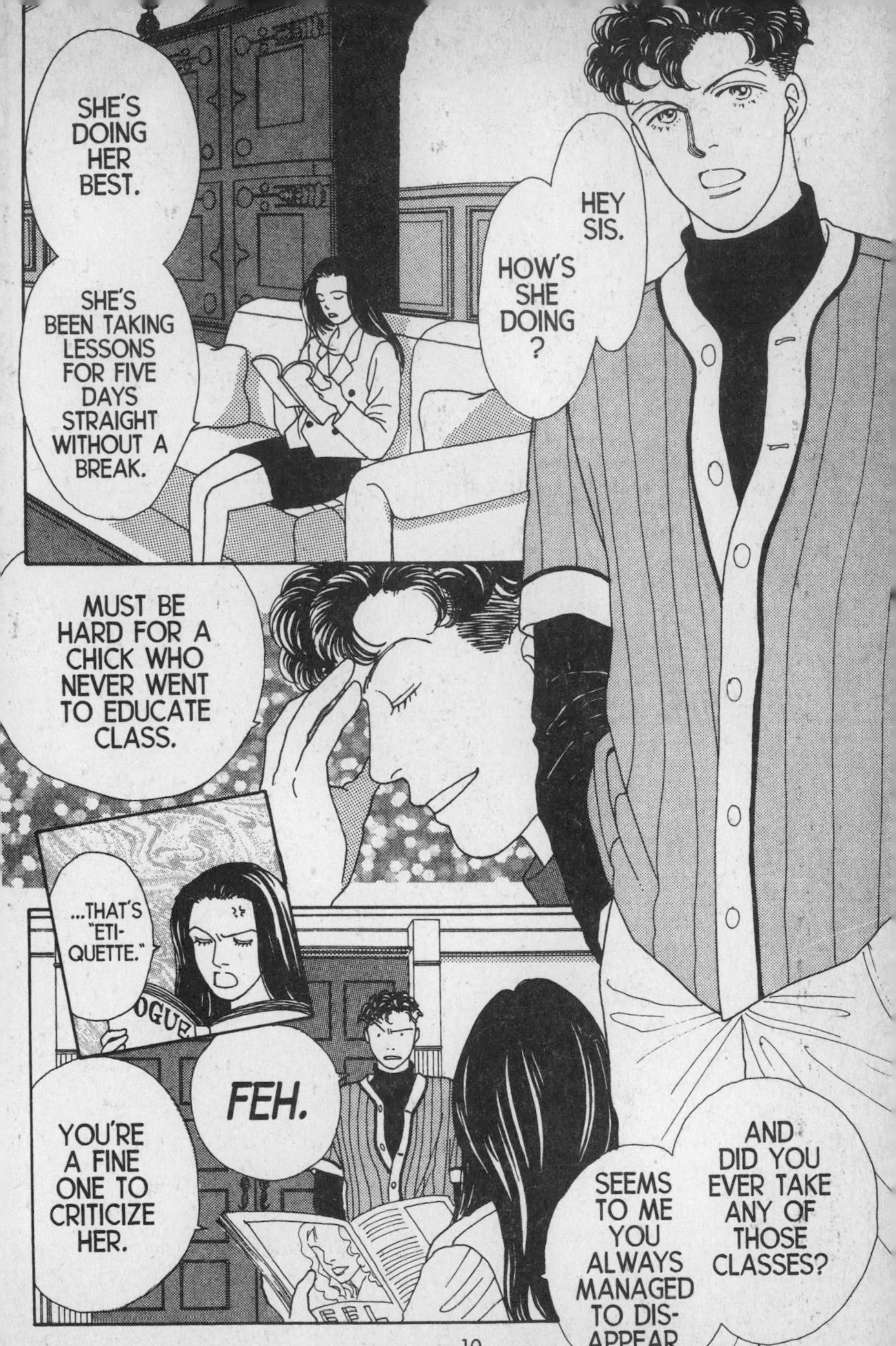
HEY SIS.
HOW'S SHE DOING?
SHE'S DOING HER BEST.
SHE'S BEEN TAKING LESSONS FOR FIVE DAYS STRAIGHT WITHOUT A BREAK.
MUST BE HARD FOR A CHICK WHO NEVER WENT TO EDUCATE CLASS.
...THAT'S "ETI-QUETTE."
YOU'RE A FINE ONE TO CRITICIZE HER.
AND DID YOU EVER TAKE ANY OF THOSE CLASSES?
SEEMS TO ME YOU ALWAYS MANAGED TO DIS-APPEAR.
FEH.

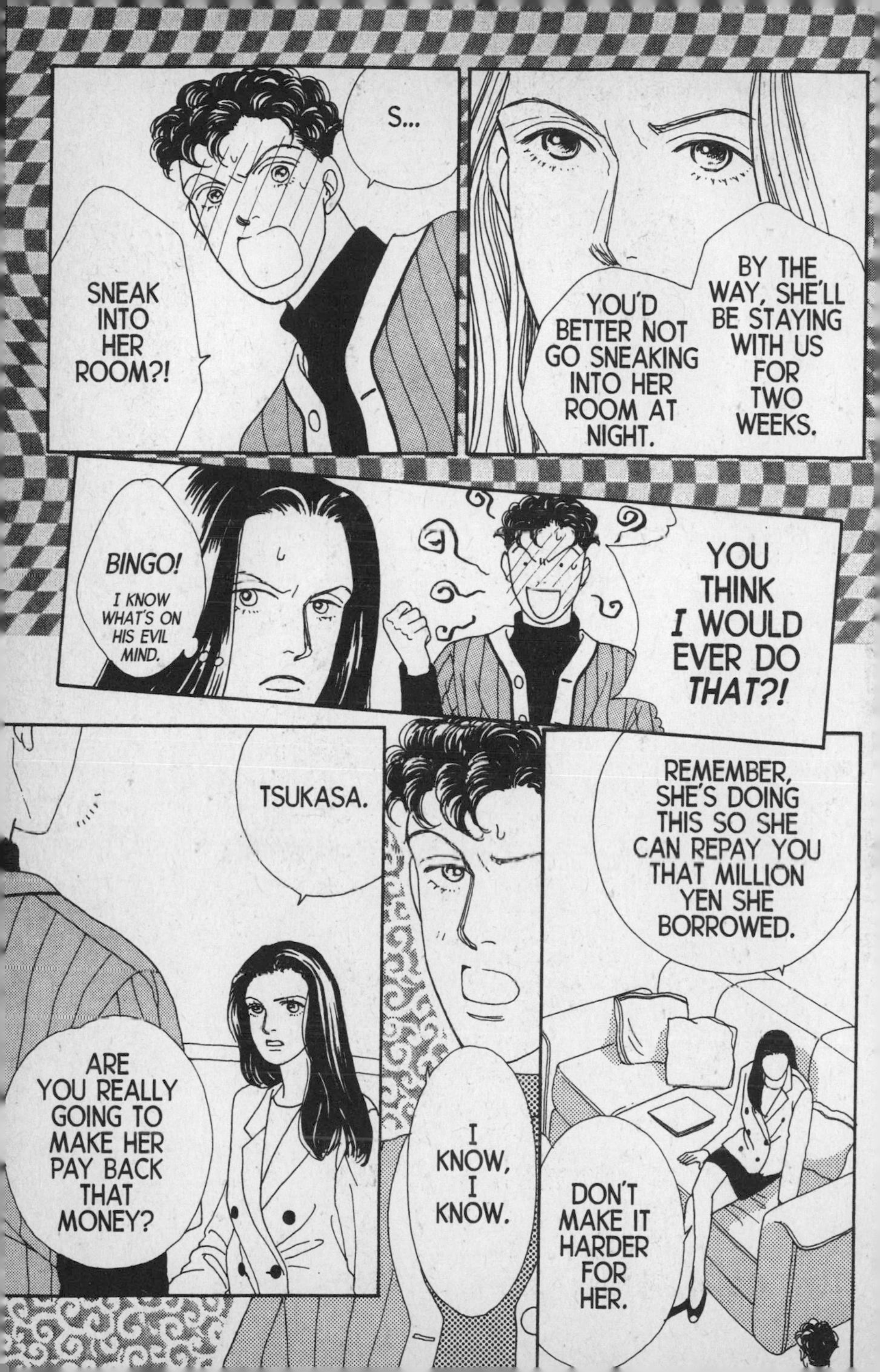
BY THE WAY, SHE'LL BE STAYING WITH US FOR TWO WEEKS.
YOU'D BETTER NOT GO SNEAKING INTO HER ROOM AT NIGHT.
S...
SNEAK INTO HER ROOM?!
YOU THINK *I* WOULD EVER DO *THAT?!*
BINGO!
I KNOW WHAT'S ON HIS EVIL MIND.
REMEMBER, SHE'S DOING THIS SO SHE CAN REPAY YOU THAT MILLION YEN SHE BORROWED.
DON'T MAKE IT HARDER FOR HER.
I KNOW, I KNOW.
TSUKASA.
ARE YOU REALLY GOING TO MAKE HER PAY BACK THAT MONEY?

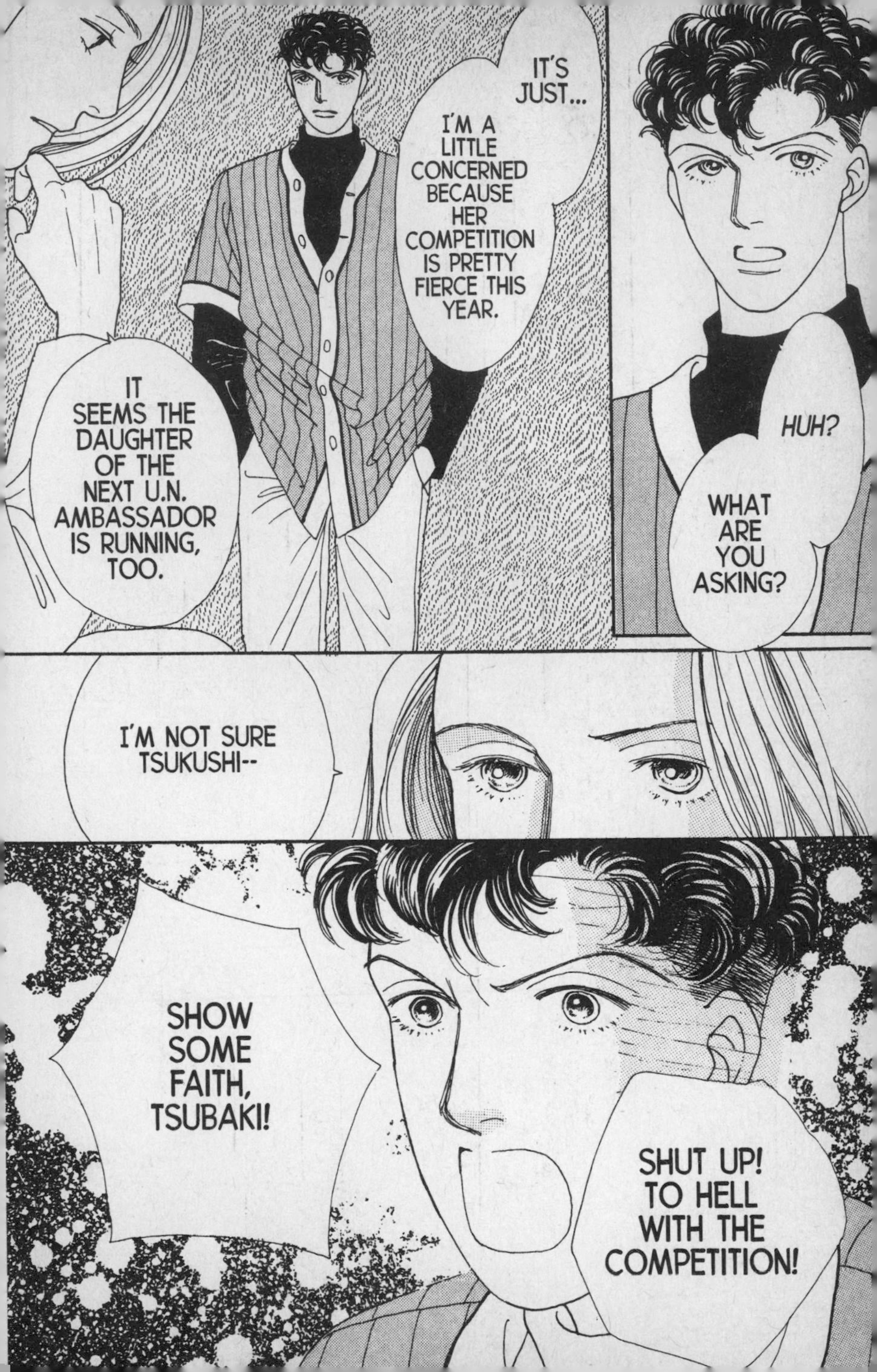
HUH?
WHAT ARE YOU ASKING?
IT'S JUST...
I'M A LITTLE CONCERNED BECAUSE HER COMPETITION IS PRETTY FIERCE THIS YEAR.
IT SEEMS THE DAUGHTER OF THE NEXT U.N. AMBASSADOR IS RUNNING, TOO.
I'M NOT SURE TSUKUSHI--
SHUT UP! TO HELL WITH THE COMPETITION!
SHOW SOME FAITH, TSUBAKI!

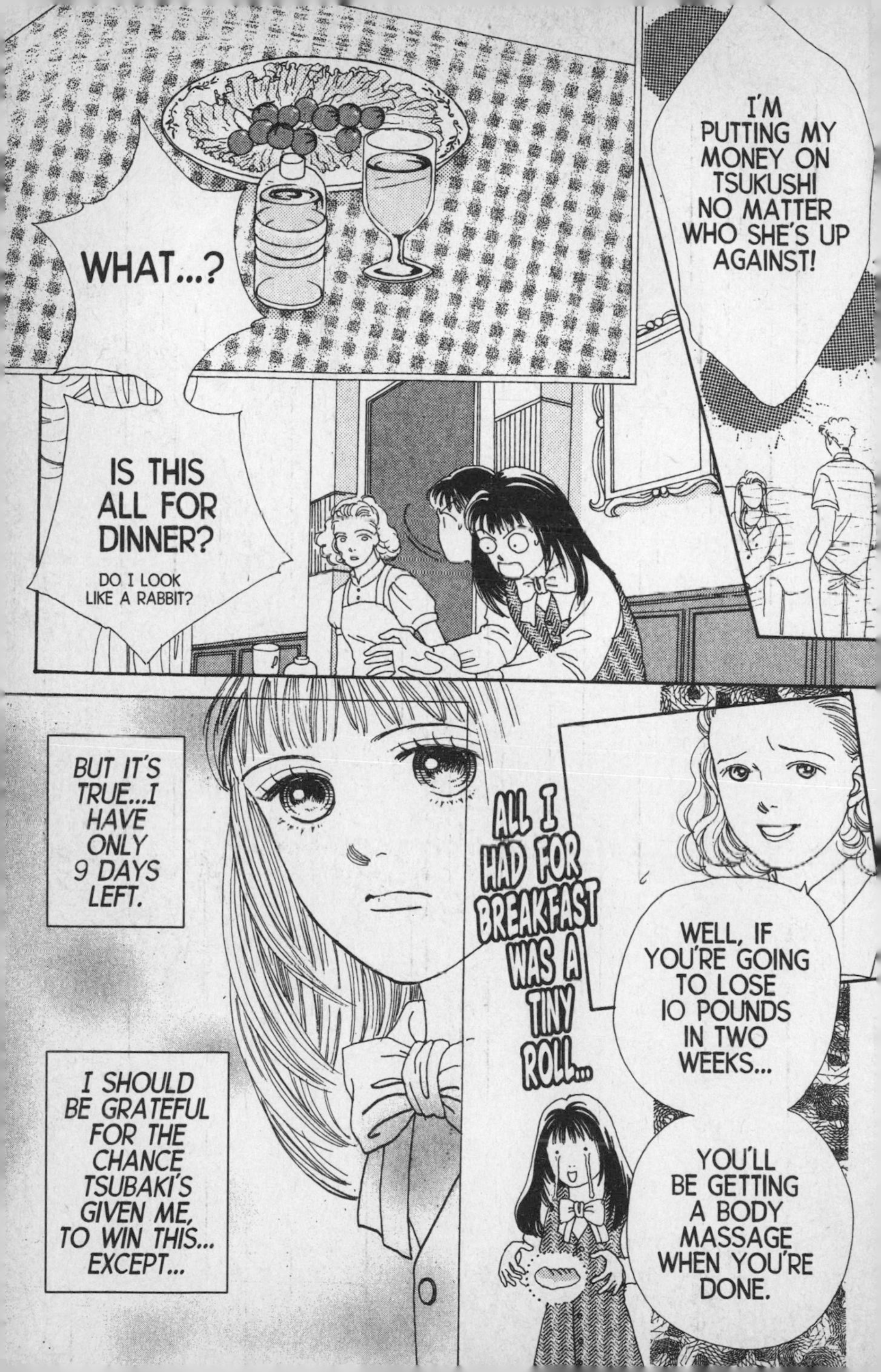
I'M PUTTING MY MONEY ON TSUKUSHI NO MATTER WHO SHE'S UP AGAINST!
WHAT...?
IS THIS ALL FOR DINNER?
DO I LOOK LIKE A RABBIT?
WELL, IF YOU'RE GOING TO LOSE 10 POUNDS IN TWO WEEKS...
YOU'LL BE GETTING A BODY MASSAGE WHEN YOU'RE DONE.
ALL I HAD FOR BREAKFAST WAS A TINY ROLL...
BUT IT'S TRUE...I HAVE ONLY 9 DAYS LEFT.
I SHOULD BE GRATEFUL FOR THE CHANCE TSUBAKI'S GIVEN ME, TO WIN THIS... EXCEPT...

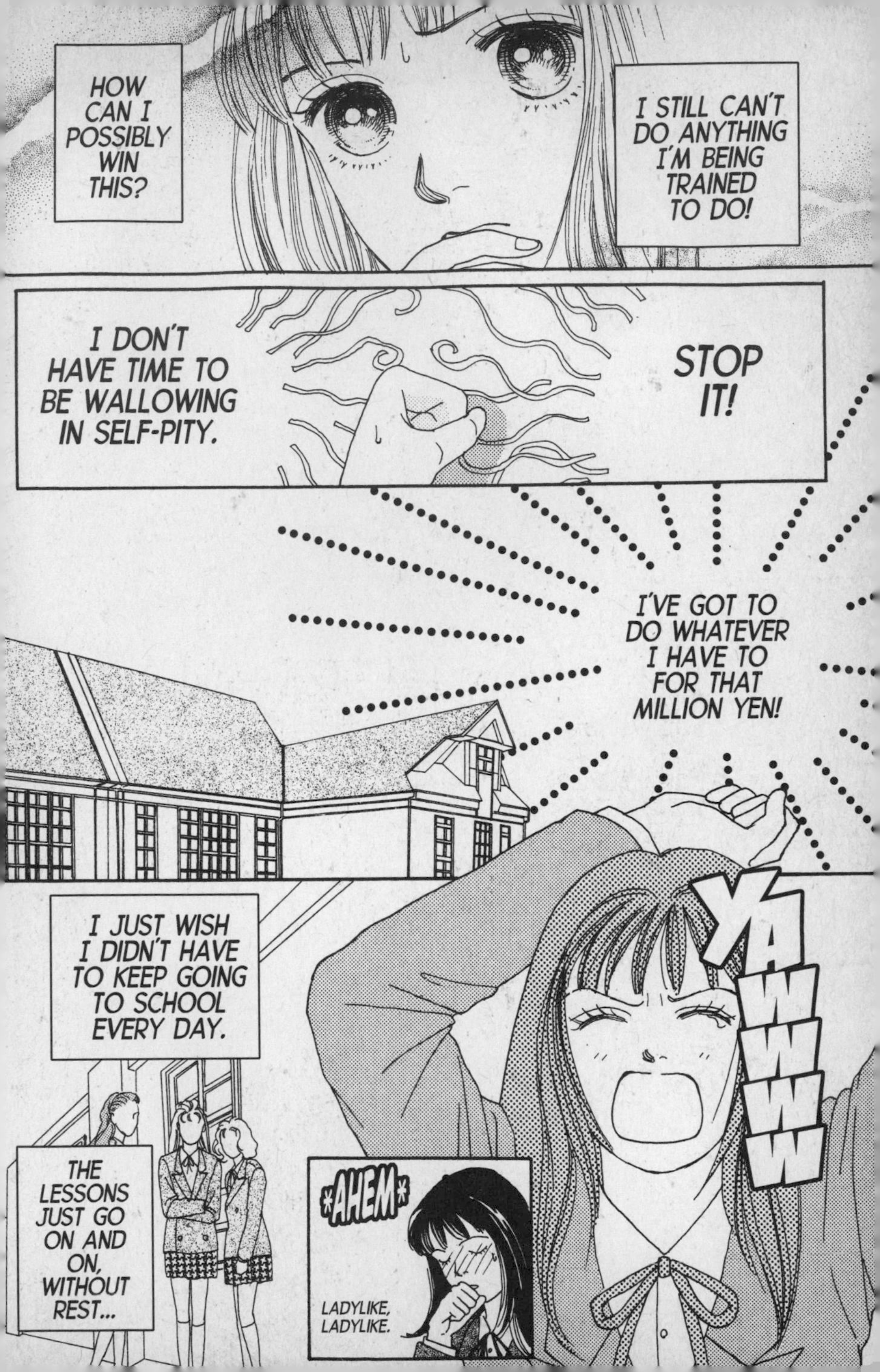
I STILL CAN'T DO ANYTHING I'M BEING TRAINED TO DO!
HOW CAN I POSSIBLY WIN THIS?
STOP IT!
I DON'T HAVE TIME TO BE WALLOWING IN SELF-PITY.
I'VE GOT TO DO WHATEVER I HAVE TO FOR THAT MILLION YEN!
YAWWWWW
I JUST WISH I DIDN'T HAVE TO KEEP GOING TO SCHOOL EVERY DAY.
THE LESSONS JUST GO ON AND ON, WITHOUT REST...
AHEM
LADYLIKE, LADYLIKE.

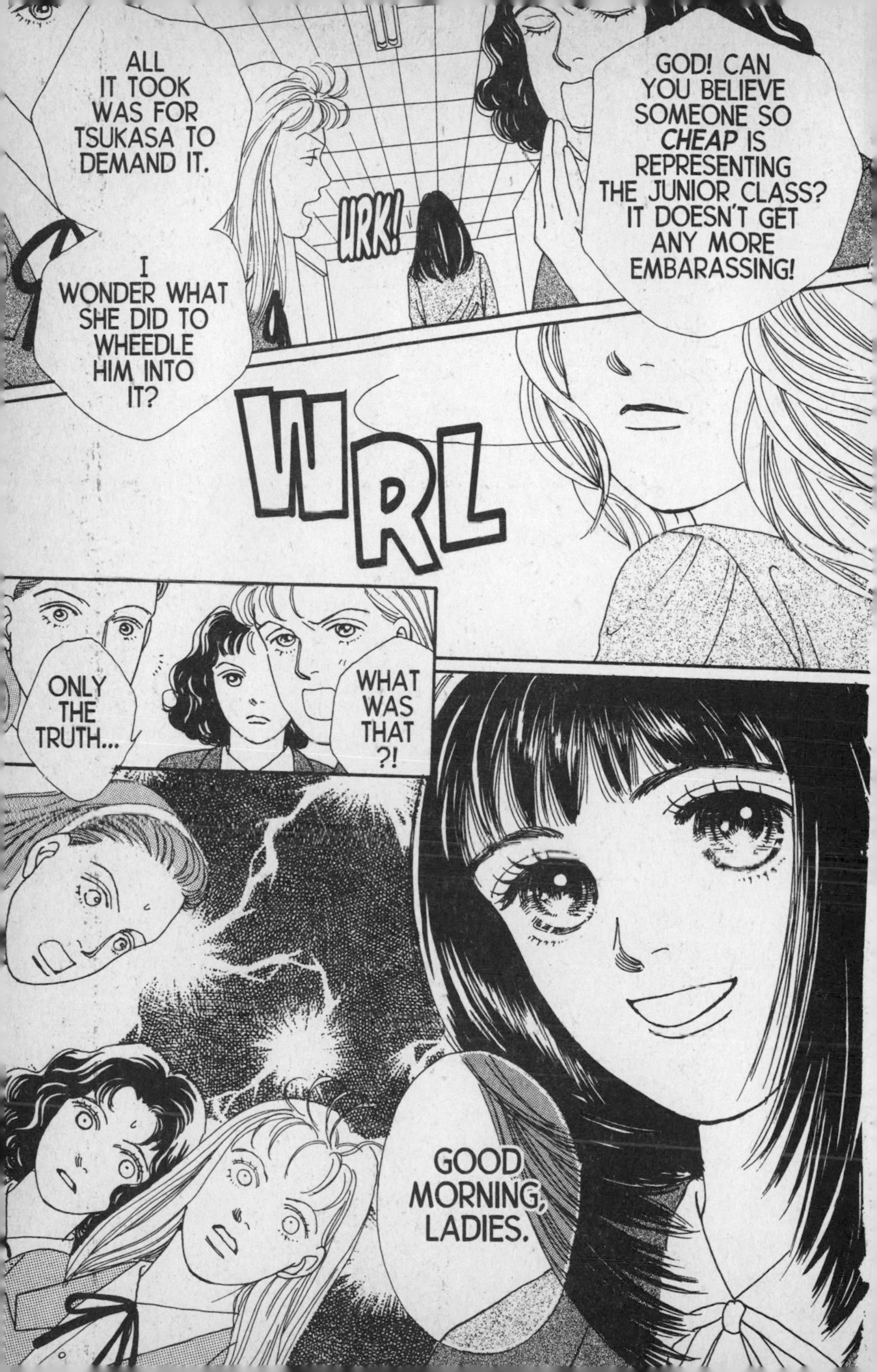
GOD! CAN YOU BELIEVE SOMEONE SO *CHEAP* IS REPRESENTING THE JUNIOR CLASS? IT DOESN'T GET ANY MORE EMBARASSING!
ALL IT TOOK WAS FOR TSUKASA TO DEMAND IT.
URK!
I WONDER WHAT SHE DID TO WHEEDLE HIM INTO IT?
WRL
WHAT WAS THAT ?!
ONLY THE TRUTH...
GOOD MORNING, LADIES.

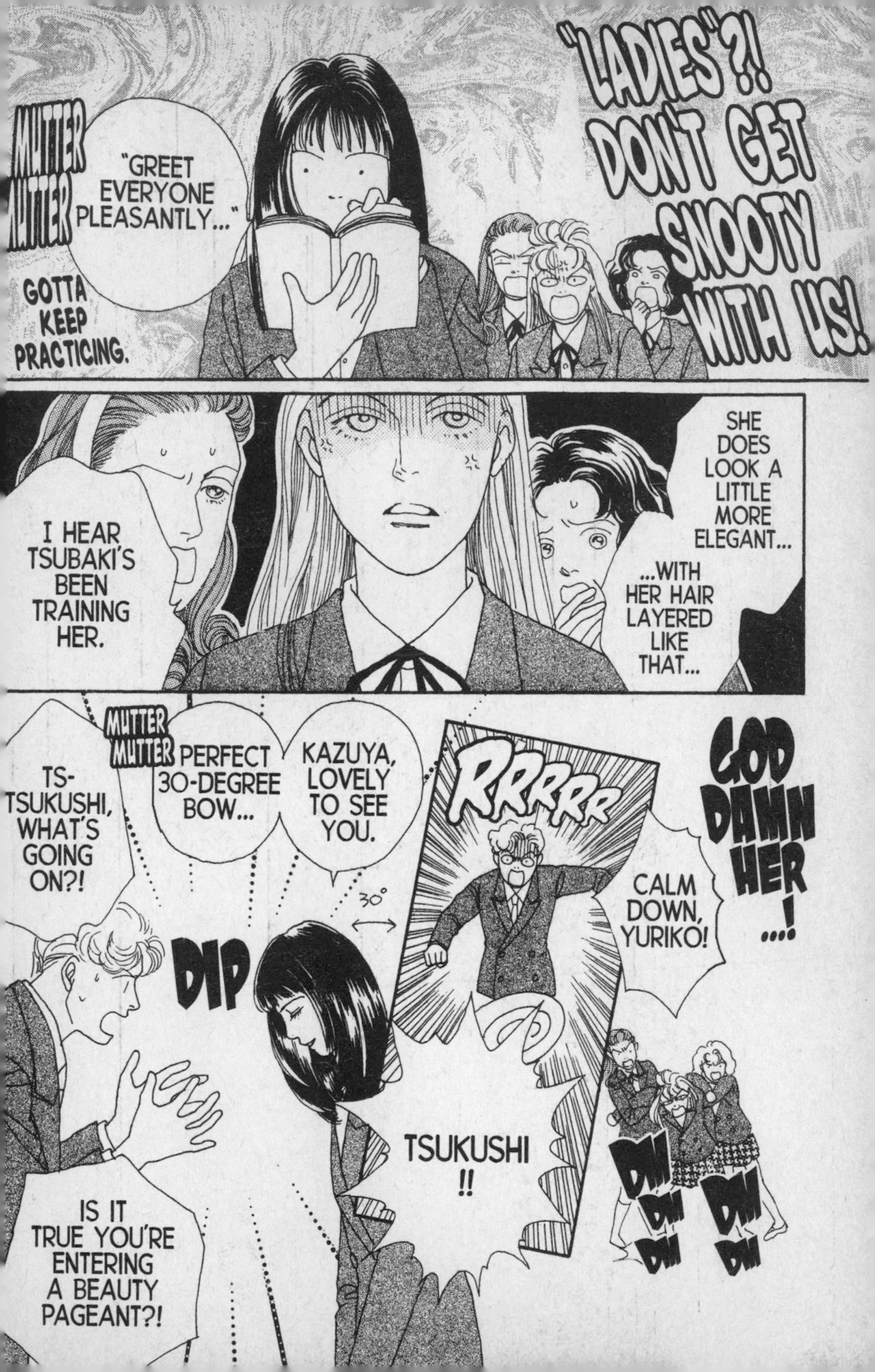
"LADIES"?! DON'T GET SNOOTY WITH US!
MUTTER MUTTER
"GREET EVERYONE PLEASANTLY..."
GOTTA KEEP PRACTICING.
SHE DOES LOOK A LITTLE MORE ELEGANT...
...WITH HER HAIR LAYERED LIKE THAT...
I HEAR TSUBAKI'S BEEN TRAINING HER.
GOD DAMN HER...!
CALM DOWN, YURIKO!
RRRRR
TSUKUSHI !!
DM DM DM
DM DM
KAZUYA, LOVELY TO SEE YOU.
MUTTER MUTTER
PERFECT 30-DEGREE BOW...
TS-TSUKUSHI, WHAT'S GOING ON?!
30°
DIP
IS IT TRUE YOU'RE ENTERING A BEAUTY PAGEANT?!

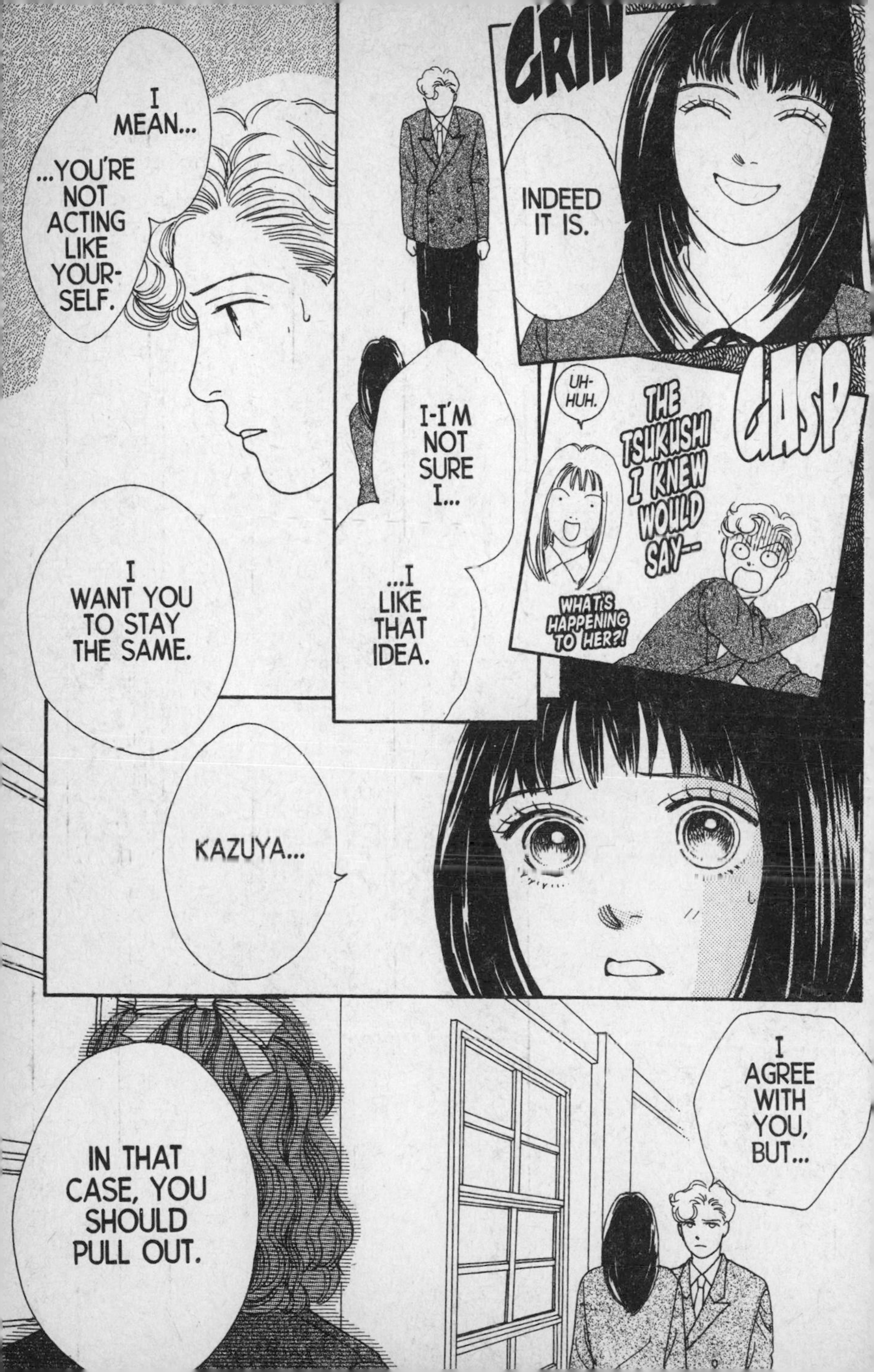
GRIN
INDEED IT IS.
GASP
THE TSUKUSHI I KNEW WOULD SAY--
UH-HUH.
WHAT'S HAPPENING TO HER?!
I-I'M NOT SURE I...
...I LIKE THAT IDEA.
I MEAN...
...YOU'RE NOT ACTING LIKE YOUR-SELF.
I WANT YOU TO STAY THE SAME.
KAZUYA...
I AGREE WITH YOU, BUT...
IN THAT CASE, YOU SHOULD PULL OUT.

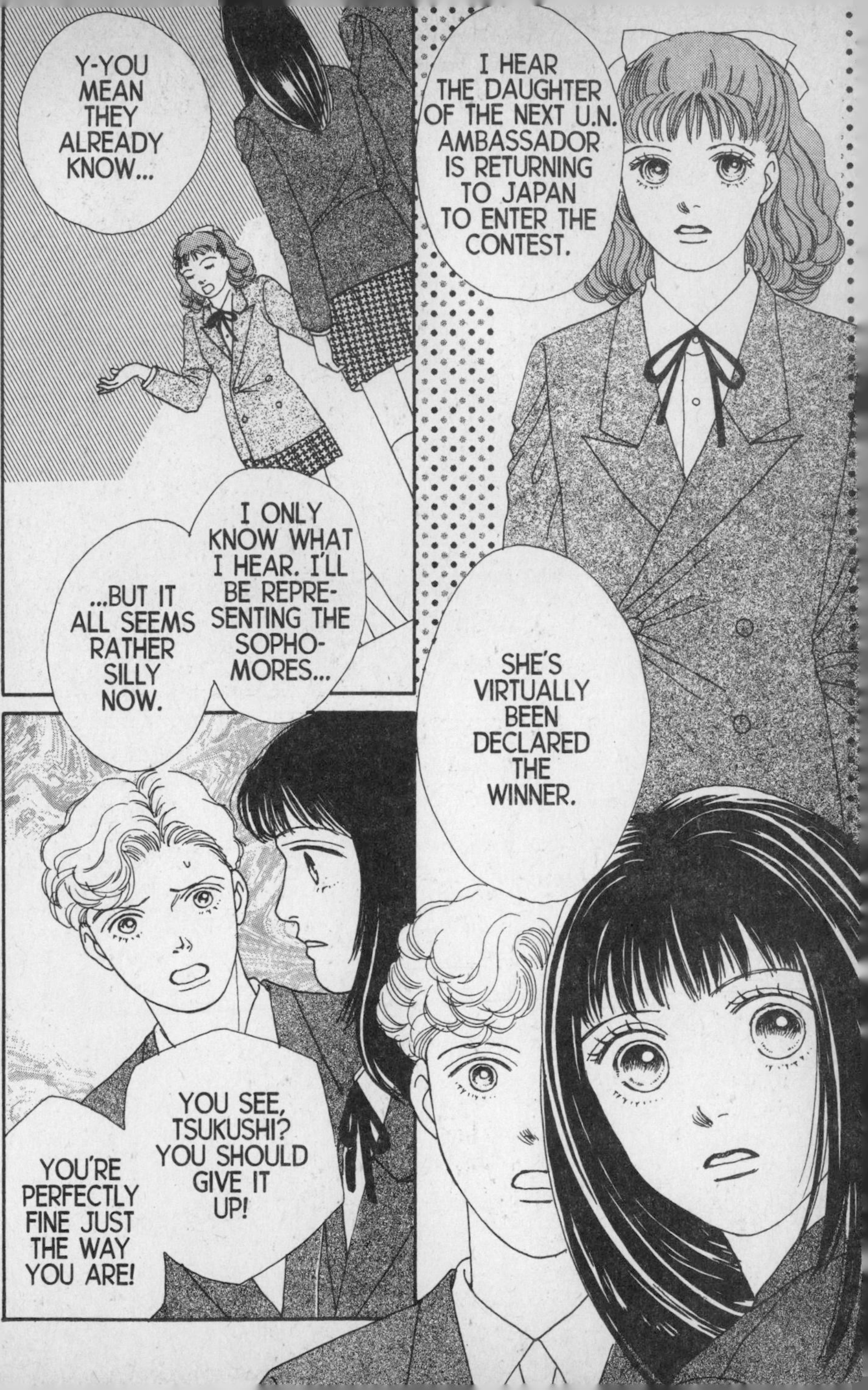
I HEAR THE DAUGHTER OF THE NEXT U.N. AMBASSADOR IS RETURNING TO JAPAN TO ENTER THE CONTEST.
SHE'S VIRTUALLY BEEN DECLARED THE WINNER.
Y-YOU MEAN THEY ALREADY KNOW...
I ONLY KNOW WHAT I HEAR. I'LL BE REPRESENTING THE SOPHOMORES...
...BUT IT ALL SEEMS RATHER SILLY NOW.
YOU SEE, TSUKUSHI? YOU SHOULD GIVE IT UP!
YOU'RE PERFECTLY FINE JUST THE WAY YOU ARE!

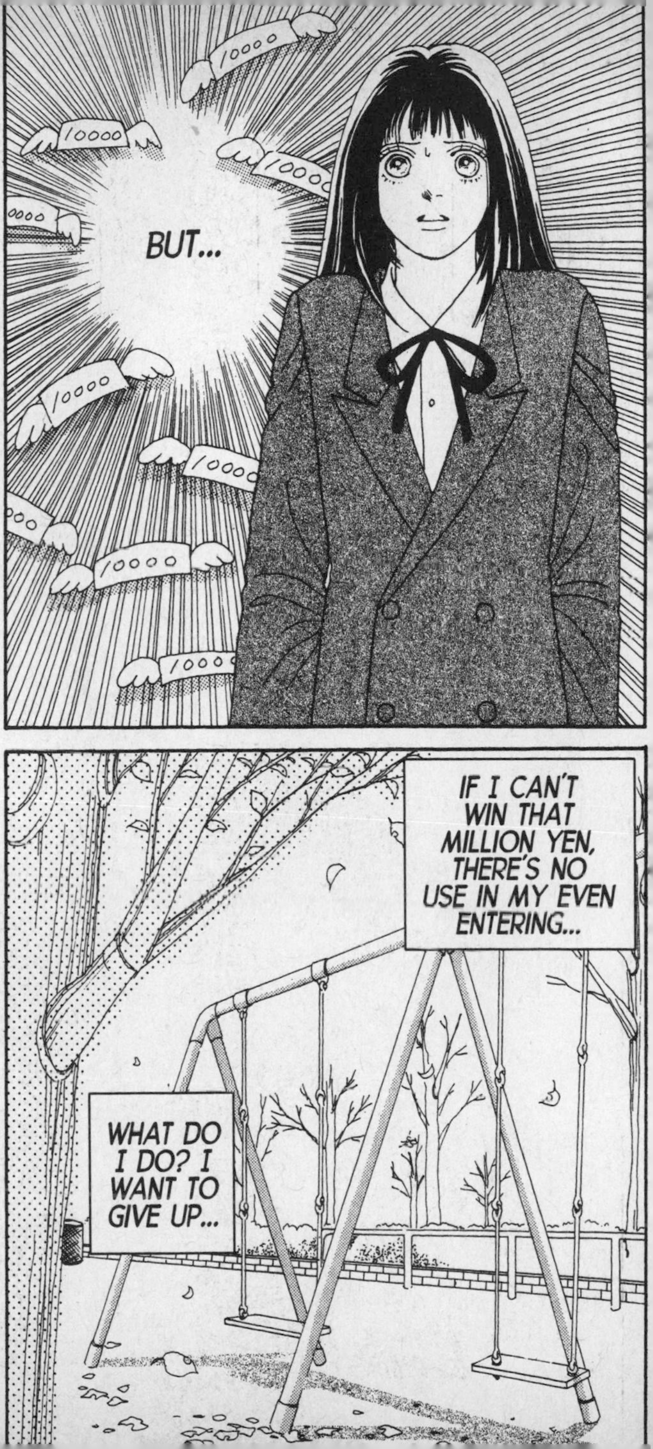
BUT...
IF I CAN'T WIN THAT MILLION YEN, THERE'S NO USE IN MY EVEN ENTERING...
WHAT DO I DO? I WANT TO GIVE UP...

Hello!

Nice to talk to you all again!

I've been writing like this in every volume, and suddenly we're in Volume 11. I never expected this would run so long!

Maybe the story keeps evolving because I've been working without thinking much about where it's going...

Your encouragement has helped too—a lot!

I've gotten some crazy letters telling me to keep drawing this story for another five years. I'll do my best, but you've got to keep supporting me.

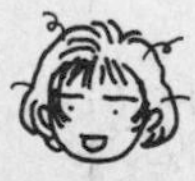

I cut my hair and now I look like a kid...

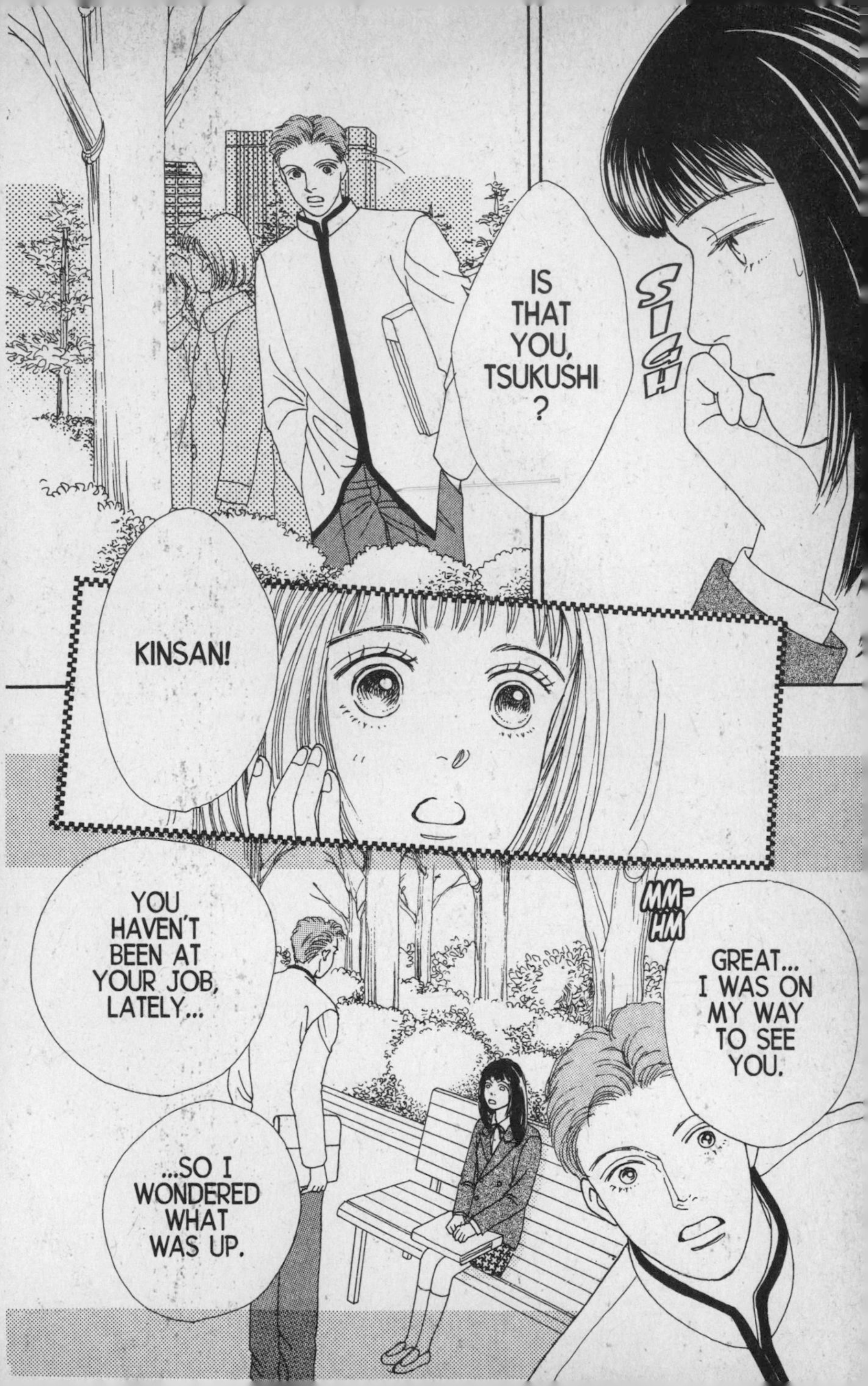
SIGH
IS THAT YOU, TSUKUSHI?
KINSAN!
GREAT... I WAS ON MY WAY TO SEE YOU.
MM-HM
YOU HAVEN'T BEEN AT YOUR JOB, LATELY...
...SO I WONDERED WHAT WAS UP.

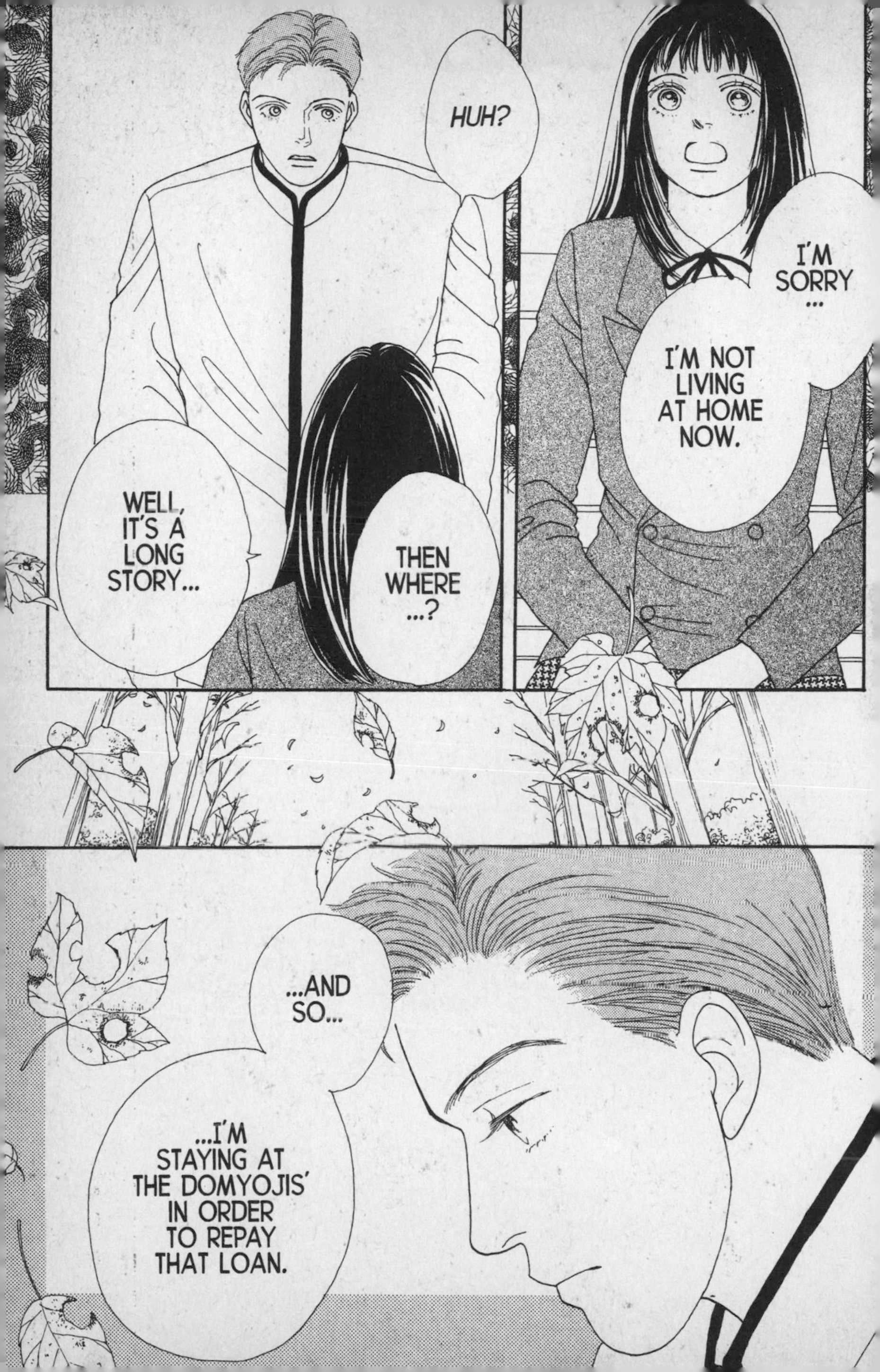
I'M SORRY ...
I'M NOT LIVING AT HOME NOW.
HUH?
THEN WHERE ...?
WELL, IT'S A LONG STORY...
...AND SO...
...I'M STAYING AT THE DOMYOJIS' IN ORDER TO REPAY THAT LOAN.

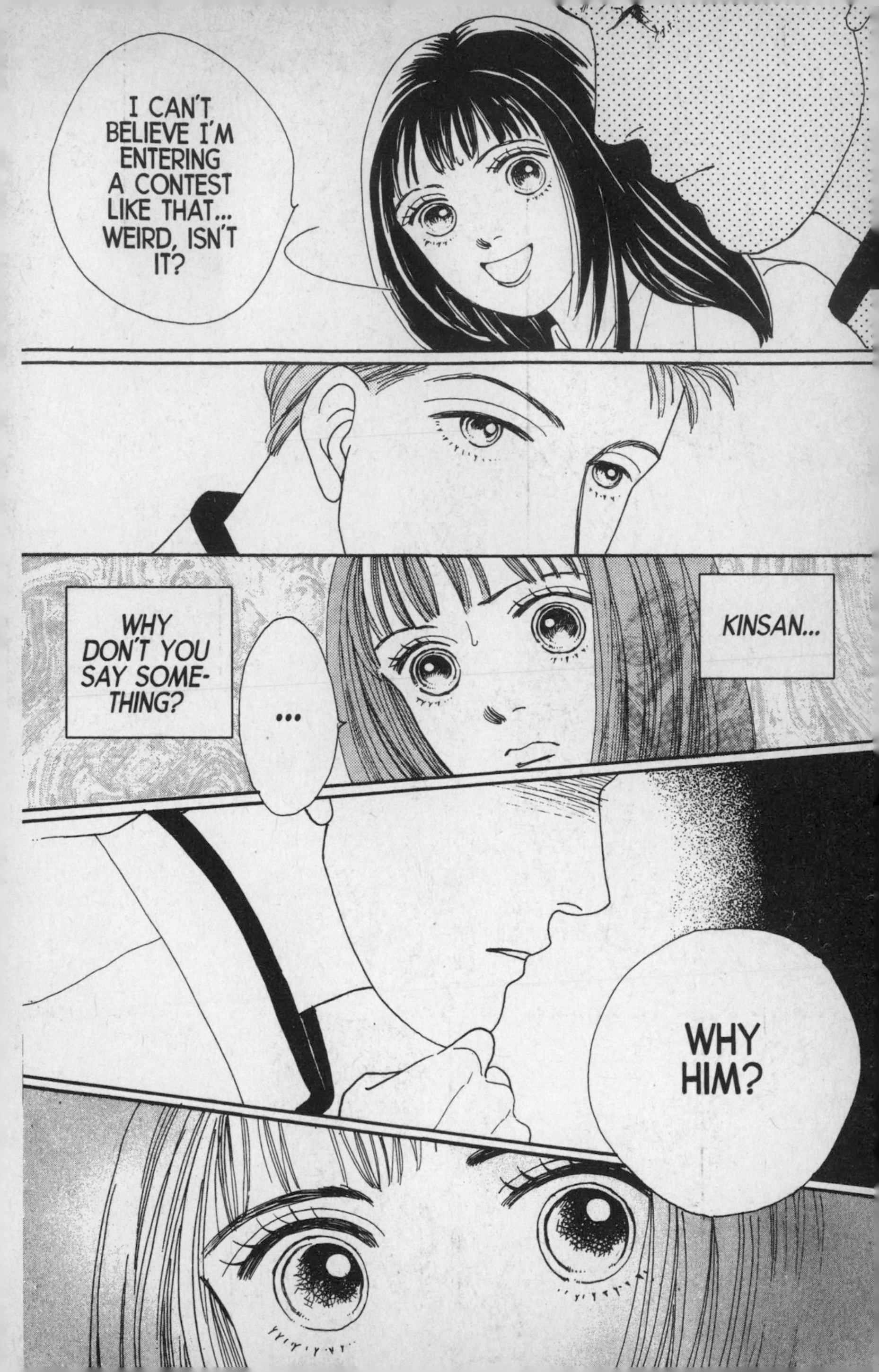
I CAN'T BELIEVE I'M ENTERING A CONTEST LIKE THAT... WEIRD, ISN'T IT?
KINSAN...
WHY DON'T YOU SAY SOME-THING?
...
WHY HIM?

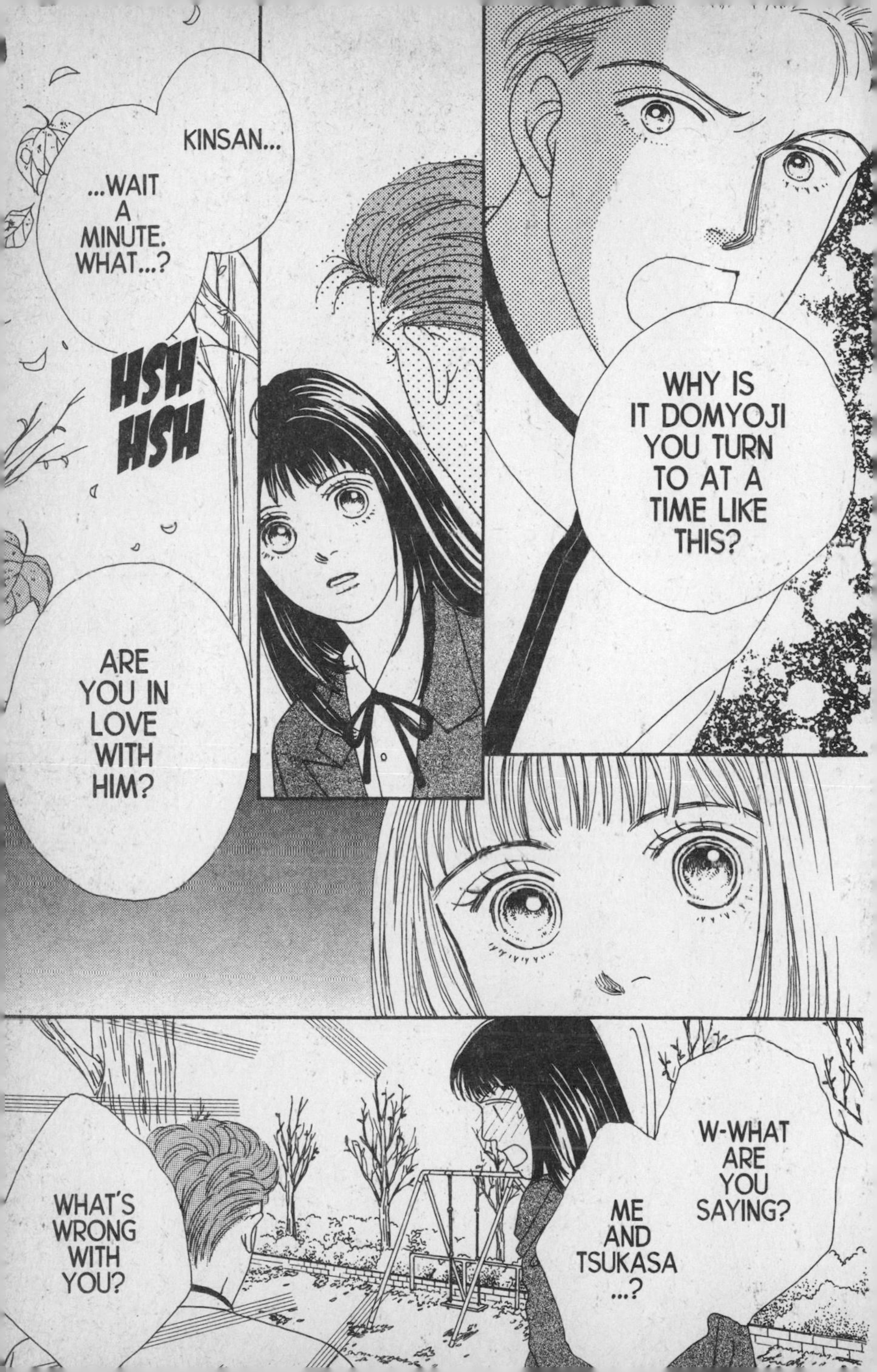
WHY IS IT DOMYOJI YOU TURN TO AT A TIME LIKE THIS?
KINSAN...
...WAIT A MINUTE. WHAT...?
HSH HSH
ARE YOU IN LOVE WITH HIM?
W-WHAT ARE YOU SAYING?
ME AND TSUKASA ...?
WHAT'S WRONG WITH YOU?

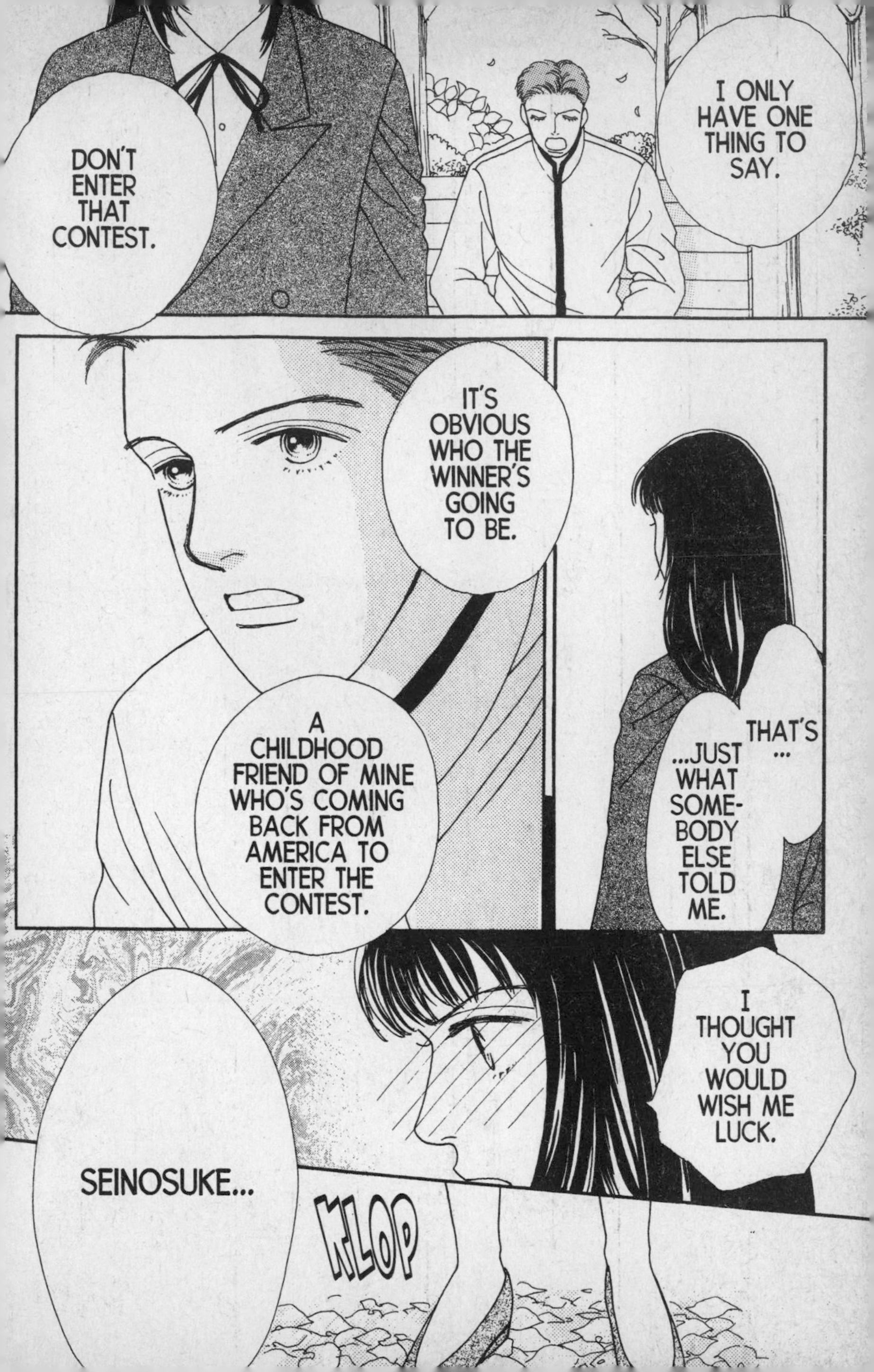
I ONLY HAVE ONE THING TO SAY.
DON'T ENTER THAT CONTEST.
THAT'S ...
...JUST WHAT SOME-BODY ELSE TOLD ME.
IT'S OBVIOUS WHO THE WINNER'S GOING TO BE.
A CHILDHOOD FRIEND OF MINE WHO'S COMING BACK FROM AMERICA TO ENTER THE CONTEST.
I THOUGHT YOU WOULD WISH ME LUCK.
SEINOSUKE...
KLOP

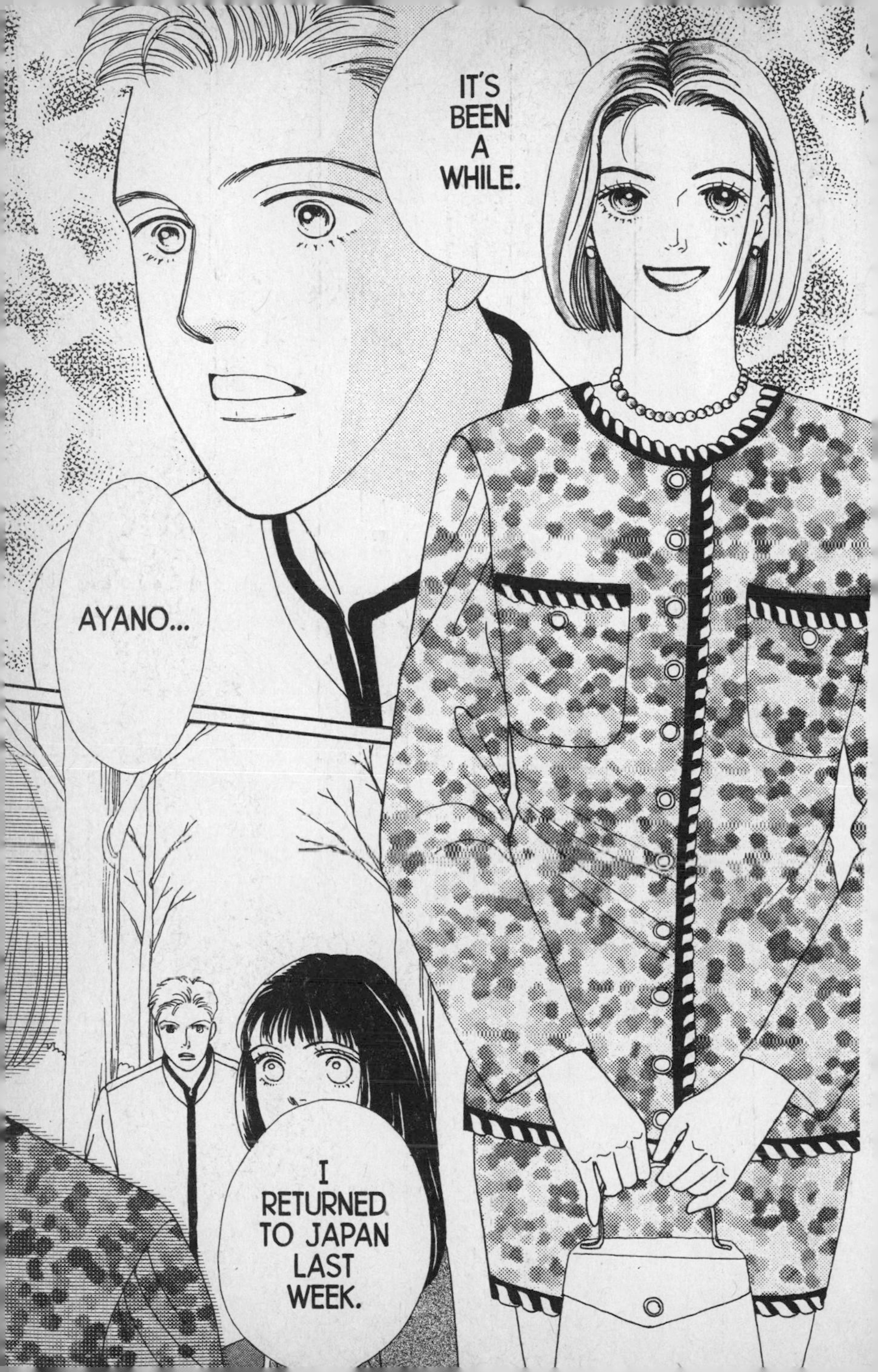
IT'S BEEN A WHILE.
AYANO...
I RETURNED TO JAPAN LAST WEEK.

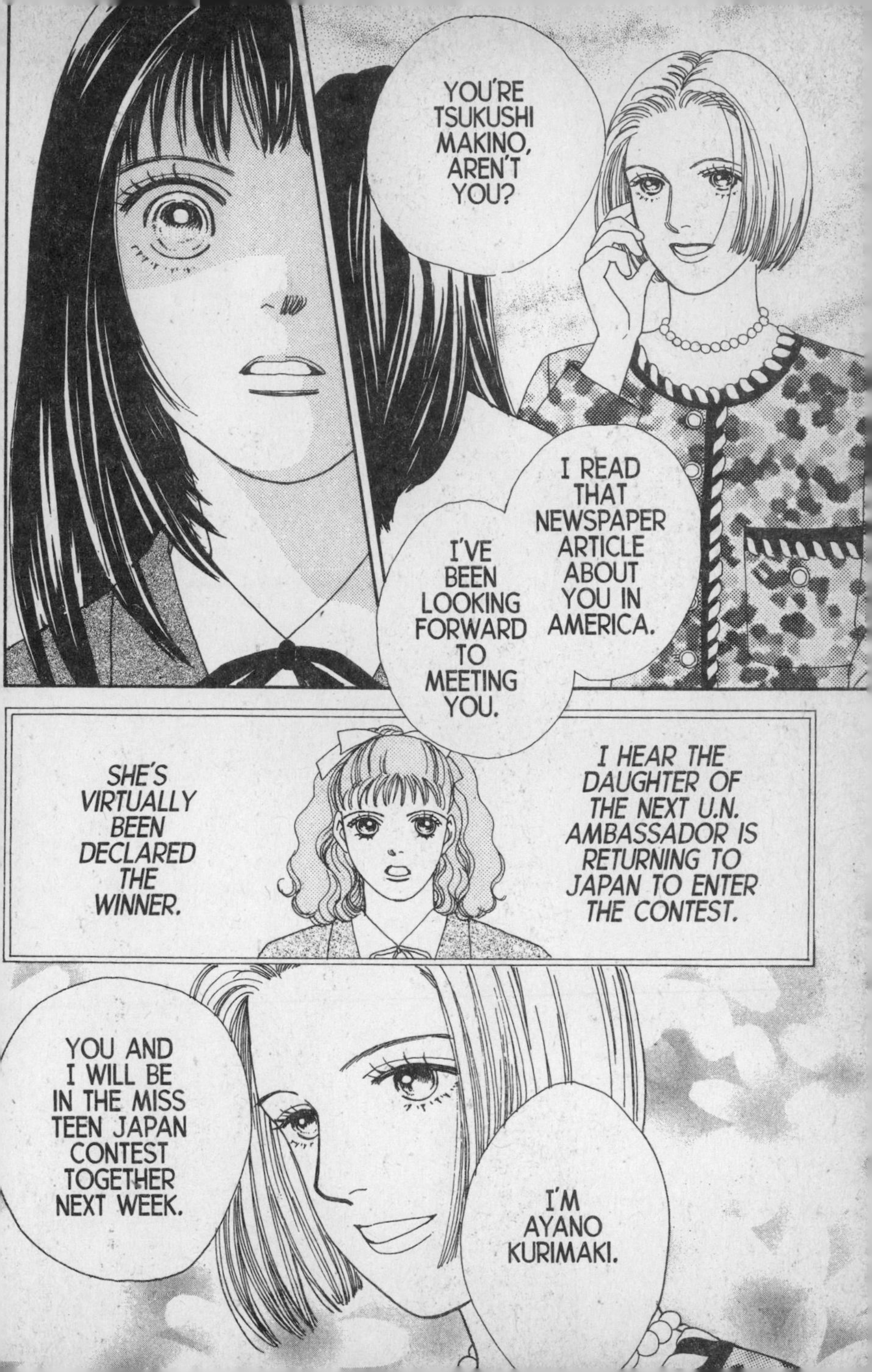
YOU'RE TSUKUSHI MAKINO, AREN'T YOU?
I READ THAT NEWSPAPER ARTICLE ABOUT YOU IN AMERICA.
I'VE BEEN LOOKING FORWARD TO MEETING YOU.
I HEAR THE DAUGHTER OF THE NEXT U.N. AMBASSADOR IS RETURNING TO JAPAN TO ENTER THE CONTEST.
SHE'S VIRTUALLY BEEN DECLARED THE WINNER.
I'M AYANO KURIMAKI.
YOU AND I WILL BE IN THE MISS TEEN JAPAN CONTEST TOGETHER NEXT WEEK.

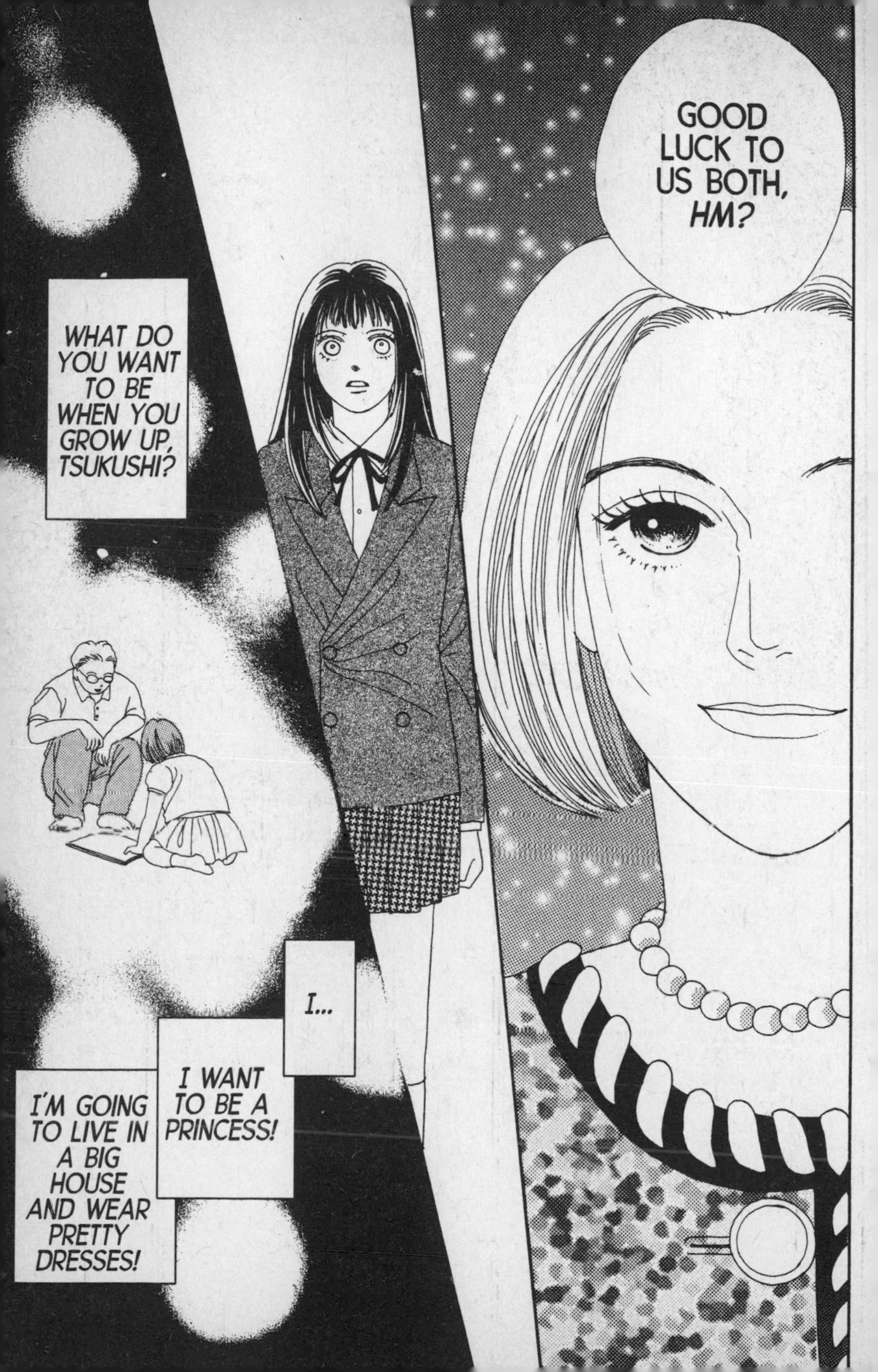
GOOD LUCK TO US BOTH, *HM?*
WHAT DO YOU WANT TO BE WHEN YOU GROW UP, TSUKUSHI?
I...
I WANT TO BE A PRINCESS!
I'M GOING TO LIVE IN A BIG HOUSE AND WEAR PRETTY DRESSES!

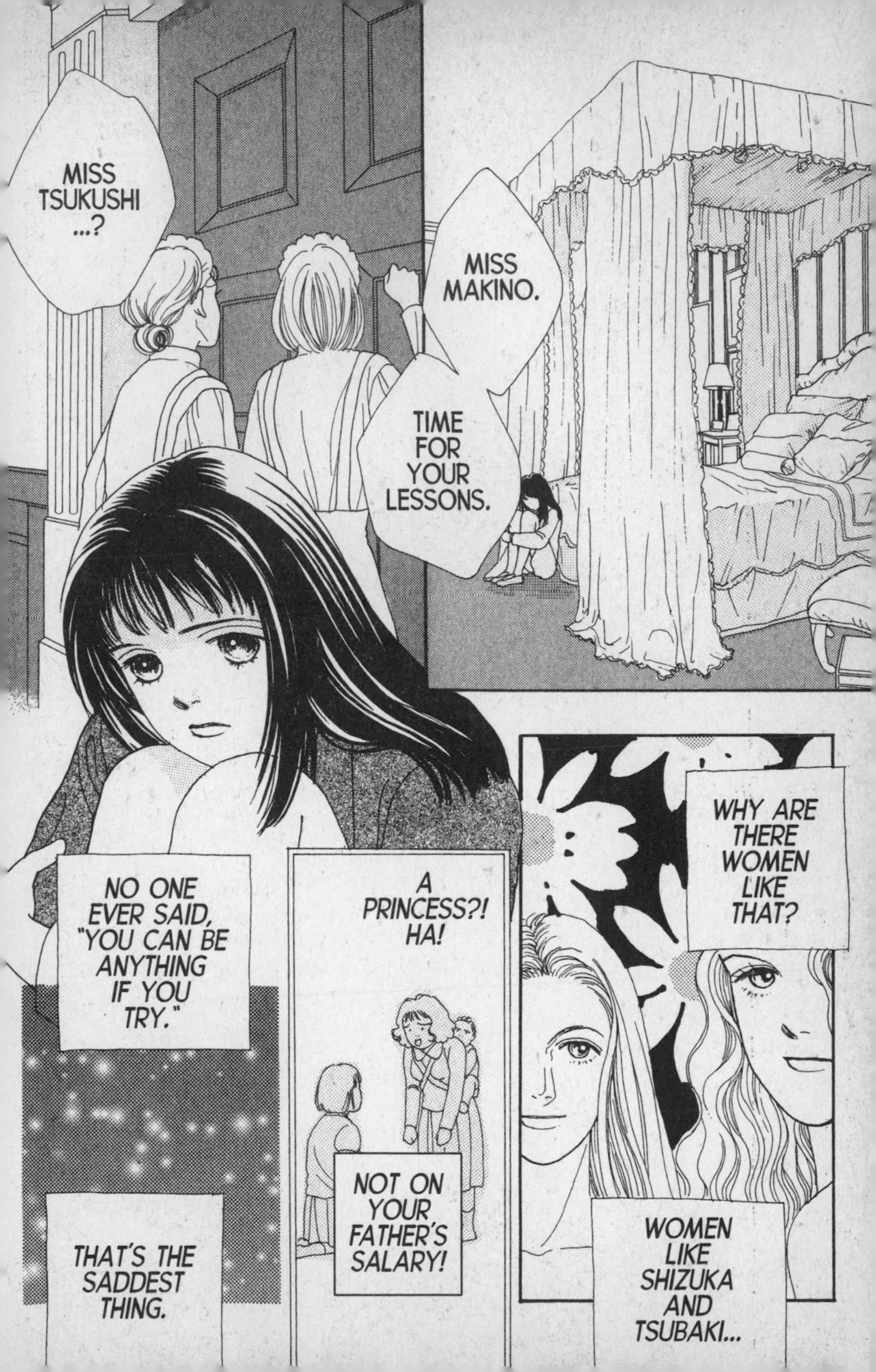
MISS MAKINO.
TIME FOR YOUR LESSONS.
MISS TSUKUSHI ...?
WHY ARE THERE WOMEN LIKE THAT?
WOMEN LIKE SHIZUKA AND TSUBAKI...
A PRINCESS?! HA!
NOT ON YOUR FATHER'S SALARY!
NO ONE EVER SAID, "YOU CAN BE ANYTHING IF YOU TRY."
THAT'S THE SADDEST THING.

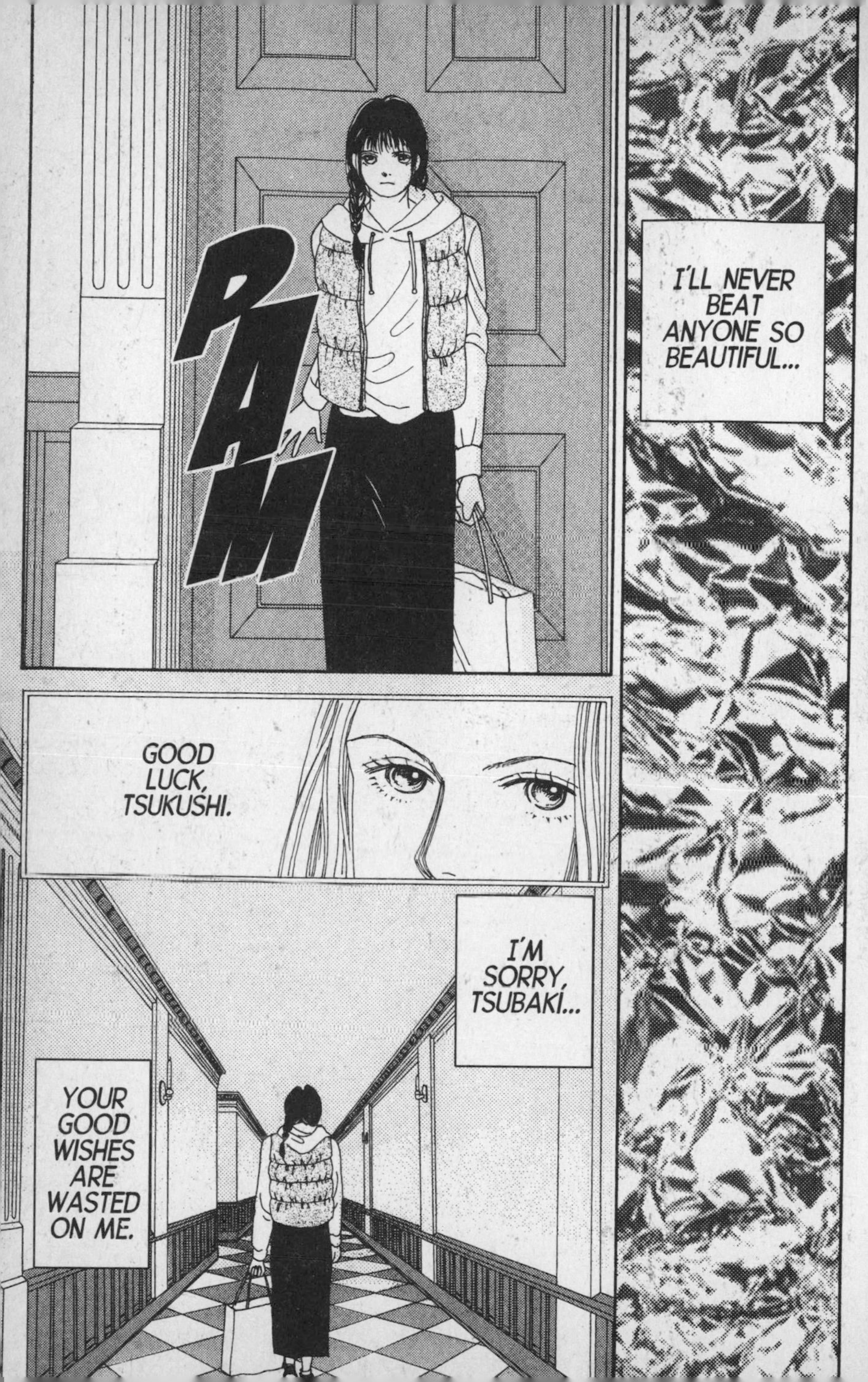
I'LL NEVER BEAT ANYONE SO BEAUTIFUL...
PAM
GOOD LUCK, TSUKUSHI.
I'M SORRY, TSUBAKI...
YOUR GOOD WISHES ARE WASTED ON ME.

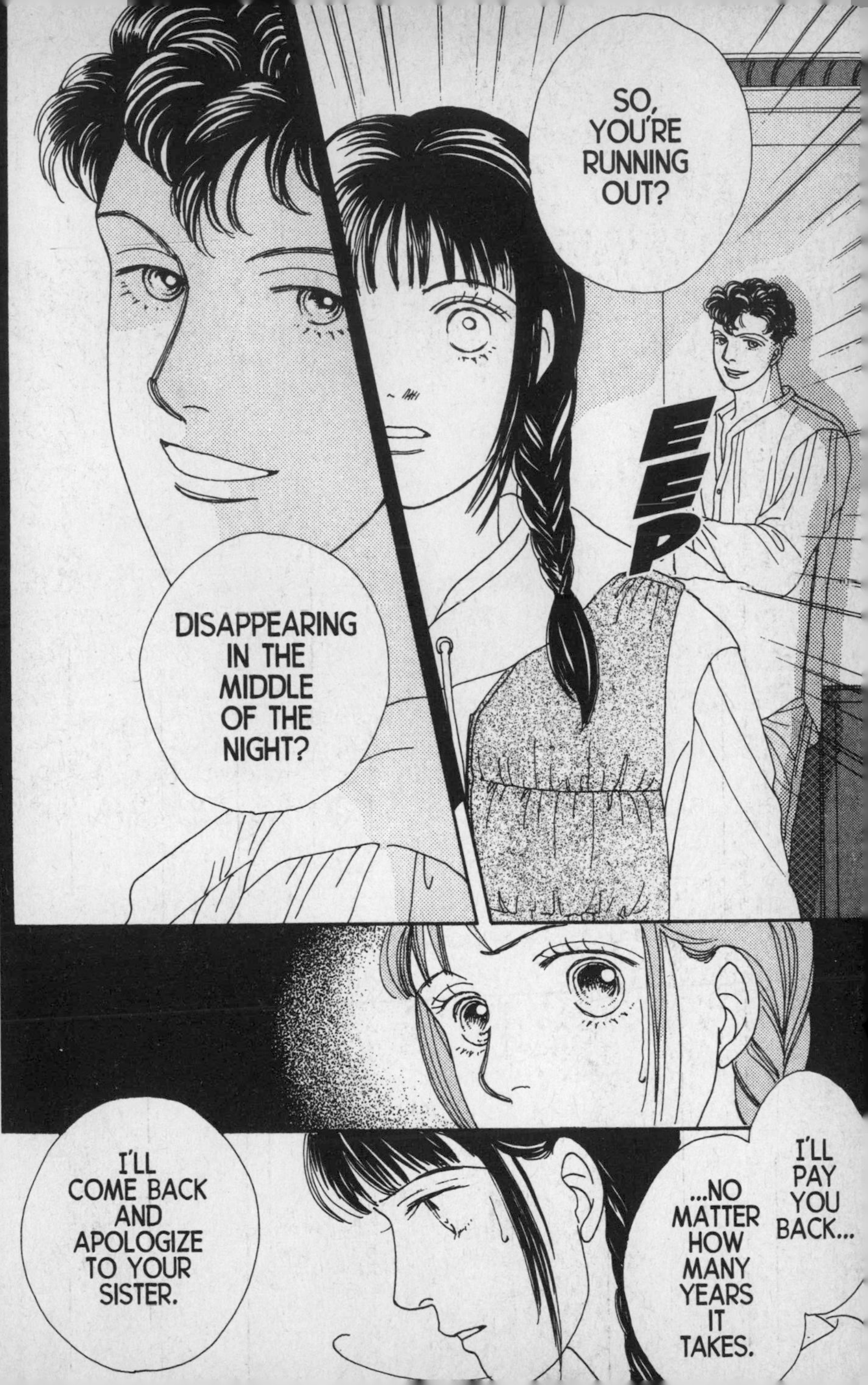
SO, YOU'RE RUNNING OUT?
EEP
DISAPPEARING IN THE MIDDLE OF THE NIGHT?
I'LL PAY YOU BACK...
...NO MATTER HOW MANY YEARS IT TAKES.
I'LL COME BACK AND APOLOGIZE TO YOUR SISTER.

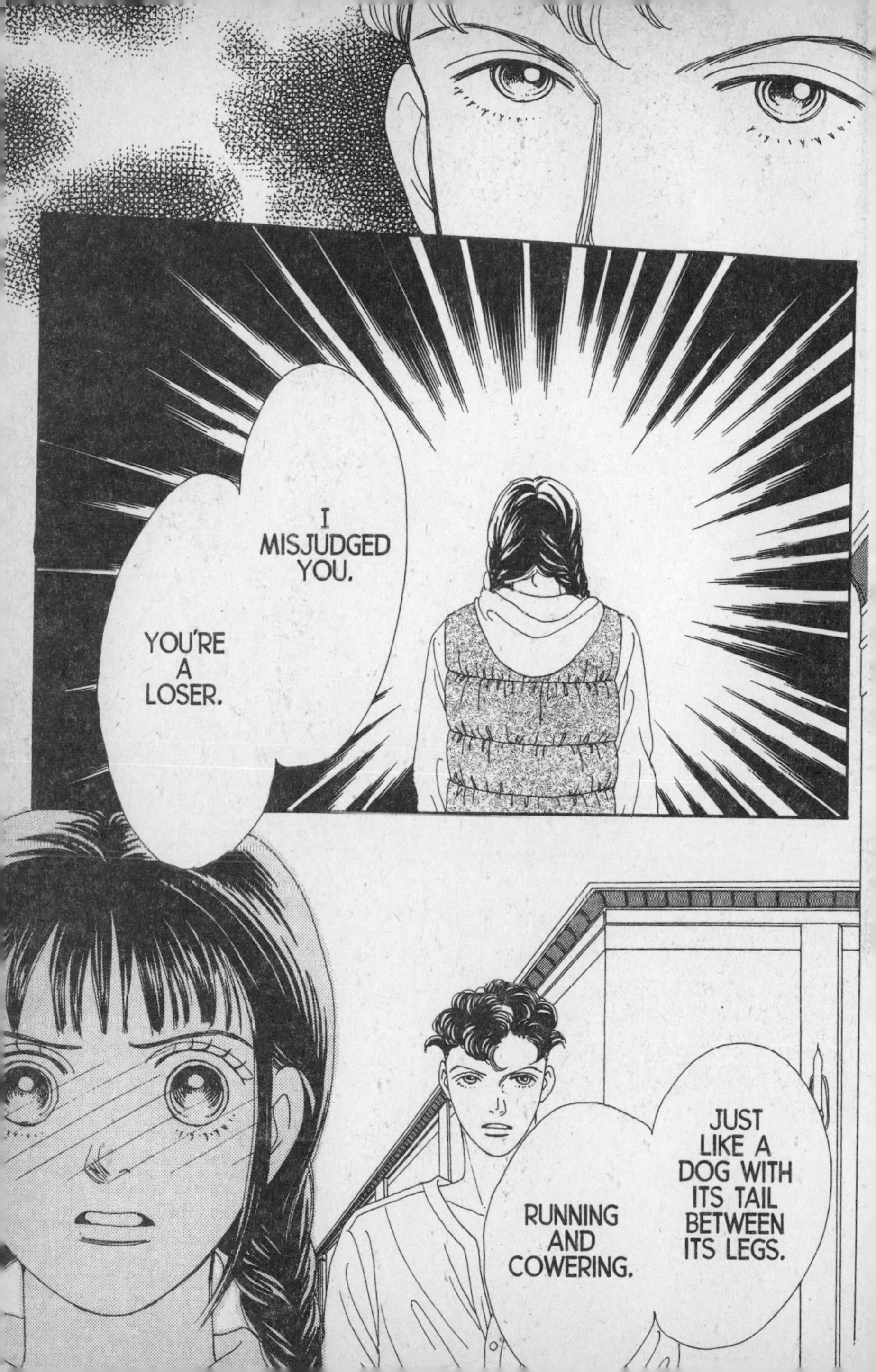
I MISJUDGED YOU.
YOU'RE A LOSER.
JUST LIKE A DOG WITH ITS TAIL BETWEEN ITS LEGS.
RUNNING AND COWERING.

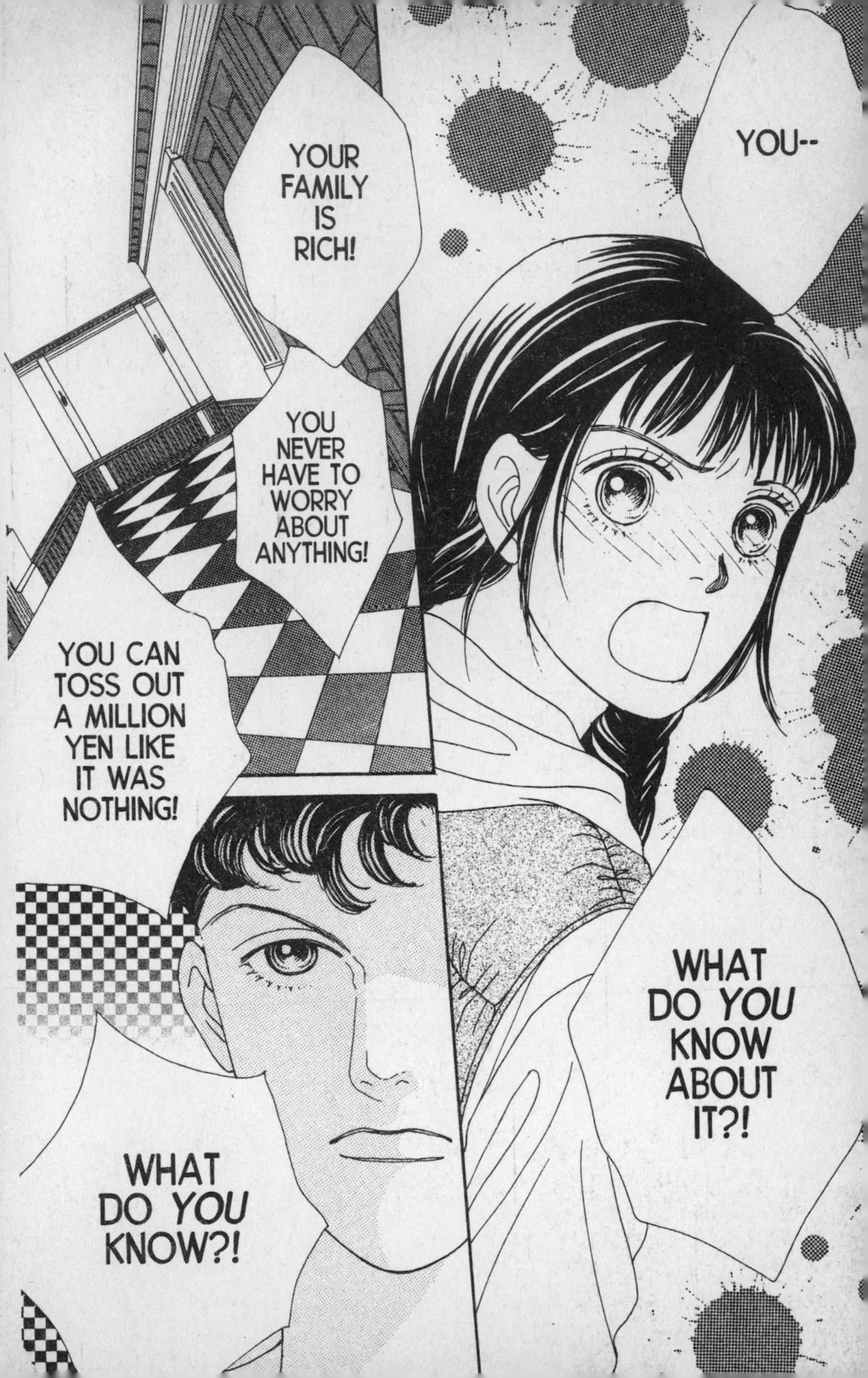
YOU--
YOUR FAMILY IS RICH!
YOU NEVER HAVE TO WORRY ABOUT ANYTHING!
YOU CAN TOSS OUT A MILLION YEN LIKE IT WAS NOTHING!
WHAT DO *YOU* KNOW ABOUT IT?!
WHAT DO *YOU* KNOW?!

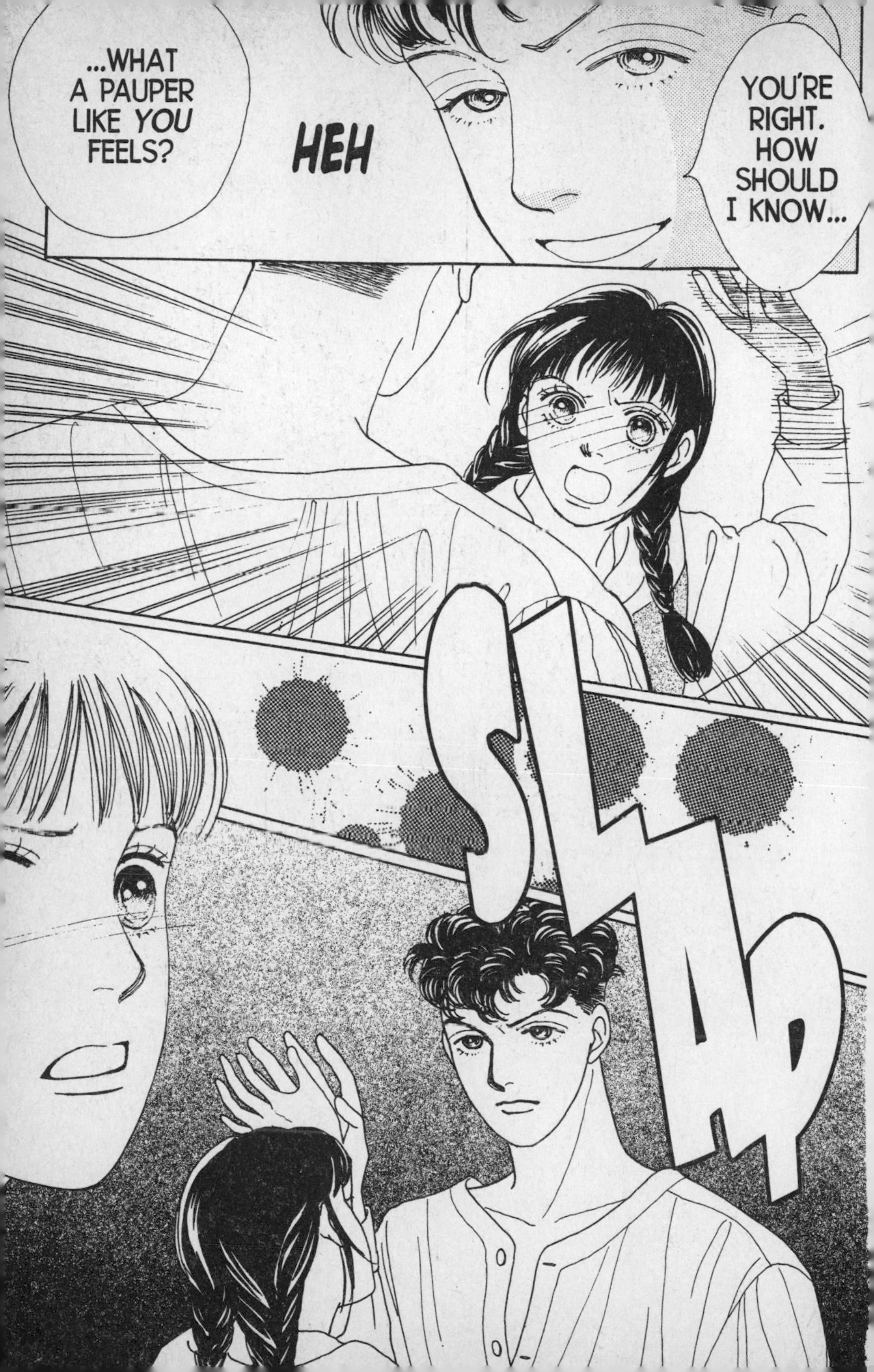
YOU'RE RIGHT. HOW SHOULD I KNOW...
HEH
...WHAT A PAUPER LIKE *YOU* FEELS?
SLAP

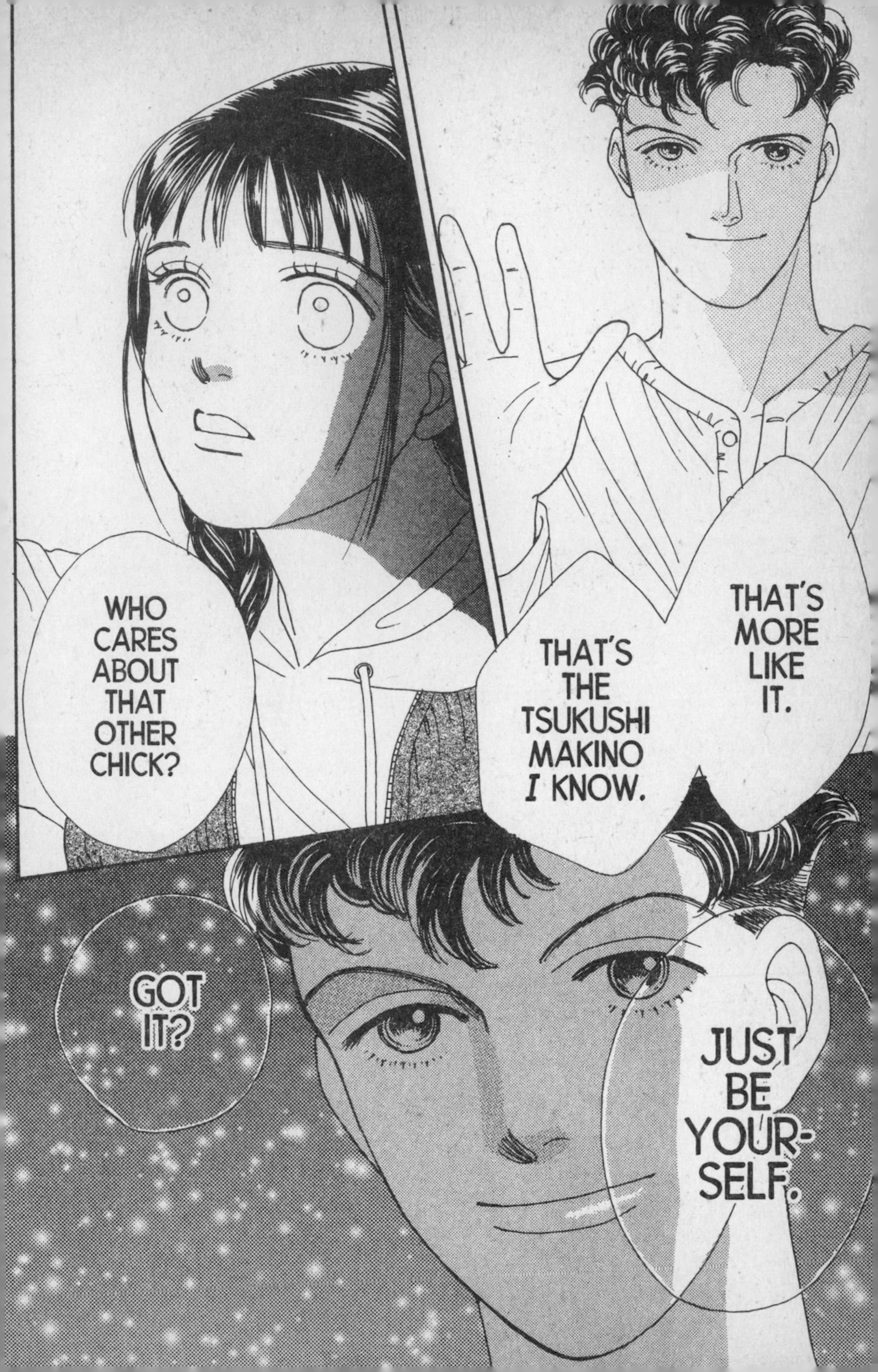
THAT'S MORE LIKE IT.
THAT'S THE TSUKUSHI MAKINO *I* KNOW.
WHO CARES ABOUT THAT OTHER CHICK?
JUST BE YOURSELF.
GOT IT?

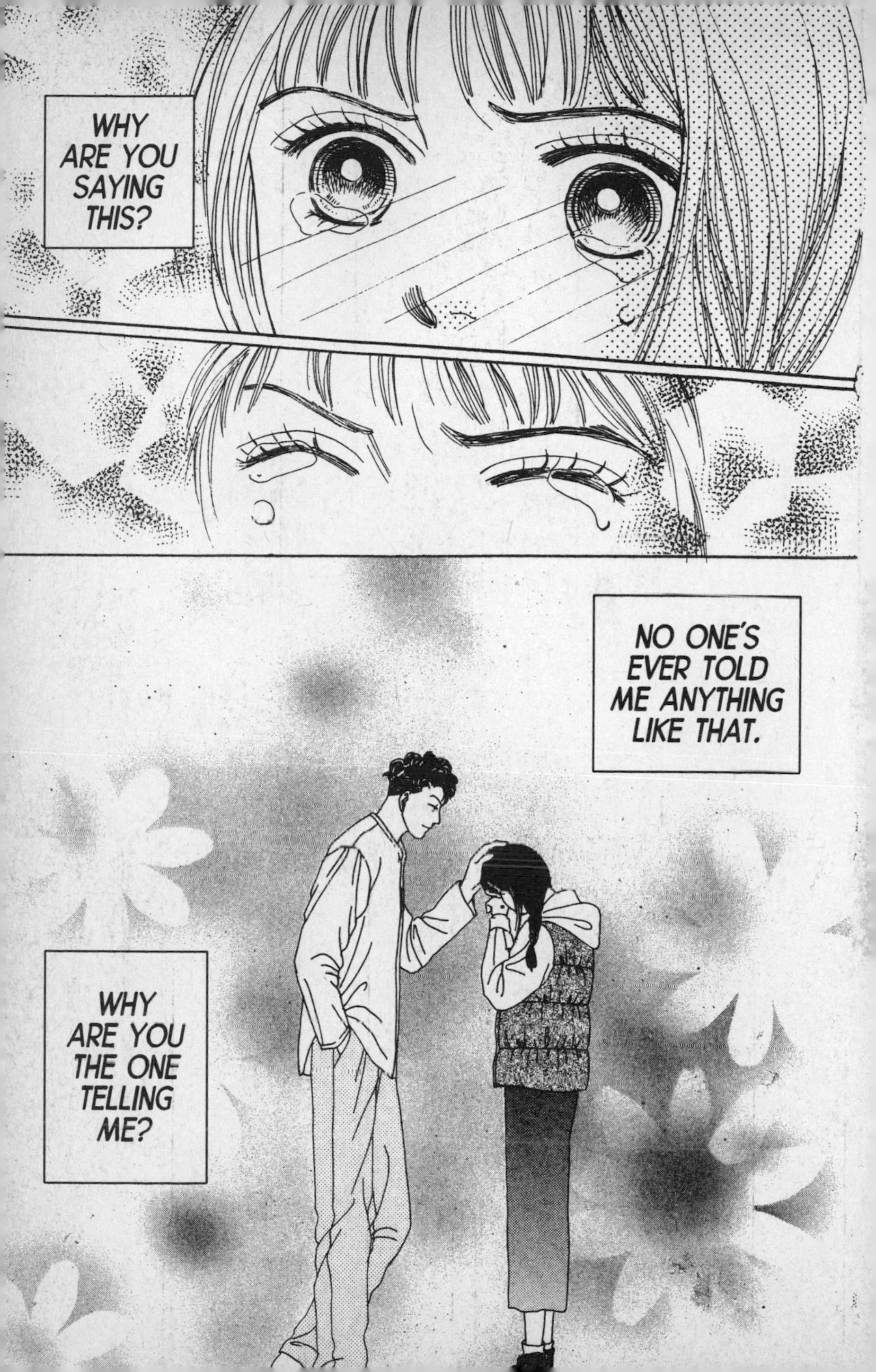
WHY ARE YOU SAYING THIS?
NO ONE'S EVER TOLD ME ANYTHING LIKE THAT.
WHY ARE YOU THE ONE TELLING ME?

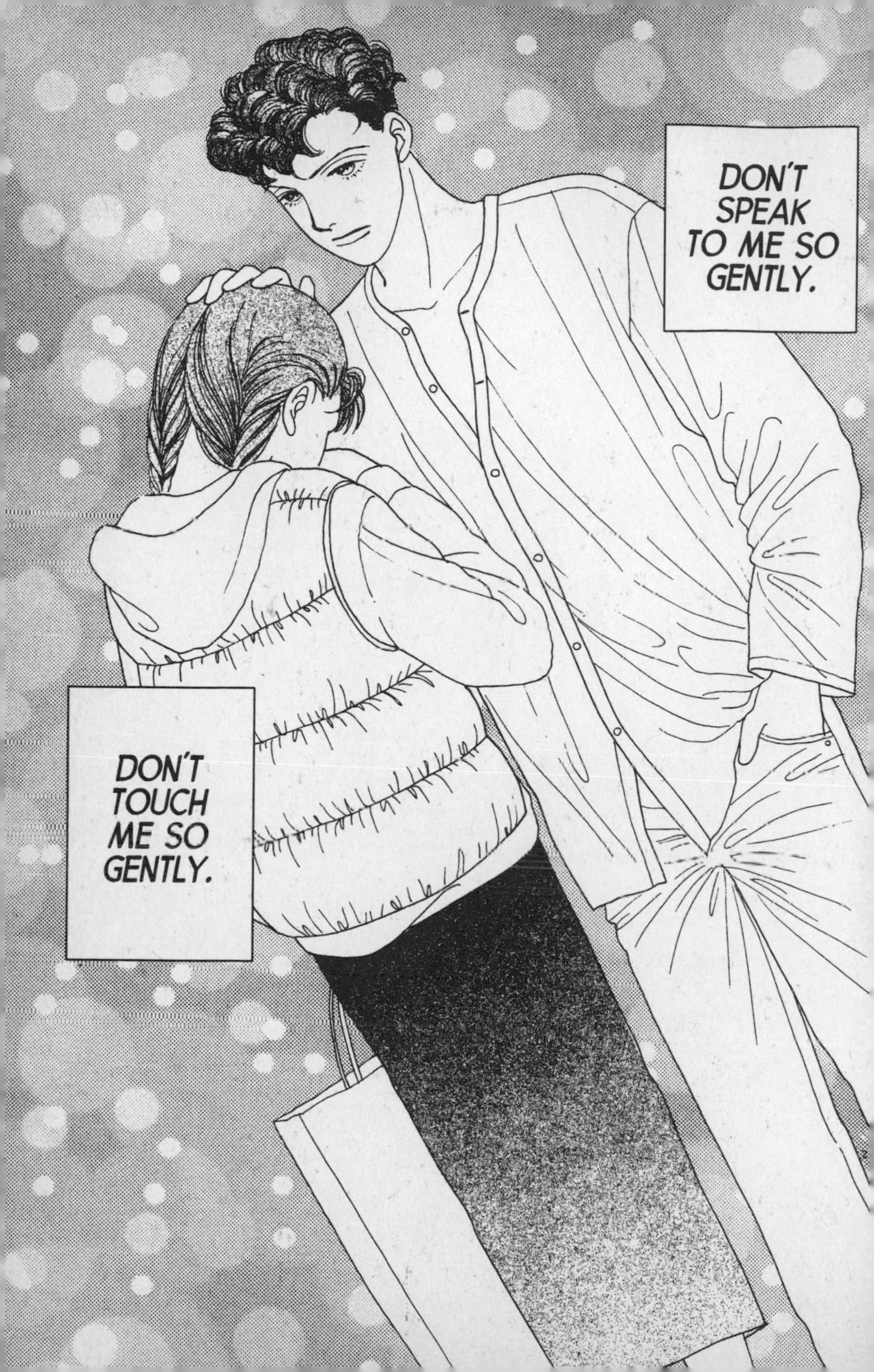
DON'T SPEAK TO ME SO GENTLY.
DON'T TOUCH ME SO GENTLY.

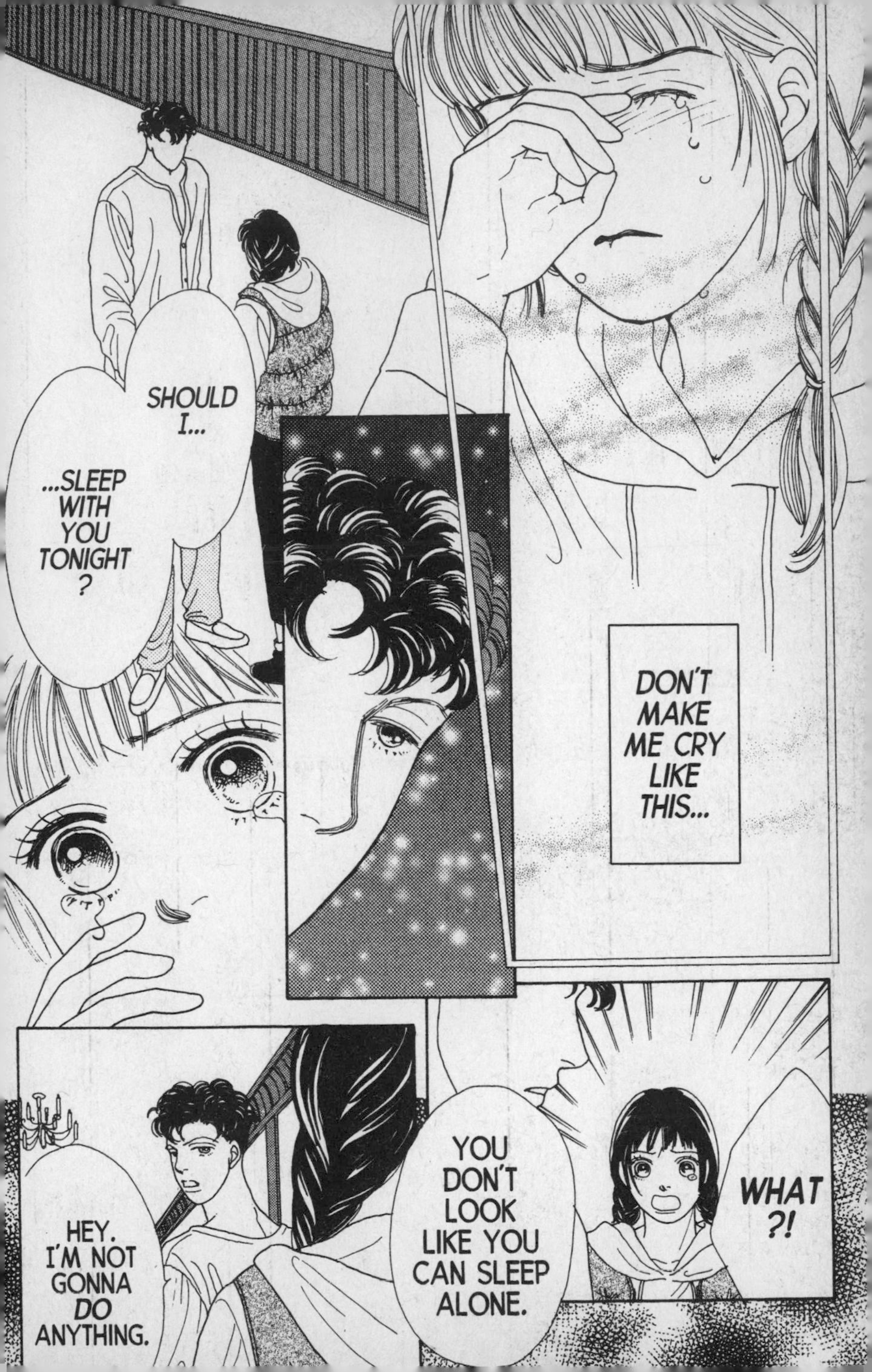
DON'T MAKE ME CRY LIKE THIS...
SHOULD I...
...SLEEP WITH YOU TONIGHT?
WHAT?!
YOU DON'T LOOK LIKE YOU CAN SLEEP ALONE.
HEY. I'M NOT GONNA *DO* ANYTHING.

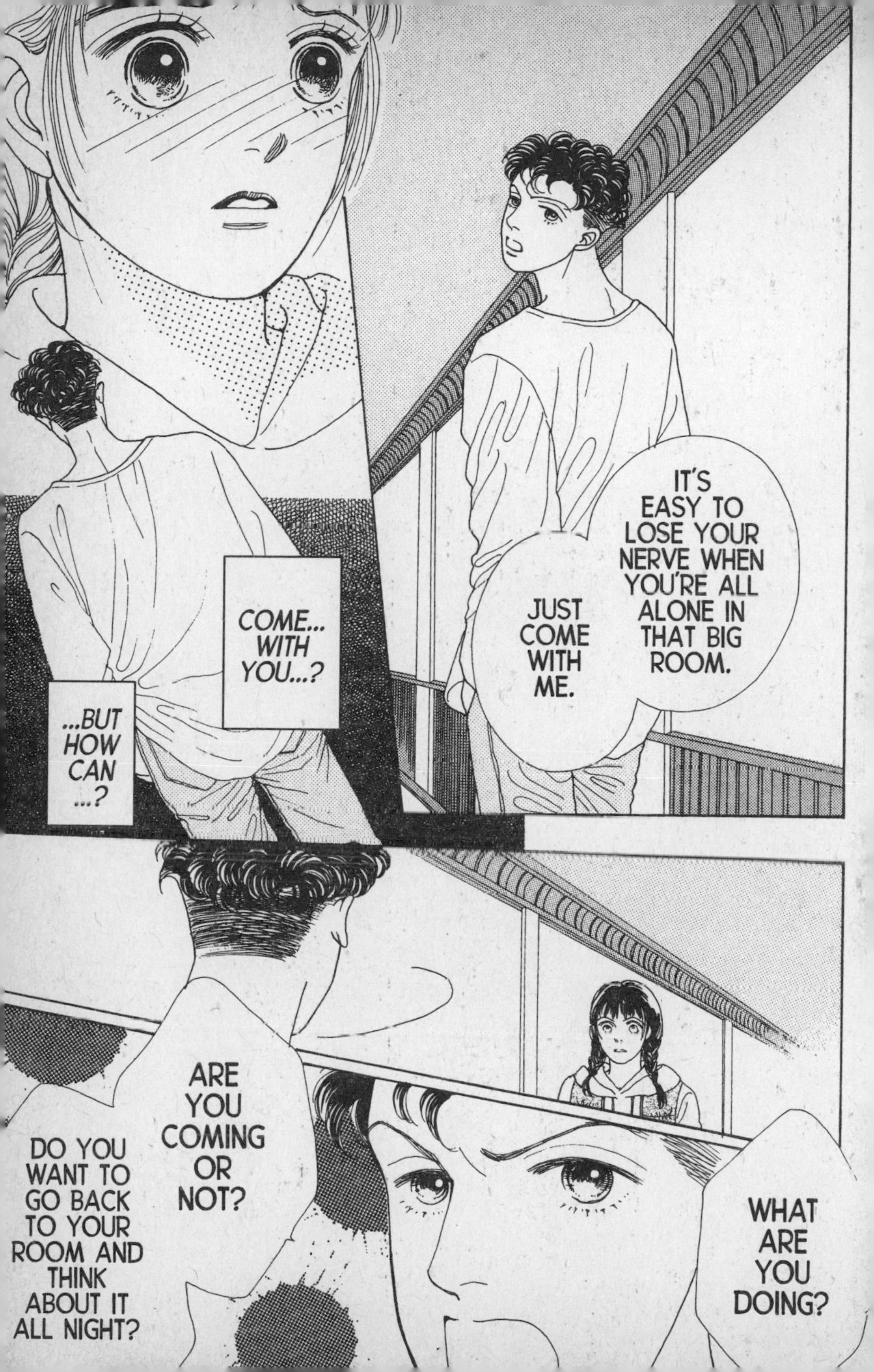
IT'S EASY TO LOSE YOUR NERVE WHEN YOU'RE ALL ALONE IN THAT BIG ROOM.
JUST COME WITH ME.
COME... WITH YOU...?
...BUT HOW CAN ...?
ARE YOU COMING OR NOT?
DO YOU WANT TO GO BACK TO YOUR ROOM AND THINK ABOUT IT ALL NIGHT?
WHAT ARE YOU DOING?

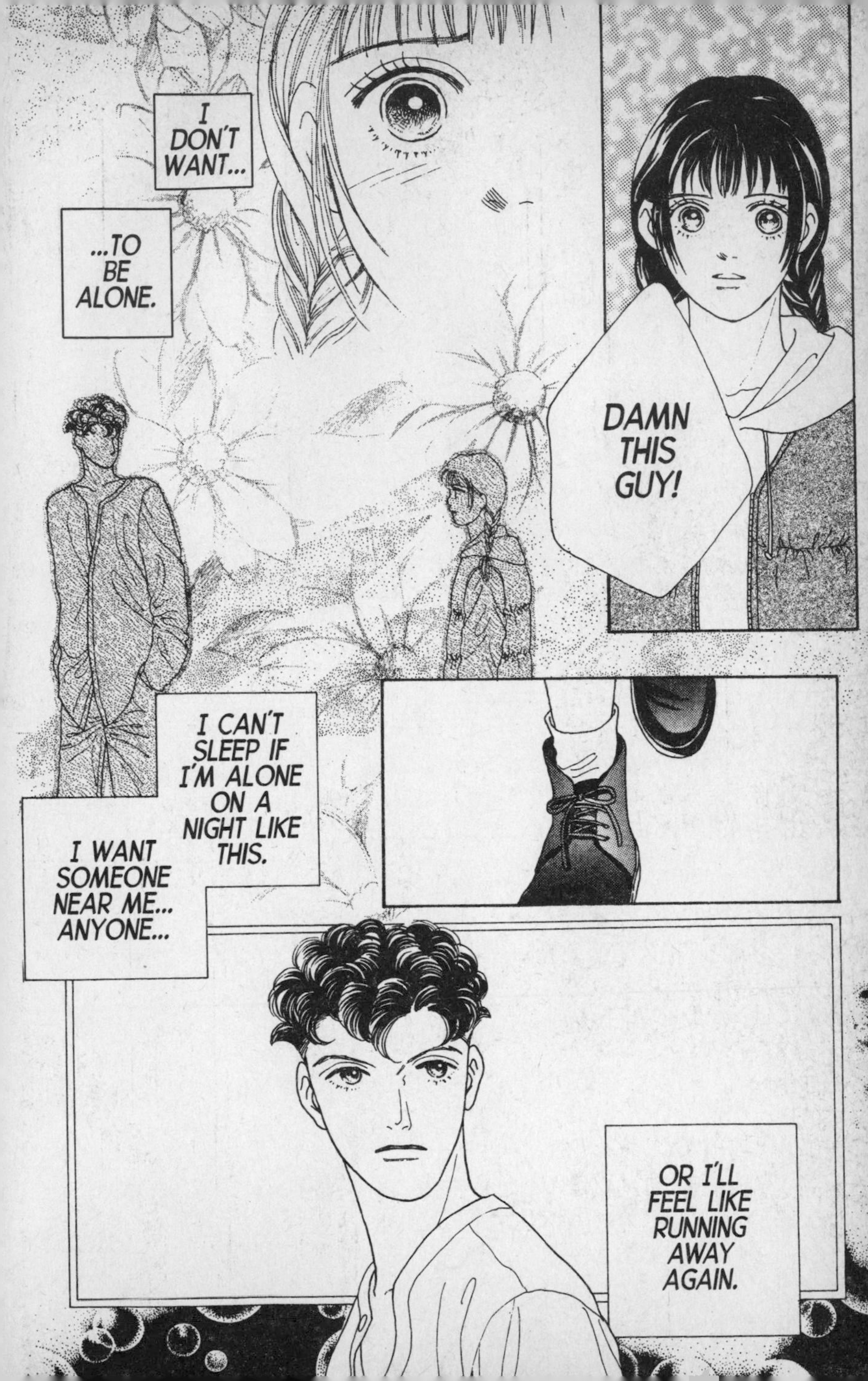
DAMN THIS GUY!
I DON'T WANT...
...TO BE ALONE.
I CAN'T SLEEP IF I'M ALONE ON A NIGHT LIKE THIS.
I WANT SOMEONE NEAR ME... ANYONE...
OR I'LL FEEL LIKE RUNNING AWAY AGAIN.

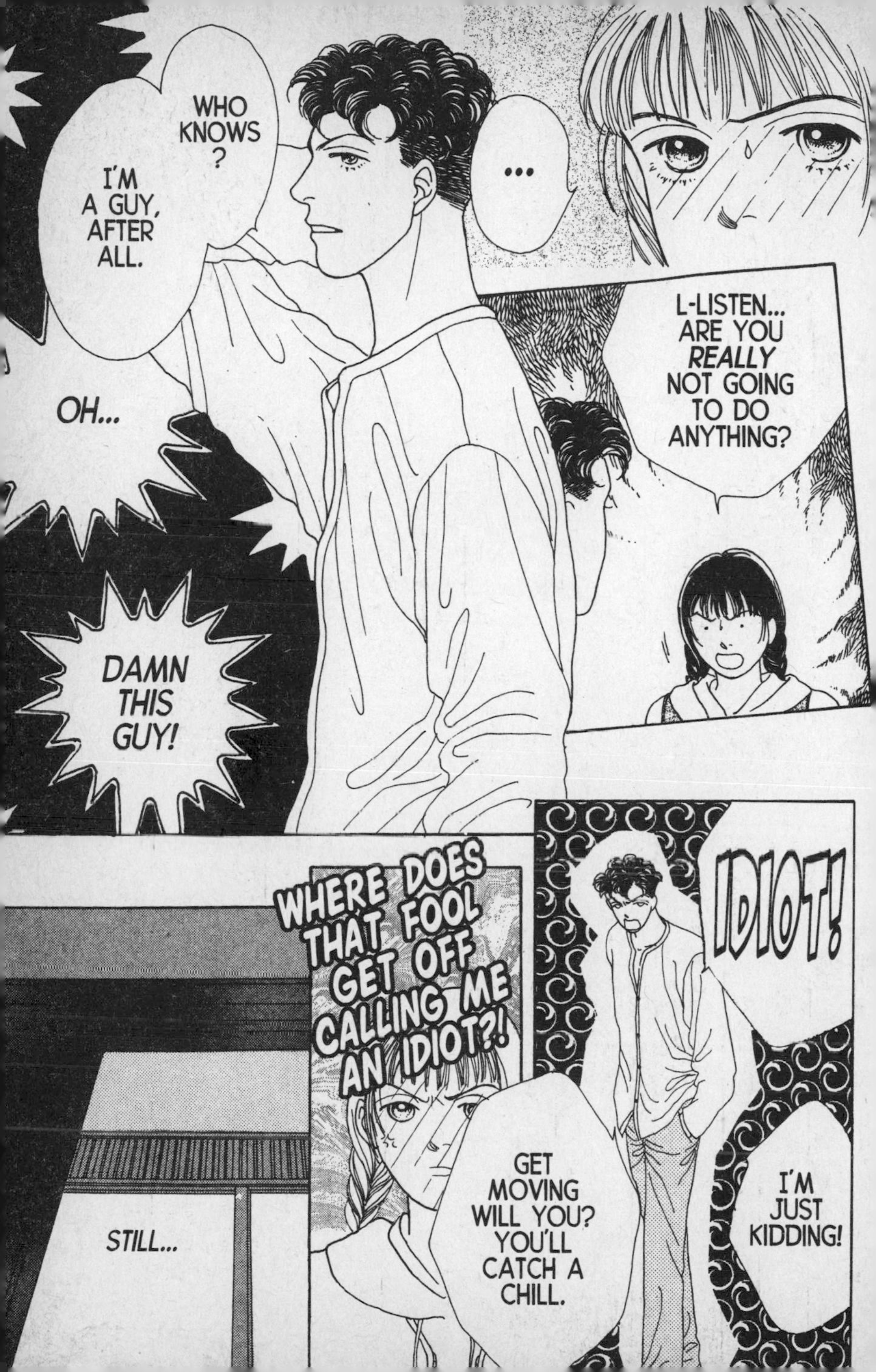
...
L-LISTEN... ARE YOU *REALLY* NOT GOING TO DO ANYTHING?
WHO KNOWS?
I'M A GUY, AFTER ALL.
OH...
DAMN THIS GUY!
IDIOT!
I'M JUST KIDDING!
GET MOVING WILL YOU? YOU'LL CATCH A CHILL.
WHERE DOES THAT FOOL GET OFF CALLING ME AN IDIOT?!
STILL...

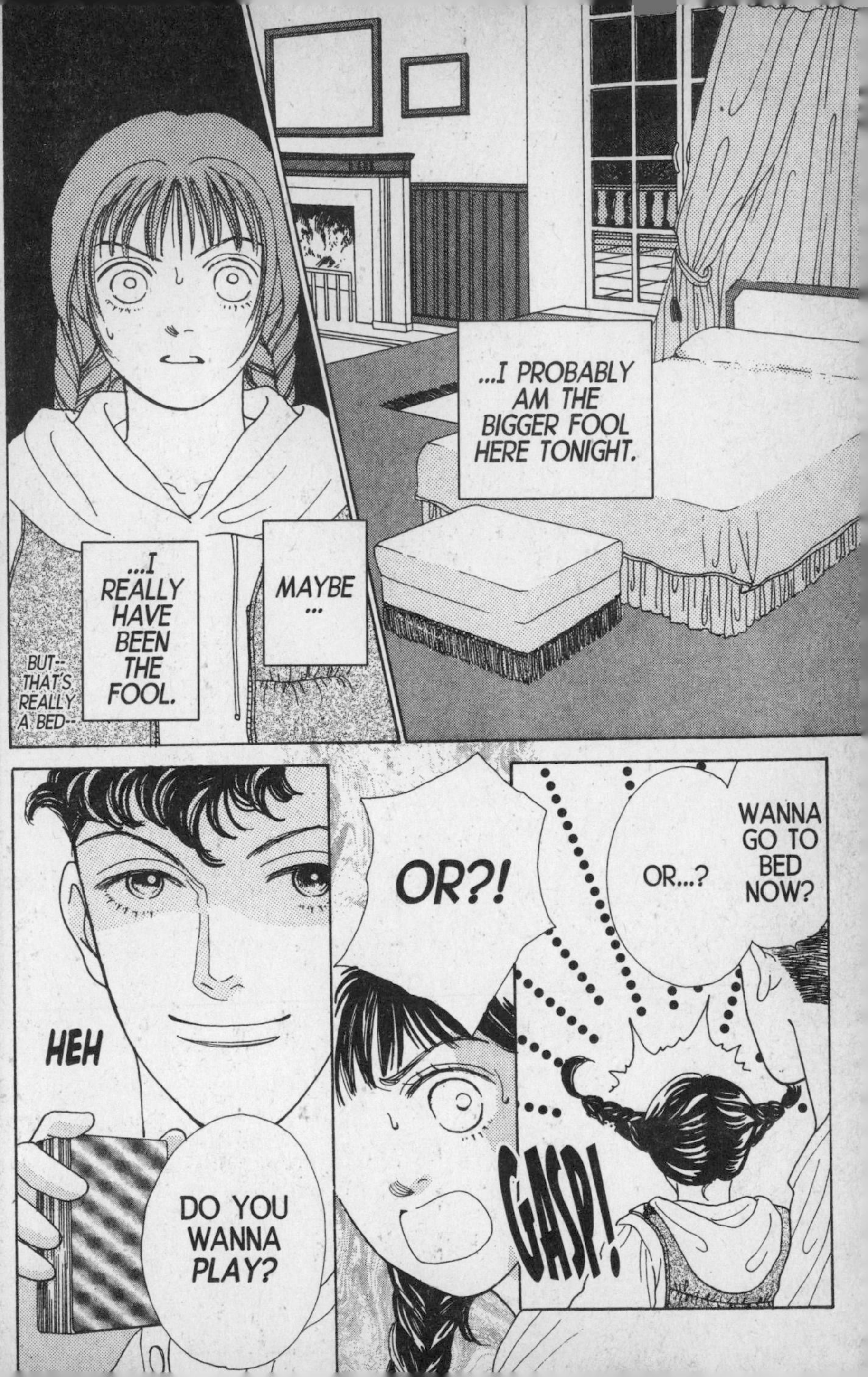
...I PROBABLY AM THE BIGGER FOOL HERE TONIGHT.
MAYBE ...
...I REALLY HAVE BEEN THE FOOL.
BUT-- THAT'S REALLY A BED--
WANNA GO TO BED NOW?
OR...?
OR?!
GASP!
HEH
DO YOU WANNA PLAY?

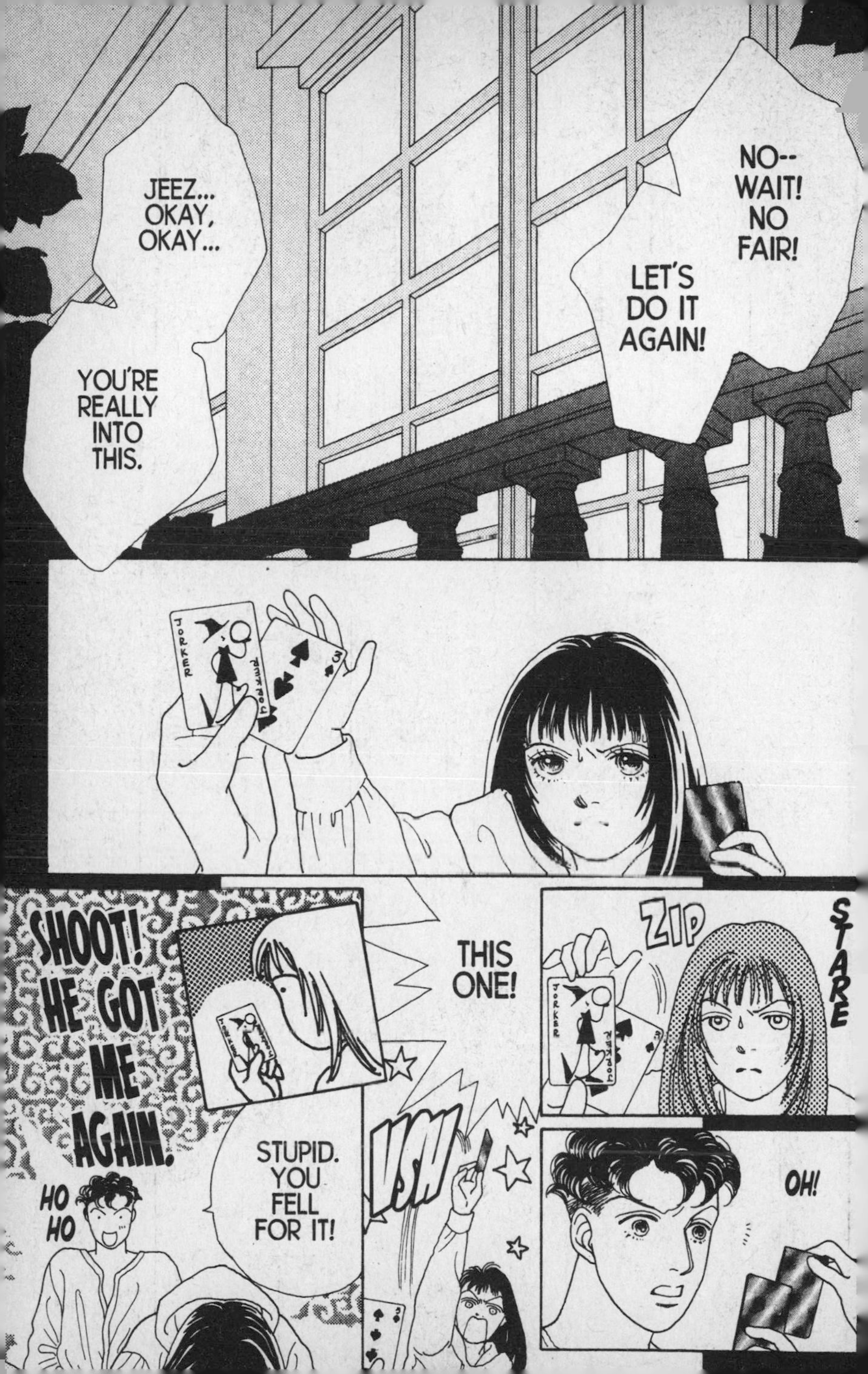
NO-- WAIT! NO FAIR!
LET'S DO IT AGAIN!
JEEZ... OKAY, OKAY...
YOU'RE REALLY INTO THIS.
JORKER
STARE
ZIP
OH!
THIS ONE!
VSH
SHOOT! HE GOT ME AGAIN.
STUPID. YOU FELL FOR IT!
HO HO

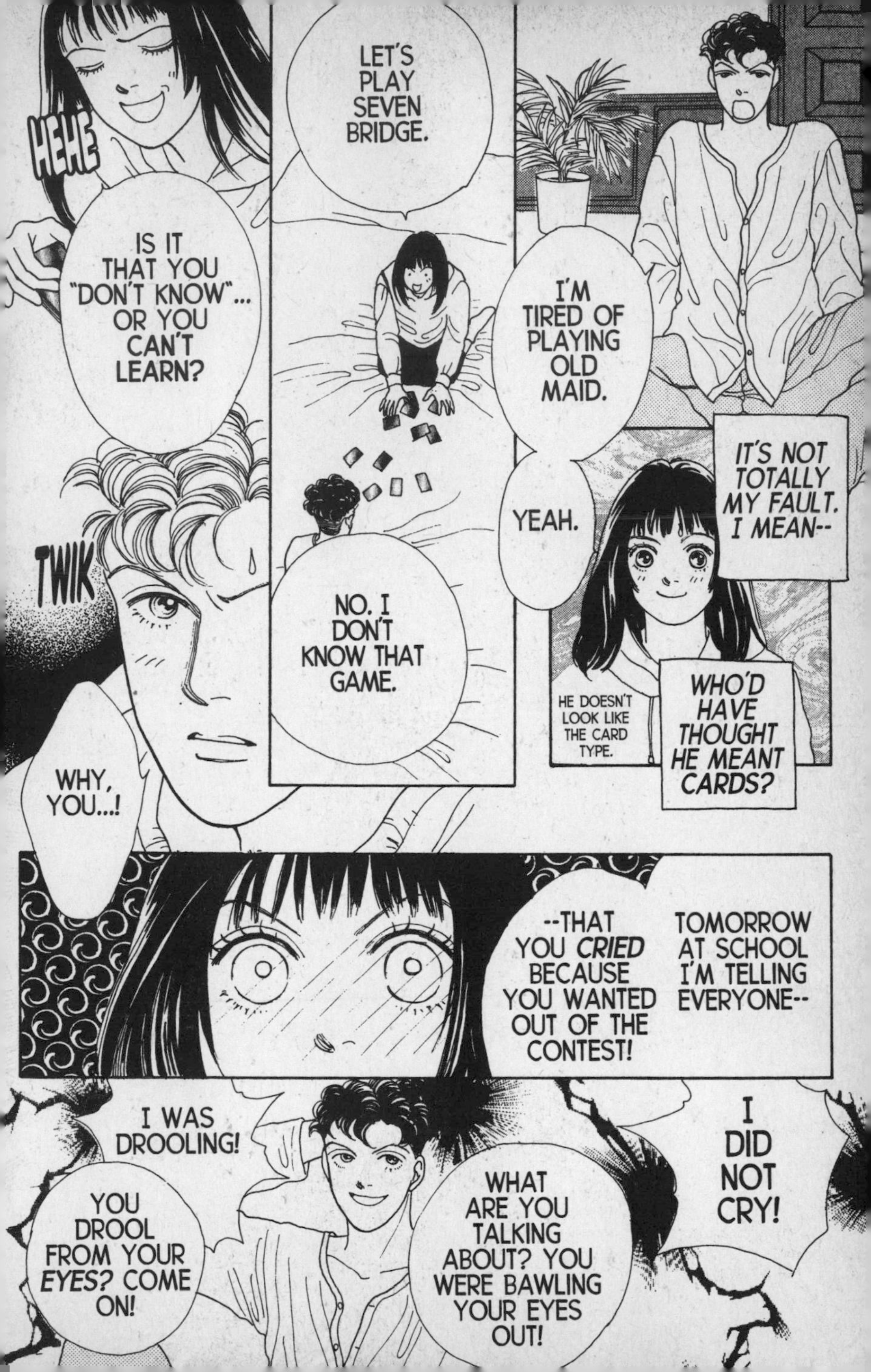
I'M TIRED OF PLAYING OLD MAID.
YEAH.
IT'S NOT TOTALLY MY FAULT. I MEAN--
HE DOESN'T LOOK LIKE THE CARD TYPE.
WHO'D HAVE THOUGHT HE MEANT CARDS?
LET'S PLAY SEVEN BRIDGE.
NO. I DON'T KNOW THAT GAME.
HEHE
IS IT THAT YOU "DON'T KNOW"... OR YOU CAN'T LEARN?
TWIK
WHY, YOU...!
TOMORROW AT SCHOOL I'M TELLING EVERYONE--
--THAT YOU CRIED BECAUSE YOU WANTED OUT OF THE CONTEST!
I DID NOT CRY!
WHAT ARE YOU TALKING ABOUT? YOU WERE BAWLING YOUR EYES OUT!
I WAS DROOLING!
YOU DROOL FROM YOUR EYES? COME ON!

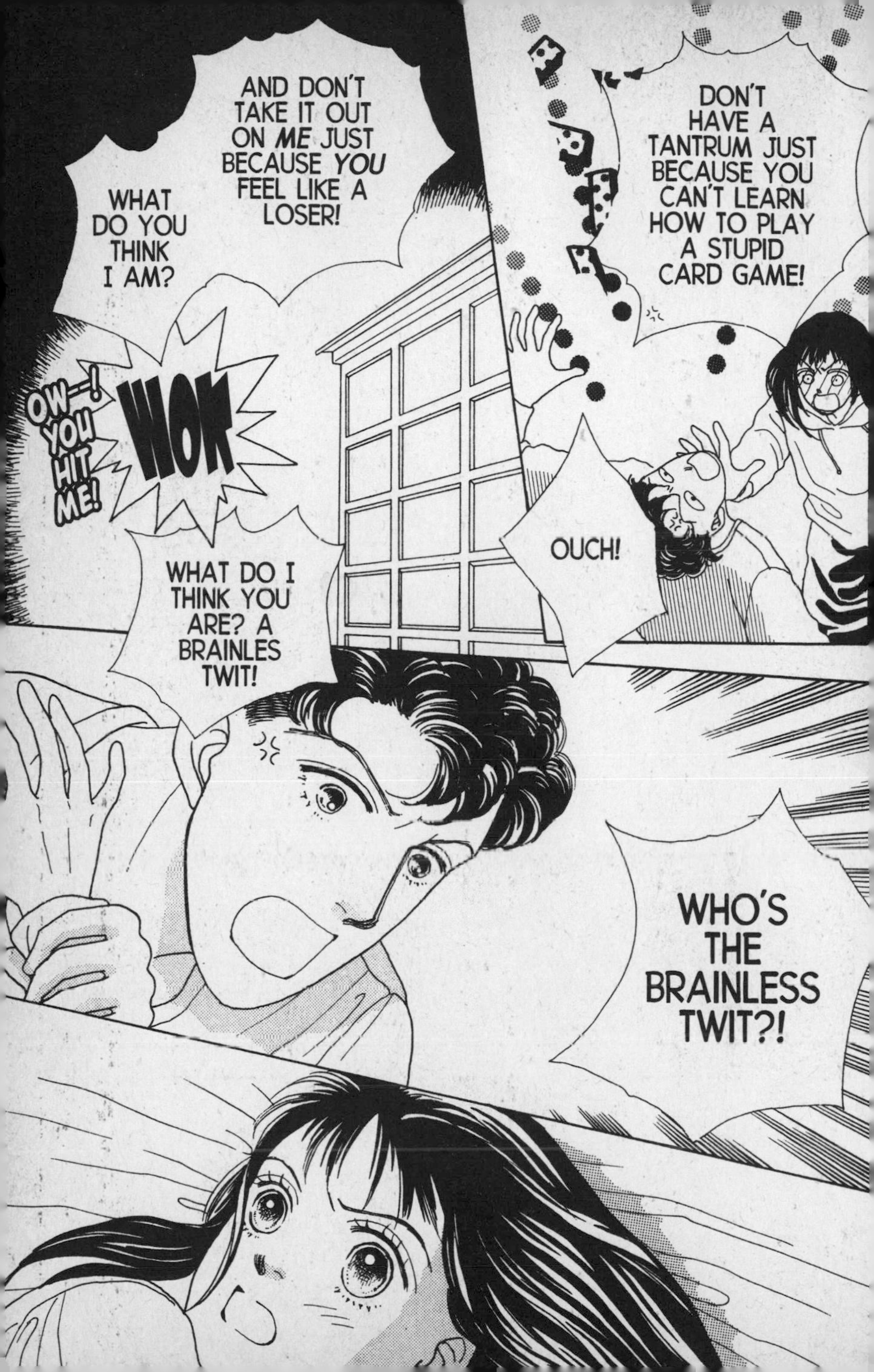
DON'T HAVE A TANTRUM JUST BECAUSE YOU CAN'T LEARN HOW TO PLAY A STUPID CARD GAME!
OUCH!
AND DON'T TAKE IT OUT ON *ME* JUST BECAUSE *YOU* FEEL LIKE A LOSER!
WHAT DO YOU THINK I AM?
WOK
OW--! YOU HIT ME!
WHAT DO I THINK YOU ARE? A BRAINLES TWIT!
WHO'S THE BRAINLESS TWIT?!

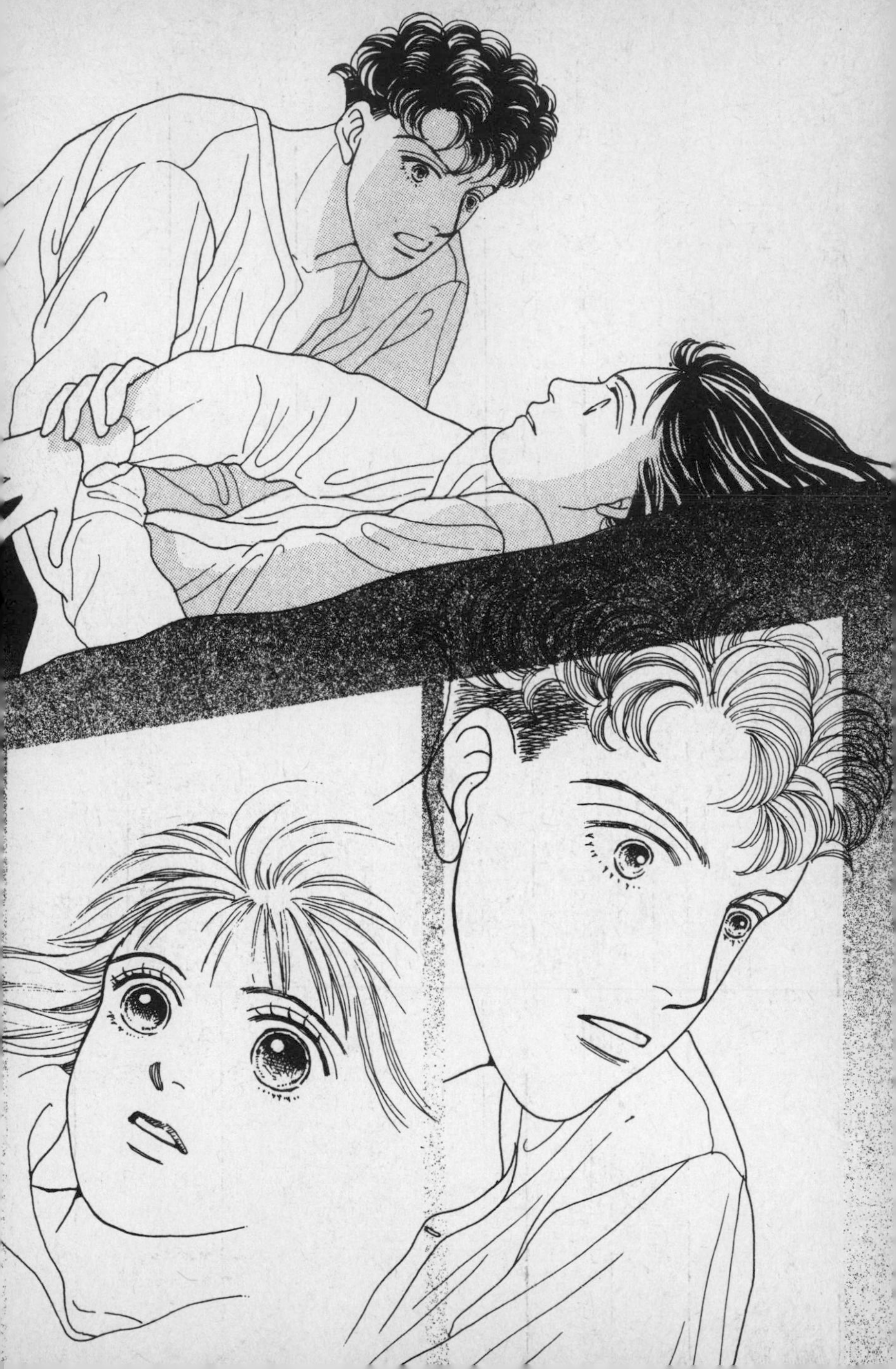

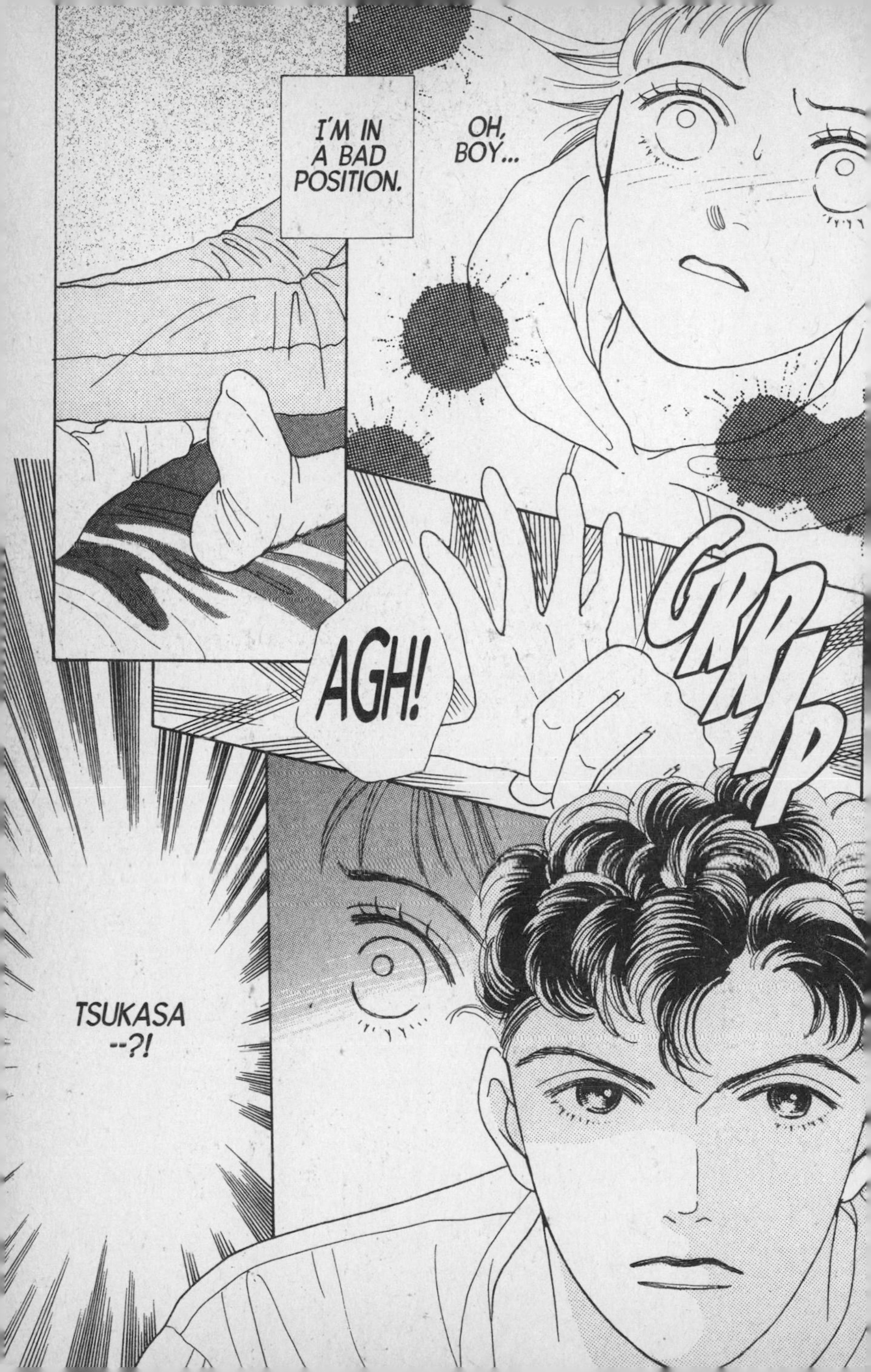
OH, BOY...
I'M IN A BAD POSITION.
GRRIP
AGH!
TSUKASA --?!

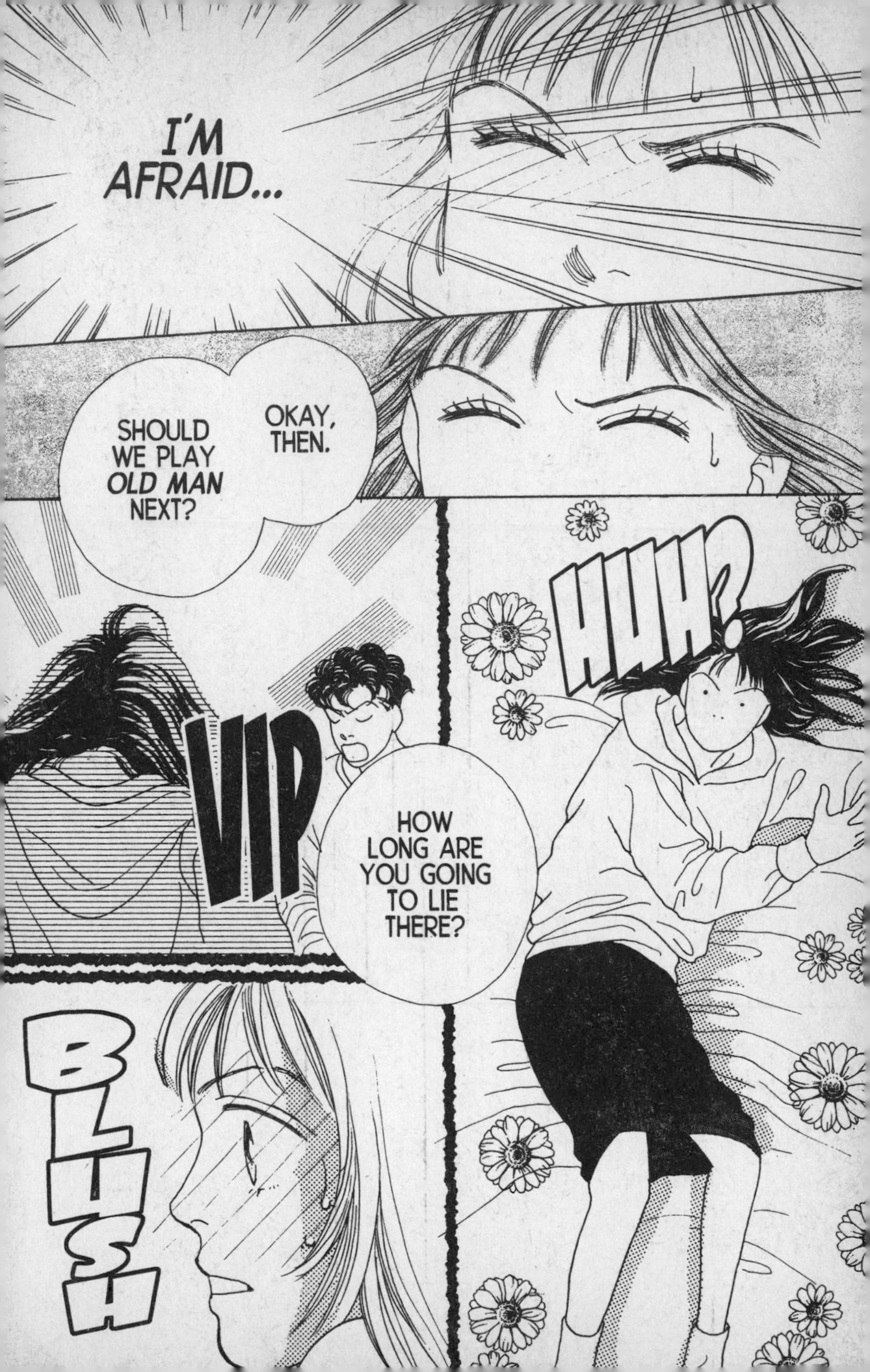

I'M AFRAID...
OKAY, THEN.
SHOULD WE PLAY *OLD MAN* NEXT?
HUH?
VIP
HOW LONG ARE YOU GOING TO LIE THERE?
BLUSH

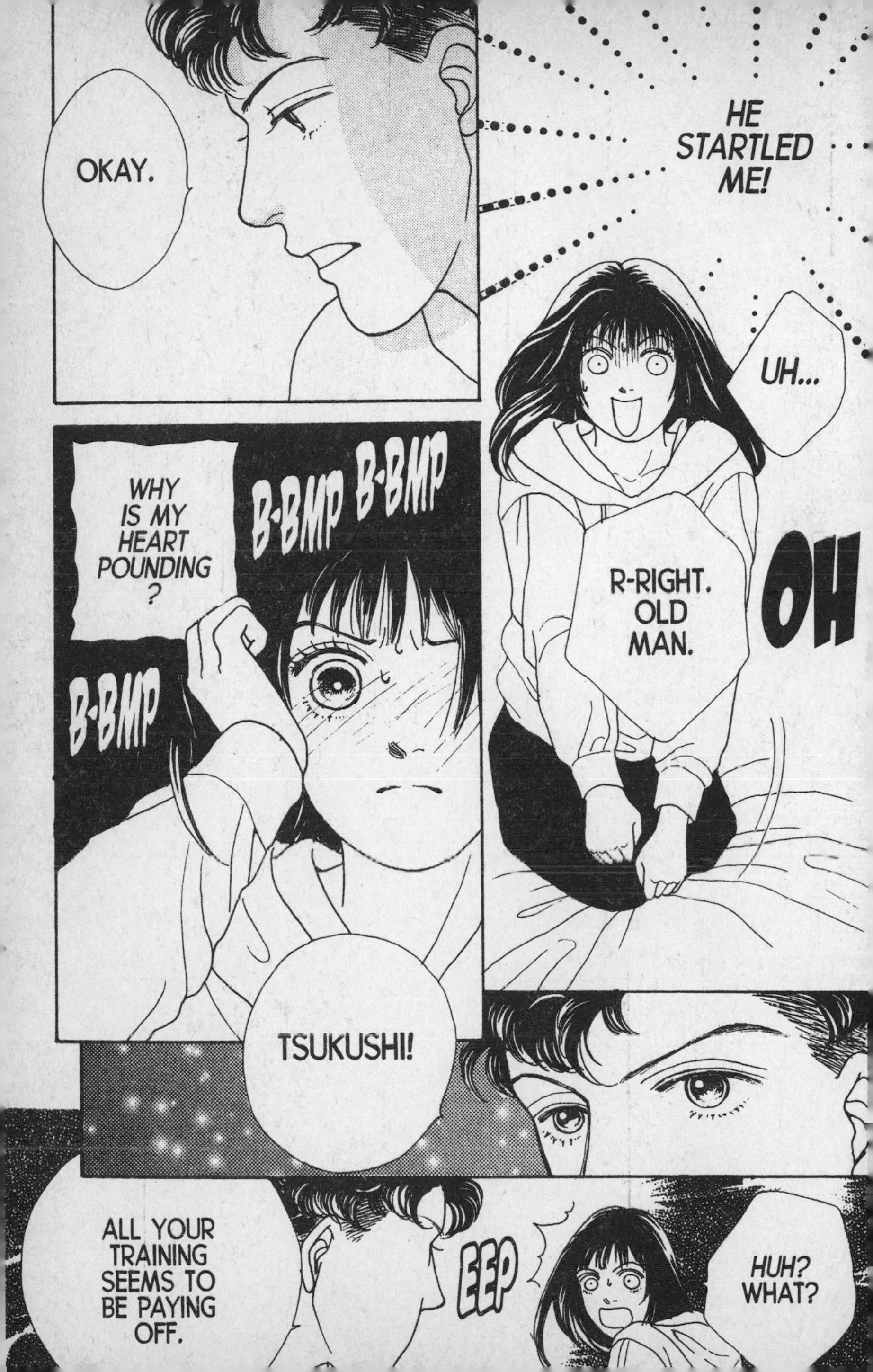
HE STARTLED ME!
UH...
R-RIGHT. OLD MAN.
OH
OKAY.
WHY IS MY HEART POUNDING?
B-BMP B-BMP
B-BMP
TSUKUSHI!
HUH? WHAT?
EEP
ALL YOUR TRAINING SEEMS TO BE PAYING OFF.

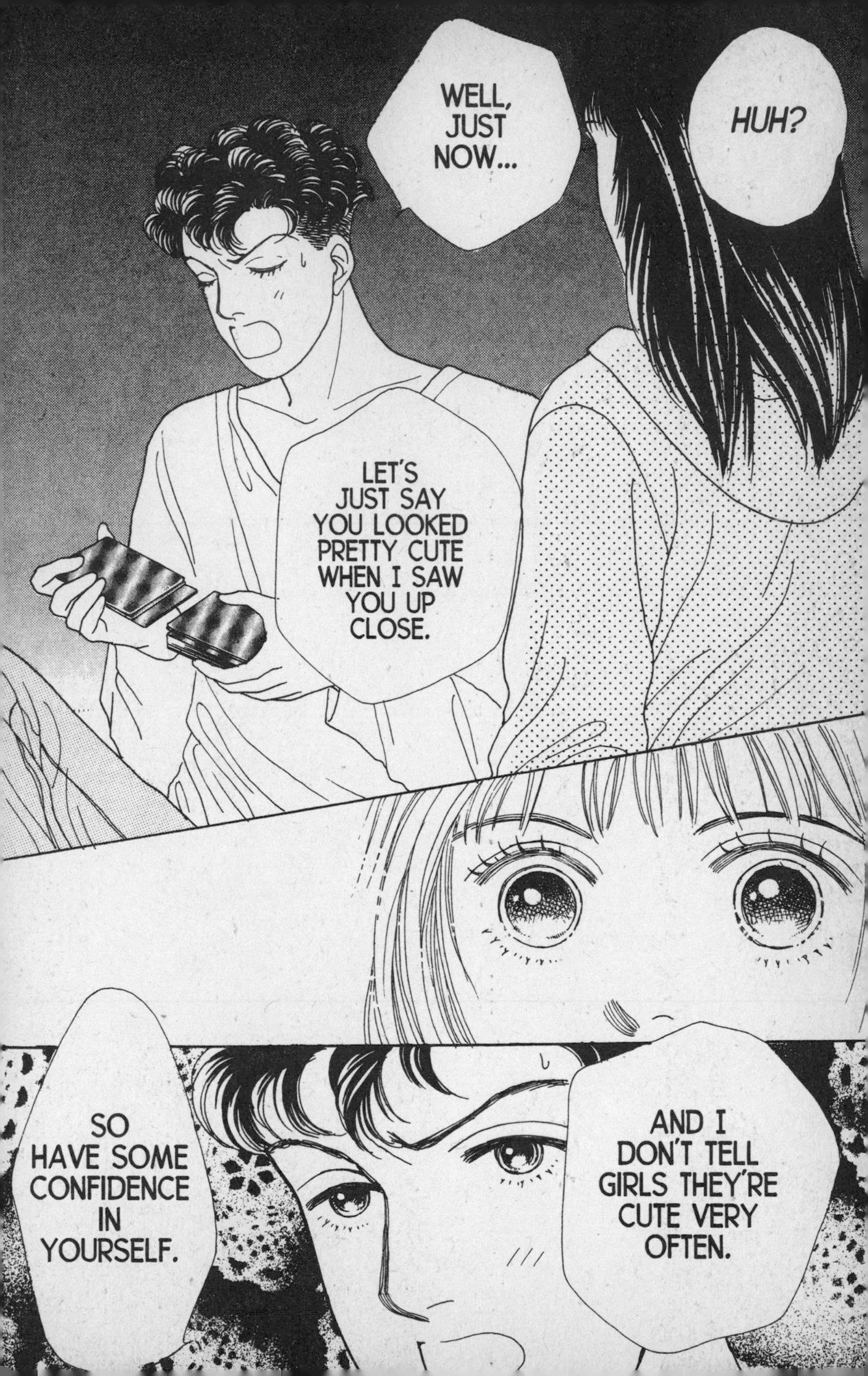
HUH?
WELL, JUST NOW...
LET'S JUST SAY YOU LOOKED PRETTY CUTE WHEN I SAW YOU UP CLOSE.
AND I DON'T TELL GIRLS THEY'RE CUTE VERY OFTEN.
SO HAVE SOME CONFIDENCE IN YOURSELF.

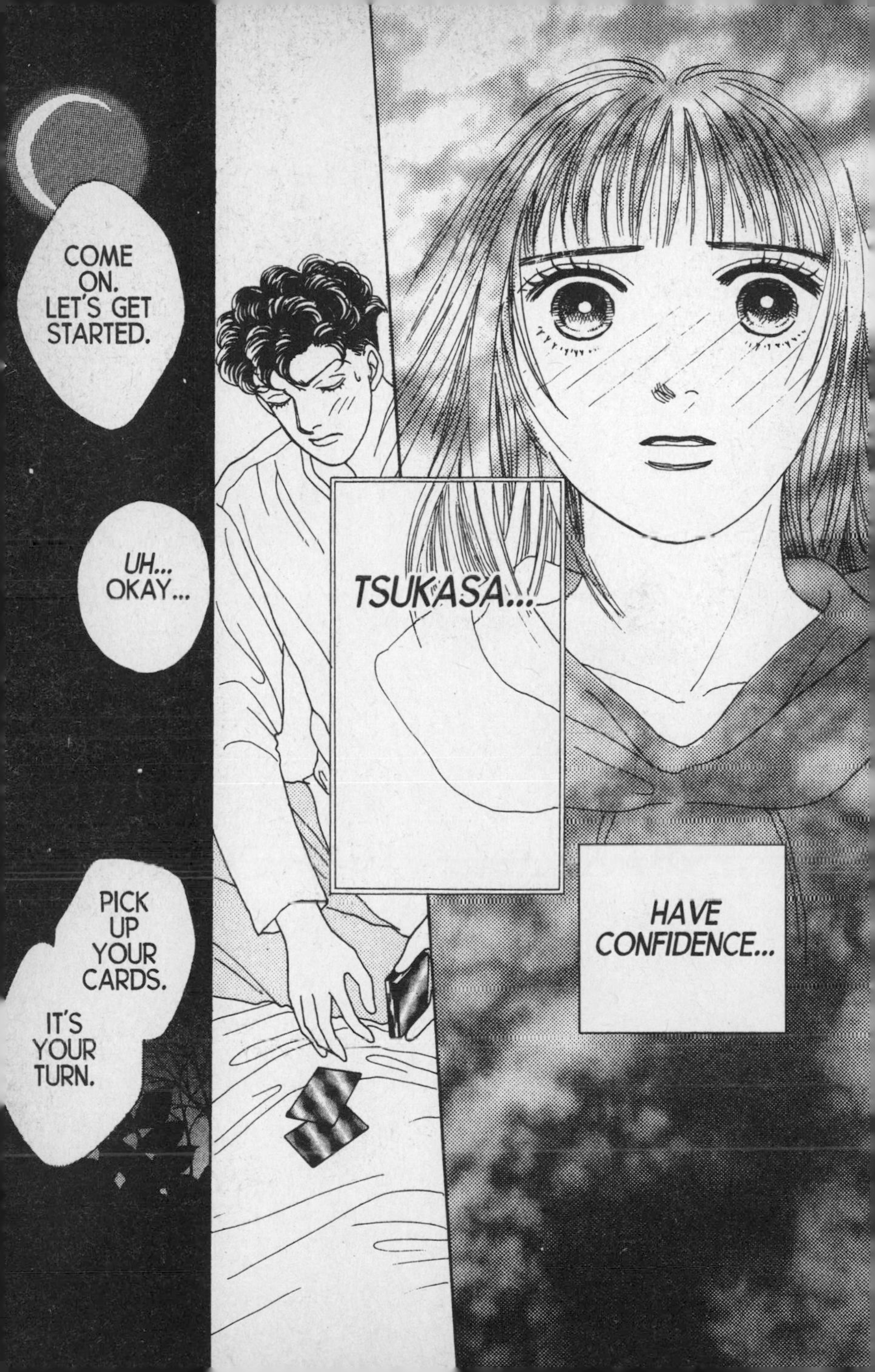
TSUKASA...
HAVE CONFIDENCE...
COME ON. LET'S GET STARTED.
UH... OKAY...
PICK UP YOUR CARDS.
IT'S YOUR TURN.

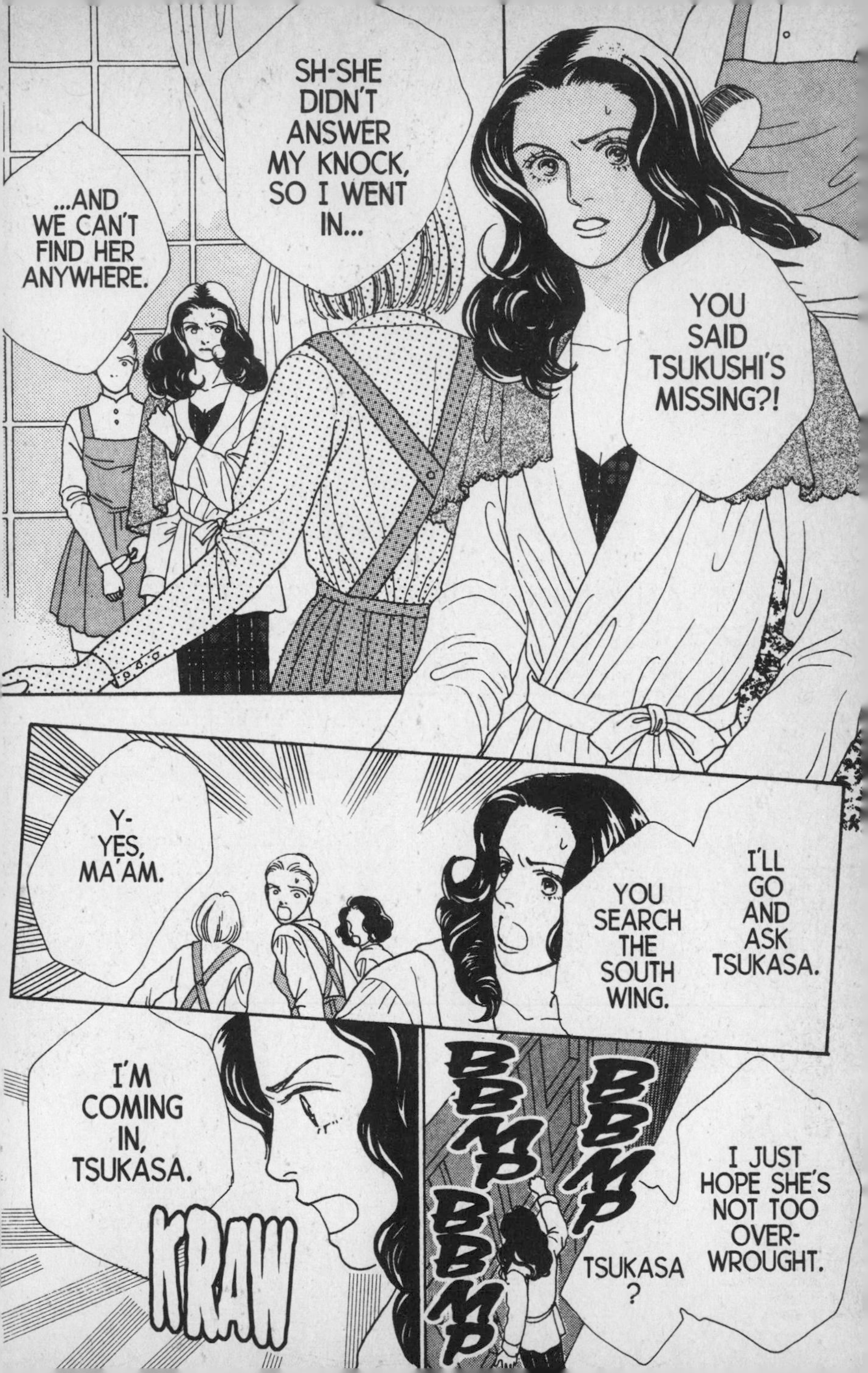
YOU SAID TSUKUSHI'S MISSING?!
SH-SHE DIDN'T ANSWER MY KNOCK, SO I WENT IN...
...AND WE CAN'T FIND HER ANYWHERE.
I'LL GO AND ASK TSUKASA.
YOU SEARCH THE SOUTH WING.
Y-YES, MA'AM.
I JUST HOPE SHE'S NOT TOO OVER-WROUGHT.
BBMP
TSUKASA?
BBMP BBMP
I'M COMING IN, TSUKASA.
KRAW

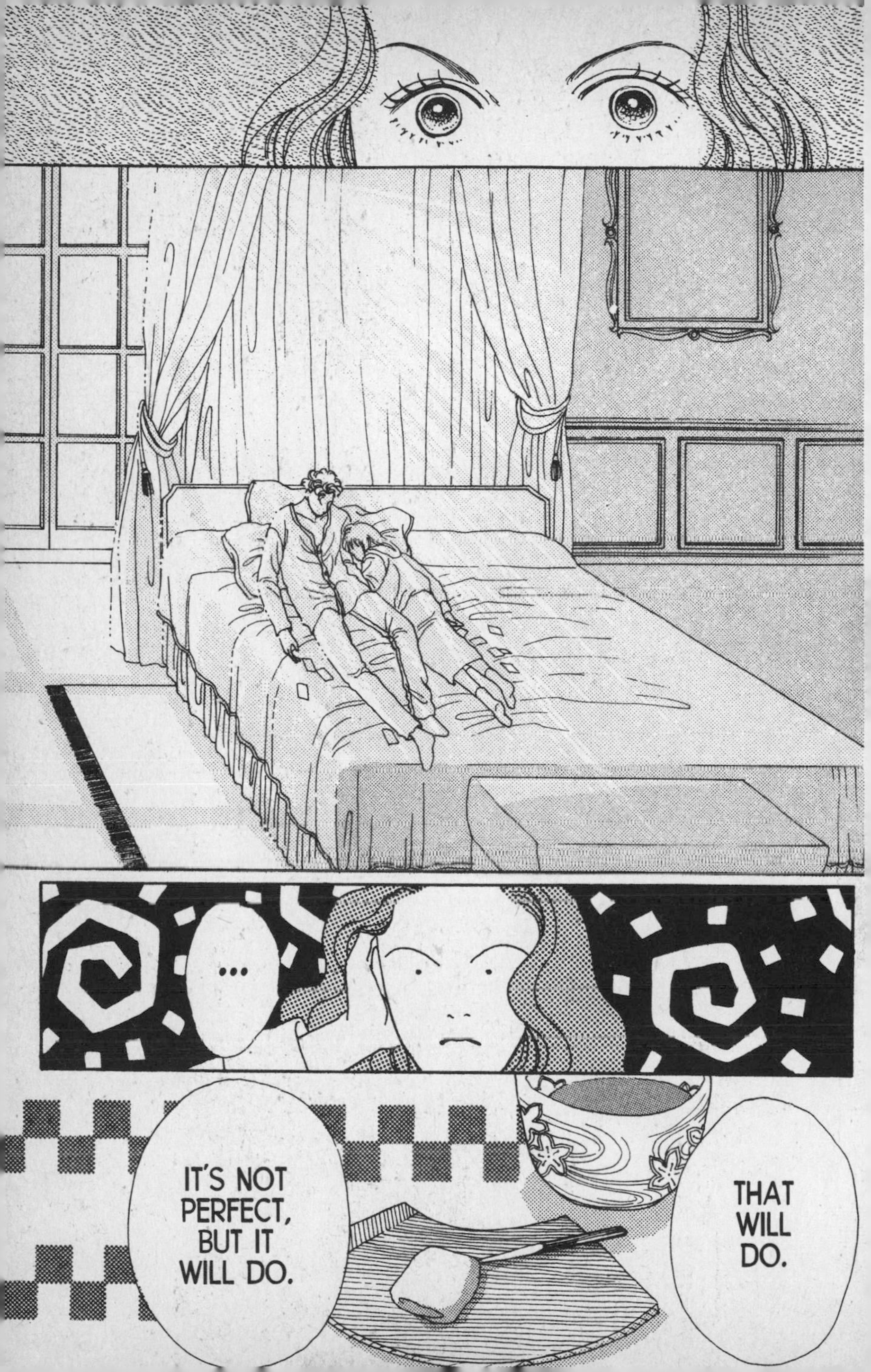
...
THAT WILL DO.
IT'S NOT PERFECT, BUT IT WILL DO.

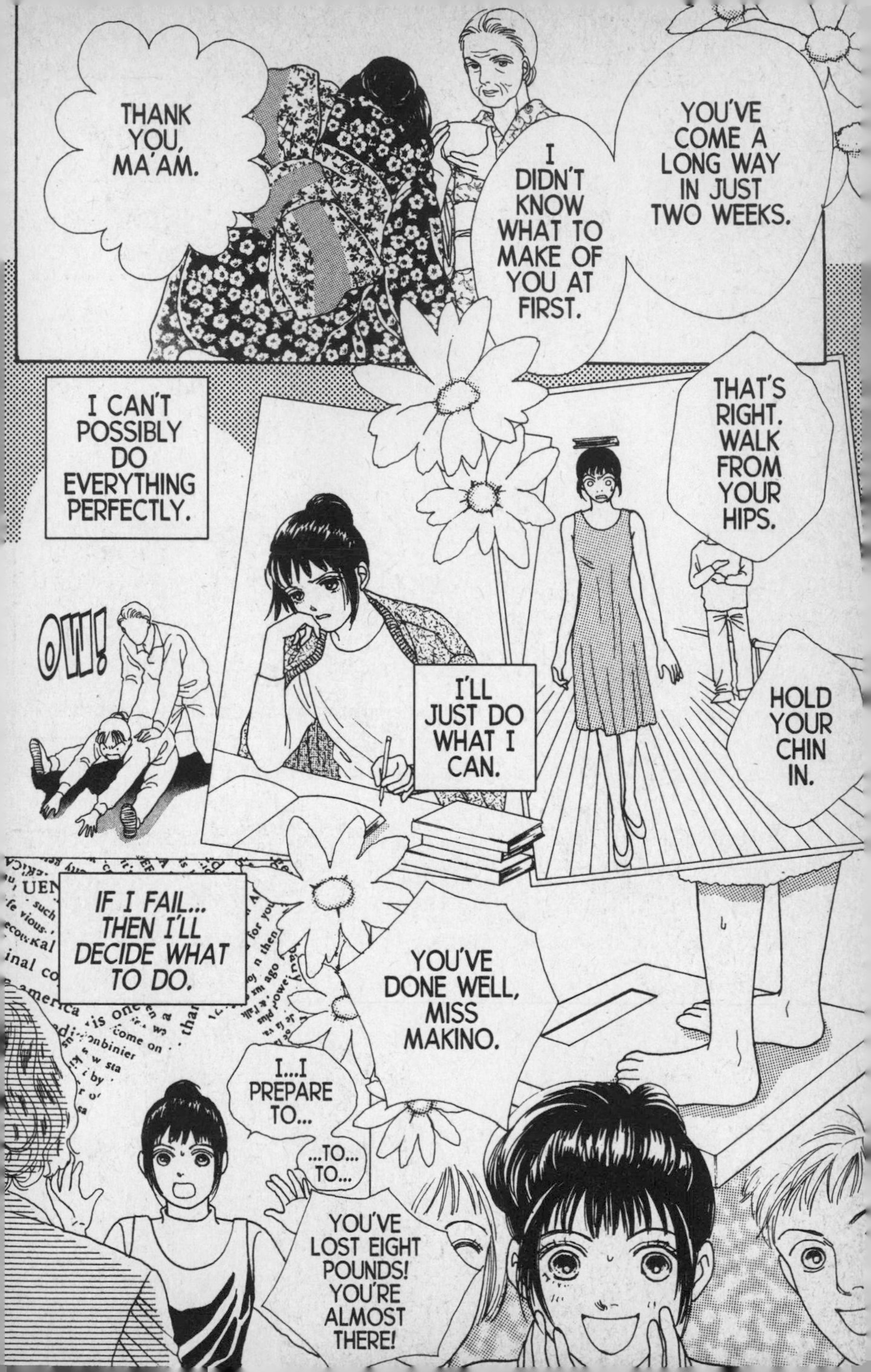
YOU'VE COME A LONG WAY IN JUST TWO WEEKS.
I DIDN'T KNOW WHAT TO MAKE OF YOU AT FIRST.
THANK YOU, MA'AM.
THAT'S RIGHT. WALK FROM YOUR HIPS.
HOLD YOUR CHIN IN.
I'LL JUST DO WHAT I CAN.
I CAN'T POSSIBLY DO EVERYTHING PERFECTLY.
OW!
YOU'VE DONE WELL, MISS MAKINO.
IF I FAIL... THEN I'LL DECIDE WHAT TO DO.
YOU'VE LOST EIGHT POUNDS! YOU'RE ALMOST THERE!
I...I PREPARE TO...
...TO... TO...

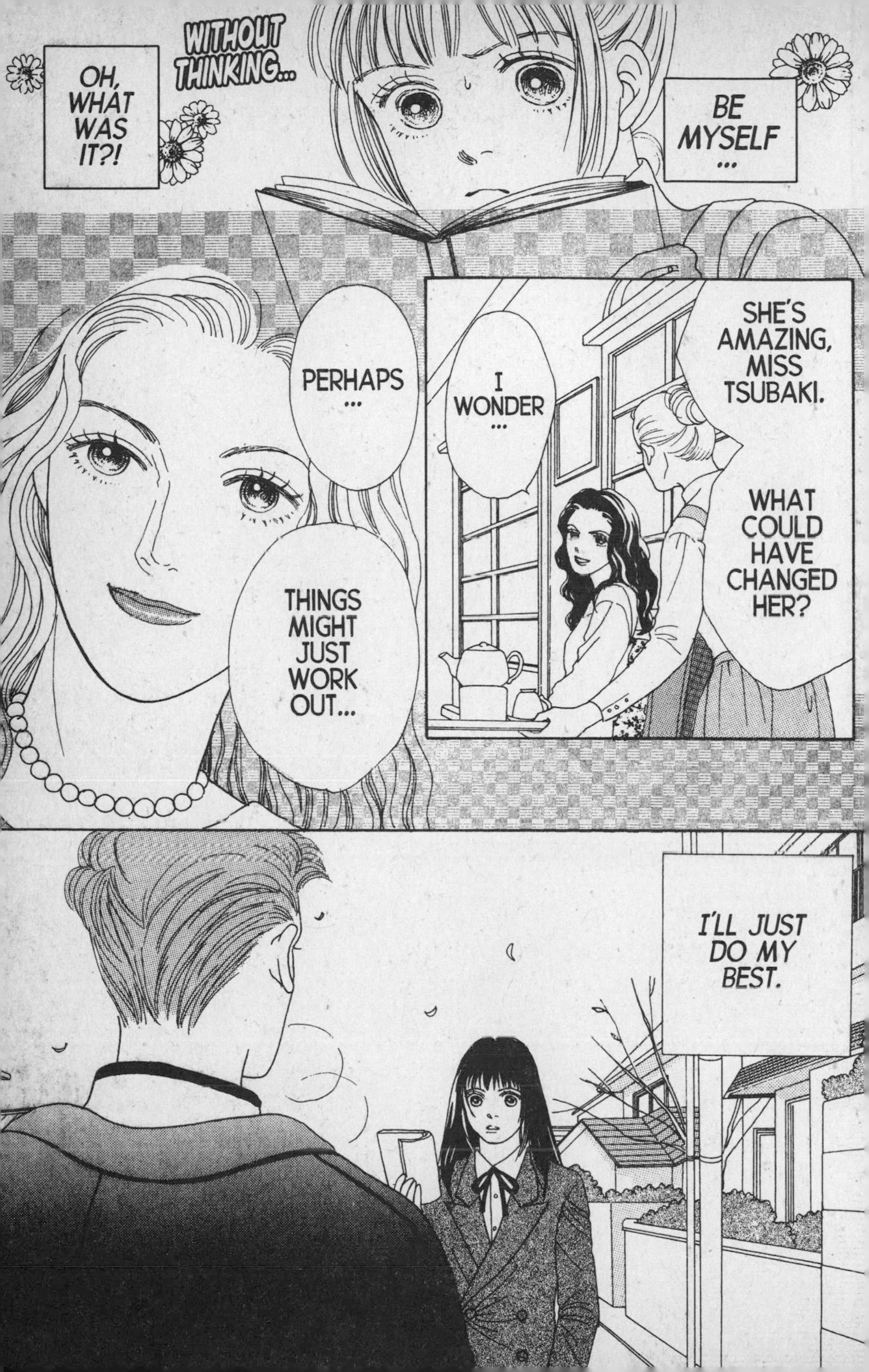
BE MYSELF ...
WITHOUT THINKING...
OH, WHAT WAS IT?!
SHE'S AMAZING, MISS TSUBAKI.
WHAT COULD HAVE CHANGED HER?
I WONDER ...
PERHAPS ...
THINGS MIGHT JUST WORK OUT...
I'LL JUST DO MY BEST.

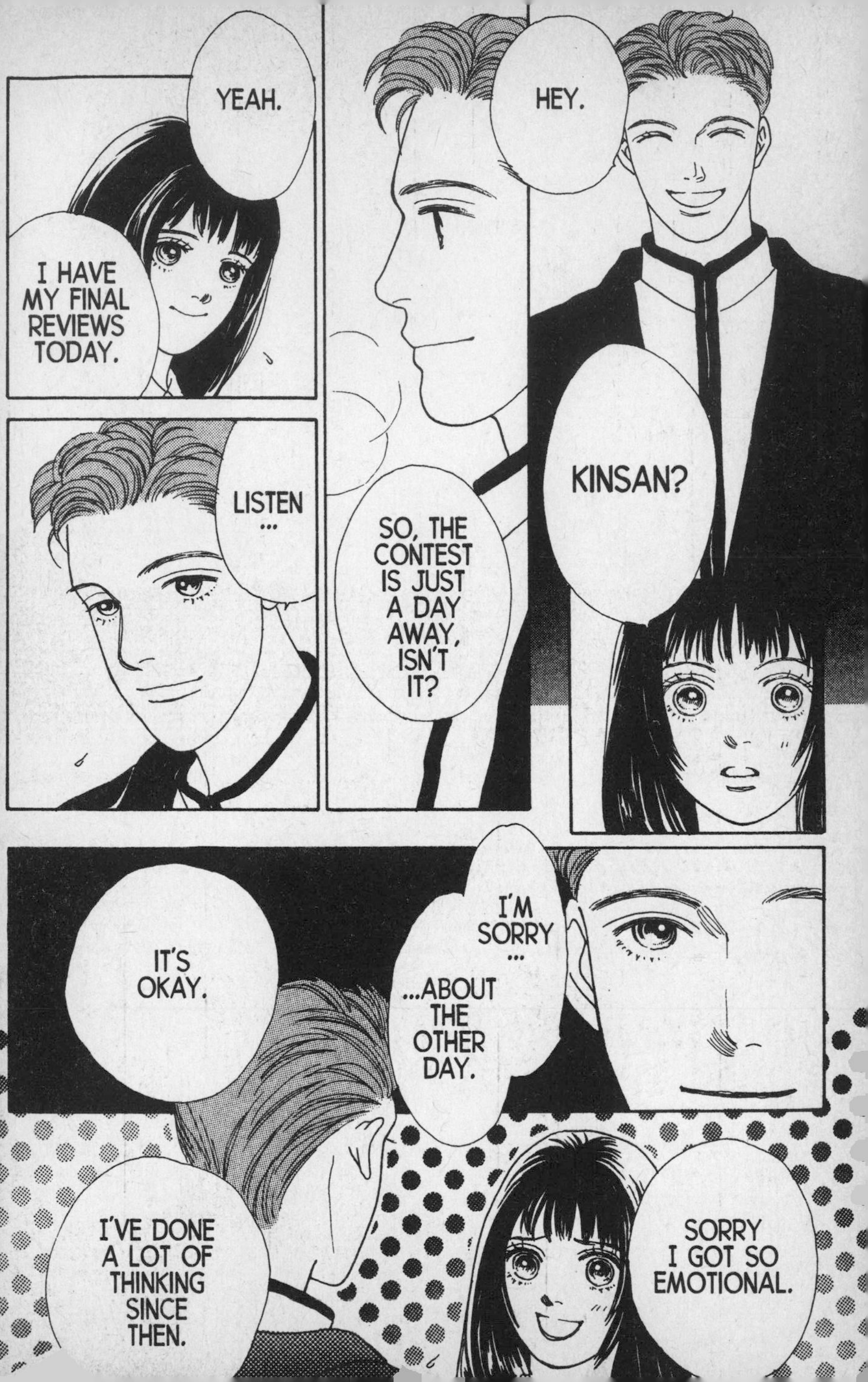
HEY.
KINSAN?
SO, THE CONTEST IS JUST A DAY AWAY, ISN'T IT?
YEAH.
I HAVE MY FINAL REVIEWS TODAY.
LISTEN...
I'M SORRY...
...ABOUT THE OTHER DAY.
IT'S OKAY.
SORRY I GOT SO EMOTIONAL.
I'VE DONE A LOT OF THINKING SINCE THEN.

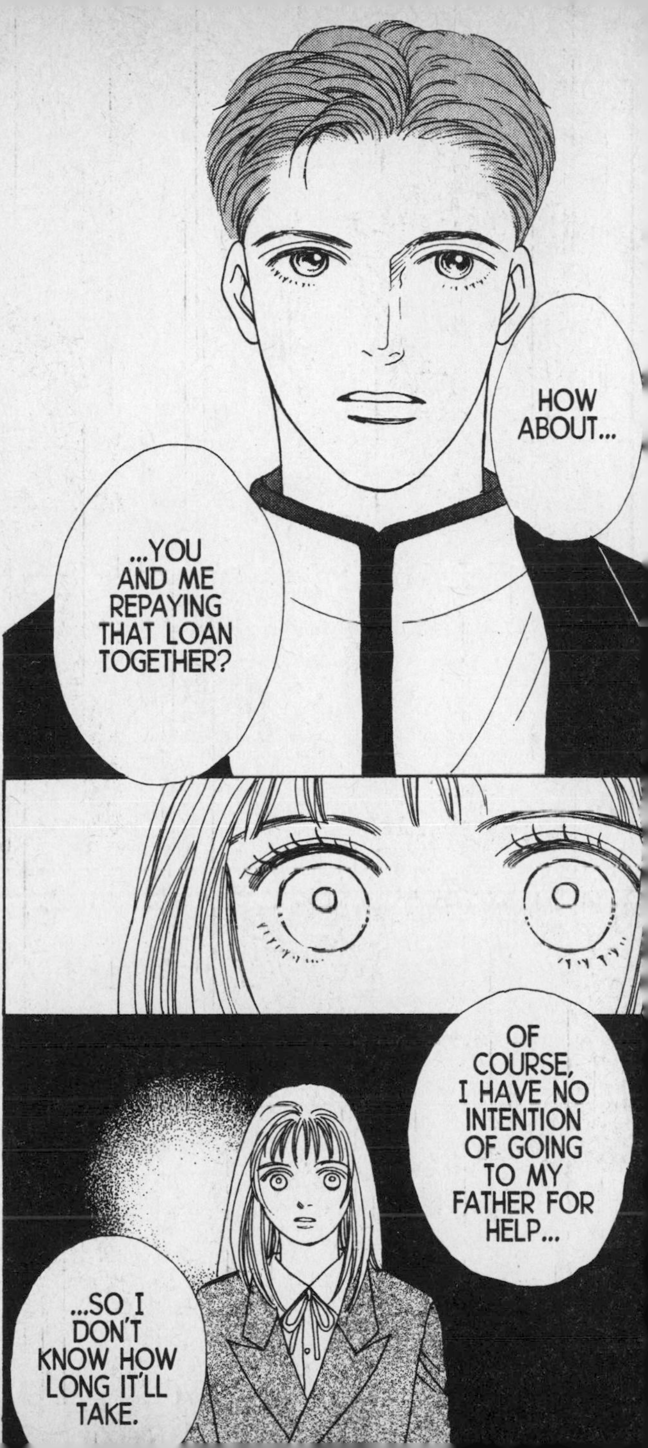
HOW ABOUT...
...YOU AND ME REPAYING THAT LOAN TOGETHER?
OF COURSE, I HAVE NO INTENTION OF GOING TO MY FATHER FOR HELP...
...SO I DON'T KNOW HOW LONG IT'LL TAKE.

☆ I Met Yuki Uchida! ☆

As I mentioned in the previous volume, Boys over Flowers is being made into a movie. The "Margaret" editorial staff and the movie company are handling everything, while I've been busily working on the manga as usual.

One day my editor said, "Let's go see how the filming is going."

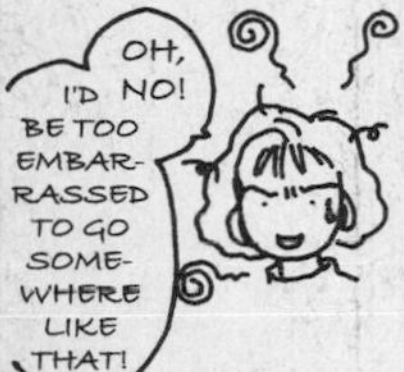
OH, NO! I'D BE TOO EMBARRASSED TO GO SOMEWHERE LIKE THAT!

I argued with her, but she dragged me there anyway. The location was a huge disco in Roppongi called Belle Faire.

What I found strange about movie making is that instead of filming from beginning to end, they can start filming from any point. So what I witnessed was the filming of the last scene of the movie.

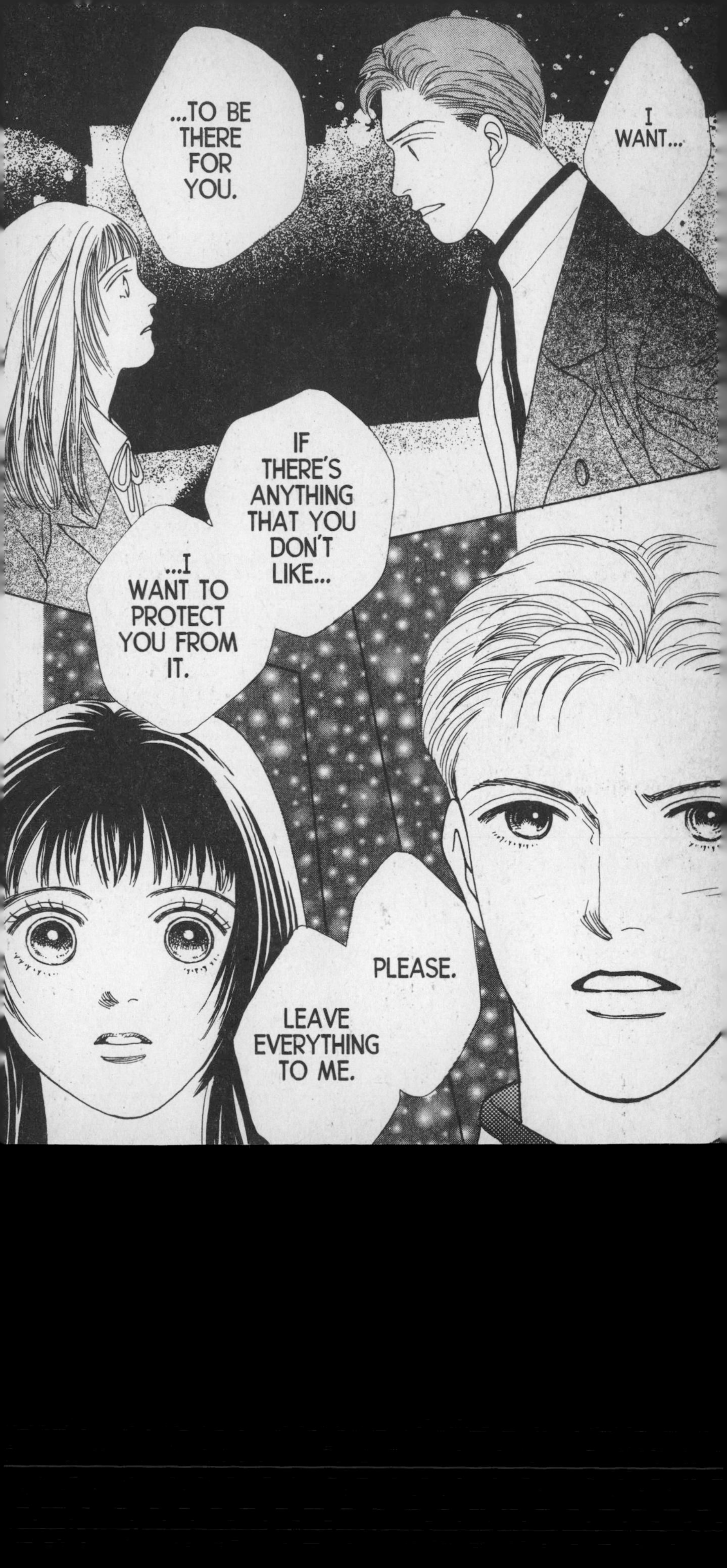
I WANT...
...TO BE THERE FOR YOU.
IF THERE'S ANYTHING THAT YOU DON'T LIKE...
...I WANT TO PROTECT YOU FROM IT.
PLEASE.
LEAVE EVERYTHING TO ME.

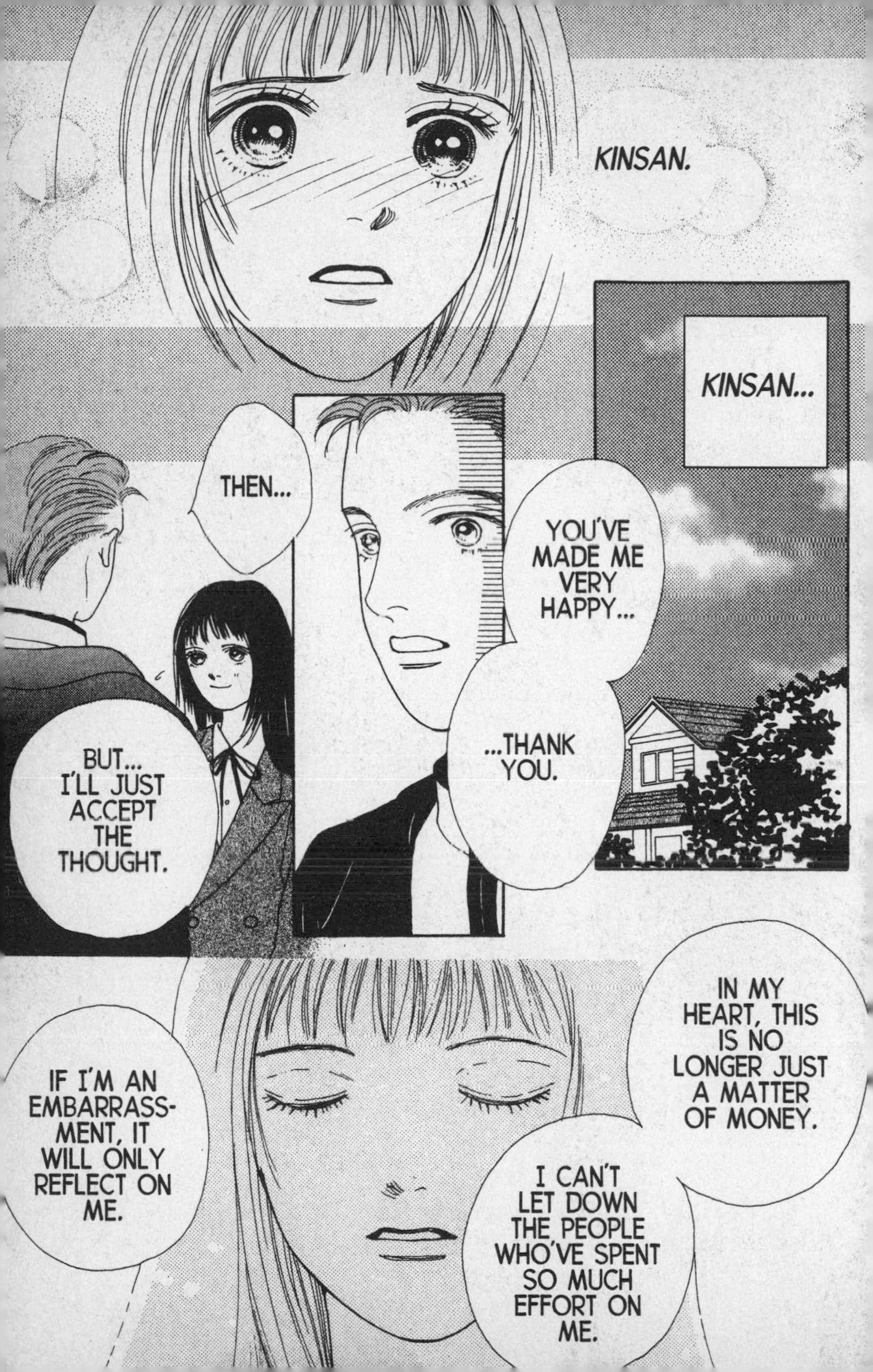
KINSAN.
KINSAN...
YOU'VE MADE ME VERY HAPPY...
...THANK YOU.
THEN...
BUT... I'LL JUST ACCEPT THE THOUGHT.
IN MY HEART, THIS IS NO LONGER JUST A MATTER OF MONEY.
I CAN'T LET DOWN THE PEOPLE WHO'VE SPENT SO MUCH EFFORT ON ME.
IF I'M AN EMBARRASS-MENT, IT WILL ONLY REFLECT ON ME.

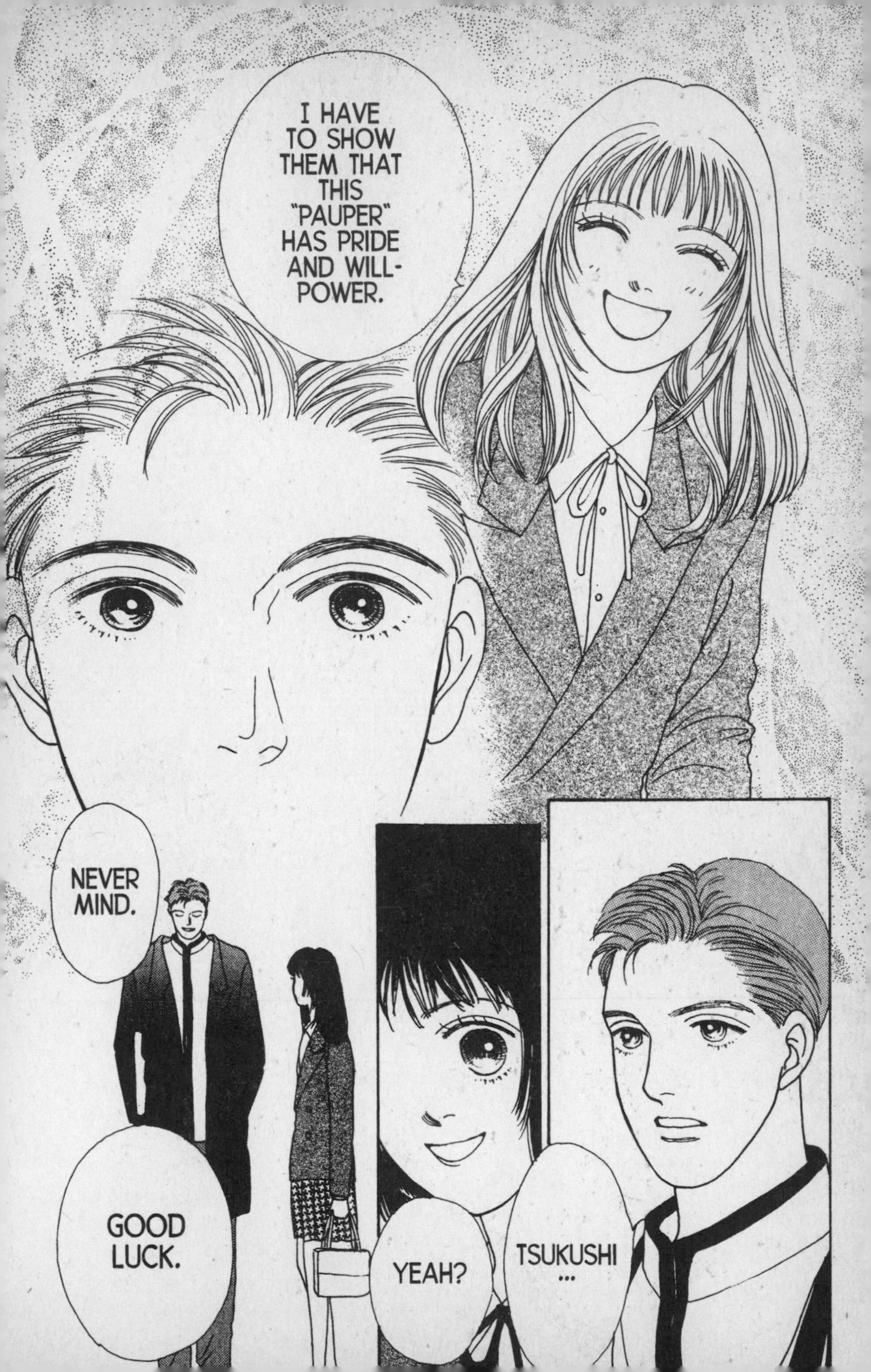
I HAVE TO SHOW THEM THAT THIS "PAUPER" HAS PRIDE AND WILL-POWER.
TSUKUSHI ...
YEAH?
NEVER MIND.
GOOD LUCK.

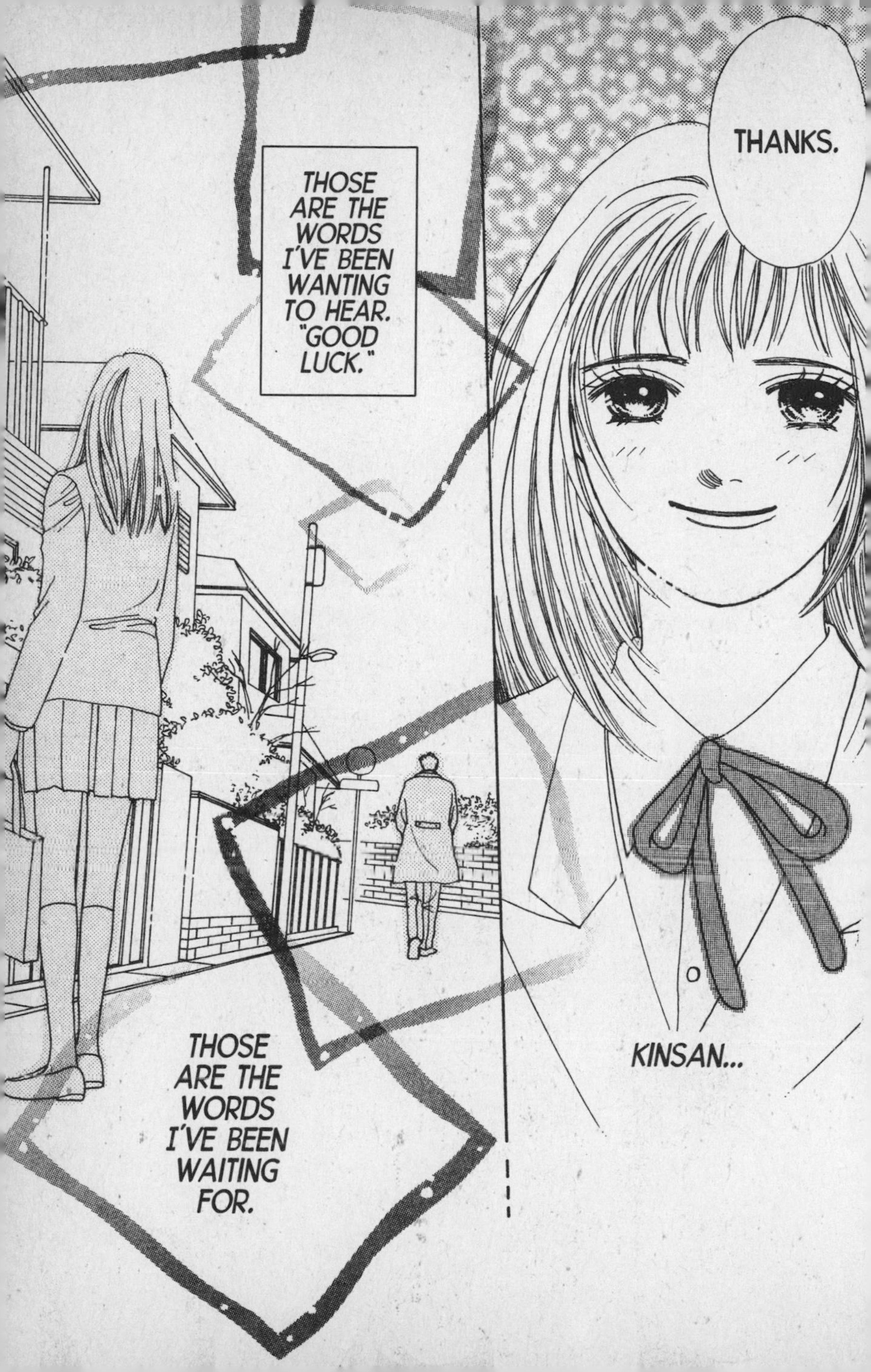
THANKS.
KINSAN...
THOSE ARE THE WORDS I'VE BEEN WANTING TO HEAR. "GOOD LUCK."
THOSE ARE THE WORDS I'VE BEEN WAITING FOR.

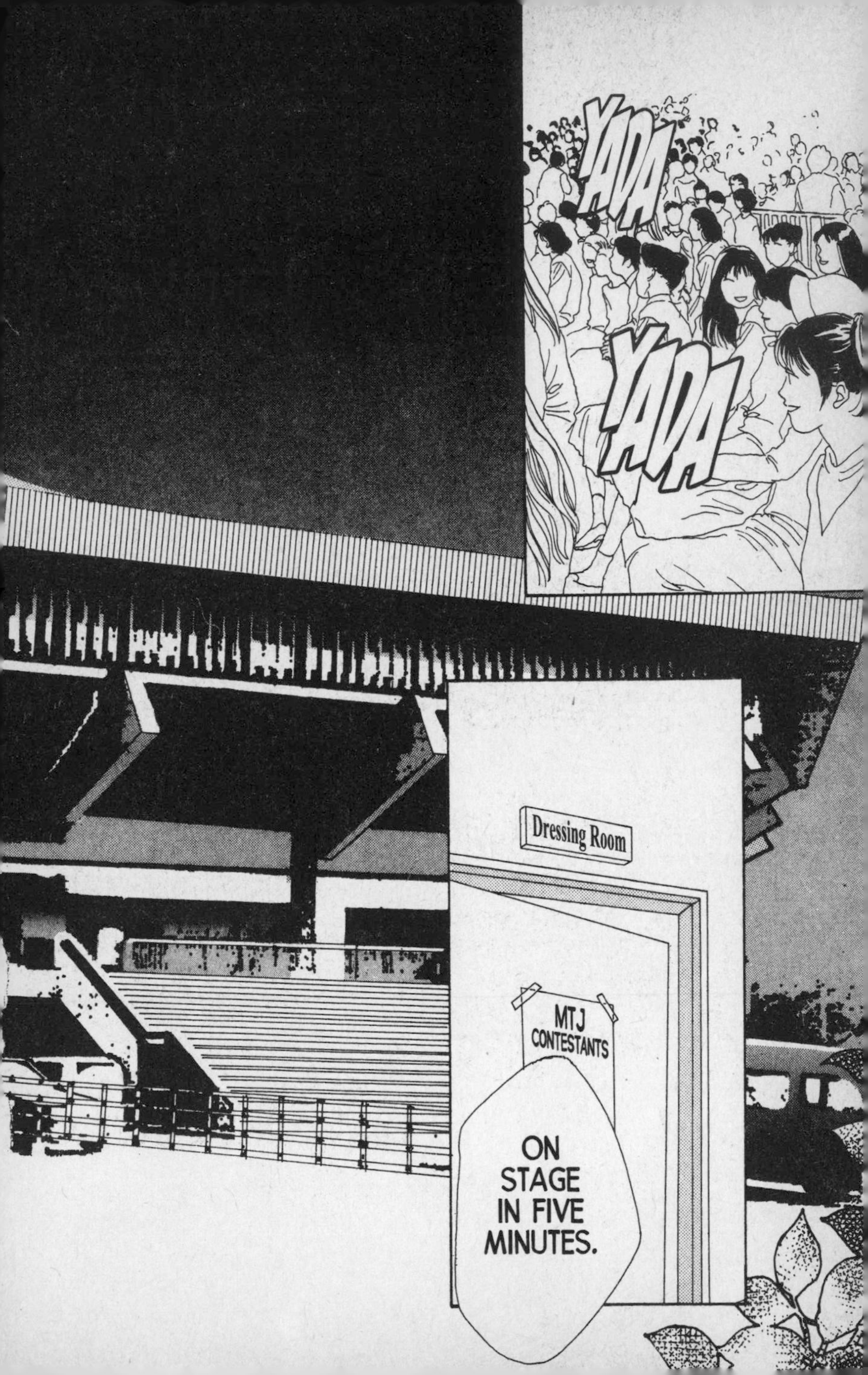
YAVA
YAVA
Dressing Room
MTJ CONTESTANTS
ON STAGE IN FIVE MINUTES.

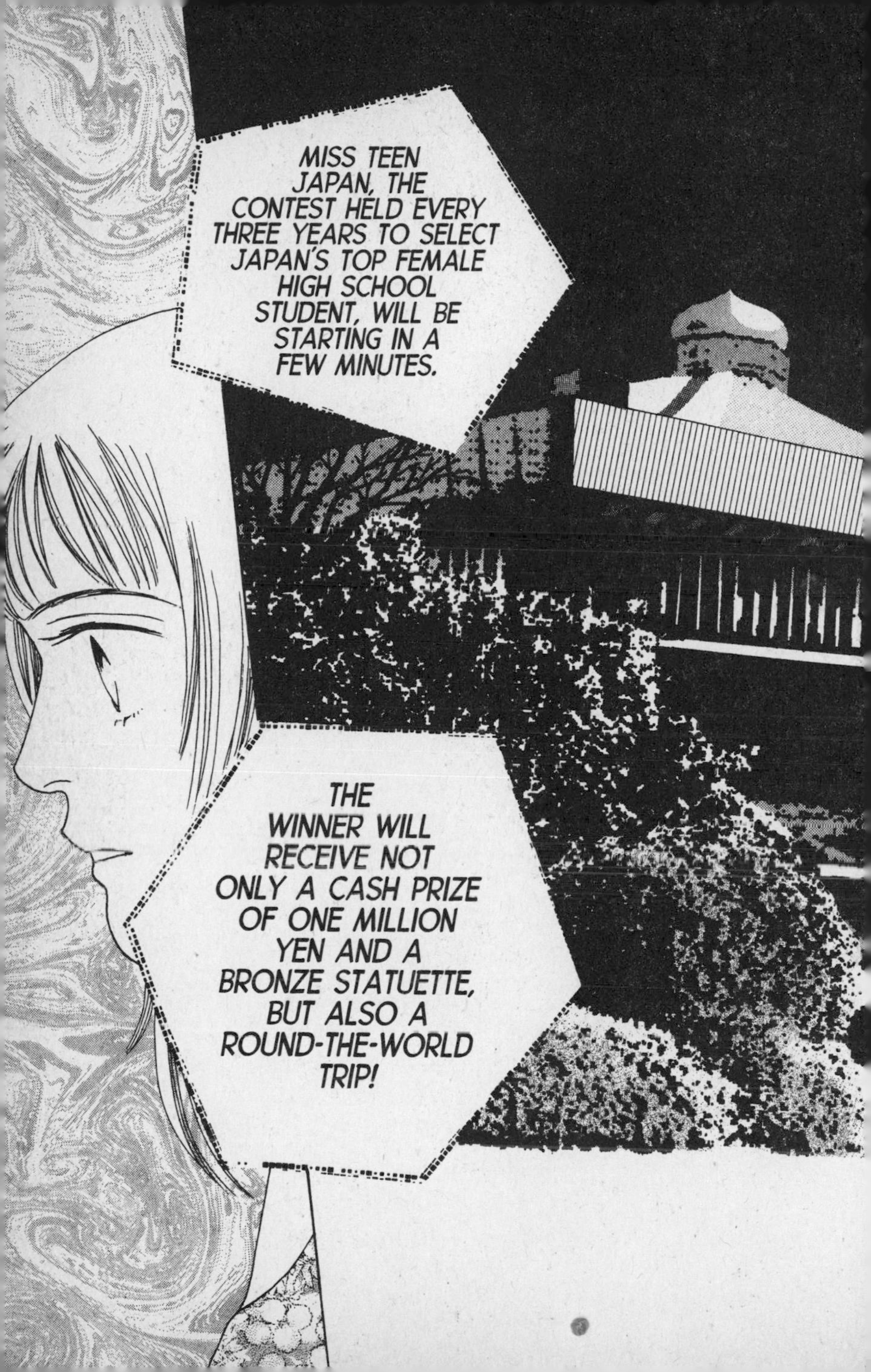
MISS TEEN JAPAN, THE CONTEST HELD EVERY THREE YEARS TO SELECT JAPAN'S TOP FEMALE HIGH SCHOOL STUDENT, WILL BE STARTING IN A FEW MINUTES.
THE WINNER WILL RECEIVE NOT ONLY A CASH PRIZE OF ONE MILLION YEN AND A BRONZE STATUETTE, BUT ALSO A ROUND-THE-WORLD TRIP!

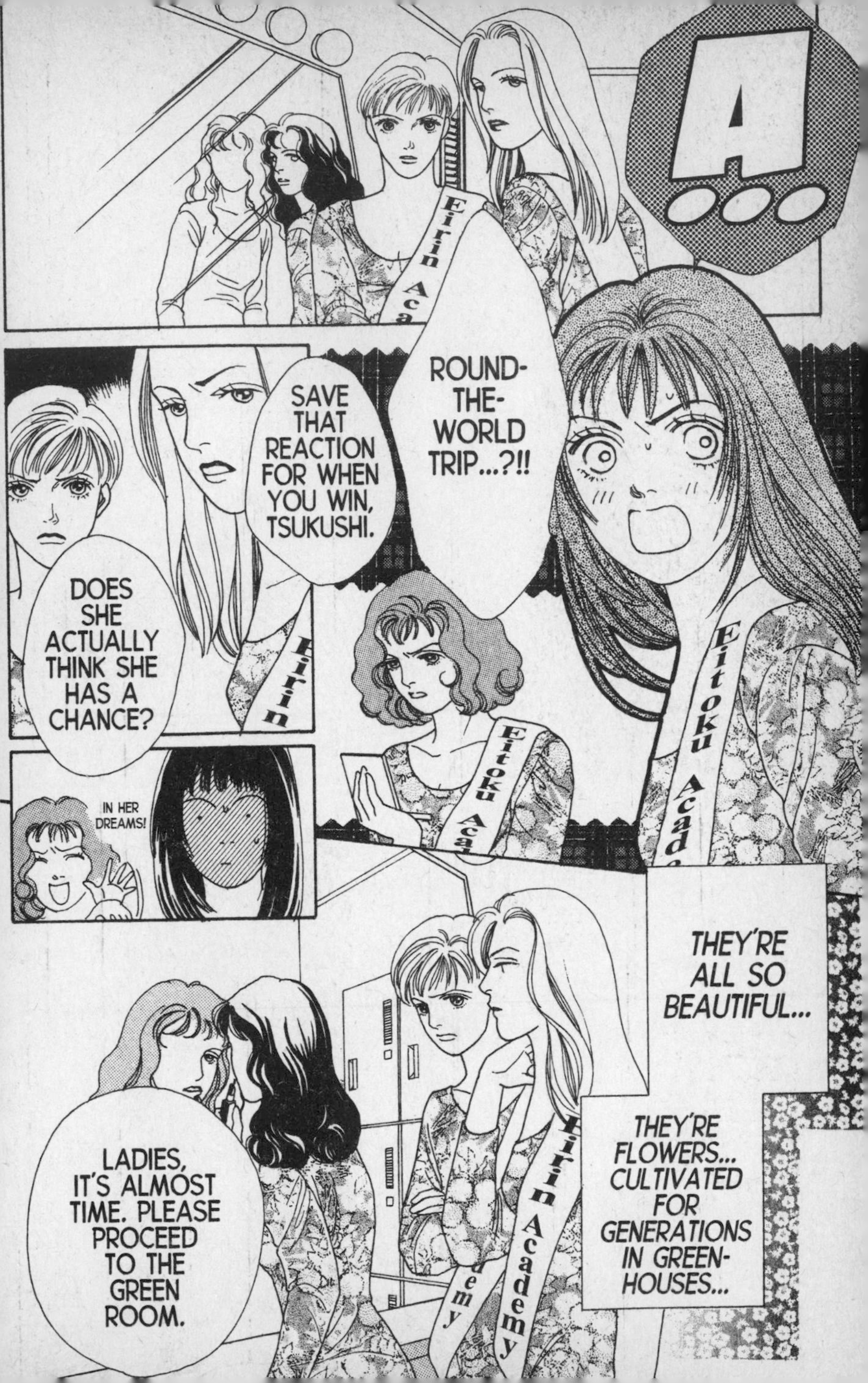
A...
ROUND-THE-WORLD TRIP...?!!
SAVE THAT REACTION FOR WHEN YOU WIN, TSUKUSHI.
DOES SHE ACTUALLY THINK SHE HAS A CHANCE?
IN HER DREAMS!
THEY'RE ALL SO BEAUTIFUL...
THEY'RE FLOWERS... CULTIVATED FOR GENERATIONS IN GREEN-HOUSES...
Eirin Academy
LADIES, IT'S ALMOST TIME. PLEASE PROCEED TO THE GREEN ROOM.

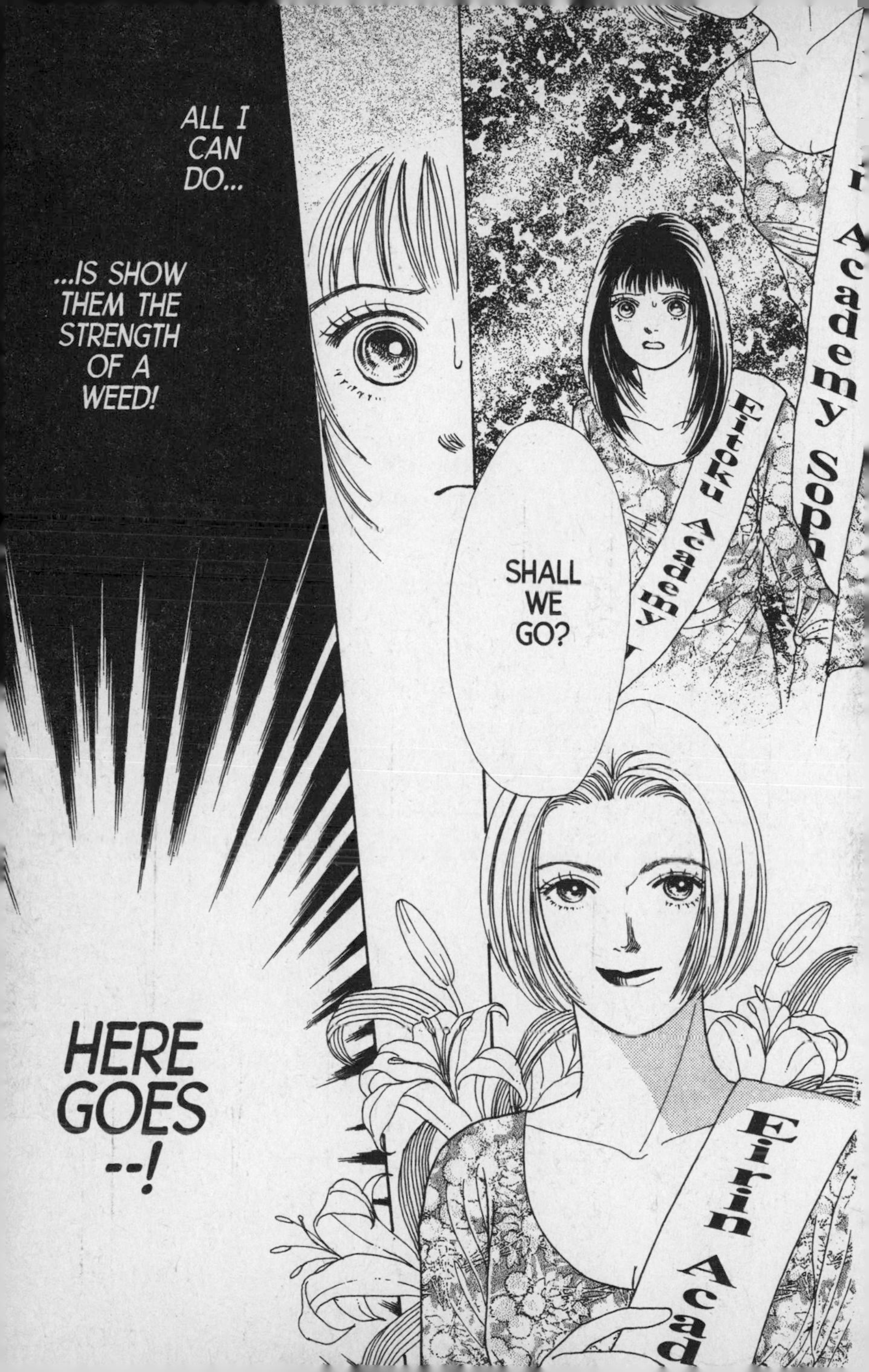
Academy Soph
Eitoku Academy
SHALL WE GO?
Eirin Acad
ALL I CAN DO...
...IS SHOW THEM THE STRENGTH OF A WEED!
HERE GOES --!

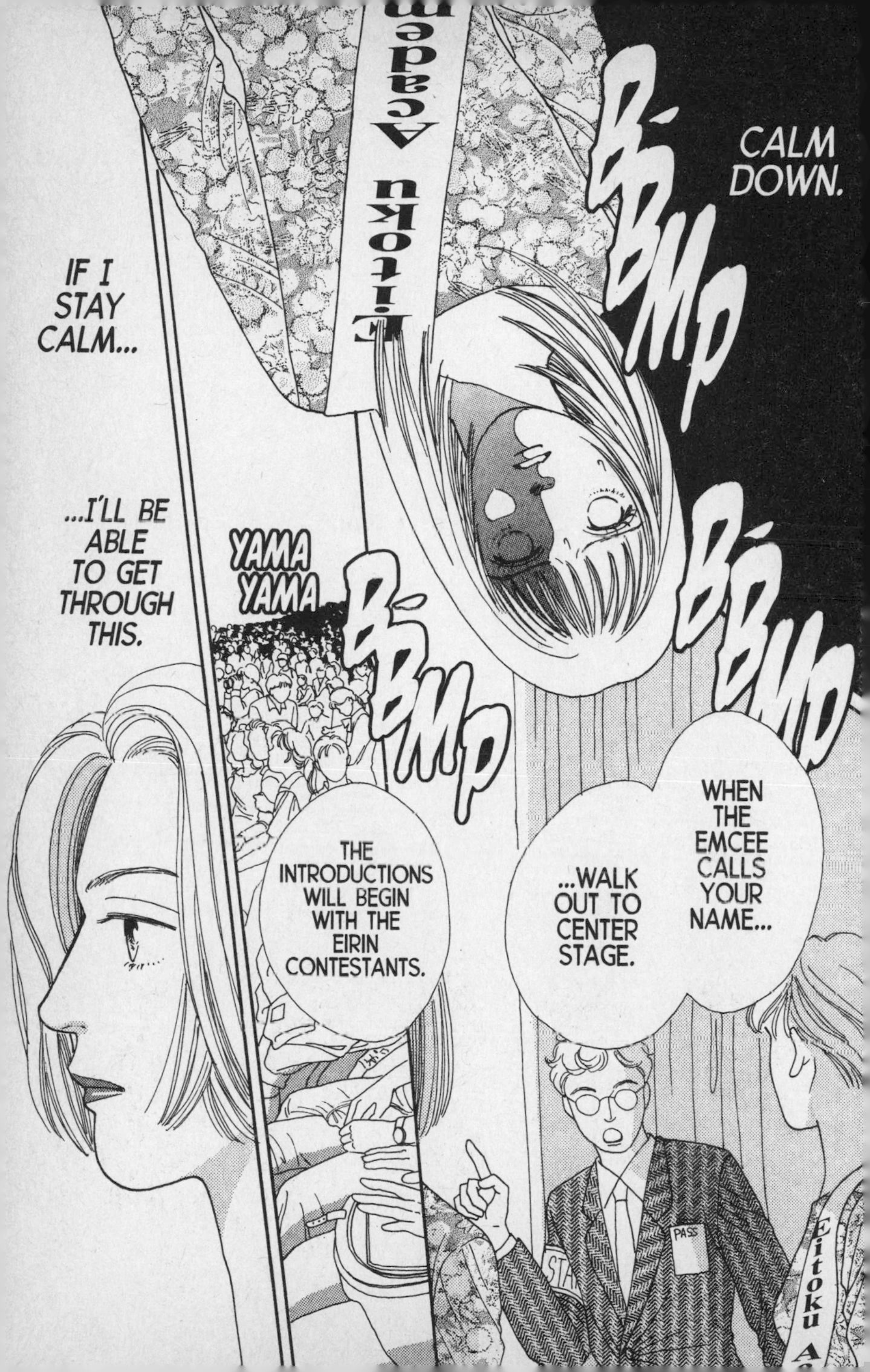

CALM DOWN.
BUMP
Eitoku Academ
BUMP BUMP
IF I STAY CALM...
...I'LL BE ABLE TO GET THROUGH THIS.
BUMP
YAMA YAMA
WHEN THE EMCEE CALLS YOUR NAME...
...WALK OUT TO CENTER STAGE.
THE INTRODUCTIONS WILL BEGIN WITH THE EIRIN CONTESTANTS.
PASS
Eitoku A

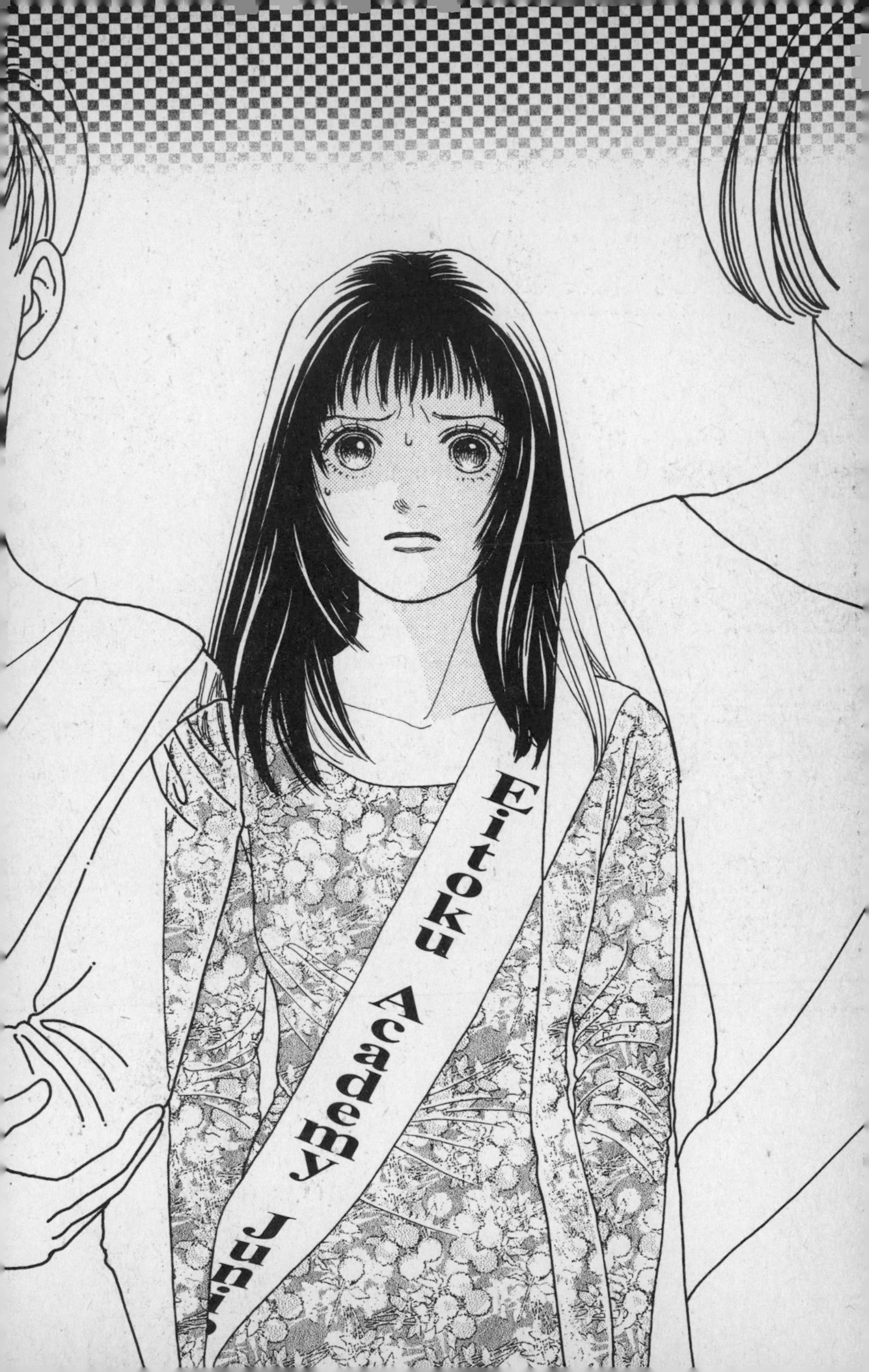
Eitoku Academy Juni

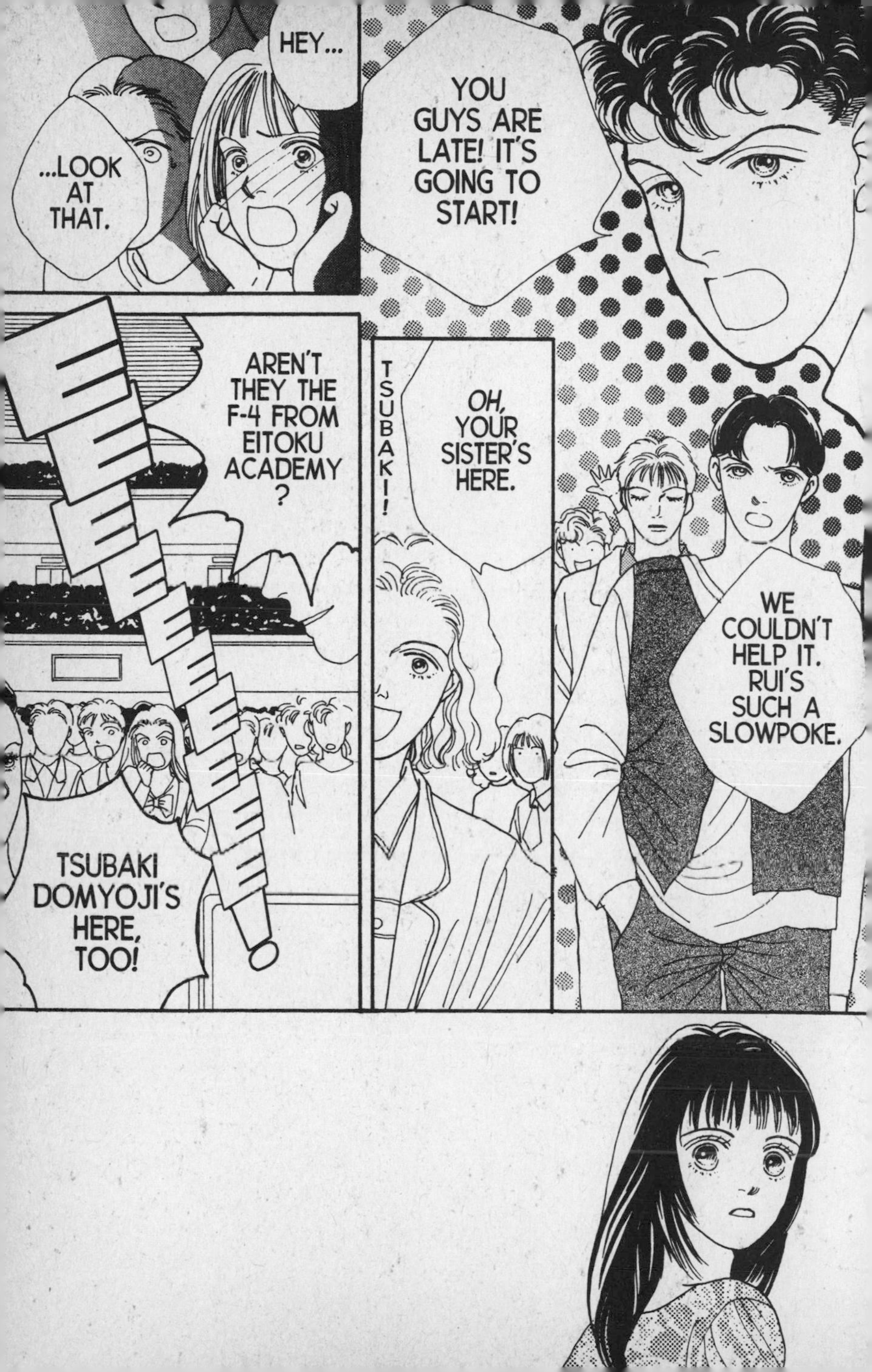
YOU GUYS ARE LATE! IT'S GOING TO START!
WE COULDN'T HELP IT. RUI'S SUCH A SLOWPOKE.
OH, YOUR SISTER'S HERE.
TSUBAKI!
HEY...
...LOOK AT THAT.
AREN'T THEY THE F-4 FROM EITOKU ACADEMY?
TSUBAKI DOMYOJI'S HERE, TOO!

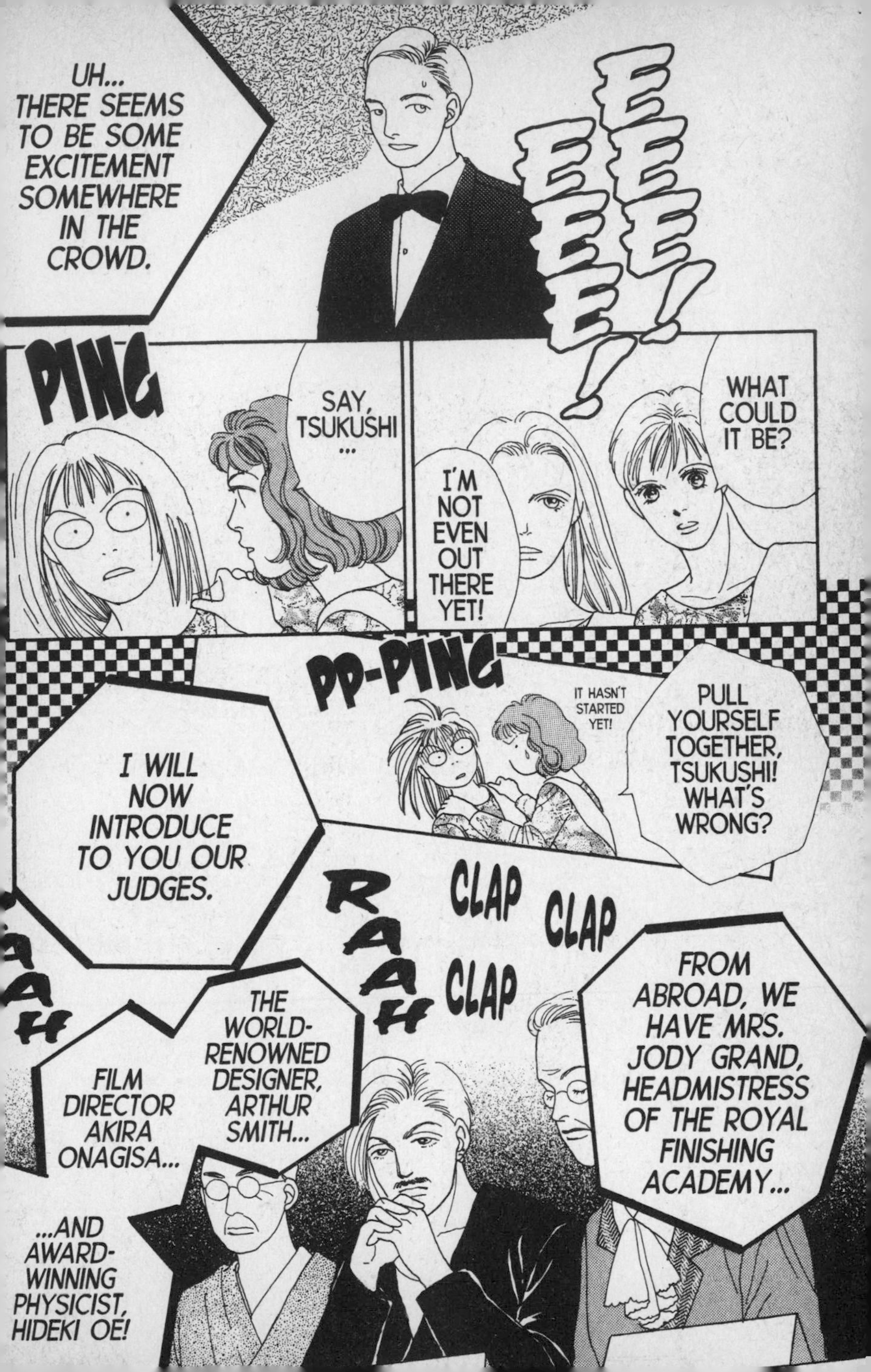
EEEEE!
UH... THERE SEEMS TO BE SOME EXCITEMENT SOMEWHERE IN THE CROWD.
WHAT COULD IT BE?
I'M NOT EVEN OUT THERE YET!
PING
SAY, TSUKUSHI...
PULL YOURSELF TOGETHER, TSUKUSHI! WHAT'S WRONG?
IT HASN'T STARTED YET!
PP-PING
I WILL NOW INTRODUCE TO YOU OUR JUDGES.
CLAP CLAP
CLAP
RAAH
FROM ABROAD, WE HAVE MRS. JODY GRAND, HEADMISTRESS OF THE ROYAL FINISHING ACADEMY...
THE WORLD-RENOWNED DESIGNER, ARTHUR SMITH...
FILM DIRECTOR AKIRA ONAGISA...
...AND AWARD-WINNING PHYSICIST, HIDEKI OE!

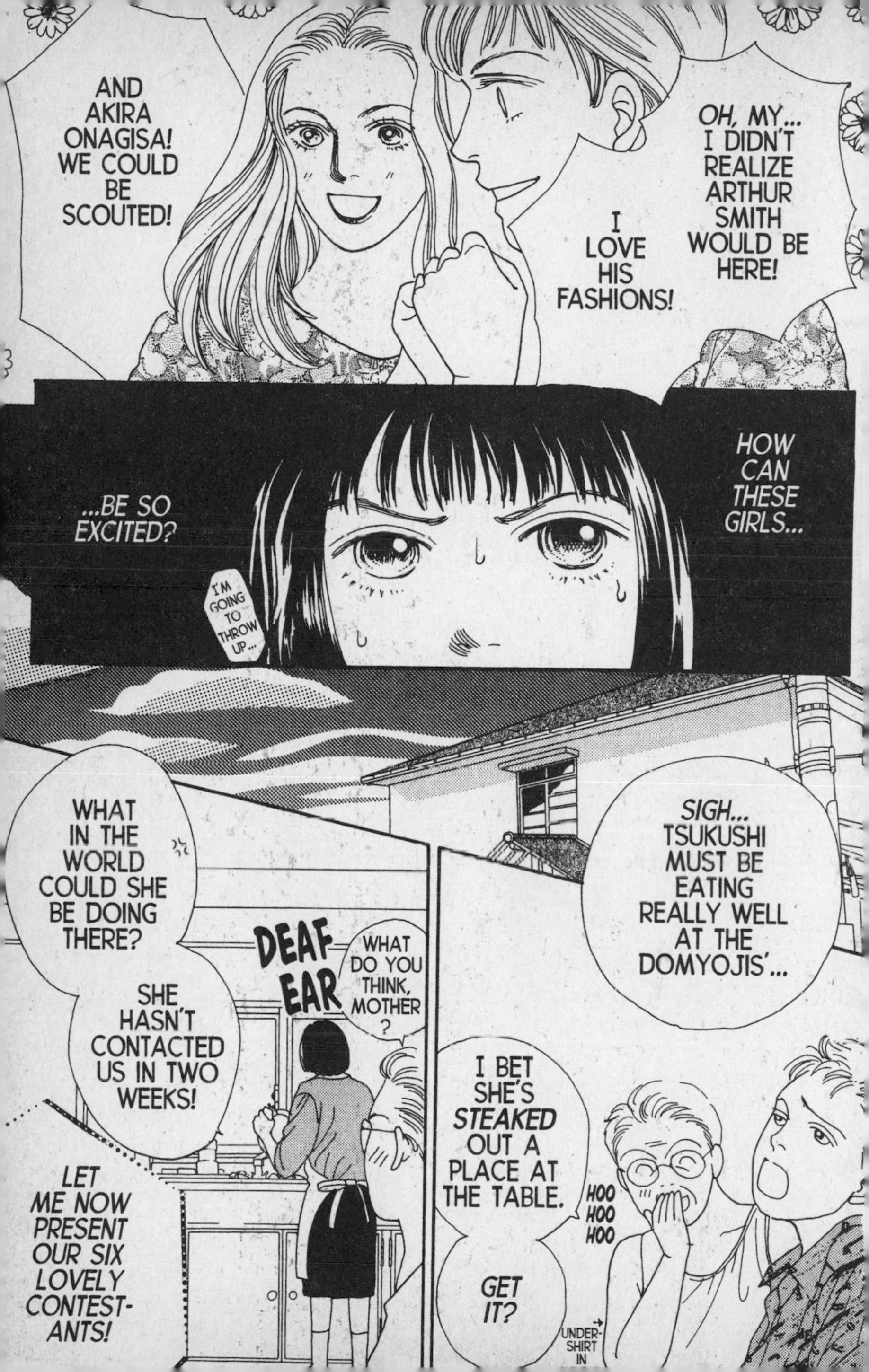
OH, MY... I DIDN'T REALIZE ARTHUR SMITH WOULD BE HERE!
I LOVE HIS FASHIONS!
AND AKIRA ONAGISA! WE COULD BE SCOUTED!
HOW CAN THESE GIRLS...
...BE SO EXCITED?
I'M GOING TO THROW UP...
SIGH... TSUKUSHI MUST BE EATING REALLY WELL AT THE DOMYOJIS'...
I BET SHE'S STEAKED OUT A PLACE AT THE TABLE.
HOO HOO HOO
GET IT?
UNDER-SHIRT IN
WHAT IN THE WORLD COULD SHE BE DOING THERE?
WHAT DO YOU THINK, MOTHER?
DEAF EAR
SHE HASN'T CONTACTED US IN TWO WEEKS!
LET ME NOW PRESENT OUR SIX LOVELY CONTEST-ANTS!

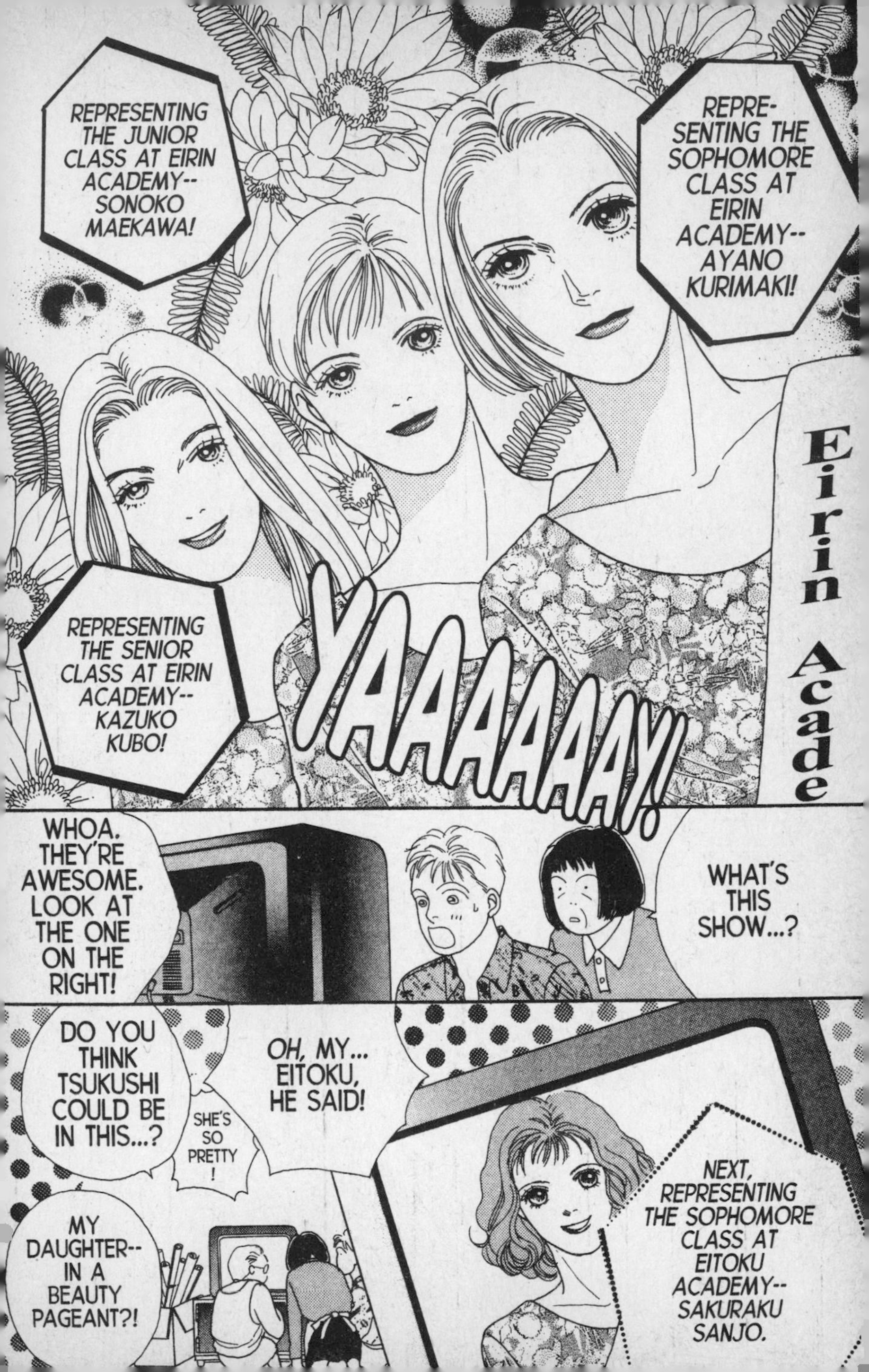
REPRESENTING THE SOPHOMORE CLASS AT EIRIN ACADEMY-- AYANO KURIMAKI!
REPRESENTING THE JUNIOR CLASS AT EIRIN ACADEMY-- SONOKO MAEKAWA!
Eirin Acade
REPRESENTING THE SENIOR CLASS AT EIRIN ACADEMY-- KAZUKO KUBO!
YAAAAAAY!
WHAT'S THIS SHOW...?
WHOA. THEY'RE AWESOME. LOOK AT THE ONE ON THE RIGHT!
NEXT, REPRESENTING THE SOPHOMORE CLASS AT EITOKU ACADEMY-- SAKURAKU SANJO.
OH, MY... EITOKU, HE SAID!
DO YOU THINK TSUKUSHI COULD BE IN THIS...?
SHE'S SO PRETTY!
MY DAUGHTER-- IN A BEAUTY PAGEANT?!

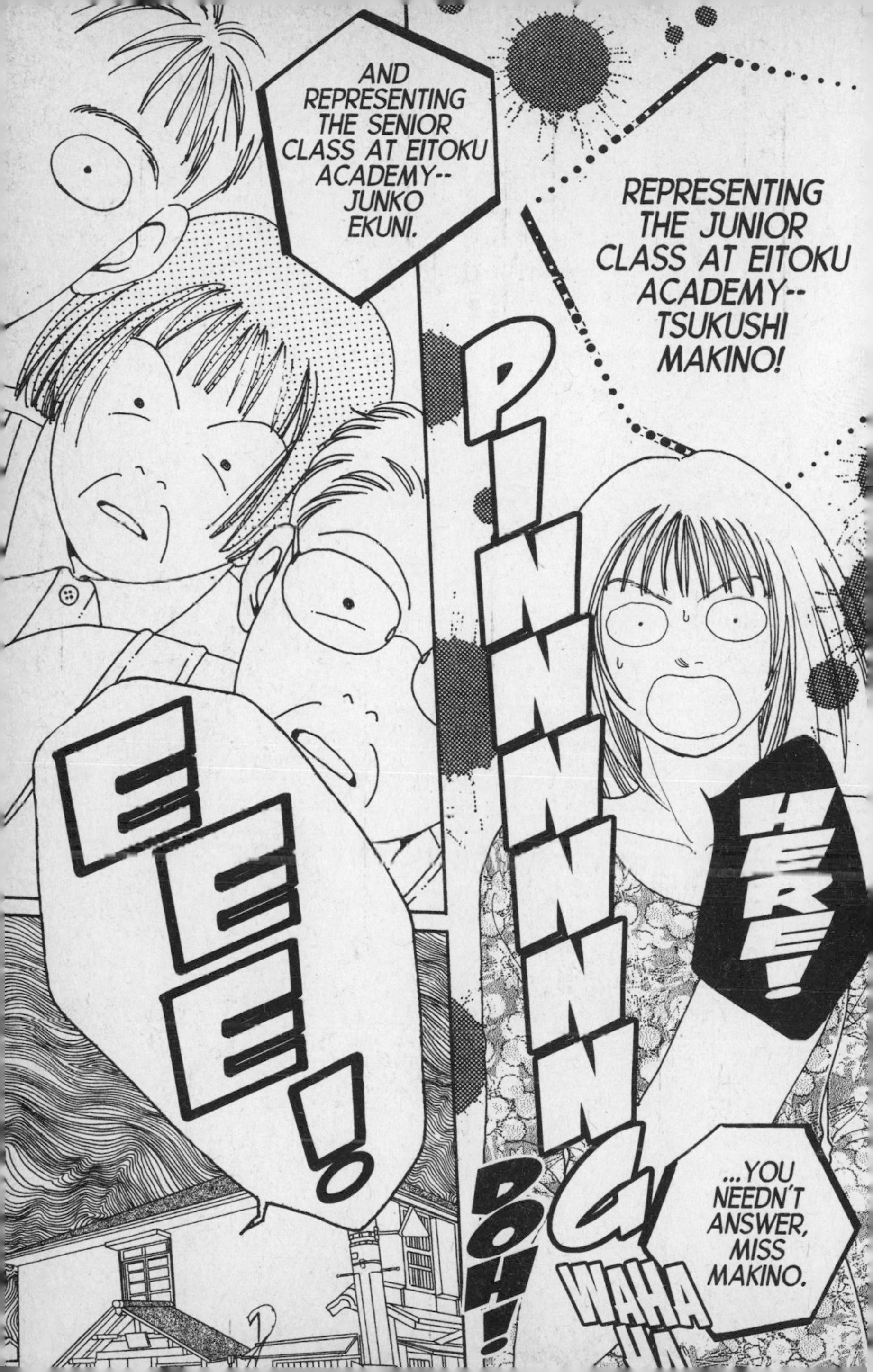
REPRESENTING THE JUNIOR CLASS AT EITOKU ACADEMY-- TSUKUSHI MAKINO!
HERE!
AND REPRESENTING THE SENIOR CLASS AT EITOKU ACADEMY-- JUNKO EKUNI.
PINNNNNG
DOH!
EEE!
...YOU NEEDN'T ANSWER, MISS MAKINO.
WAHA

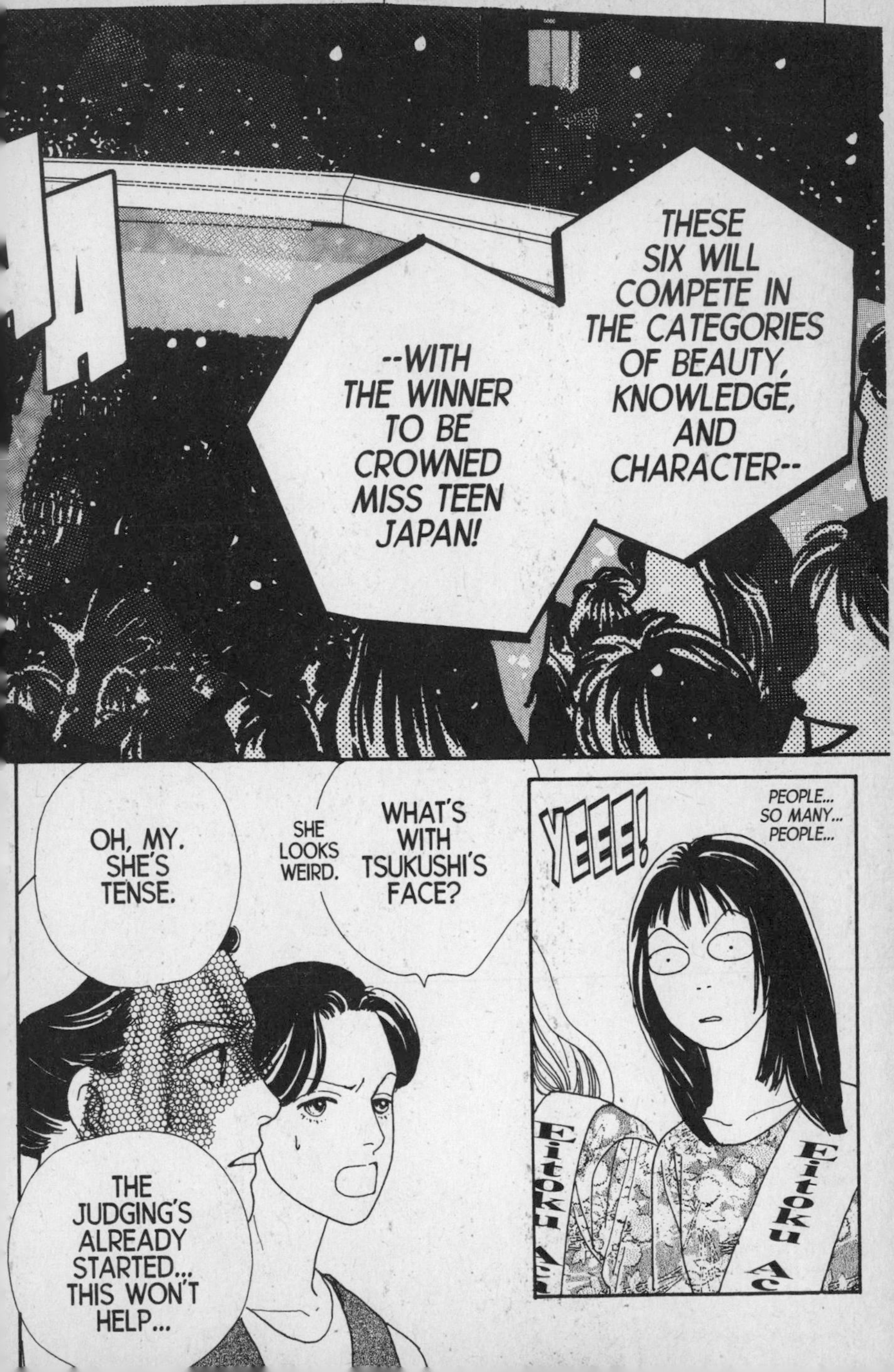
THESE SIX WILL COMPETE IN THE CATEGORIES OF BEAUTY, KNOWLEDGE, AND CHARACTER--
--WITH THE WINNER TO BE CROWNED MISS TEEN JAPAN!
YEEE!
PEOPLE... SO MANY... PEOPLE...
Eitoku
Eitoku
WHAT'S WITH TSUKUSHI'S FACE?
SHE LOOKS WEIRD.
OH, MY. SHE'S TENSE.
THE JUDGING'S ALREADY STARTED... THIS WON'T HELP...

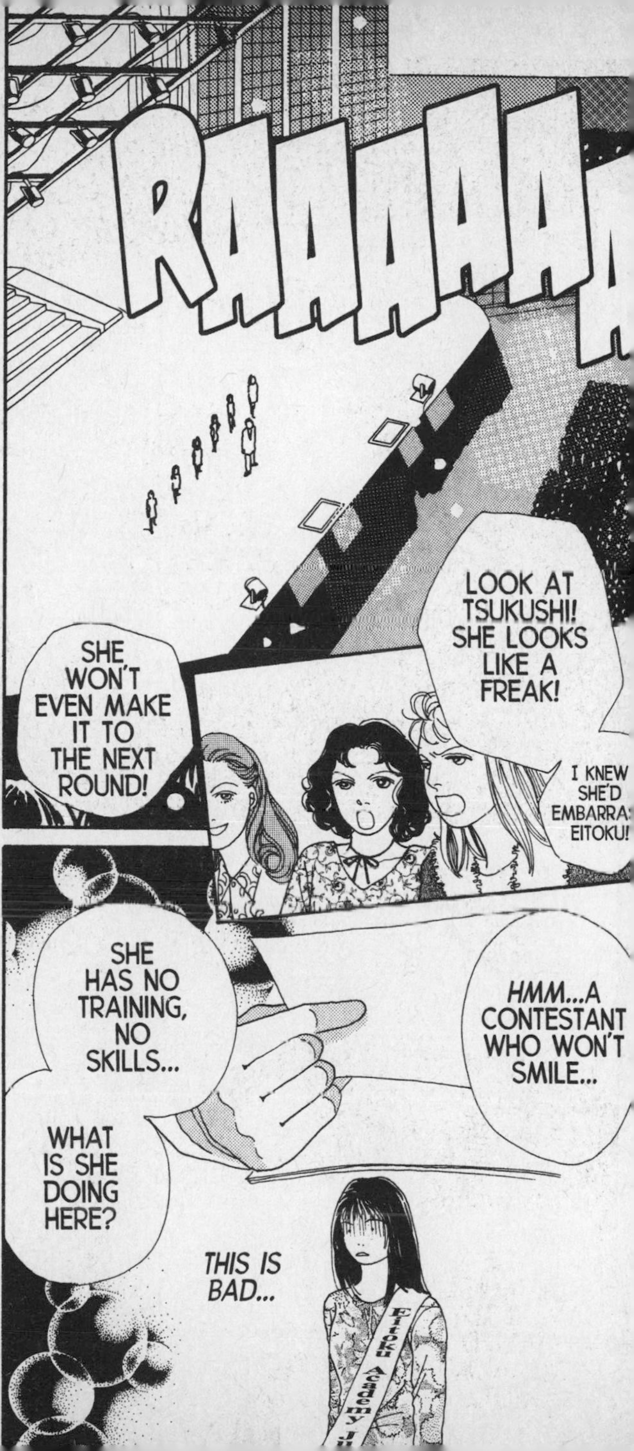
RAAAAA
LOOK AT TSUKUSHI! SHE LOOKS LIKE A FREAK!
I KNEW SHE'D EMBARRAS EITOKU!
SHE WON'T EVEN MAKE IT TO THE NEXT ROUND!
HMM...A CONTESTANT WHO WON'T SMILE...
SHE HAS NO TRAINING, NO SKILLS...
WHAT IS SHE DOING HERE?
THIS IS BAD...

☆

I hadn't been to a disco in years. (I went to Juliana about two years before to gather background data.) I normally lead a very dull life, so the instant I entered the disco, I felt lightheaded.

I used to love going to discos when I was a student. Am I getting old...? Sob!

The place was packed with cast and crew. I was dizzy from the density of the population, when...

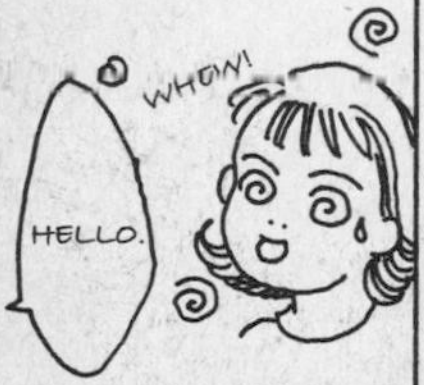
WHEW!
HELLO.

I heard a cute voice.

It turned out to be Yuki Uchida, the actress!

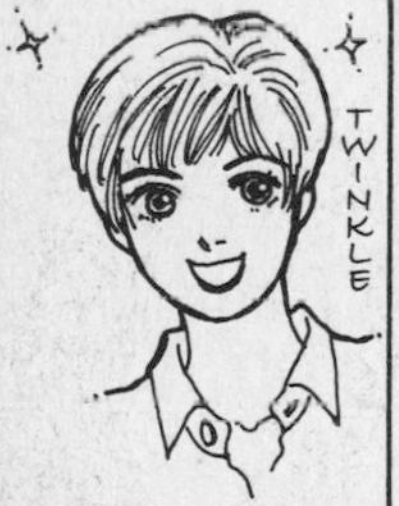
TWINKLE

Picture doesn't look like her. I'm sorry!

She was so pretty--like a character out of a girls' comic book! Her face was so tiny, and her arms and legs were so long. Everything about her said "teen idol." What's more, she seemed to have a great personality. I thought she was perfect!

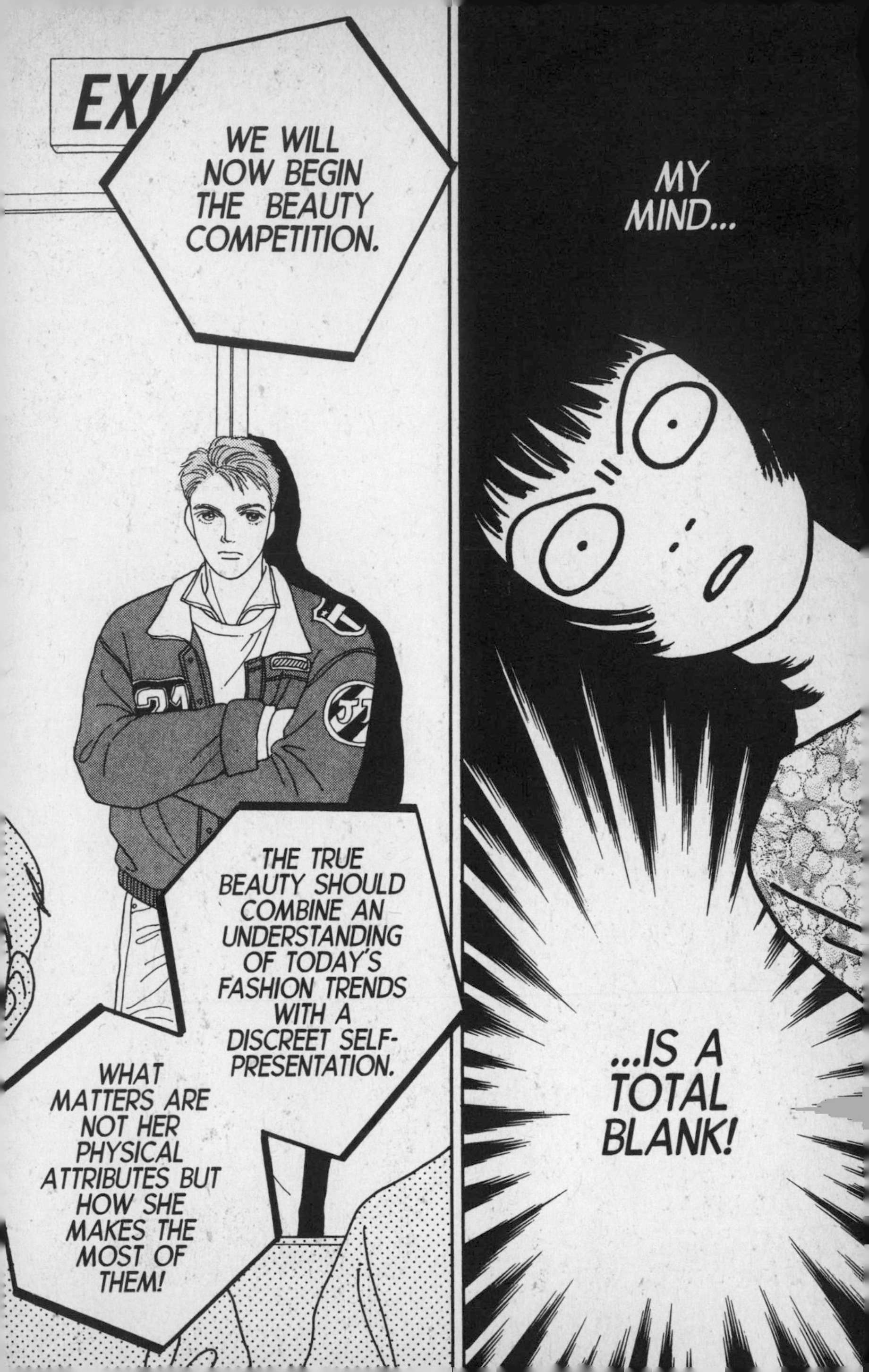
MY MIND...
...IS A TOTAL BLANK!
WE WILL NOW BEGIN THE BEAUTY COMPETITION.
THE TRUE BEAUTY SHOULD COMBINE AN UNDERSTANDING OF TODAY'S FASHION TRENDS WITH A DISCREET SELF-PRESENTATION.
WHAT MATTERS ARE NOT HER PHYSICAL ATTRIBUTES BUT HOW SHE MAKES THE MOST OF THEM!

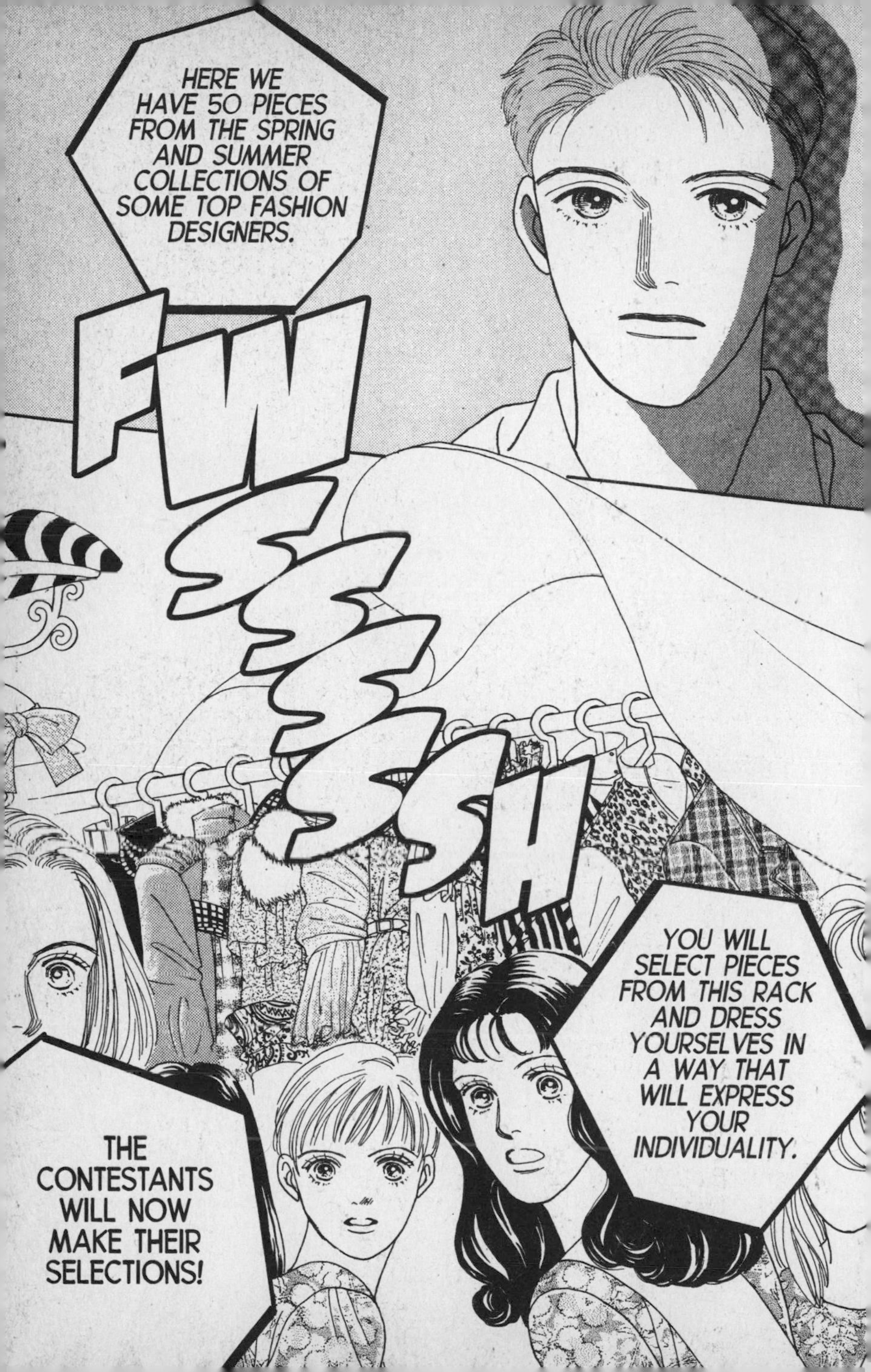
HERE WE HAVE 50 PIECES FROM THE SPRING AND SUMMER COLLECTIONS OF SOME TOP FASHION DESIGNERS.
FWSSSSSH
YOU WILL SELECT PIECES FROM THIS RACK AND DRESS YOURSELVES IN A WAY THAT WILL EXPRESS YOUR INDIVIDUALITY.
THE CONTESTANTS WILL NOW MAKE THEIR SELECTIONS!

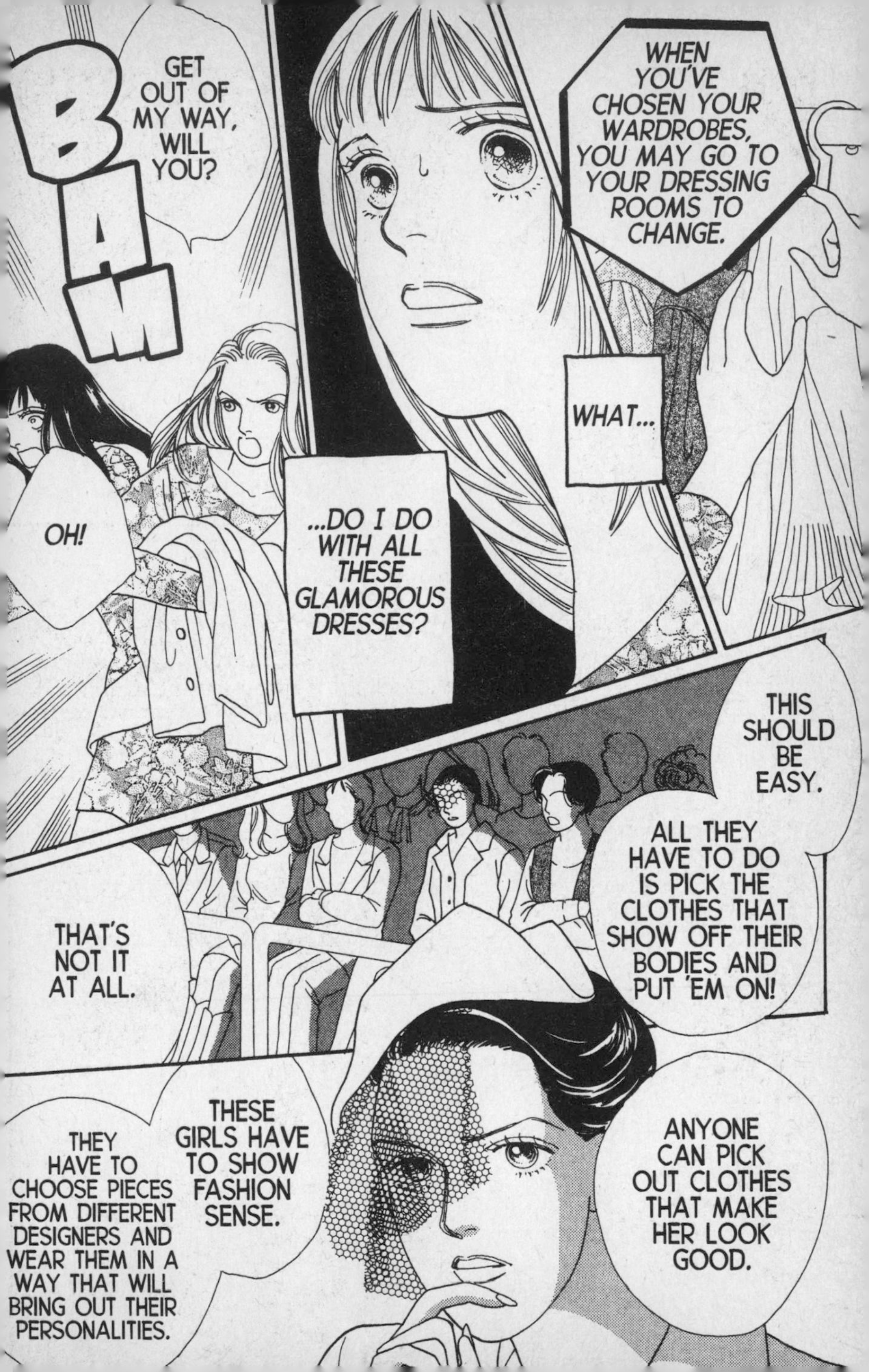
WHEN YOU'VE CHOSEN YOUR WARDROBES, YOU MAY GO TO YOUR DRESSING ROOMS TO CHANGE.
WHAT...
...DO I DO WITH ALL THESE GLAMOROUS DRESSES?
GET OUT OF MY WAY, WILL YOU?
BAM
OH!
THIS SHOULD BE EASY.
ALL THEY HAVE TO DO IS PICK THE CLOTHES THAT SHOW OFF THEIR BODIES AND PUT 'EM ON!
THAT'S NOT IT AT ALL.
ANYONE CAN PICK OUT CLOTHES THAT MAKE HER LOOK GOOD.
THESE GIRLS HAVE TO SHOW FASHION SENSE.
THEY HAVE TO CHOOSE PIECES FROM DIFFERENT DESIGNERS AND WEAR THEM IN A WAY THAT WILL BRING OUT THEIR PERSONALITIES.

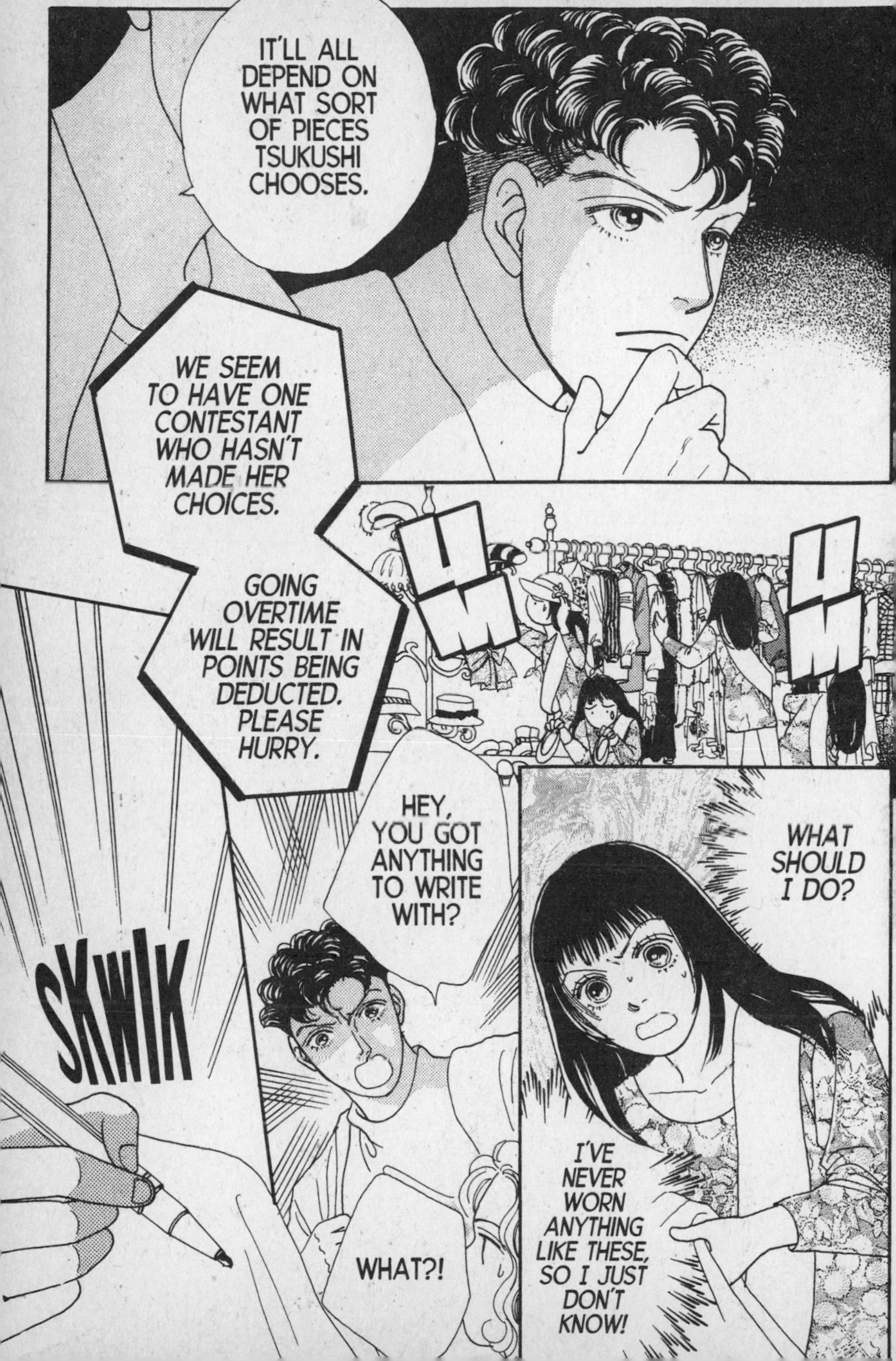
IT'LL ALL DEPEND ON WHAT SORT OF PIECES TSUKUSHI CHOOSES.
WE SEEM TO HAVE ONE CONTESTANT WHO HASN'T MADE HER CHOICES.
GOING OVERTIME WILL RESULT IN POINTS BEING DEDUCTED. PLEASE HURRY.
UM
UM
WHAT SHOULD I DO?
I'VE NEVER WORN ANYTHING LIKE THESE, SO I JUST DON'T KNOW!
HEY, YOU GOT ANYTHING TO WRITE WITH?
WHAT?!
SKWIK

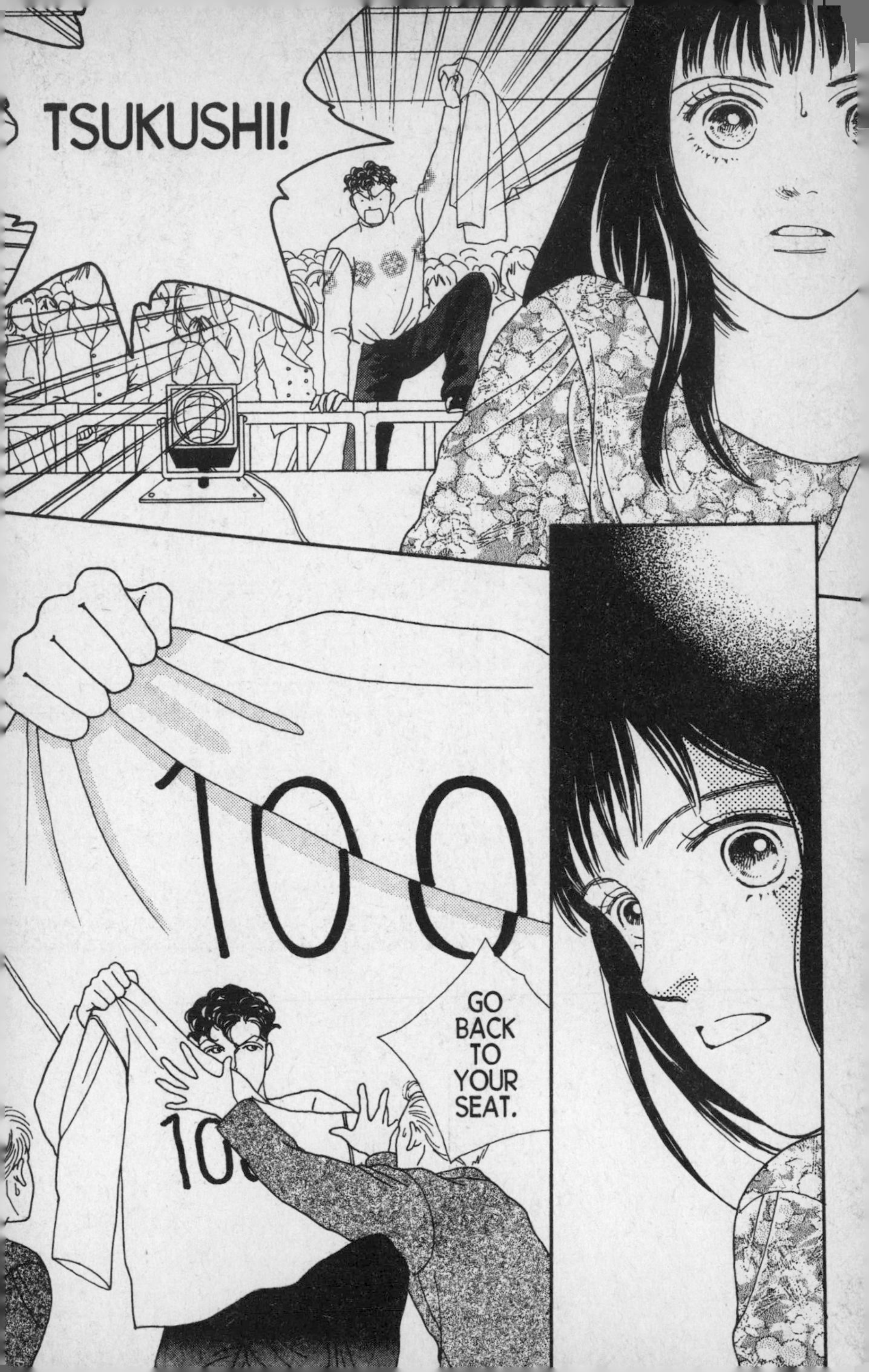
TSUKUSHI!
100
GO BACK TO YOUR SEAT.

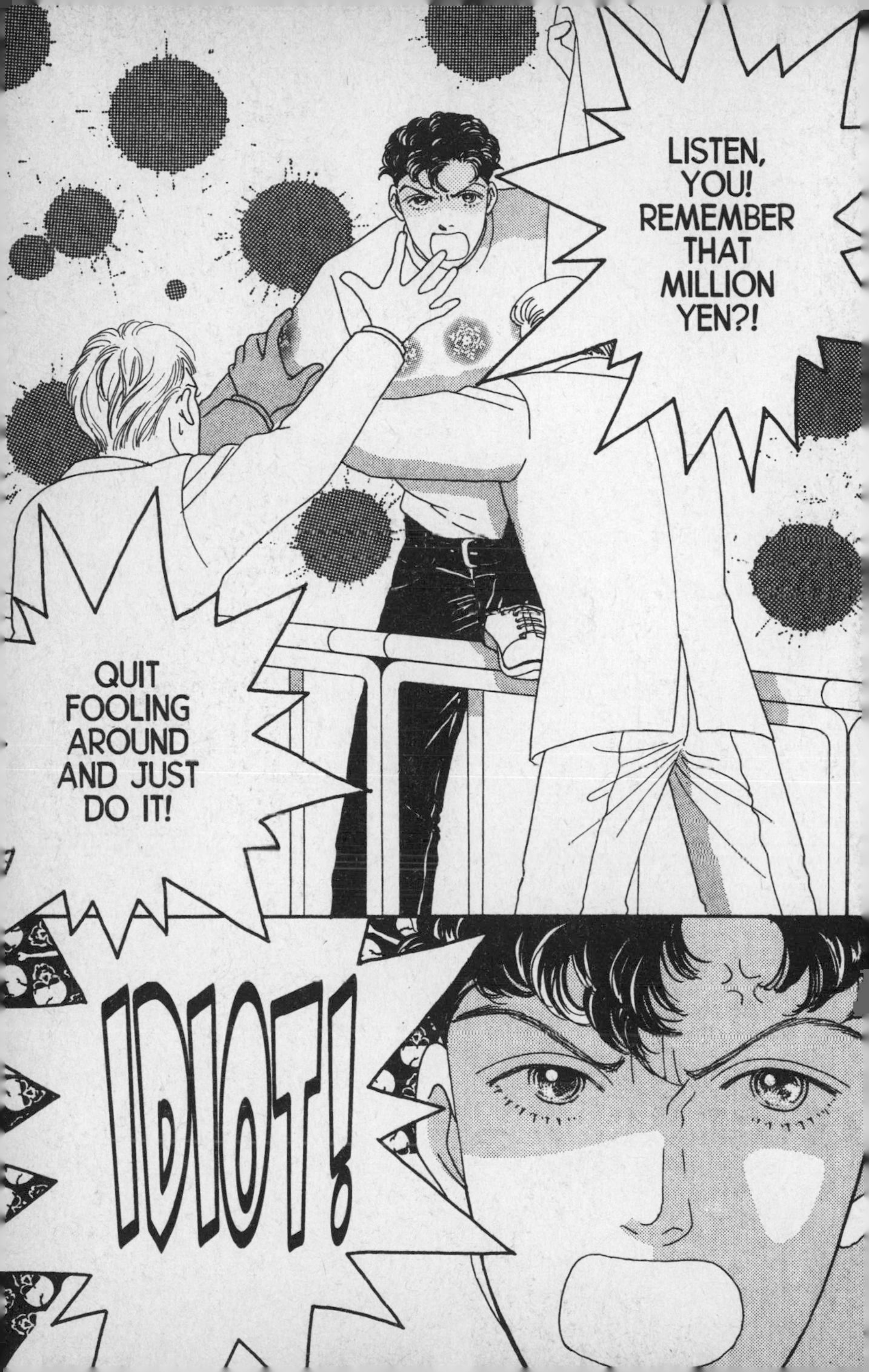
LISTEN, YOU! REMEMBER THAT MILLION YEN?!
QUIT FOOLING AROUND AND JUST DO IT!
IDIOT!

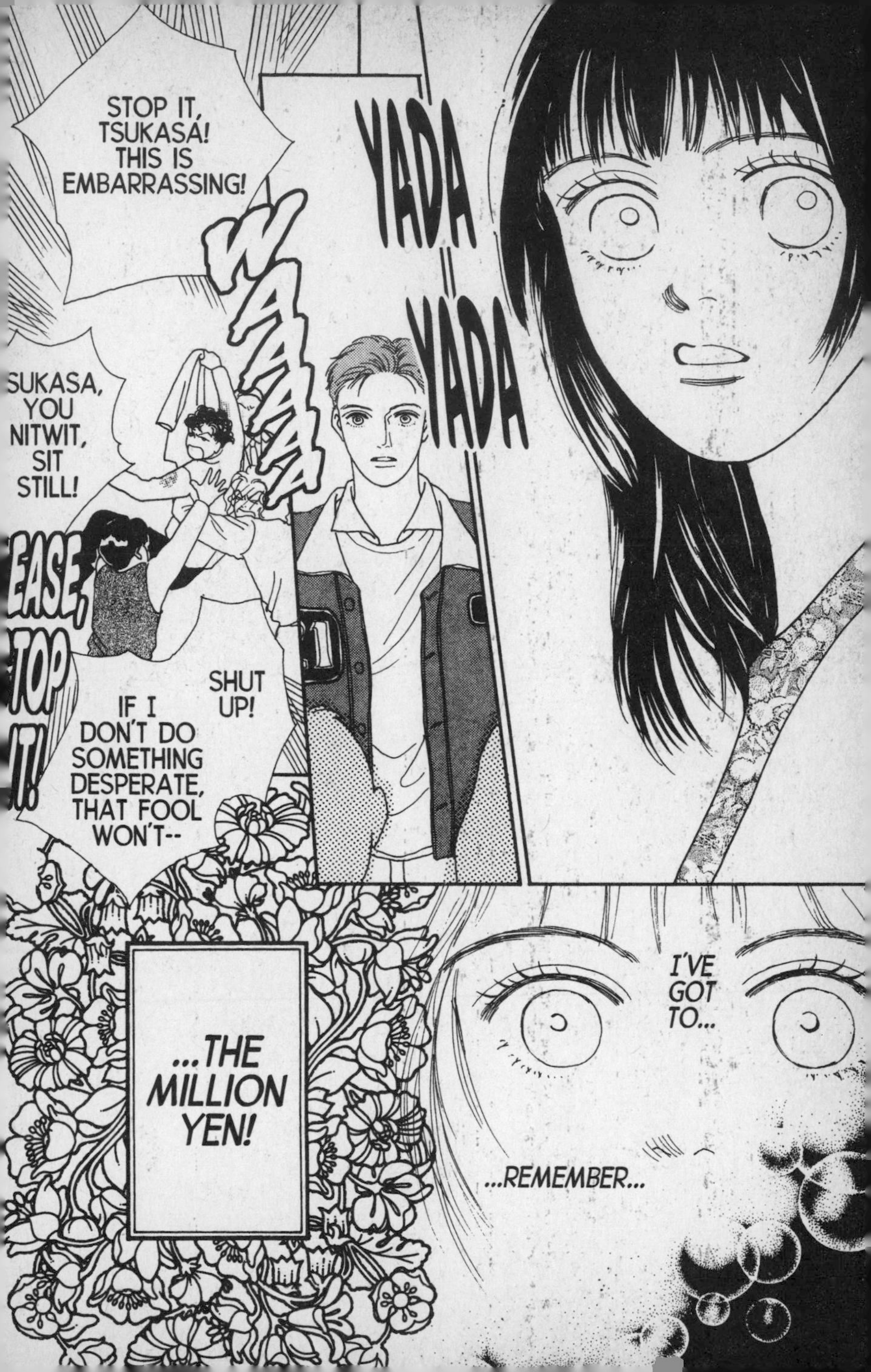
YADA YADA
STOP IT, TSUKASA! THIS IS EMBARRASSING!
SUKASA, YOU NITWIT, SIT STILL!
SHUT UP!
IF I DON'T DO SOMETHING DESPERATE, THAT FOOL WON'T--
EASE, TOP IT!
I'VE GOT TO...
...REMEMBER...
...THE MILLION YEN!

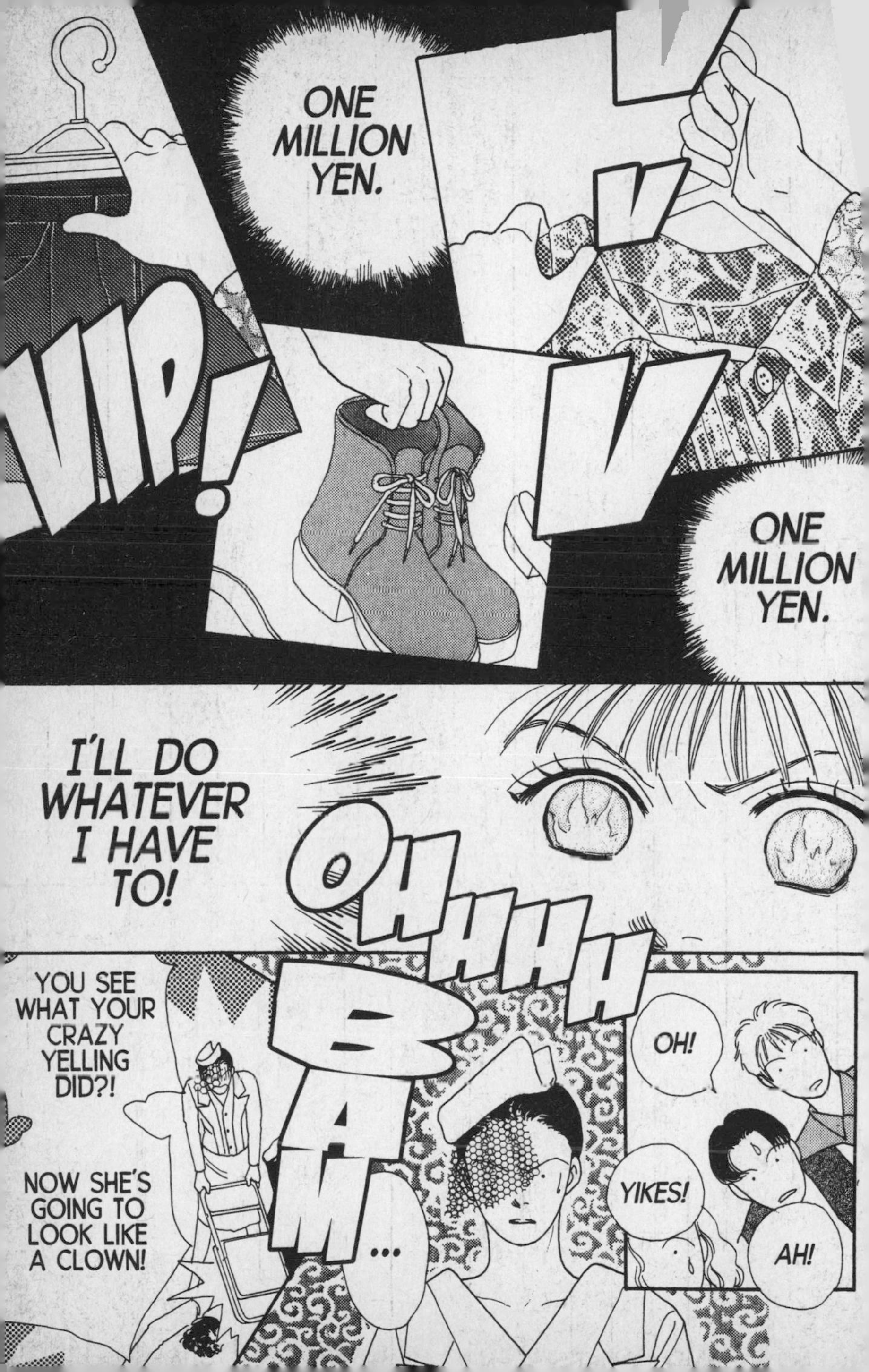
ONE MILLION YEN.
V
V
ONE MILLION YEN.
VIP!
OHHHHH
I'LL DO WHATEVER I HAVE TO!
OH!
YIKES!
AH!
BAM...
YOU SEE WHAT YOUR CRAZY YELLING DID?!
NOW SHE'S GOING TO LOOK LIKE A CLOWN!

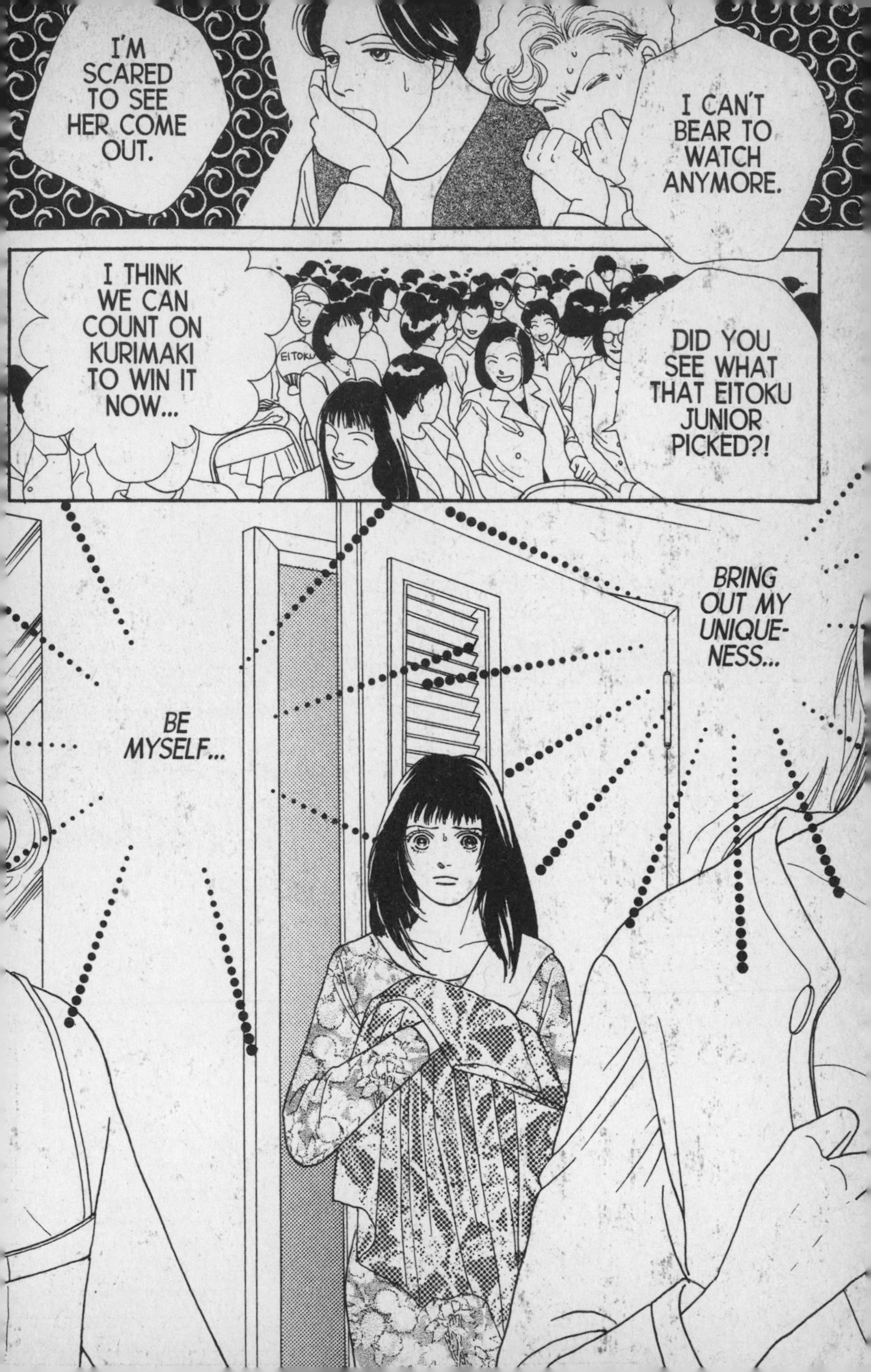
I CAN'T BEAR TO WATCH ANYMORE.
I'M SCARED TO SEE HER COME OUT.
DID YOU SEE WHAT THAT EITOKU JUNIOR PICKED?!
EITOKU
I THINK WE CAN COUNT ON KURIMAKI TO WIN IT NOW...
BRING OUT MY UNIQUE-NESS...
BE MYSELF...

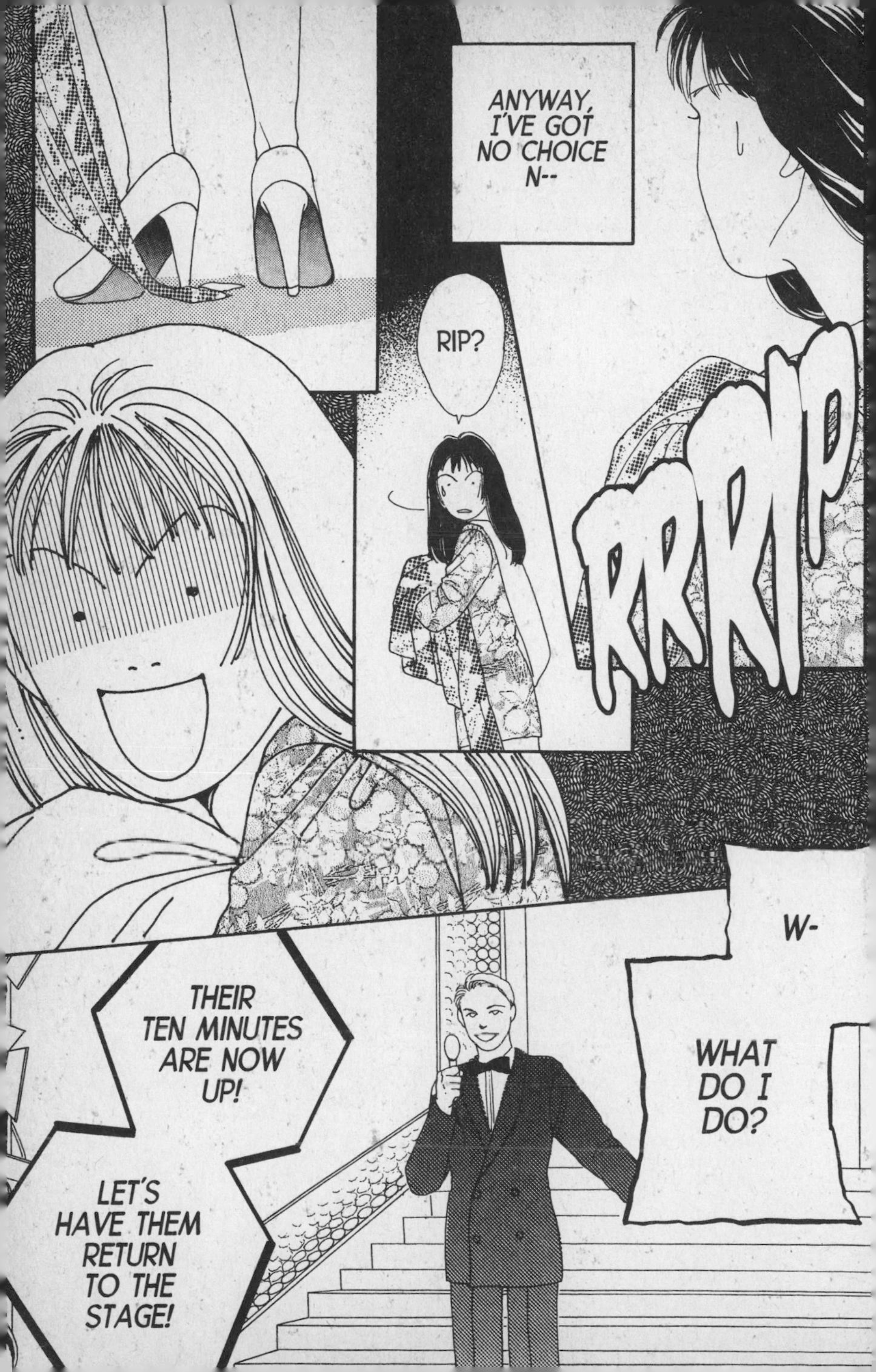
ANYWAY, I'VE GOT NO CHOICE N--
RRRIP
RIP?
W-
WHAT DO I DO?
THEIR TEN MINUTES ARE NOW UP!
LET'S HAVE THEM RETURN TO THE STAGE!

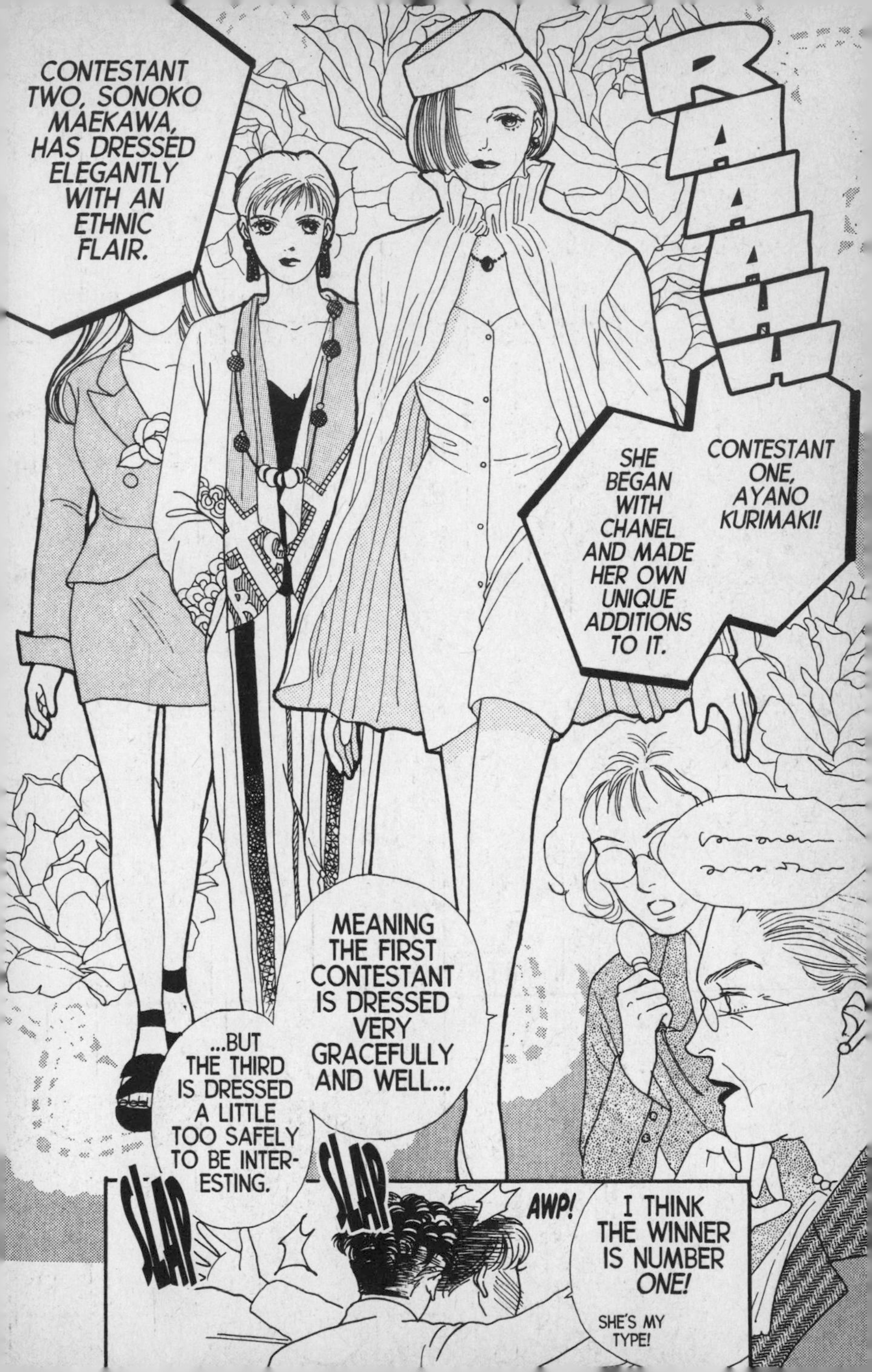
RAAAHH
CONTESTANT ONE, AYANO KURIMAKI!
SHE BEGAN WITH CHANEL AND MADE HER OWN UNIQUE ADDITIONS TO IT.
CONTESTANT TWO, SONOKO MAEKAWA, HAS DRESSED ELEGANTLY WITH AN ETHNIC FLAIR.
MEANING THE FIRST CONTESTANT IS DRESSED VERY GRACEFULLY AND WELL...
...BUT THE THIRD IS DRESSED A LITTLE TOO SAFELY TO BE INTER-ESTING.
I THINK THE WINNER IS NUMBER ONE!
SHE'S MY TYPE!
AWP!
SLAP
SLAP

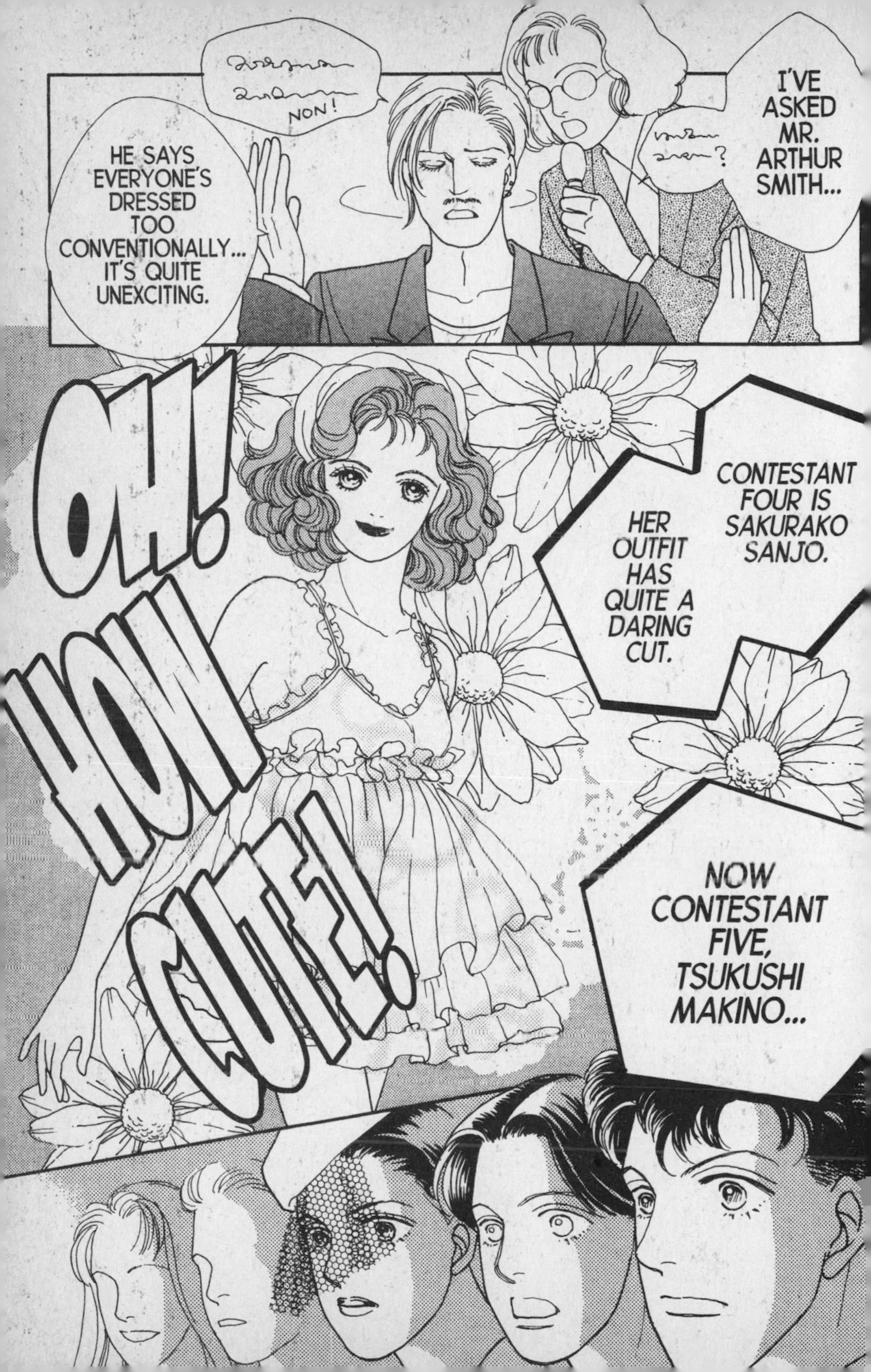
I'VE ASKED MR. ARTHUR SMITH...
NON!
HE SAYS EVERYONE'S DRESSED TOO CONVENTIONALLY... IT'S QUITE UNEXCITING.
CONTESTANT FOUR IS SAKURAKO SANJO.
HER OUTFIT HAS QUITE A DARING CUT.
OH! HOW CUTE!!
NOW CONTESTANT FIVE, TSUKUSHI MAKINO...

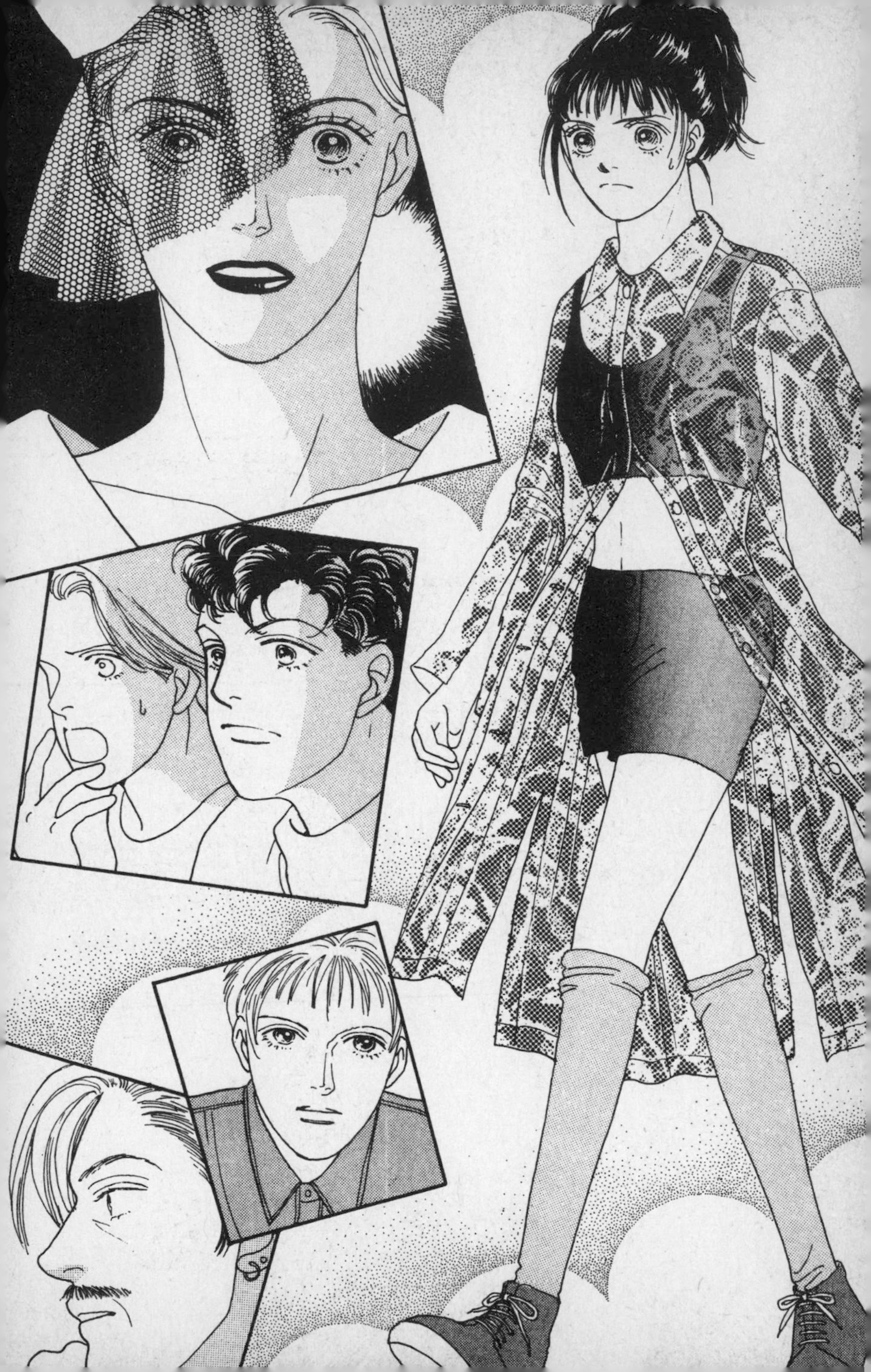

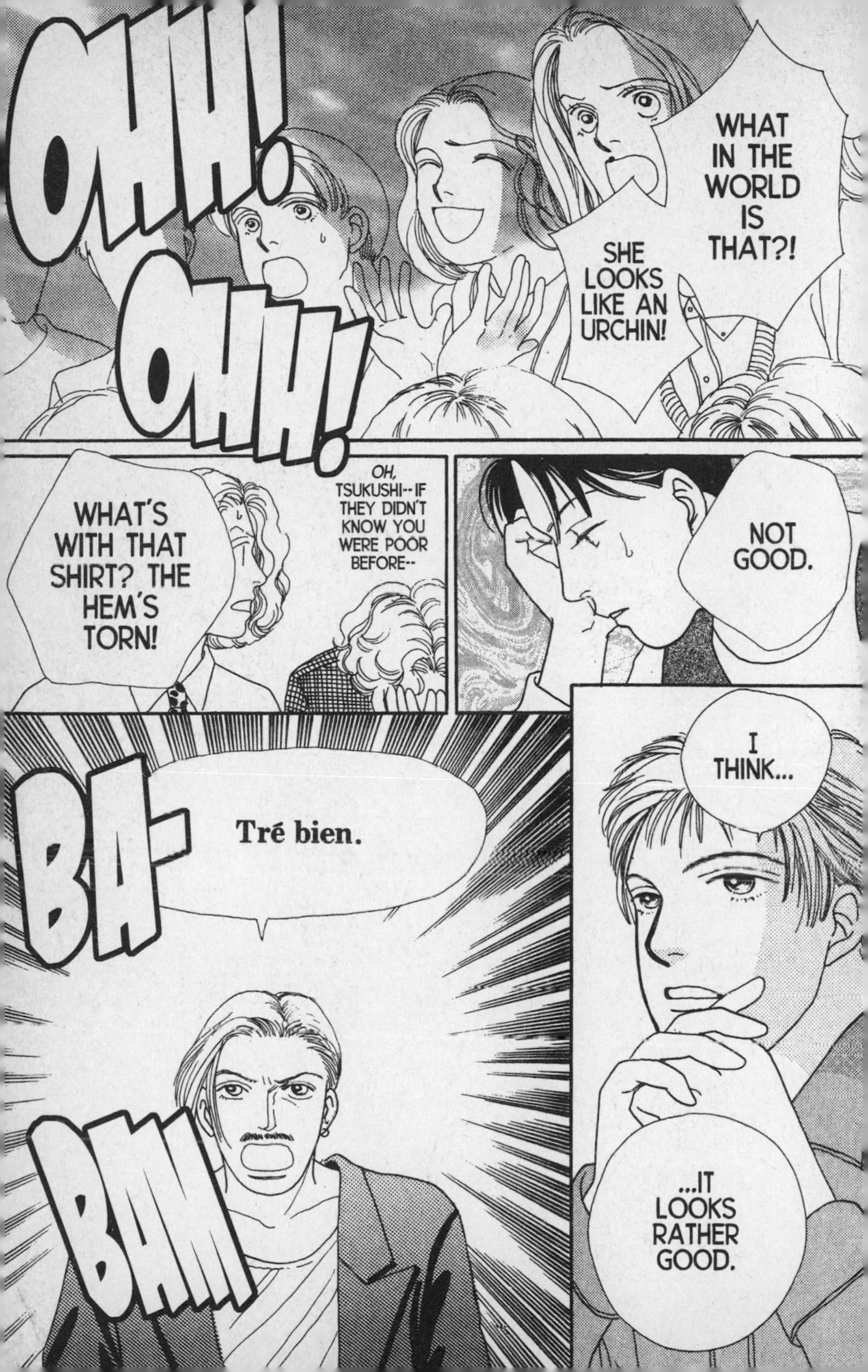
WHAT IN THE WORLD IS THAT?!
SHE LOOKS LIKE AN URCHIN!
OHH! OHH!
NOT GOOD.
OH, TSUKUSHI--IF THEY DIDN'T KNOW YOU WERE POOR BEFORE--
WHAT'S WITH THAT SHIRT? THE HEM'S TORN!
I THINK...
...IT LOOKS RATHER GOOD.
Tré bien.
BA-BAM

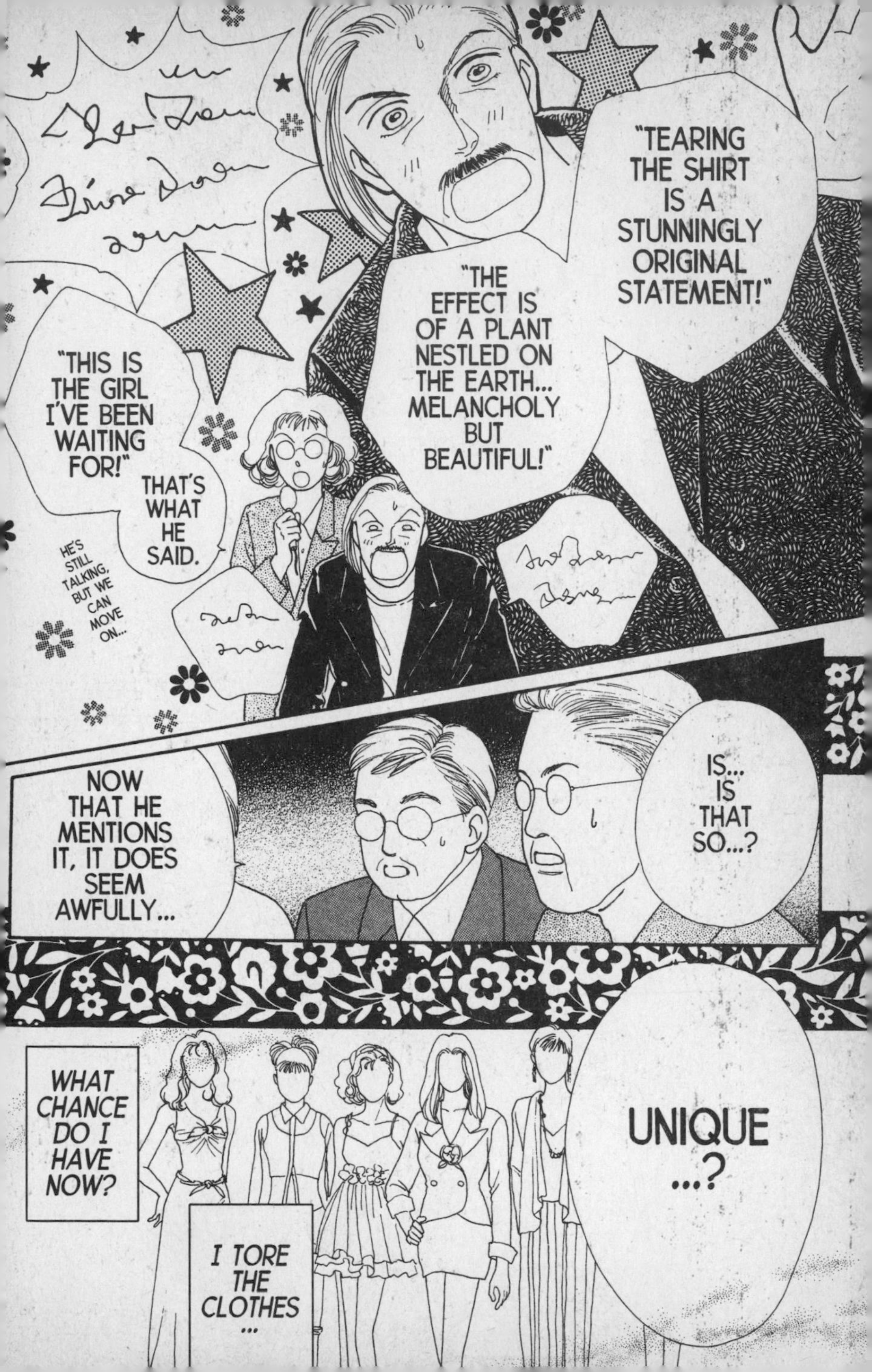
"TEARING THE SHIRT IS A STUNNINGLY ORIGINAL STATEMENT!"
"THE EFFECT IS OF A PLANT NESTLED ON THE EARTH... MELANCHOLY BUT BEAUTIFUL!"
"THIS IS THE GIRL I'VE BEEN WAITING FOR!"
THAT'S WHAT HE SAID.
HE'S STILL TALKING, BUT WE CAN MOVE ON...
IS... IS THAT SO...?
NOW THAT HE MENTIONS IT, IT DOES SEEM AWFULLY...
UNIQUE ...?
WHAT CHANCE DO I HAVE NOW?
I TORE THE CLOTHES ...

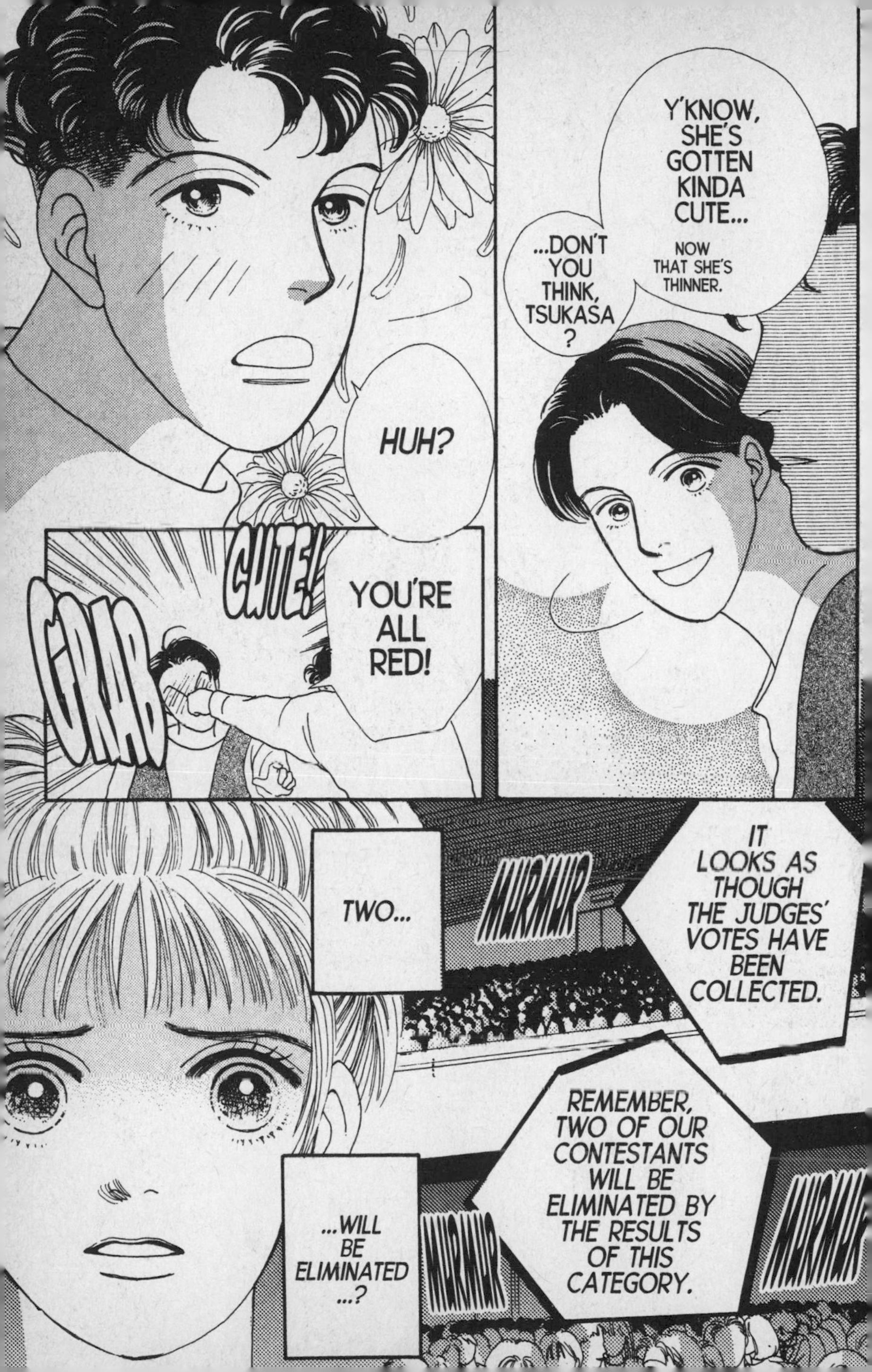
Y'KNOW, SHE'S GOTTEN KINDA CUTE...
NOW THAT SHE'S THINNER.
...DON'T YOU THINK, TSUKASA?
HUH?
CUTE!
GRAB
YOU'RE ALL RED!
IT LOOKS AS THOUGH THE JUDGES' VOTES HAVE BEEN COLLECTED.
MURMUR
TWO...
REMEMBER, TWO OF OUR CONTESTANTS WILL BE ELIMINATED BY THE RESULTS OF THIS CATEGORY.
MURMUR
MURMUR
...WILL BE ELIMINATED ...?

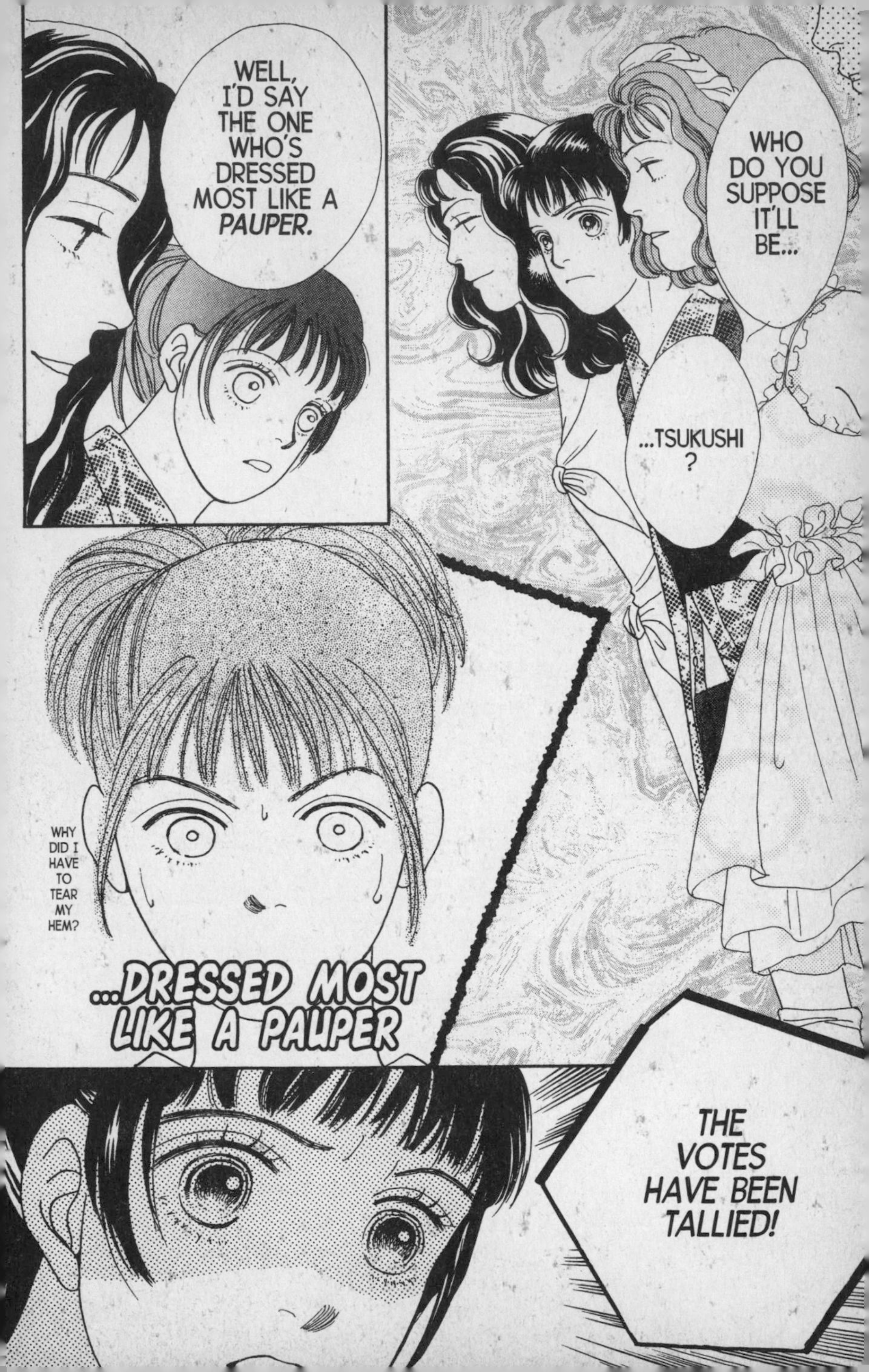
WHO DO YOU SUPPOSE IT'LL BE...
...TSUKUSHI?
WELL, I'D SAY THE ONE WHO'S DRESSED MOST LIKE A *PAUPER.*
WHY DID I HAVE TO TEAR MY HEM?
...DRESSED MOST LIKE A PAUPER
THE VOTES HAVE BEEN TALLIED!

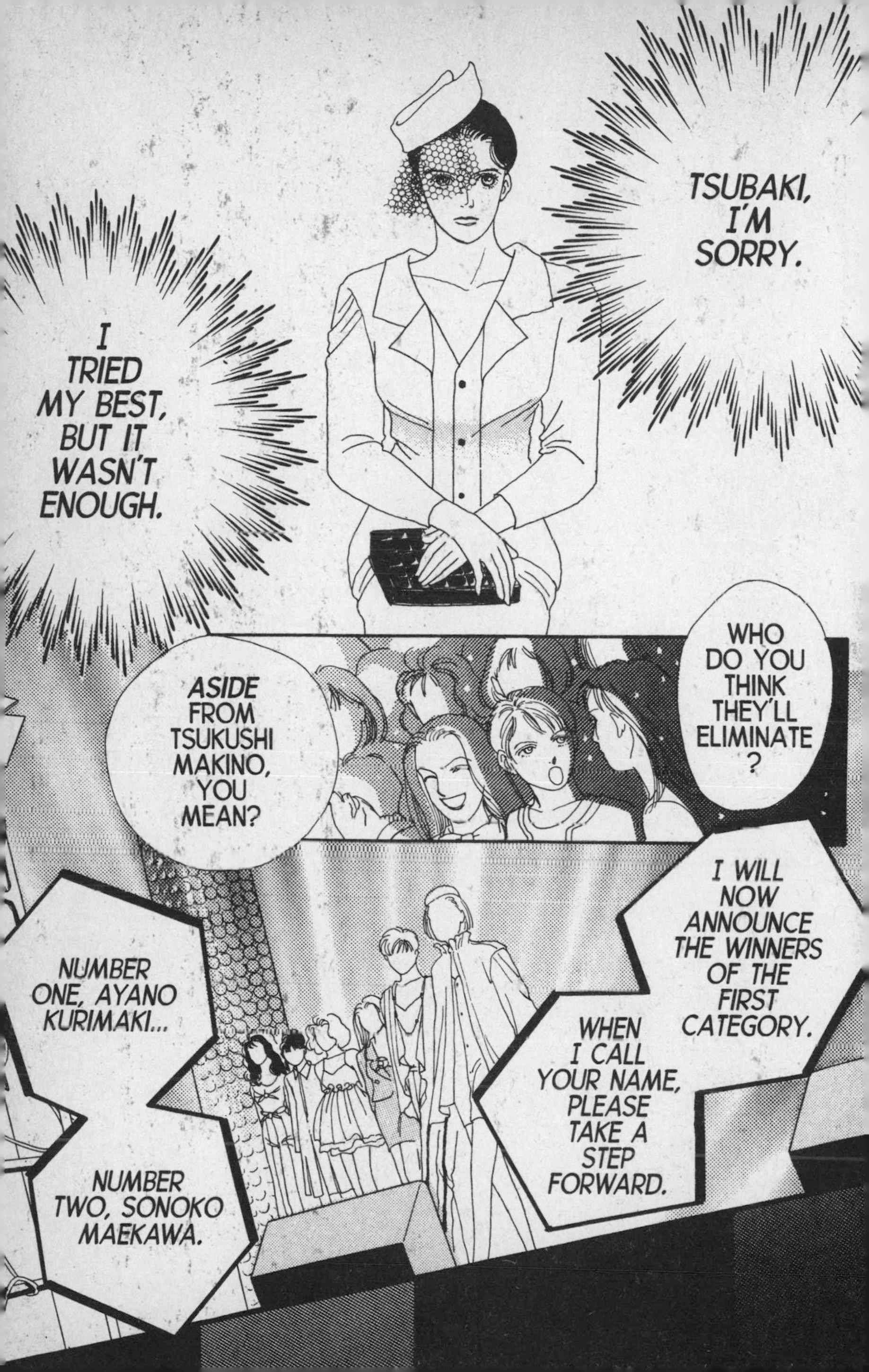
TSUBAKI, I'M SORRY.
I TRIED MY BEST, BUT IT WASN'T ENOUGH.
WHO DO YOU THINK THEY'LL ELIMINATE?
ASIDE FROM TSUKUSHI MAKINO, YOU MEAN?
I WILL NOW ANNOUNCE THE WINNERS OF THE FIRST CATEGORY.
WHEN I CALL YOUR NAME, PLEASE TAKE A STEP FORWARD.
NUMBER ONE, AYANO KURIMAKI...
NUMBER TWO, SONOKO MAEKAWA.

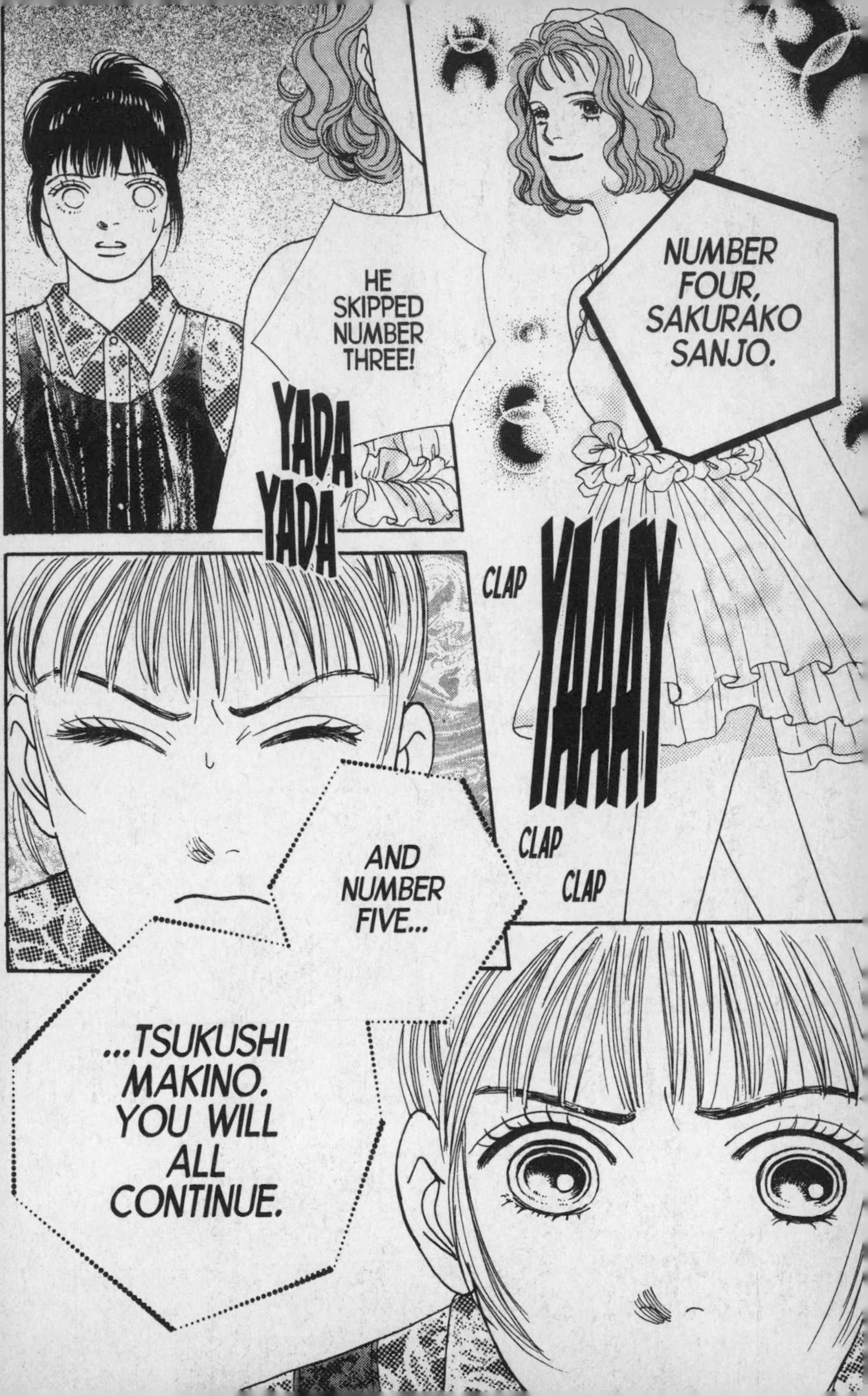
NUMBER FOUR, SAKURAKO SANJO.
CLAP
YAAAY
CLAP
CLAP
HE SKIPPED NUMBER THREE!
YADA YADA
AND NUMBER FIVE...
...TSUKUSHI MAKINO. YOU WILL ALL CONTINUE.

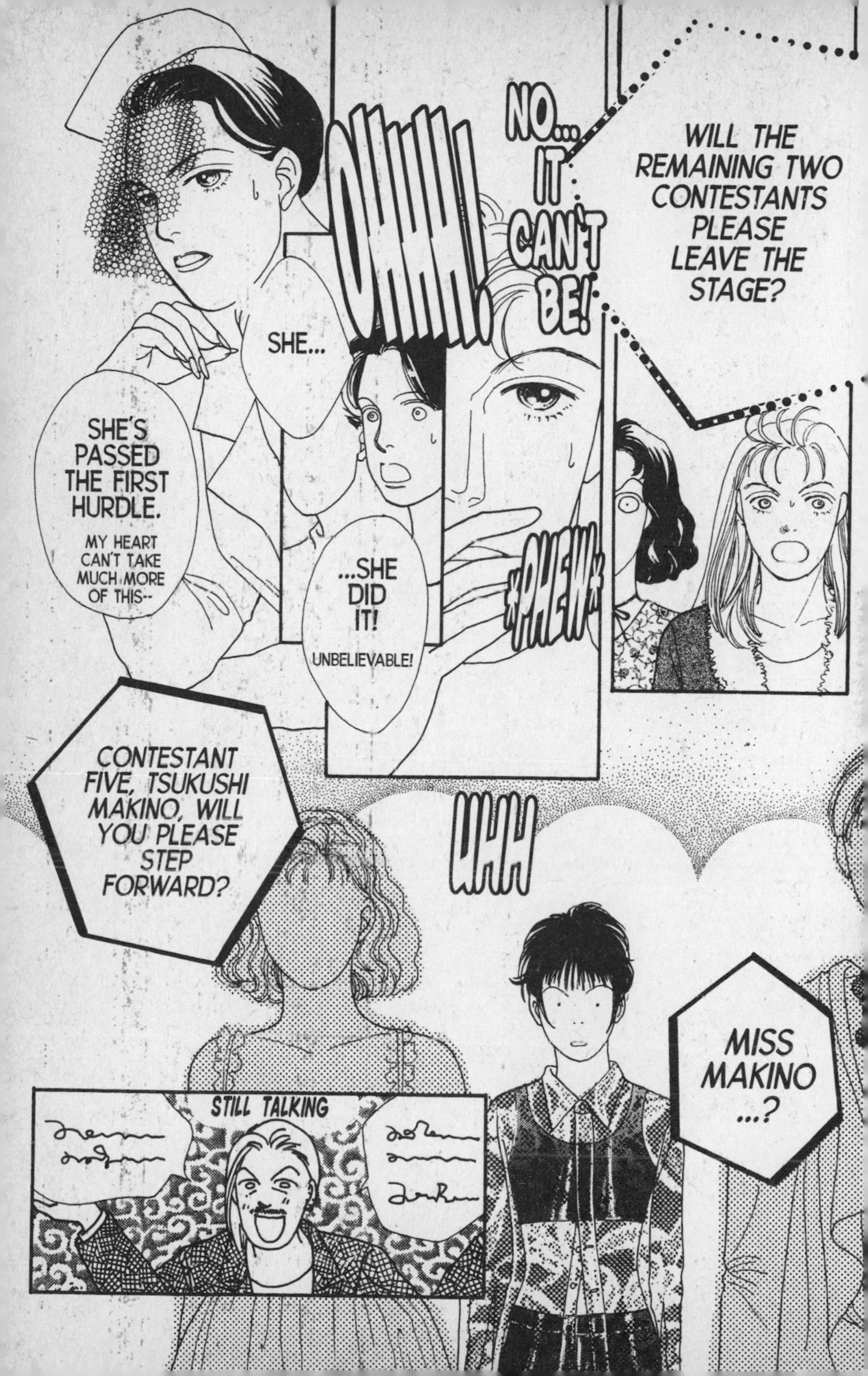
WILL THE REMAINING TWO CONTESTANTS PLEASE LEAVE THE STAGE?
NO... IT CAN'T BE!
OHHH!
SHE...
...SHE DID IT!
UNBELIEVABLE!
PHEW
SHE'S PASSED THE FIRST HURDLE.
MY HEART CAN'T TAKE MUCH MORE OF THIS--
CONTESTANT FIVE, TSUKUSHI MAKINO, WILL YOU PLEASE STEP FORWARD?
UHH
MISS MAKINO ...?
STILL TALKING

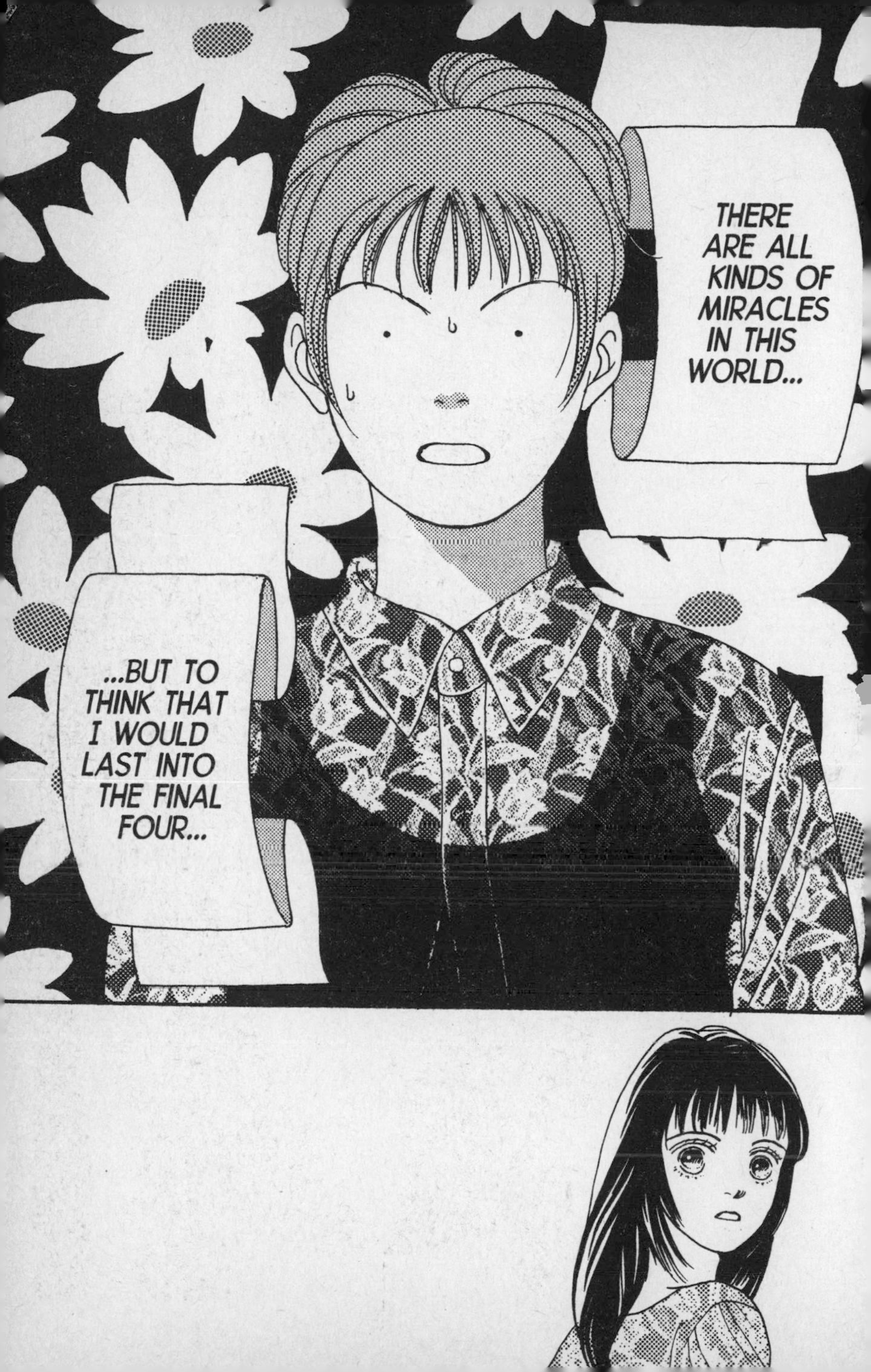
THERE ARE ALL KINDS OF MIRACLES IN THIS WORLD...
...BUT TO THINK THAT I WOULD LAST INTO THE FINAL FOUR...

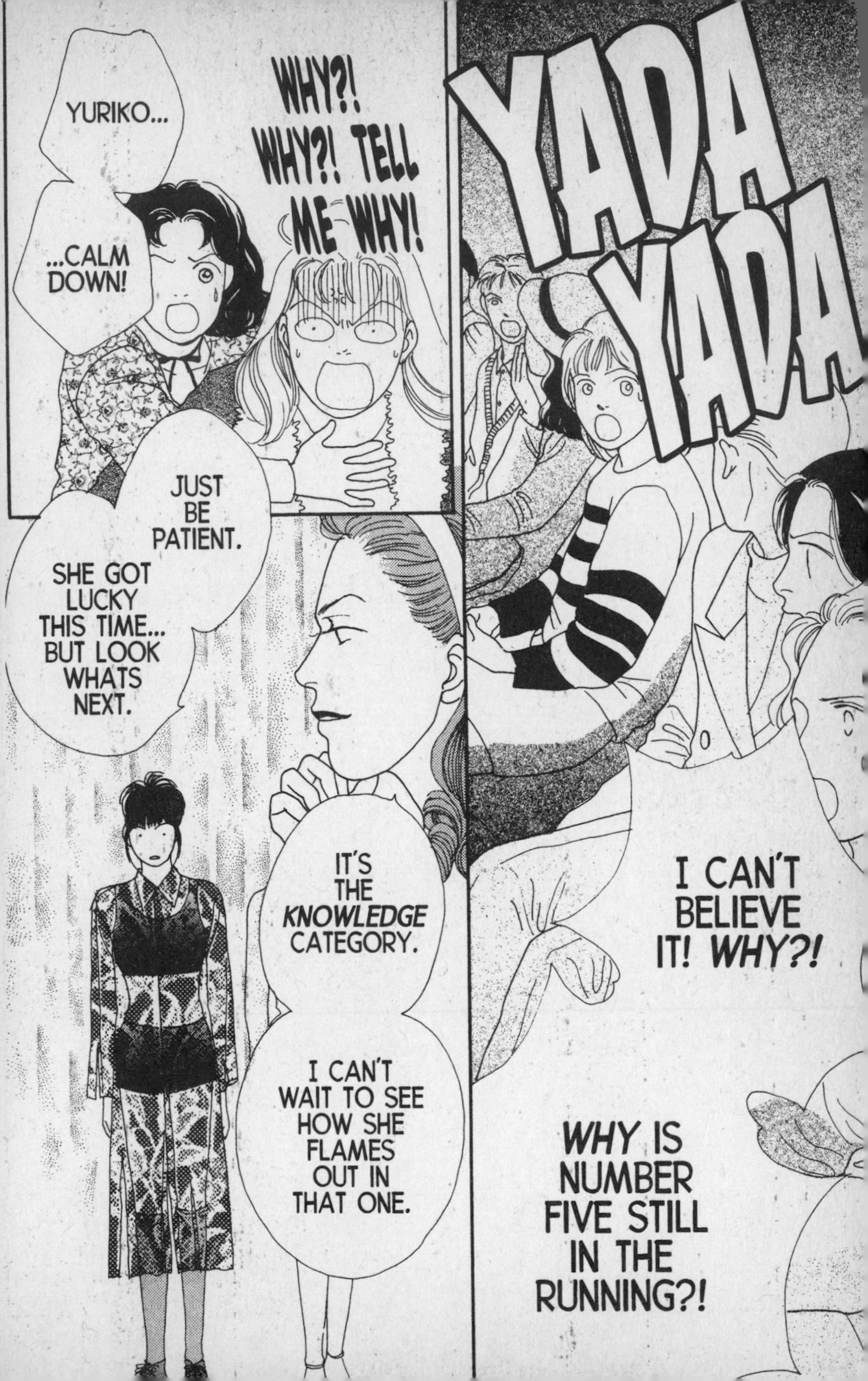
YADA YADA
I CAN'T BELIEVE IT! *WHY?!*
WHY IS NUMBER FIVE STILL IN THE RUNNING?!
WHY?! WHY?! TELL ME WHY!
YURIKO...
...CALM DOWN!
JUST BE PATIENT.
SHE GOT LUCKY THIS TIME... BUT LOOK WHATS NEXT.
IT'S THE *KNOWLEDGE* CATEGORY.
I CAN'T WAIT TO SEE HOW SHE FLAMES OUT IN THAT ONE.

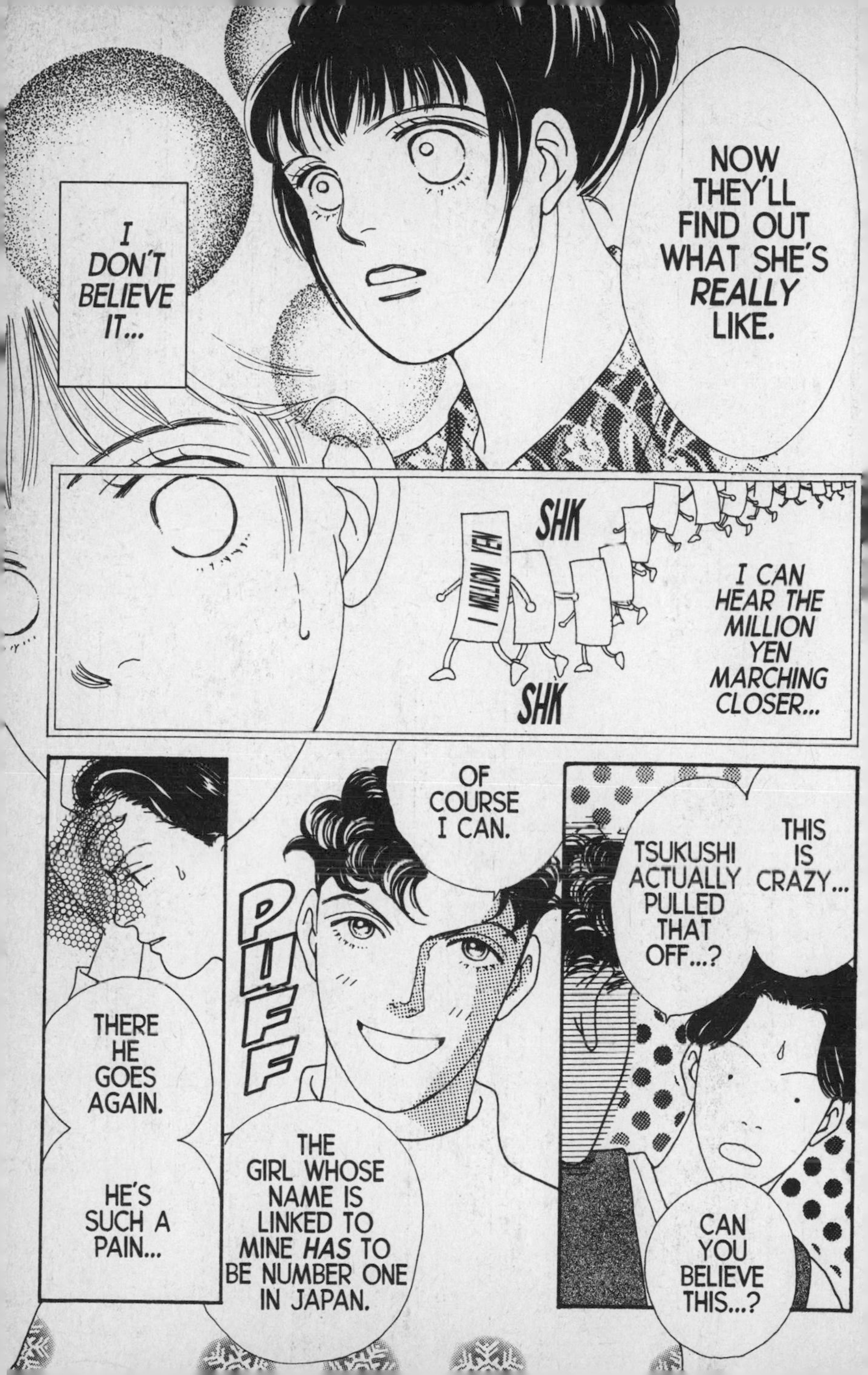
NOW THEY'LL FIND OUT WHAT SHE'S *REALLY* LIKE.
I DON'T BELIEVE IT...
I CAN HEAR THE MILLION YEN MARCHING CLOSER...
SHK
SHK
THIS IS CRAZY...
TSUKUSHI ACTUALLY PULLED THAT OFF...?
CAN YOU BELIEVE THIS...?
OF COURSE I CAN.
PUFF
THE GIRL WHOSE NAME IS LINKED TO MINE *HAS* TO BE NUMBER ONE IN JAPAN.
THERE HE GOES AGAIN.
HE'S SUCH A PAIN...

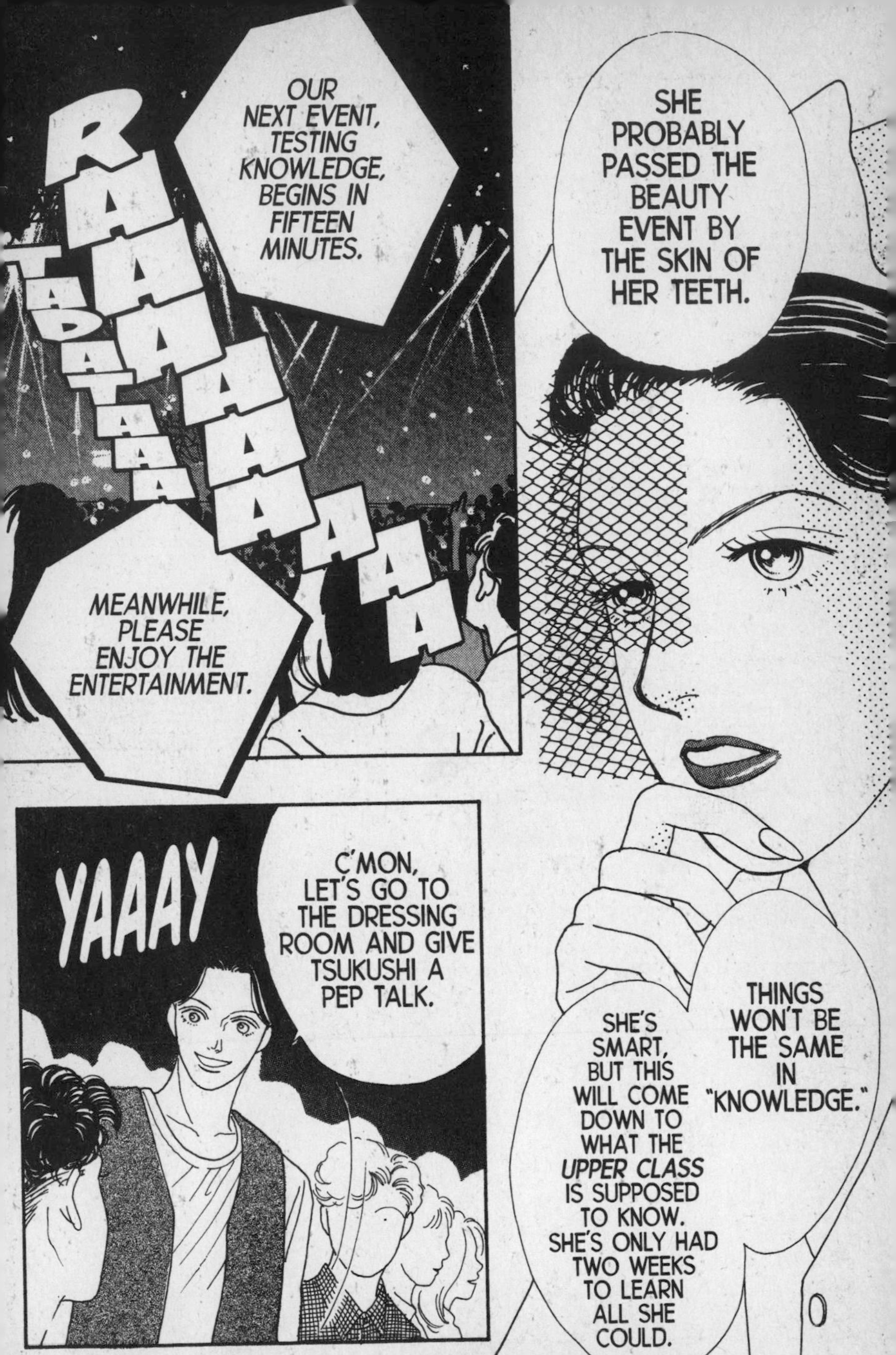
SHE PROBABLY PASSED THE BEAUTY EVENT BY THE SKIN OF HER TEETH.
THINGS WON'T BE THE SAME IN "KNOWLEDGE."
SHE'S SMART, BUT THIS WILL COME DOWN TO WHAT THE *UPPER CLASS* IS SUPPOSED TO KNOW. SHE'S ONLY HAD TWO WEEKS TO LEARN ALL SHE COULD.
OUR NEXT EVENT, TESTING KNOWLEDGE, BEGINS IN FIFTEEN MINUTES.
RAAAAAAAAA
TADATAAA
MEANWHILE, PLEASE ENJOY THE ENTERTAINMENT.
YAAAY
C'MON, LET'S GO TO THE DRESSING ROOM AND GIVE TSUKUSHI A PEP TALK.

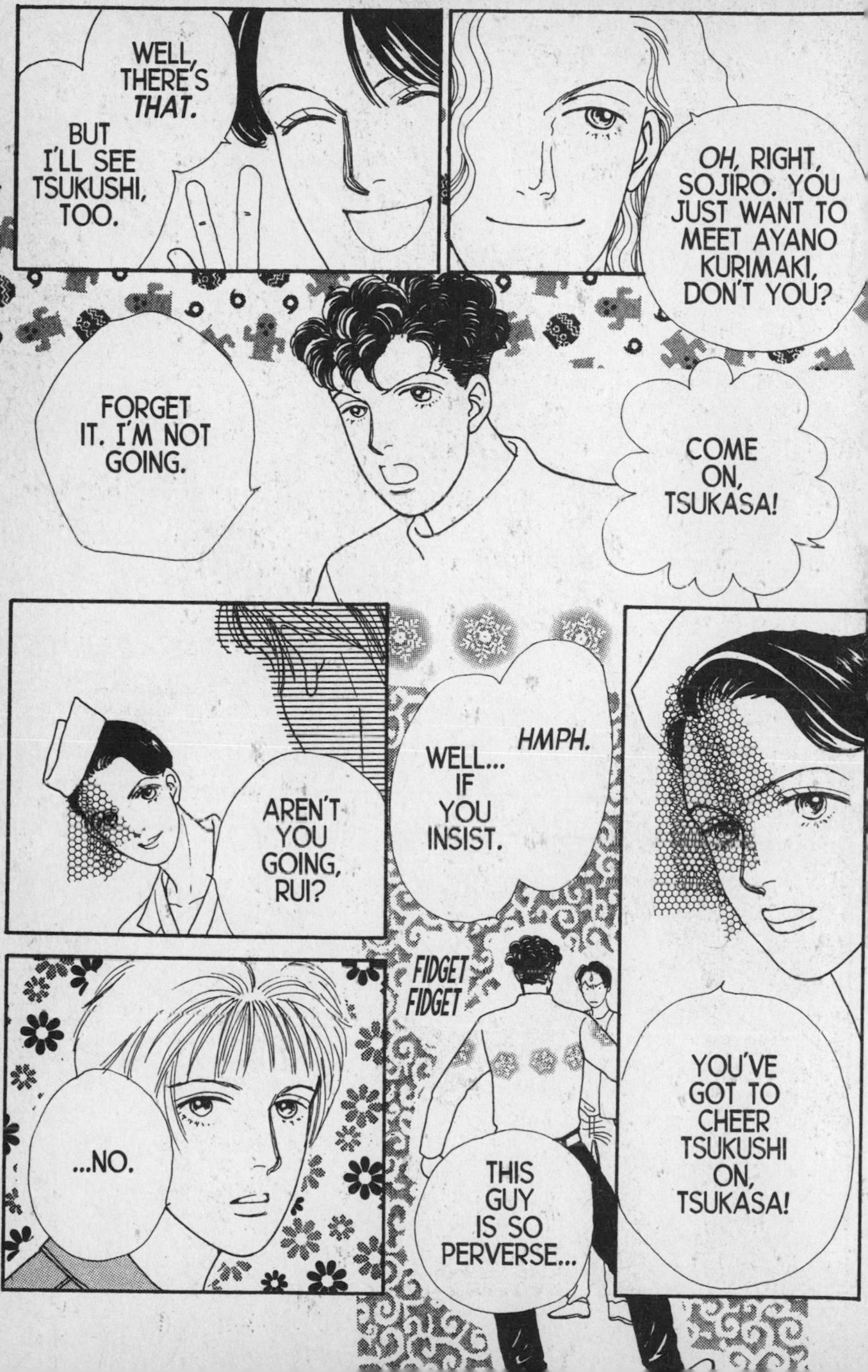
OH, RIGHT, SOJIRO. YOU JUST WANT TO MEET AYANO KURIMAKI, DON'T YOU?
WELL, THERE'S *THAT.*
BUT I'LL SEE TSUKUSHI, TOO.
COME ON, TSUKASA!
FORGET IT. I'M NOT GOING.
YOU'VE GOT TO CHEER TSUKUSHI ON, TSUKASA!
HMPH.
WELL... IF YOU INSIST.
FIDGET FIDGET
THIS GUY IS SO PERVERSE...
AREN'T YOU GOING, RUI?
...NO.

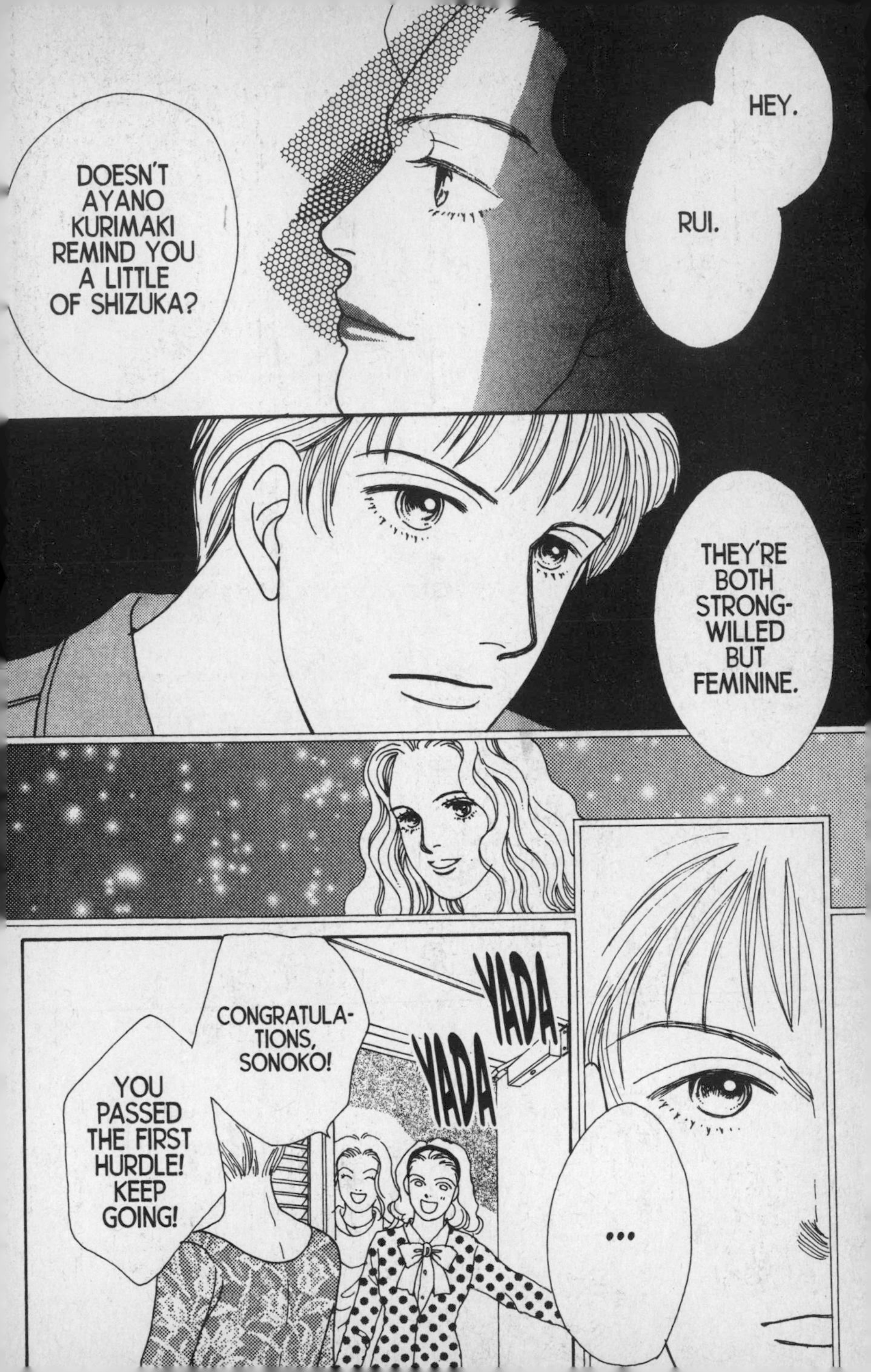
HEY.
RUI.
DOESN'T AYANO KURIMAKI REMIND YOU A LITTLE OF SHIZUKA?
THEY'RE BOTH STRONG-WILLED BUT FEMININE.
...
YADA
YADA
CONGRATULA-TIONS, SONOKO!
YOU PASSED THE FIRST HURDLE! KEEP GOING!

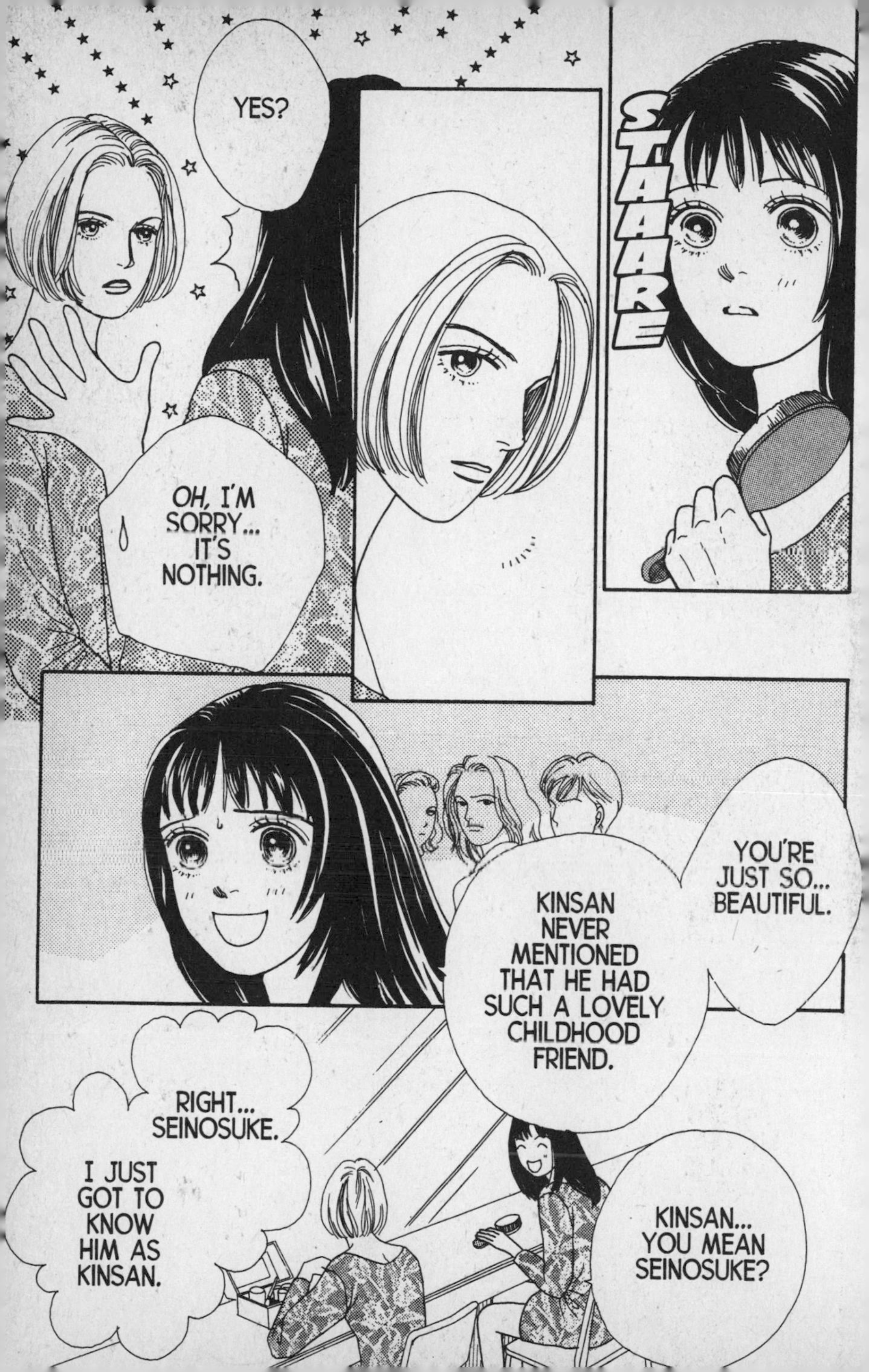
STAARE
YES?
OH, I'M SORRY... IT'S NOTHING.
YOU'RE JUST SO... BEAUTIFUL.
KINSAN NEVER MENTIONED THAT HE HAD SUCH A LOVELY CHILDHOOD FRIEND.
KINSAN... YOU MEAN SEINOSUKE?
RIGHT... SEINOSUKE.
I JUST GOT TO KNOW HIM AS KINSAN.

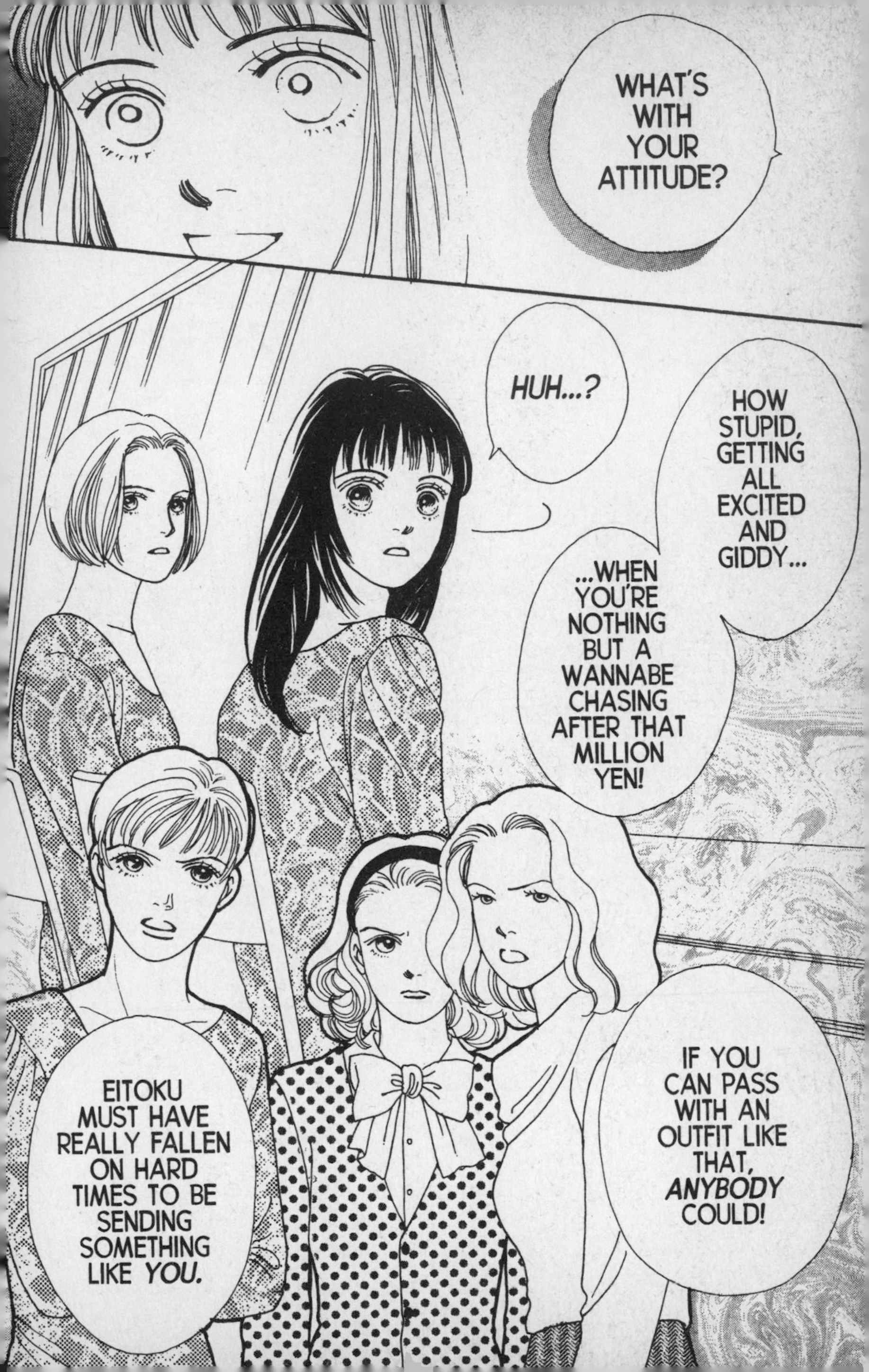
WHAT'S WITH YOUR ATTITUDE?
HUH...?
HOW STUPID, GETTING ALL EXCITED AND GIDDY...
...WHEN YOU'RE NOTHING BUT A WANNABE CHASING AFTER THAT MILLION YEN!
IF YOU CAN PASS WITH AN OUTFIT LIKE THAT, *ANYBODY* COULD!
EITOKU MUST HAVE REALLY FALLEN ON HARD TIMES TO BE SENDING SOMETHING LIKE *YOU.*

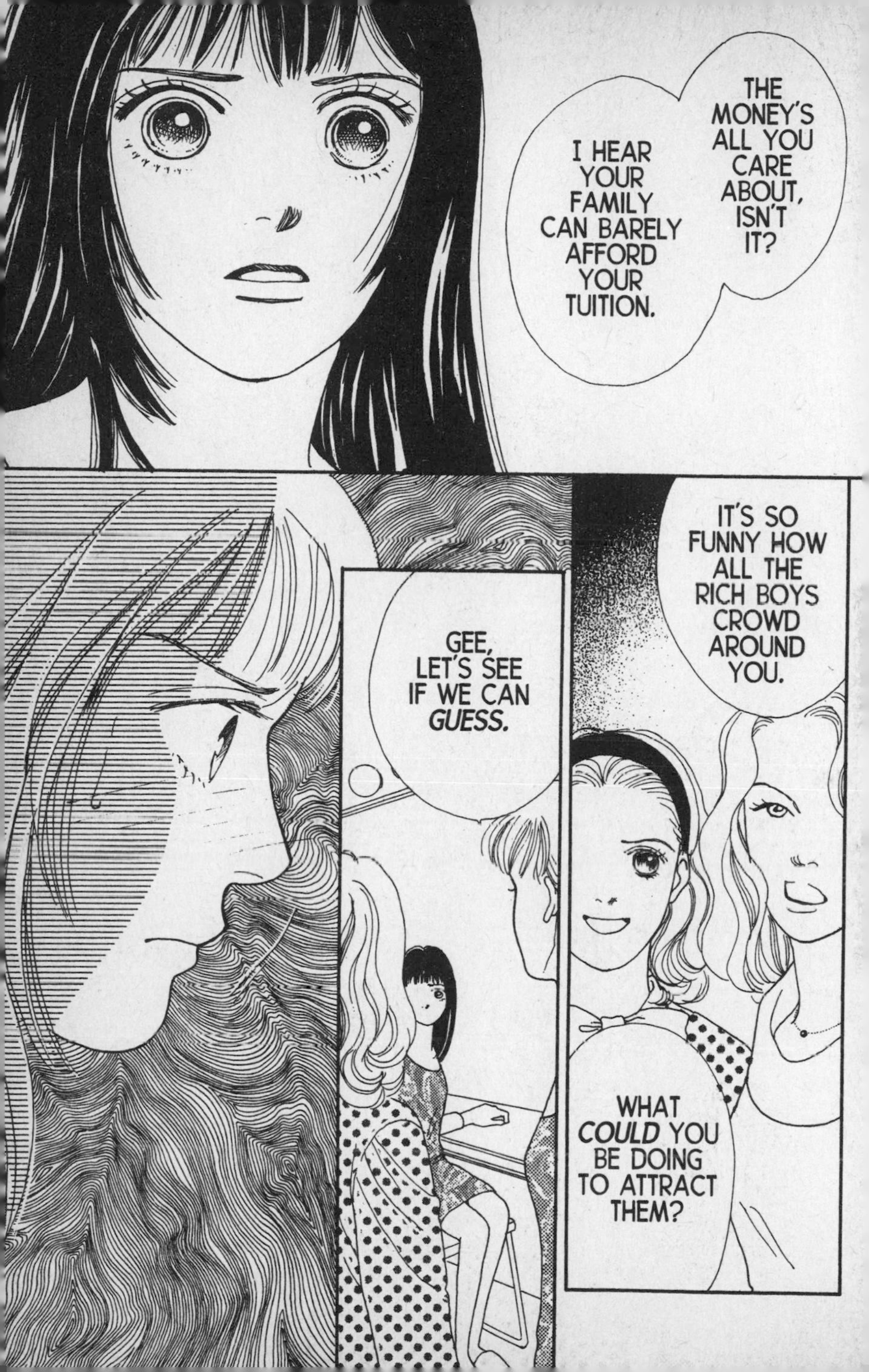
THE MONEY'S ALL YOU CARE ABOUT, ISN'T IT?
I HEAR YOUR FAMILY CAN BARELY AFFORD YOUR TUITION.
IT'S SO FUNNY HOW ALL THE RICH BOYS CROWD AROUND YOU.
WHAT *COULD* YOU BE DOING TO ATTRACT THEM?
GEE, LET'S SEE IF WE CAN *GUESS.*

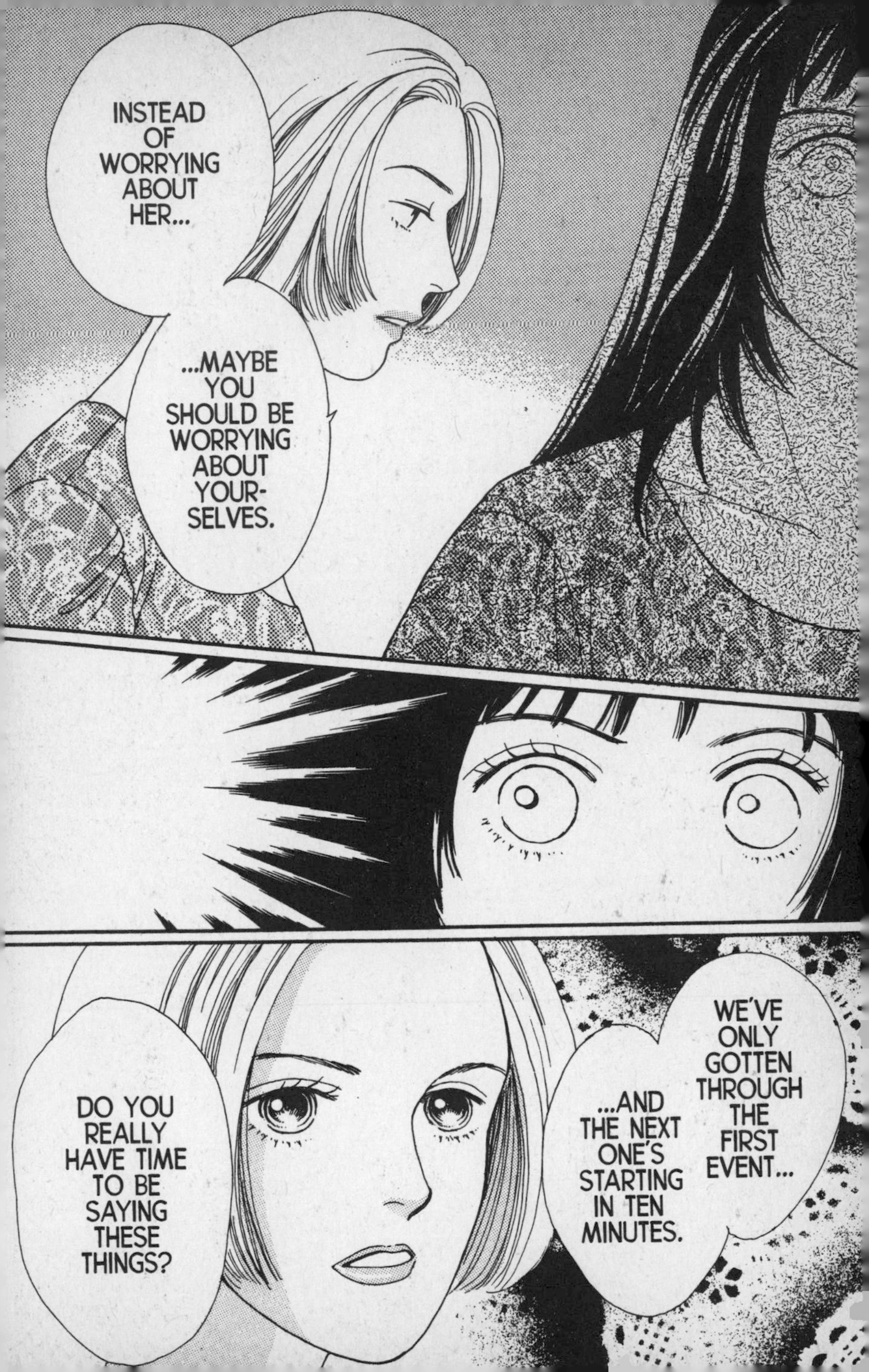
INSTEAD OF WORRYING ABOUT HER...
...MAYBE YOU SHOULD BE WORRYING ABOUT YOUR-SELVES.
WE'VE ONLY GOTTEN THROUGH THE FIRST EVENT...
...AND THE NEXT ONE'S STARTING IN TEN MINUTES.
DO YOU REALLY HAVE TIME TO BE SAYING THESE THINGS?

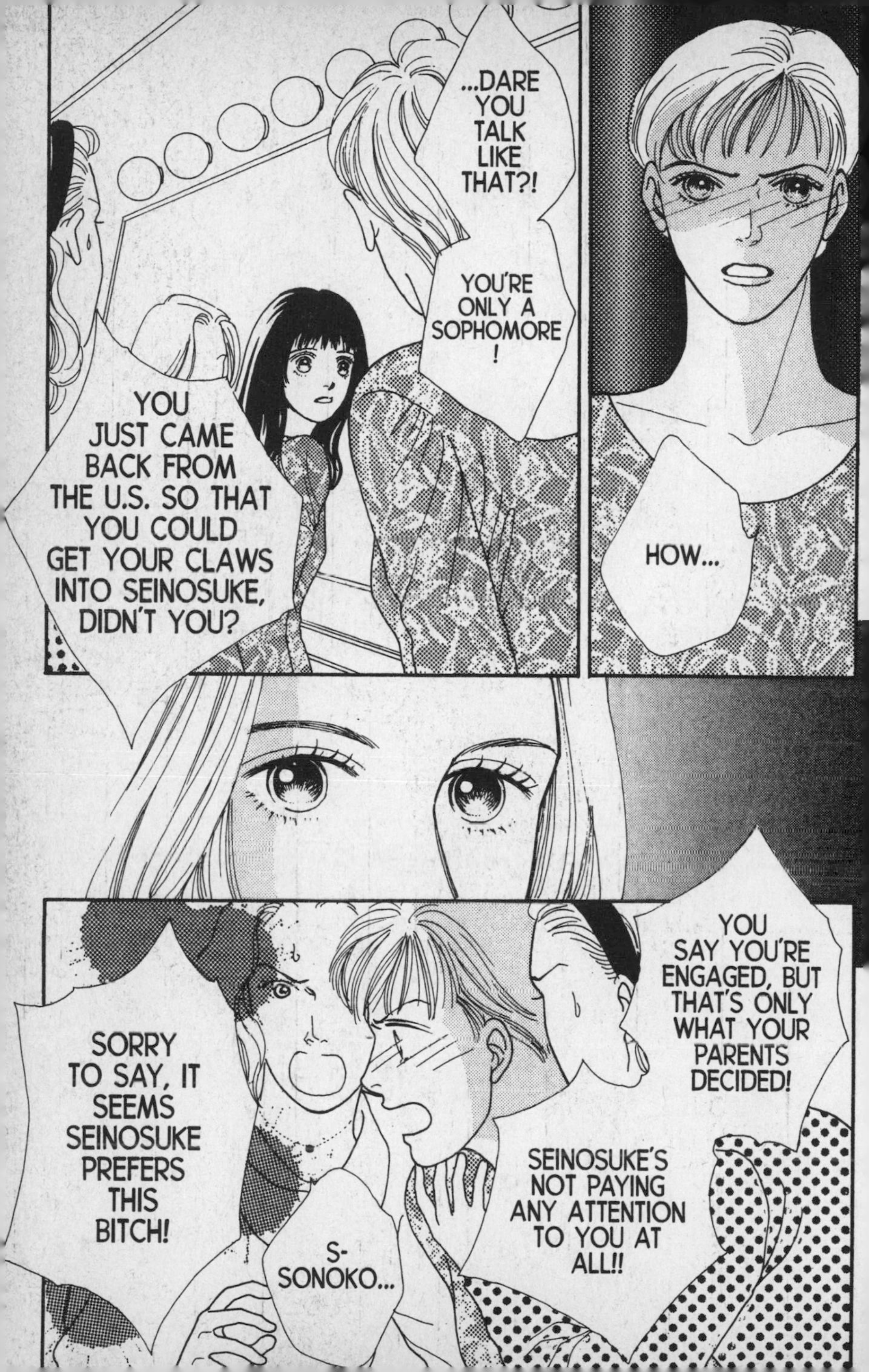
HOW...
...DARE YOU TALK LIKE THAT?!
YOU'RE ONLY A SOPHOMORE!
YOU JUST CAME BACK FROM THE U.S. SO THAT YOU COULD GET YOUR CLAWS INTO SEINOSUKE, DIDN'T YOU?
YOU SAY YOU'RE ENGAGED, BUT THAT'S ONLY WHAT YOUR PARENTS DECIDED!
SEINOSUKE'S NOT PAYING ANY ATTENTION TO YOU AT ALL!!
SORRY TO SAY, IT SEEMS SEINOSUKE PREFERS THIS BITCH!
S- SONOKO...

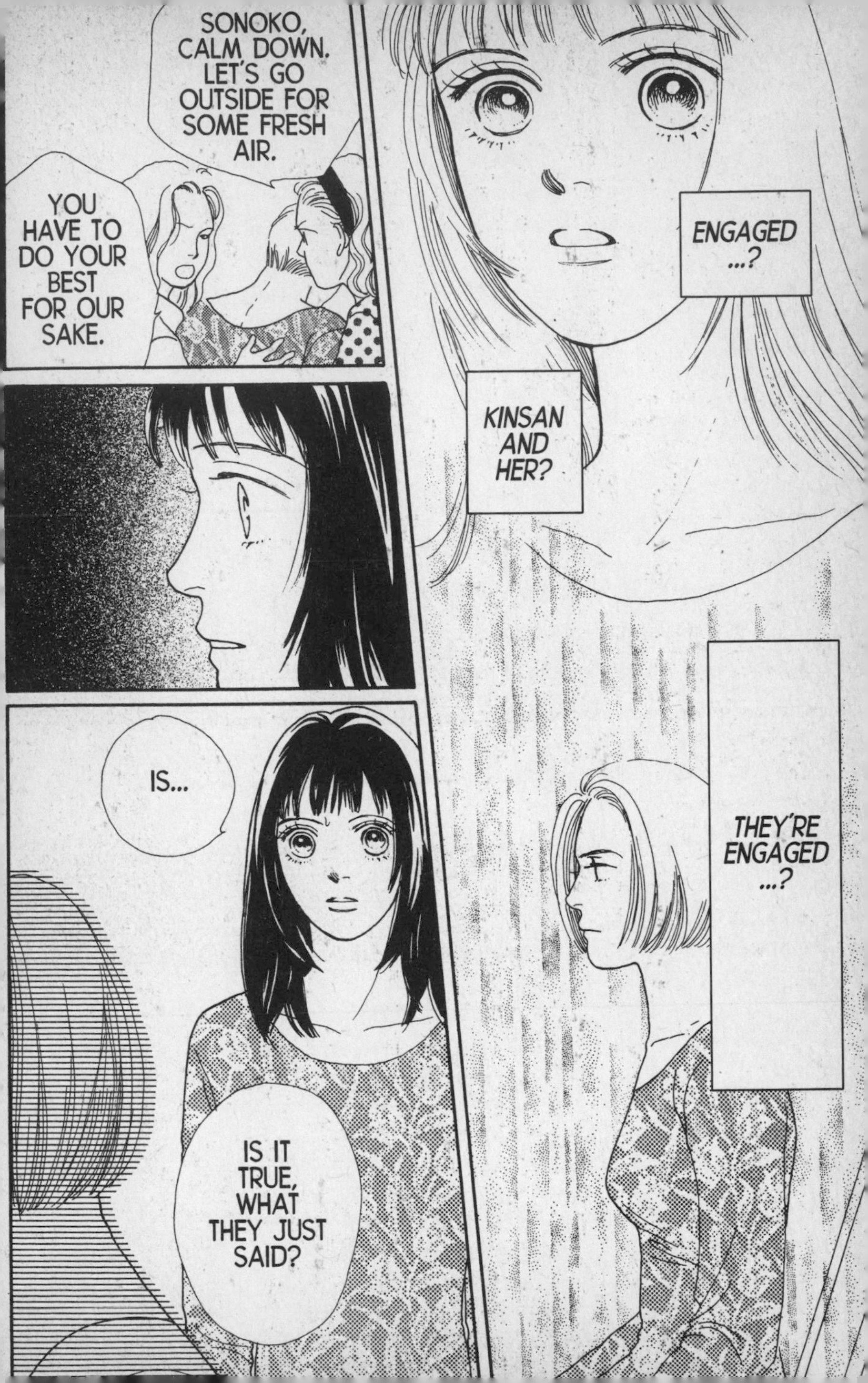
ENGAGED ...?
KINSAN AND HER?
THEY'RE ENGAGED ...?
SONOKO, CALM DOWN. LET'S GO OUTSIDE FOR SOME FRESH AIR.
YOU HAVE TO DO YOUR BEST FOR OUR SAKE.
IS...
IS IT TRUE, WHAT THEY JUST SAID?

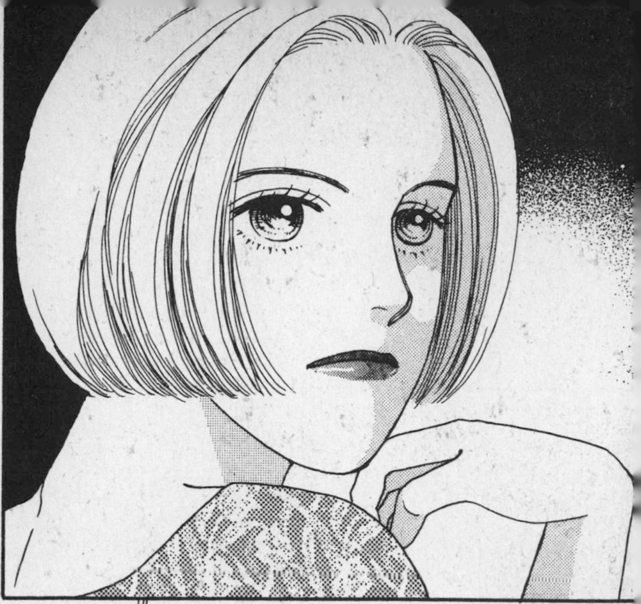

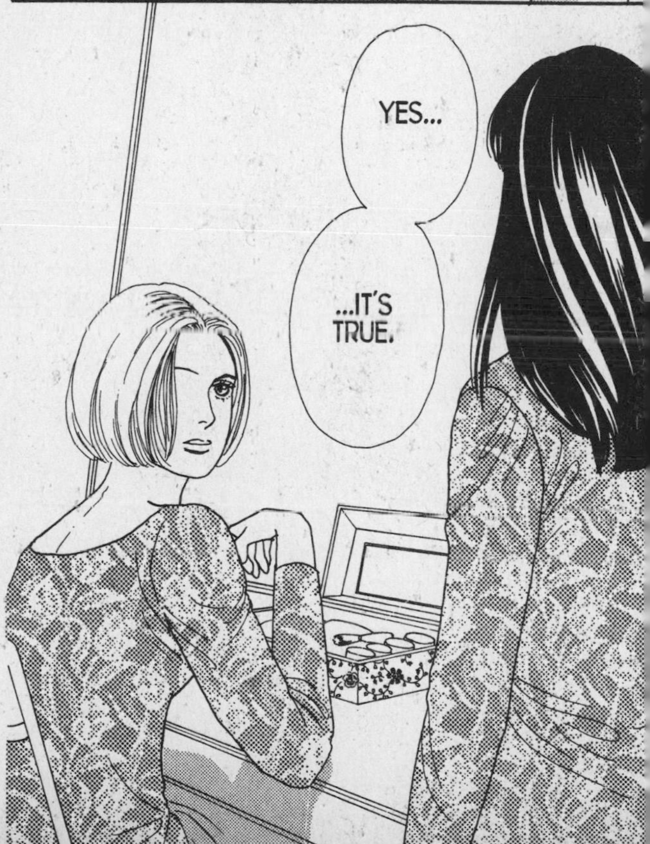
YES...
...IT'S TRUE.

☆ I Met All the F4 Members! ☆

I met all the actors playing the roles of the F4. Being that they were so carefully selected, they were all studs.

I'd checked out Naoto Fujiki in the commercials he was in, so I was happy that he was chosen to play Rui.

Everyone on the shoot seemed to get along really well.

There was such a camaraderie that even an outsider like me could have fun!

I still haven't seen the movie, but I have a feeling that the fun atmosphere during the shoot will show up on screen. I'm really looking forward to seeing it!

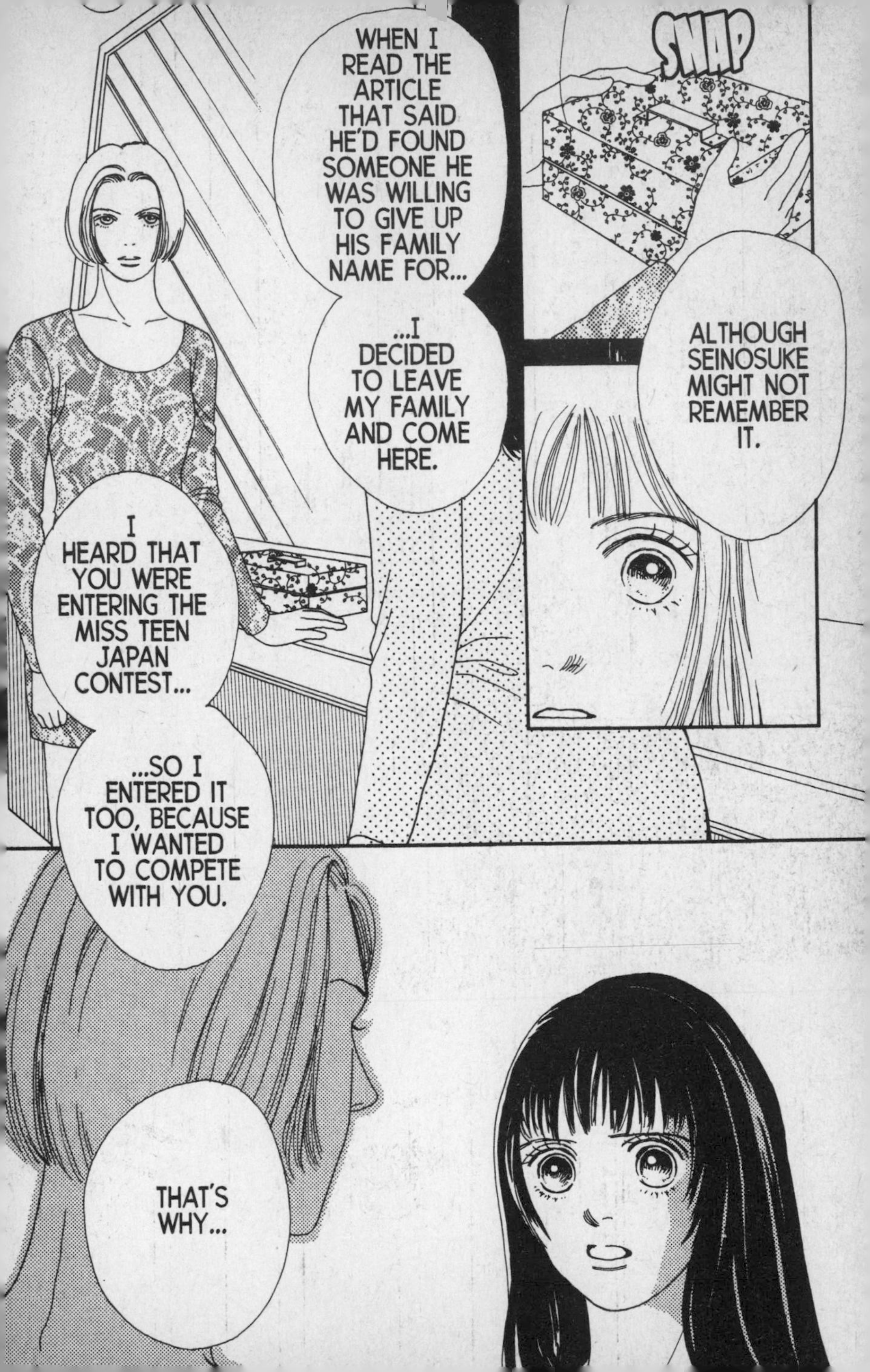
SNAP
ALTHOUGH SEINOSUKE MIGHT NOT REMEMBER IT.
WHEN I READ THE ARTICLE THAT SAID HE'D FOUND SOMEONE HE WAS WILLING TO GIVE UP HIS FAMILY NAME FOR...
...I DECIDED TO LEAVE MY FAMILY AND COME HERE.
I HEARD THAT YOU WERE ENTERING THE MISS TEEN JAPAN CONTEST...
...SO I ENTERED IT TOO, BECAUSE I WANTED TO COMPETE WITH YOU.
THAT'S WHY...

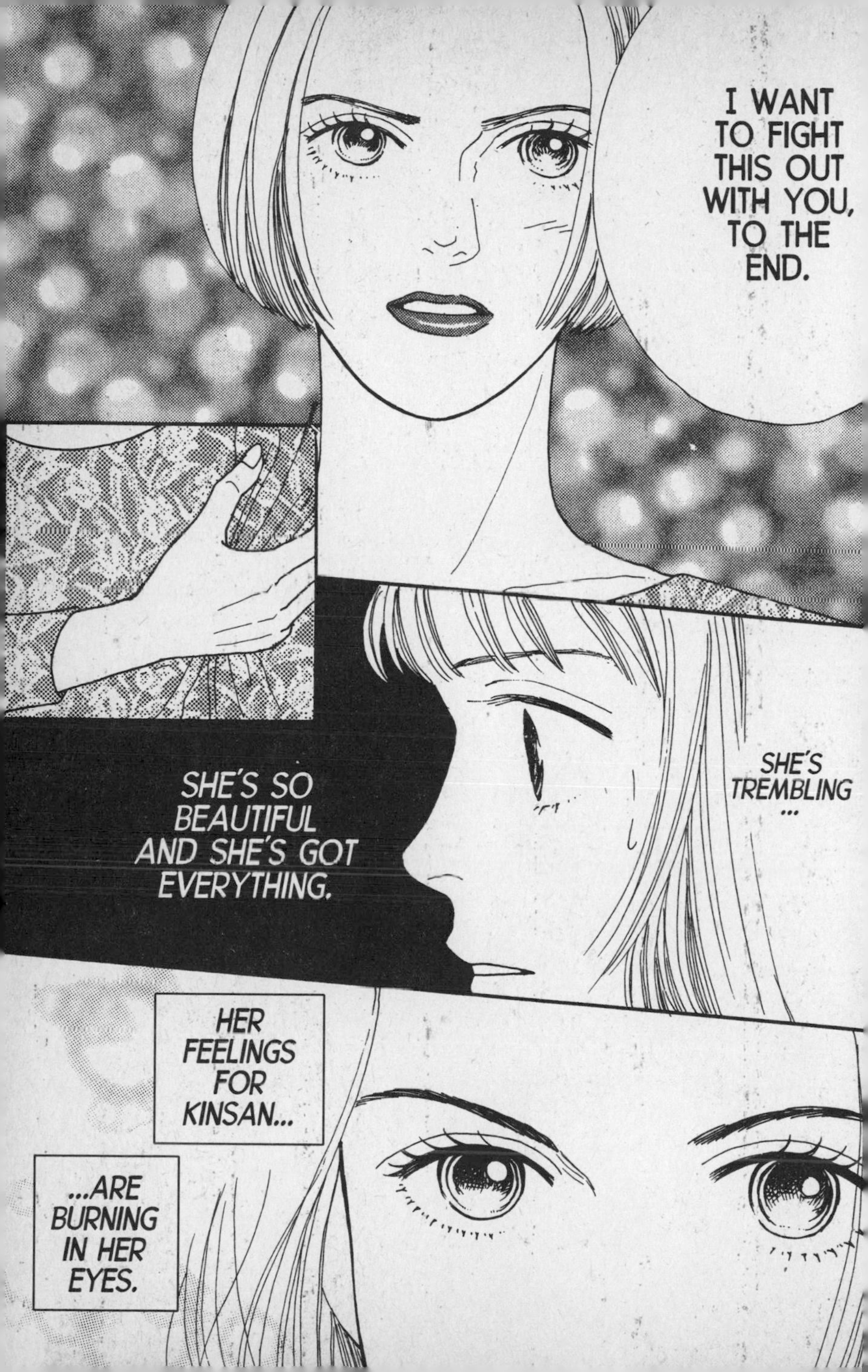
I WANT TO FIGHT THIS OUT WITH YOU, TO THE END.
SHE'S TREMBLING ...
SHE'S SO BEAUTIFUL AND SHE'S GOT EVERYTHING.
HER FEELINGS FOR KINSAN...
...ARE BURNING IN HER EYES.

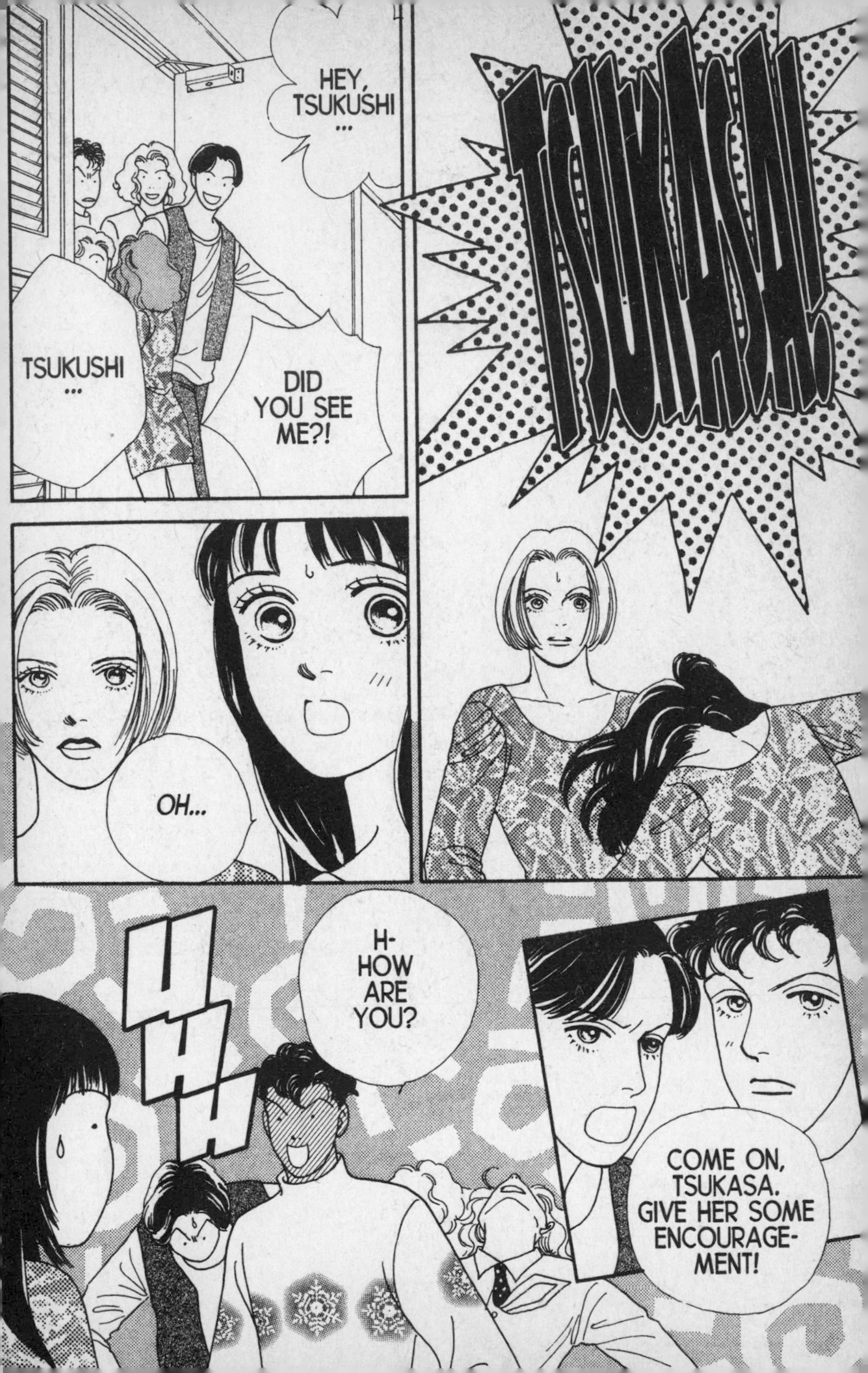
HEY, TSUKUSHI ...
DID YOU SEE ME?!
TSUKUSHI ...
OH...
COME ON, TSUKASA. GIVE HER SOME ENCOURAGE-MENT!
H- HOW ARE YOU?
UHHH

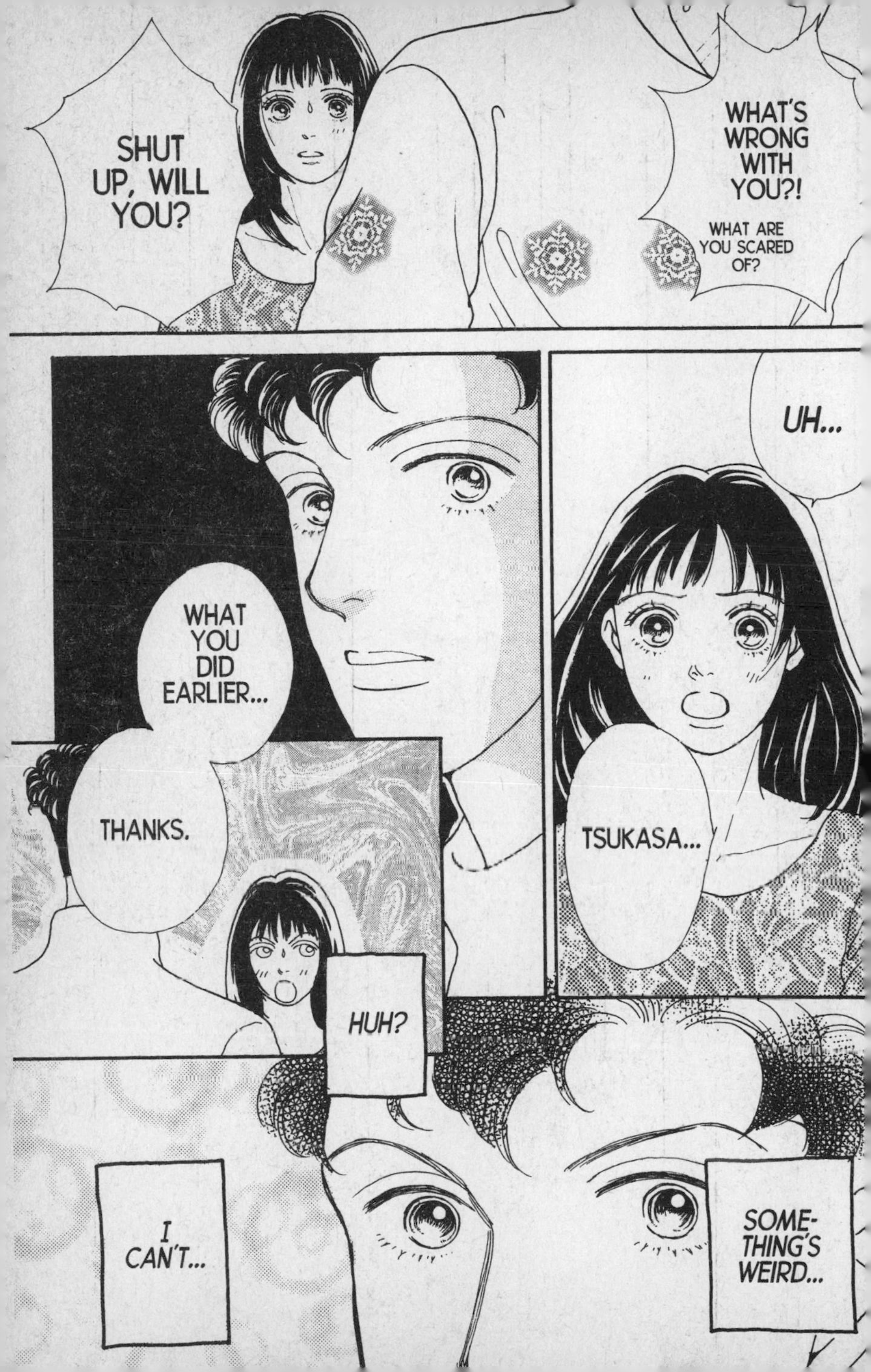
WHAT'S WRONG WITH YOU?!
WHAT ARE YOU SCARED OF?
SHUT UP, WILL YOU?
UH...
TSUKASA...
WHAT YOU DID EARLIER...
THANKS.
HUH?
SOME-THING'S WEIRD...
I CAN'T...

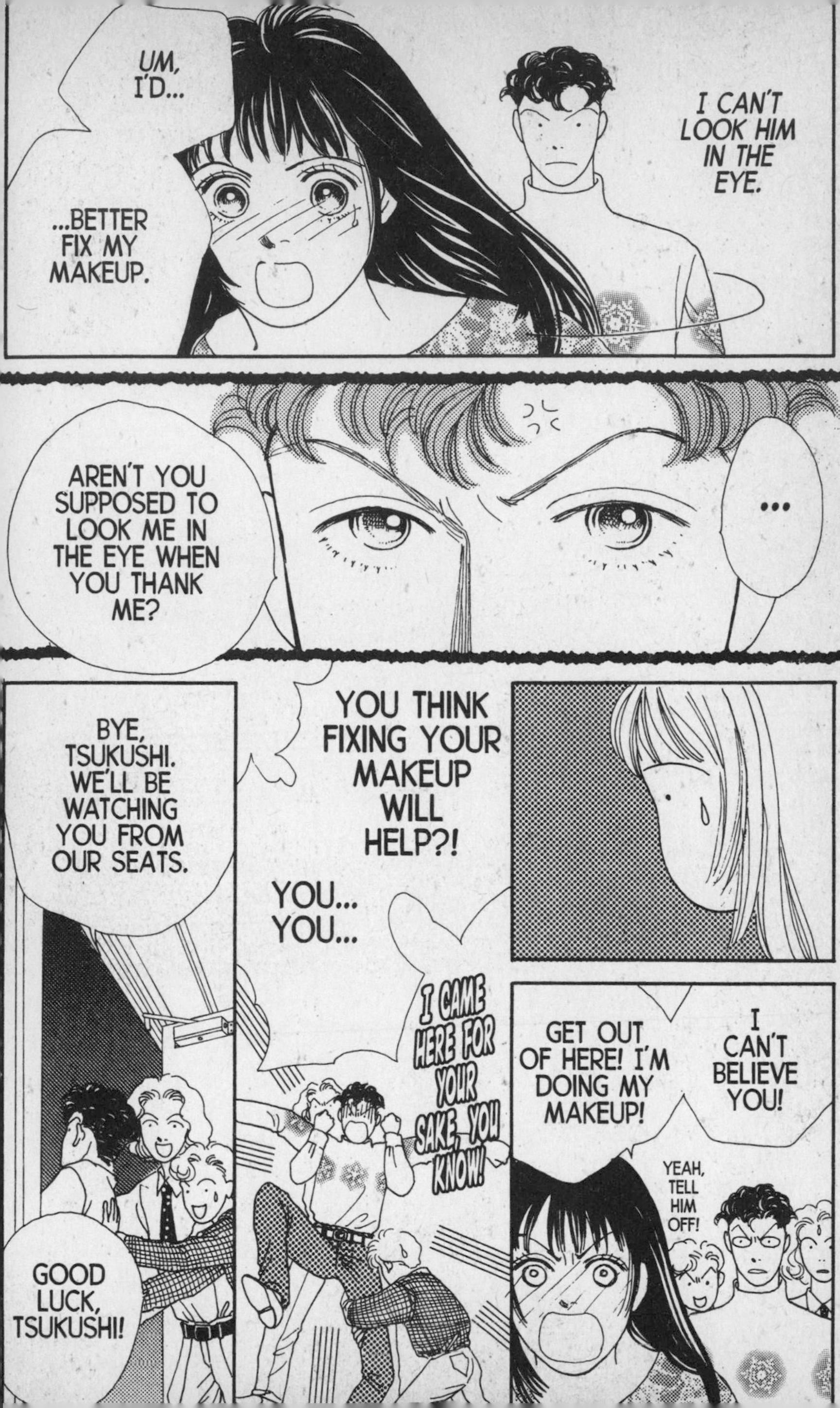
I CAN'T LOOK HIM IN THE EYE.
UM, I'D...
...BETTER FIX MY MAKEUP.
...
AREN'T YOU SUPPOSED TO LOOK ME IN THE EYE WHEN YOU THANK ME?
I CAN'T BELIEVE YOU!
GET OUT OF HERE! I'M DOING MY MAKEUP!
YEAH, TELL HIM OFF!
YOU THINK FIXING YOUR MAKEUP WILL HELP?!
YOU... YOU...
I CAME HERE FOR YOUR SAKE, YOU KNOW!
BYE, TSUKUSHI. WE'LL BE WATCHING YOU FROM OUR SEATS.
GOOD LUCK, TSUKUSHI!

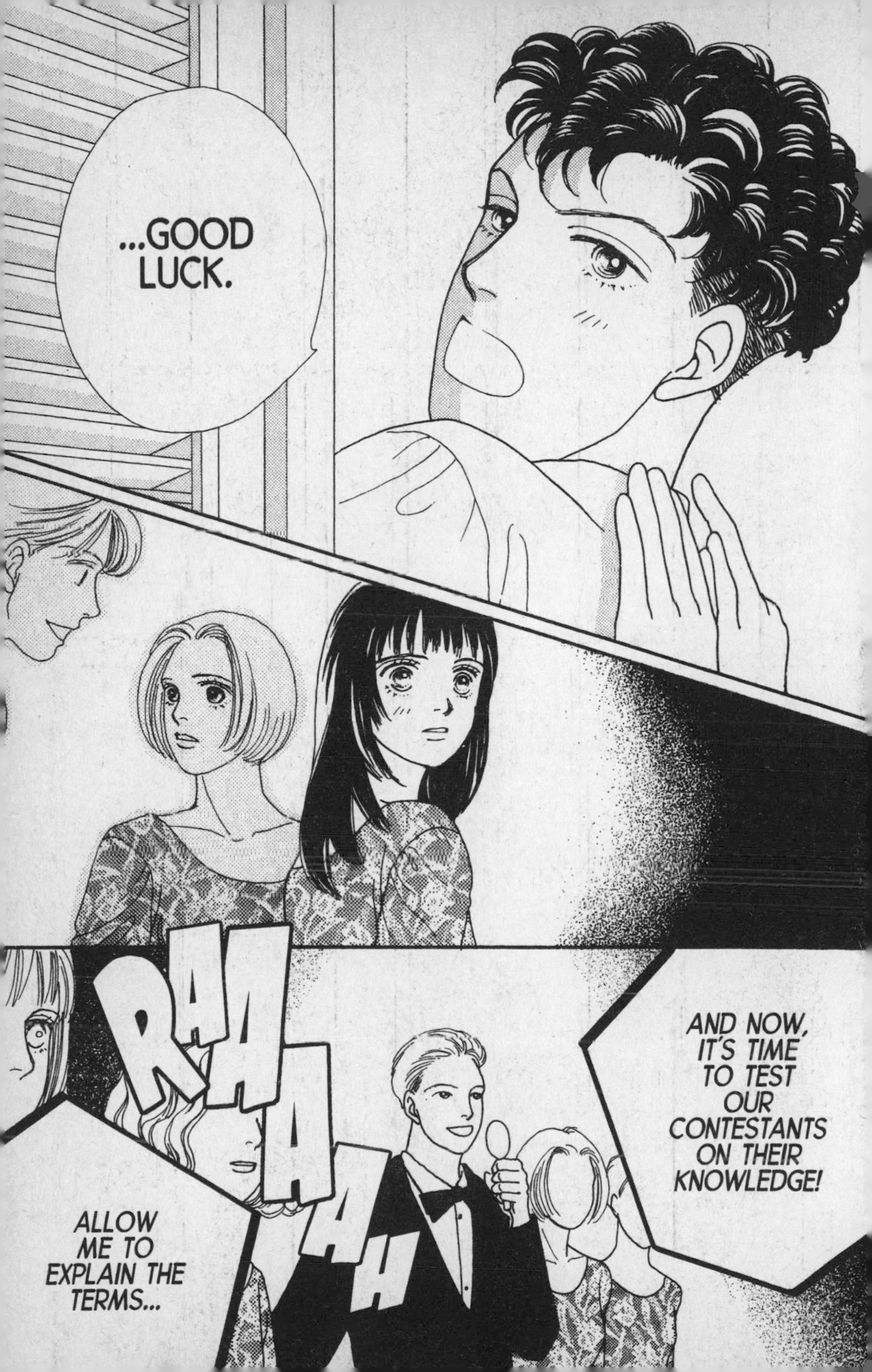
...GOOD LUCK.
AND NOW, IT'S TIME TO TEST OUR CONTESTANTS ON THEIR KNOWLEDGE!
ALLOW ME TO EXPLAIN THE TERMS...

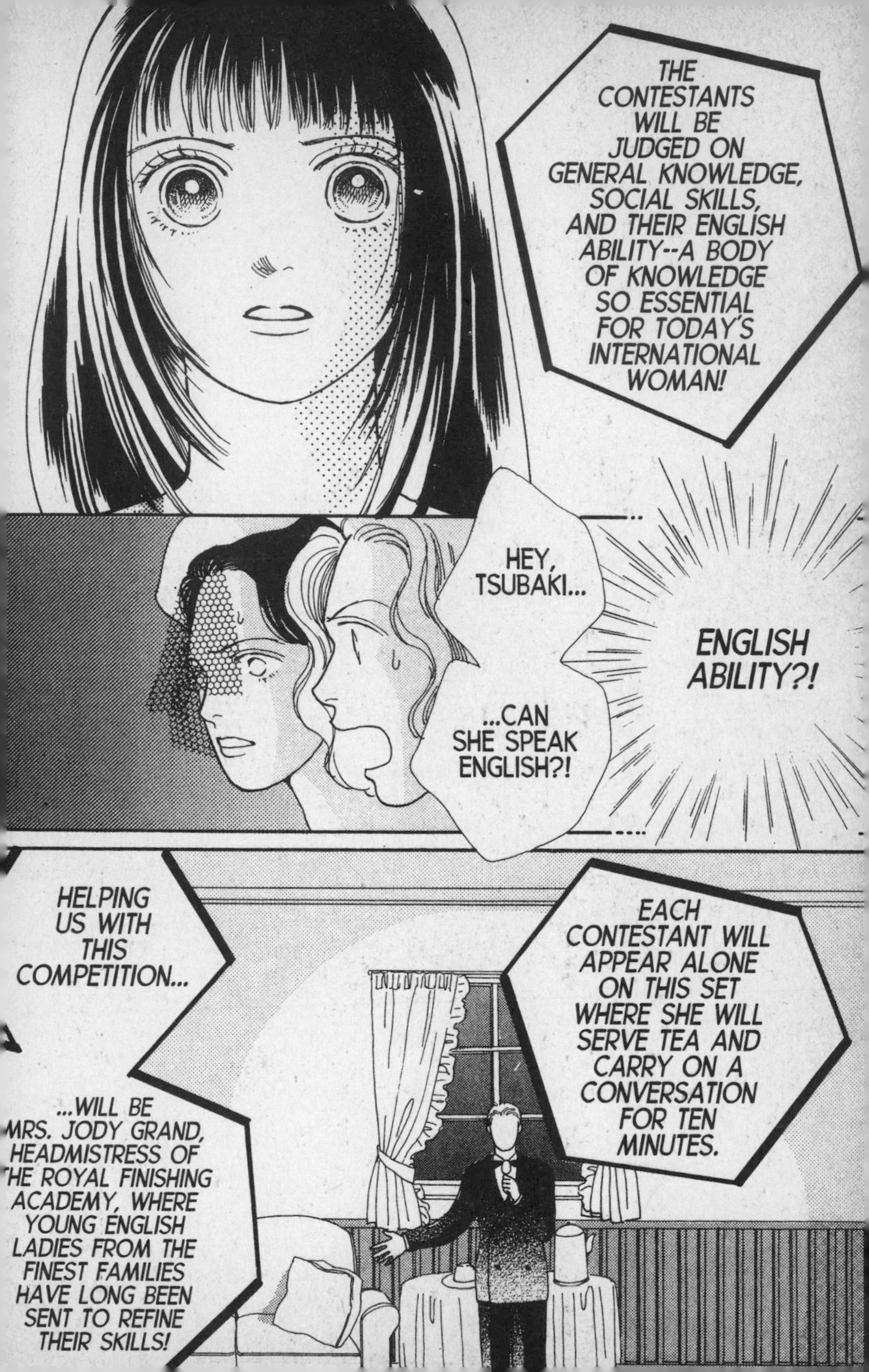
THE CONTESTANTS WILL BE JUDGED ON GENERAL KNOWLEDGE, SOCIAL SKILLS, AND THEIR ENGLISH ABILITY--A BODY OF KNOWLEDGE SO ESSENTIAL FOR TODAY'S INTERNATIONAL WOMAN!
ENGLISH ABILITY?!
HEY, TSUBAKI...
...CAN SHE SPEAK ENGLISH?!
EACH CONTESTANT WILL APPEAR ALONE ON THIS SET WHERE SHE WILL SERVE TEA AND CARRY ON A CONVERSATION FOR TEN MINUTES.
HELPING US WITH THIS COMPETITION...
...WILL BE MRS. JODY GRAND, HEADMISTRESS OF THE ROYAL FINISHING ACADEMY, WHERE YOUNG ENGLISH LADIES FROM THE FINEST FAMILIES HAVE LONG BEEN SENT TO REFINE THEIR SKILLS!

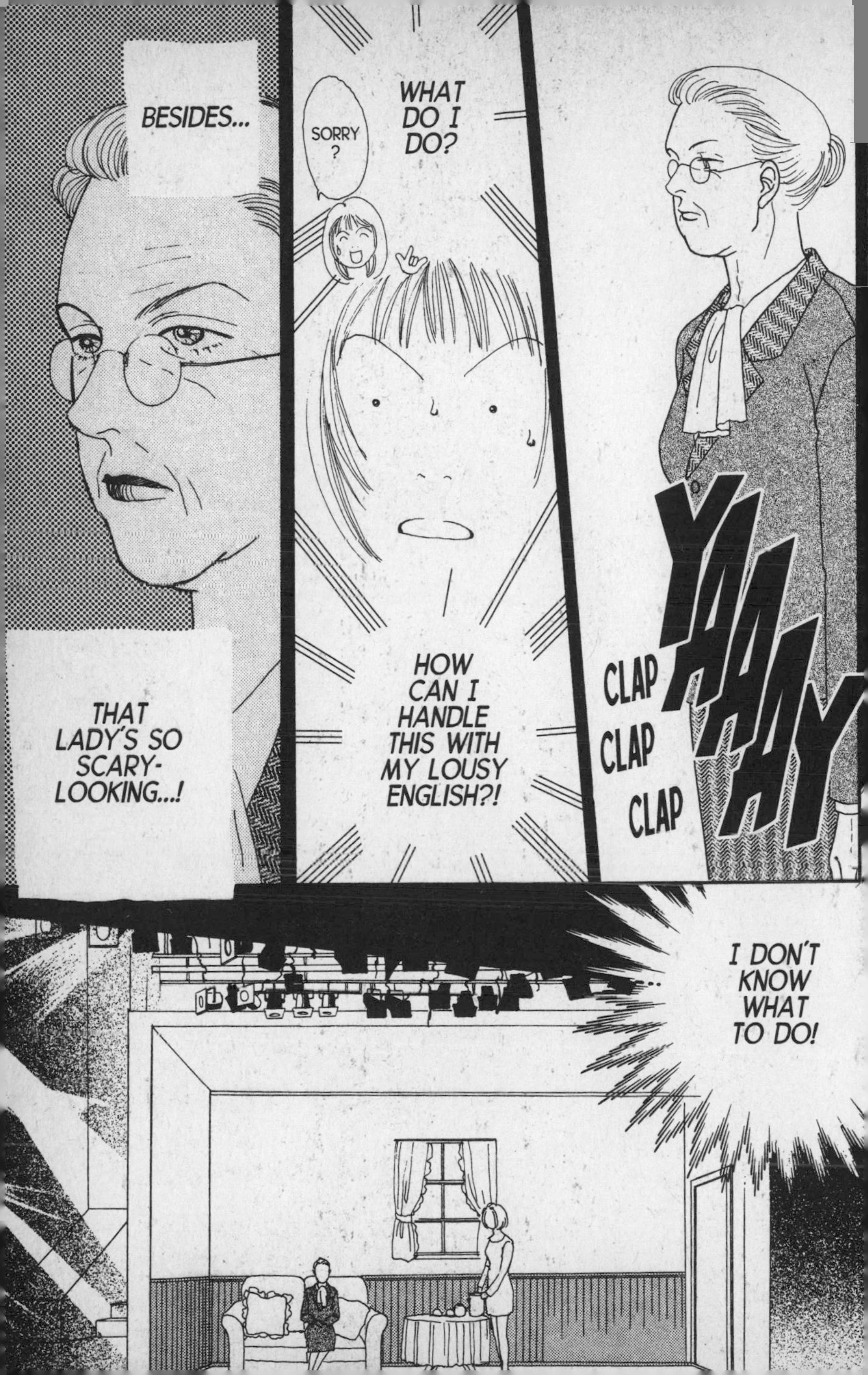
CLAP
CLAP
CLAP
YAAAY
WHAT DO I DO?
SORRY ?
HOW CAN I HANDLE THIS WITH MY LOUSY ENGLISH?!
BESIDES...
THAT LADY'S SO SCARY-LOOKING...!
I DON'T KNOW WHAT TO DO!

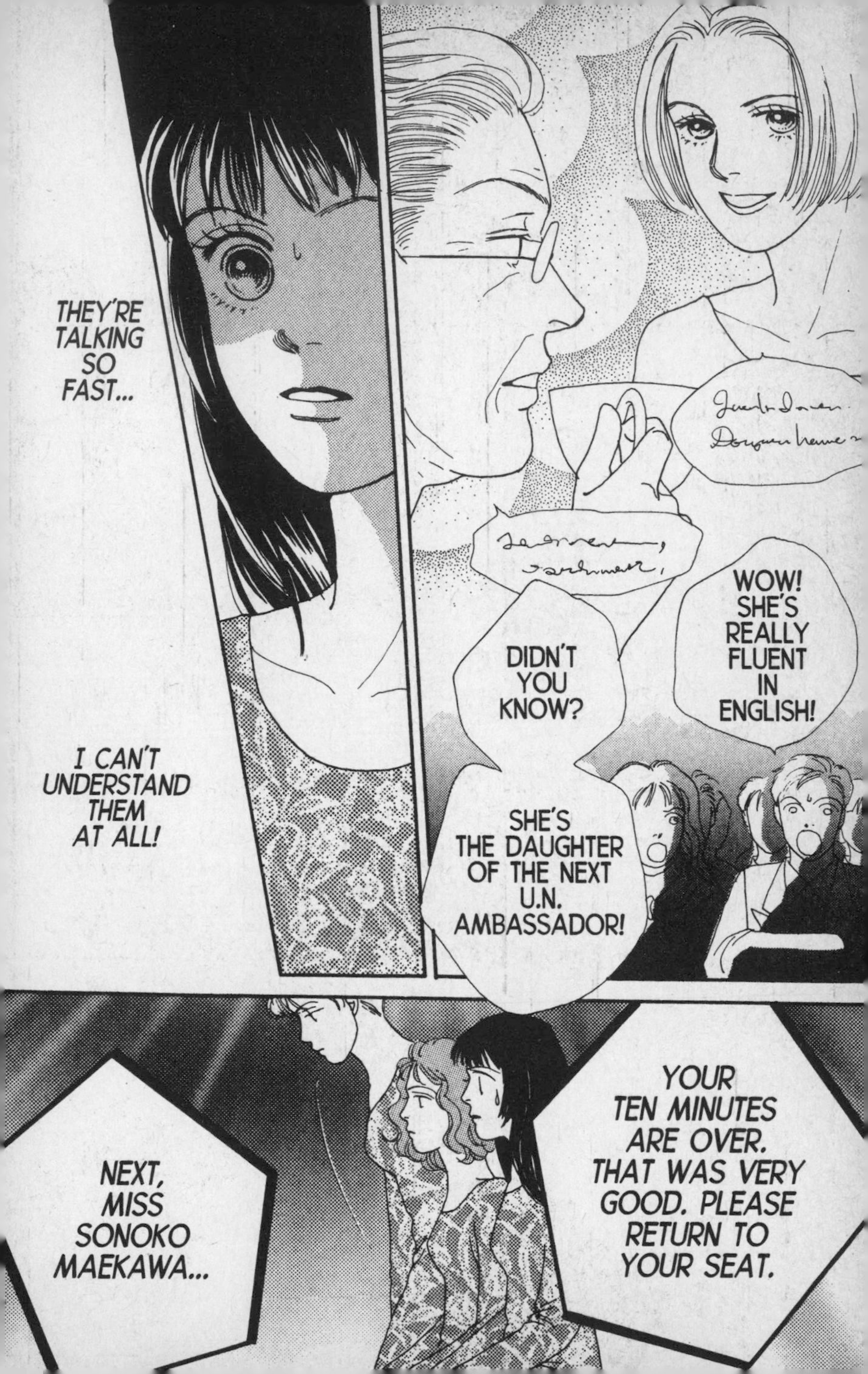
WOW! SHE'S REALLY FLUENT IN ENGLISH!
DIDN'T YOU KNOW?
SHE'S THE DAUGHTER OF THE NEXT U.N. AMBASSADOR!
THEY'RE TALKING SO FAST...
I CAN'T UNDERSTAND THEM AT ALL!
YOUR TEN MINUTES ARE OVER. THAT WAS VERY GOOD. PLEASE RETURN TO YOUR SEAT.
NEXT, MISS SONOKO MAEKAWA...

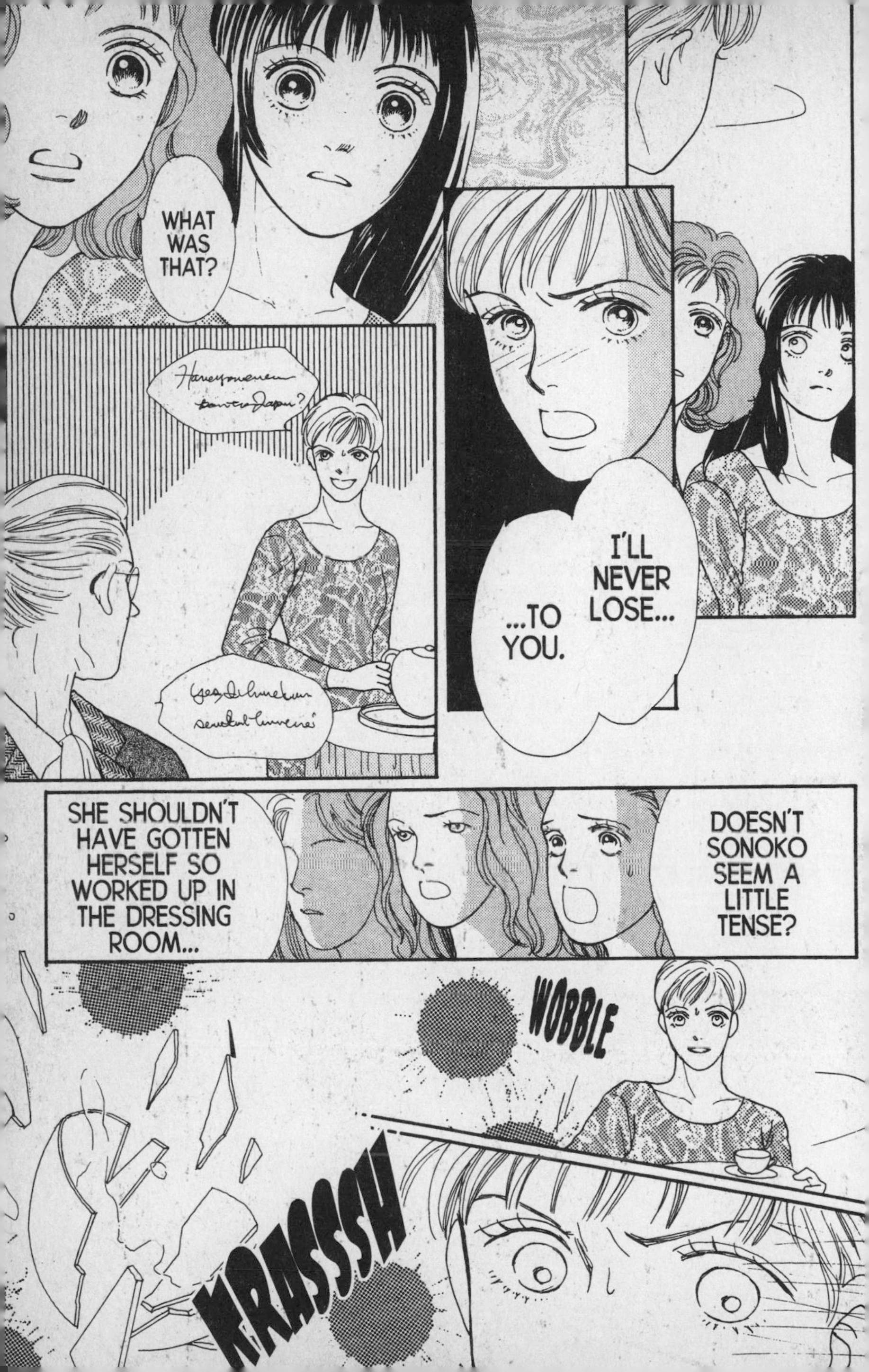
WHAT WAS THAT?
I'LL NEVER LOSE...
...TO YOU.
DOESN'T SONOKO SEEM A LITTLE TENSE?
SHE SHOULDN'T HAVE GOTTEN HERSELF SO WORKED UP IN THE DRESSING ROOM...
WOBBLE
KRASSSH

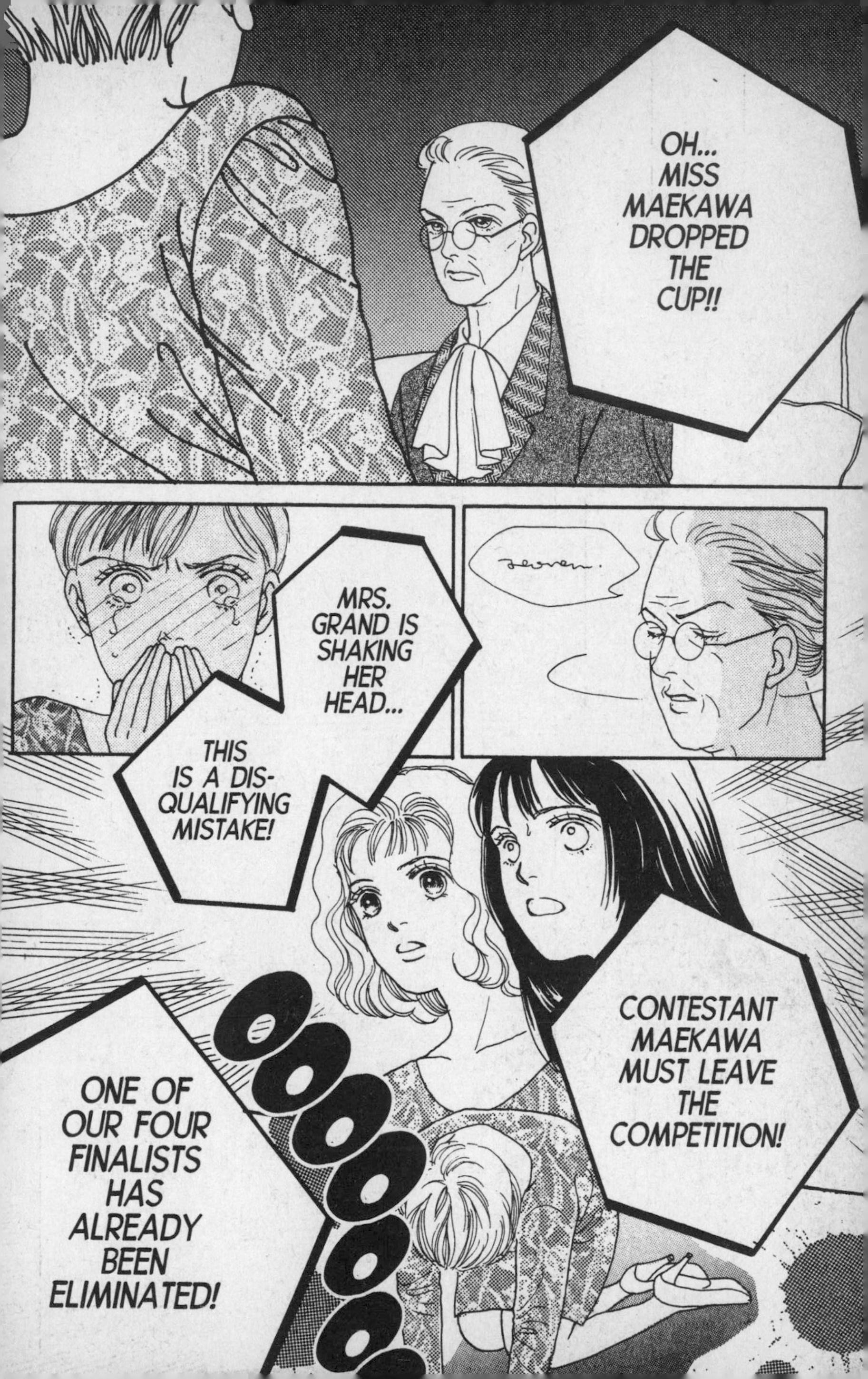
OH... MISS MAEKAWA DROPPED THE CUP!!
MRS. GRAND IS SHAKING HER HEAD...
THIS IS A DIS-QUALIFYING MISTAKE!
CONTESTANT MAEKAWA MUST LEAVE THE COMPETITION!
OOOOOOOO
ONE OF OUR FOUR FINALISTS HAS ALREADY BEEN ELIMINATED!

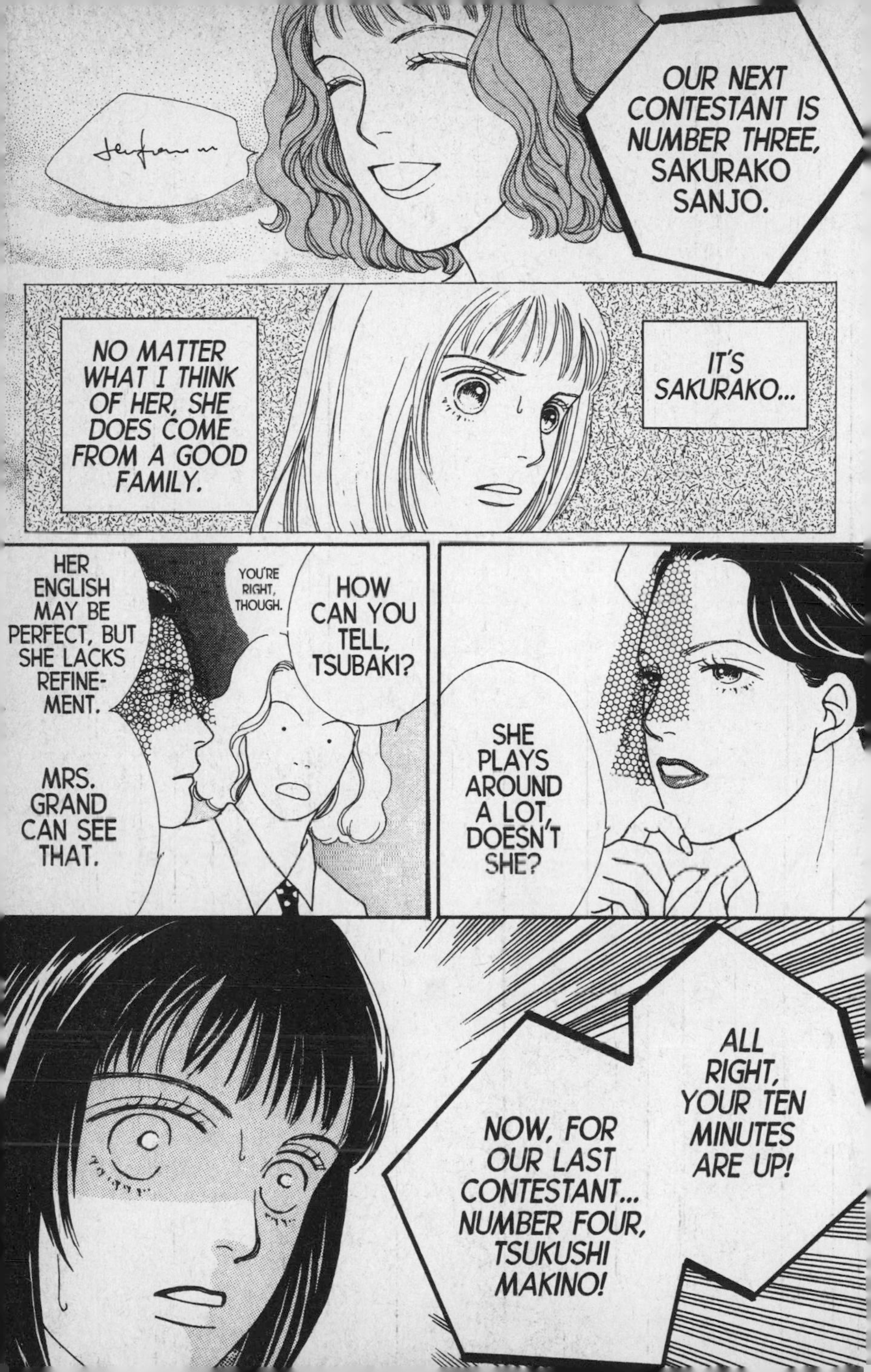
OUR NEXT CONTESTANT IS NUMBER THREE, SAKURAKO SANJO.
IT'S SAKURAKO...
NO MATTER WHAT I THINK OF HER, SHE DOES COME FROM A GOOD FAMILY.
SHE PLAYS AROUND A LOT, DOESN'T SHE?
HOW CAN YOU TELL, TSUBAKI?
YOU'RE RIGHT, THOUGH.
HER ENGLISH MAY BE PERFECT, BUT SHE LACKS REFINE-MENT.
MRS. GRAND CAN SEE THAT.
ALL RIGHT, YOUR TEN MINUTES ARE UP!
NOW, FOR OUR LAST CONTESTANT... NUMBER FOUR, TSUKUSHI MAKINO!

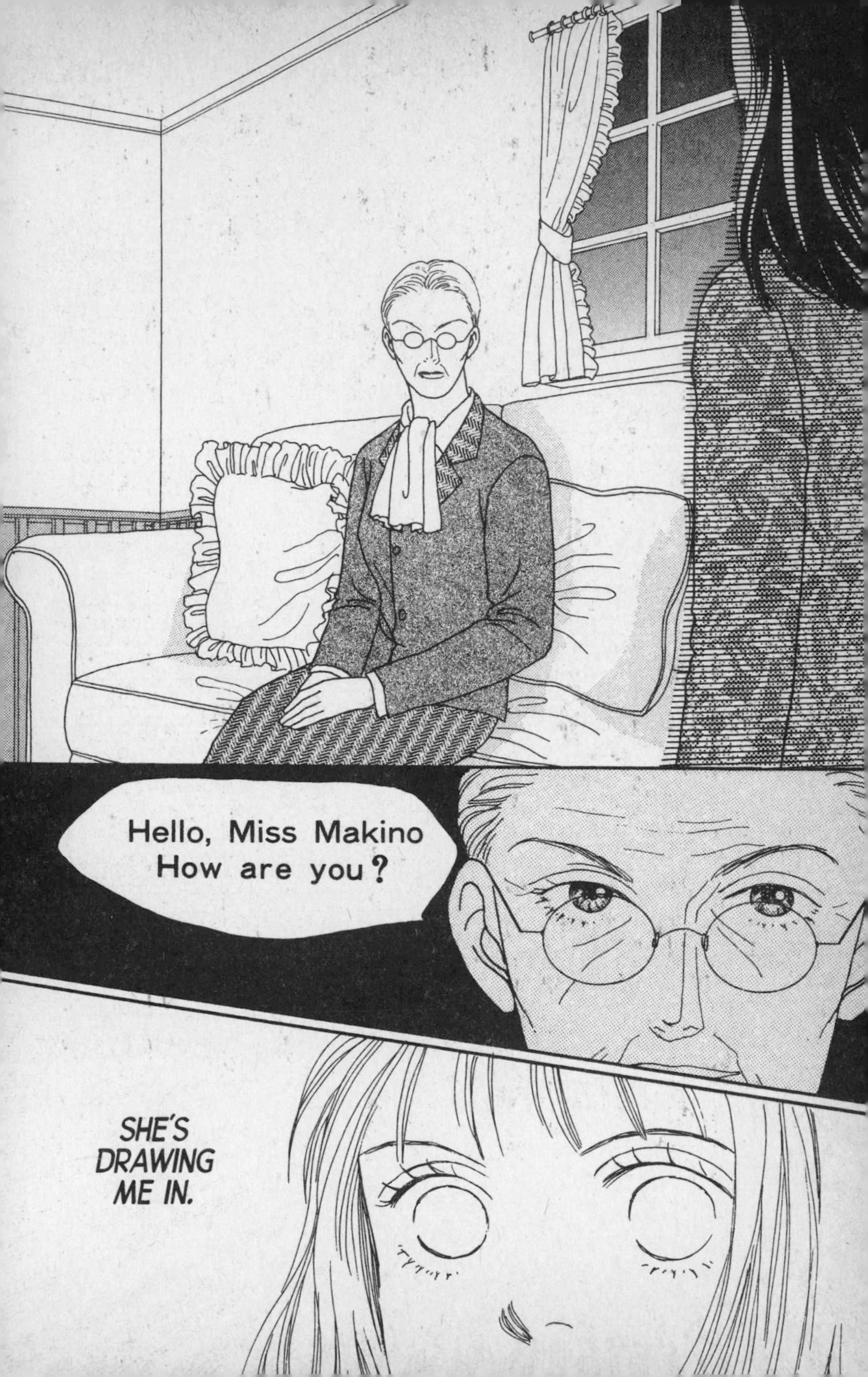
Hello, Miss Makino How are you?
SHE'S DRAWING ME IN.

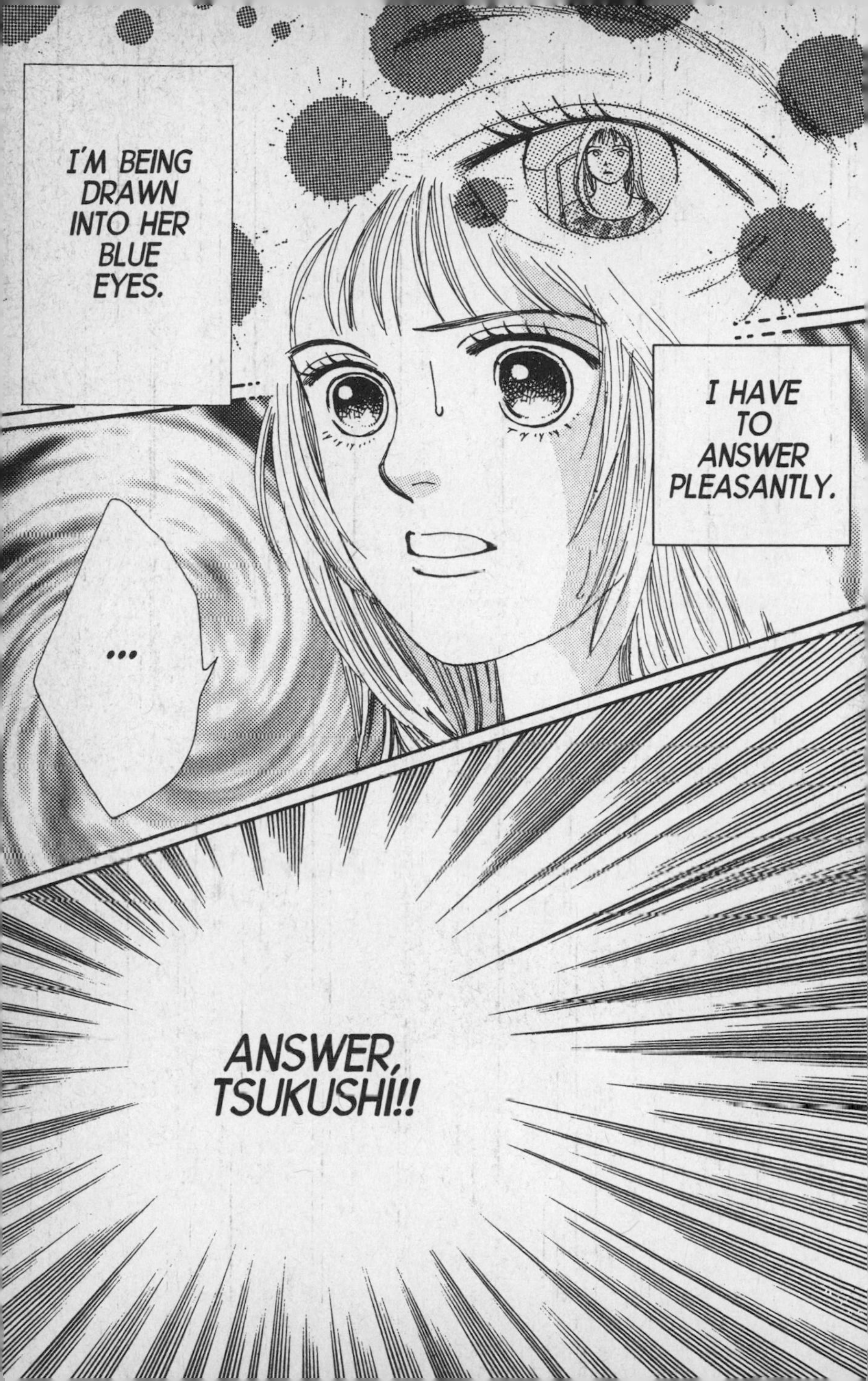
I'M BEING DRAWN INTO HER BLUE EYES.
I HAVE TO ANSWER PLEASANTLY.
...
ANSWER, TSUKUSHI!!

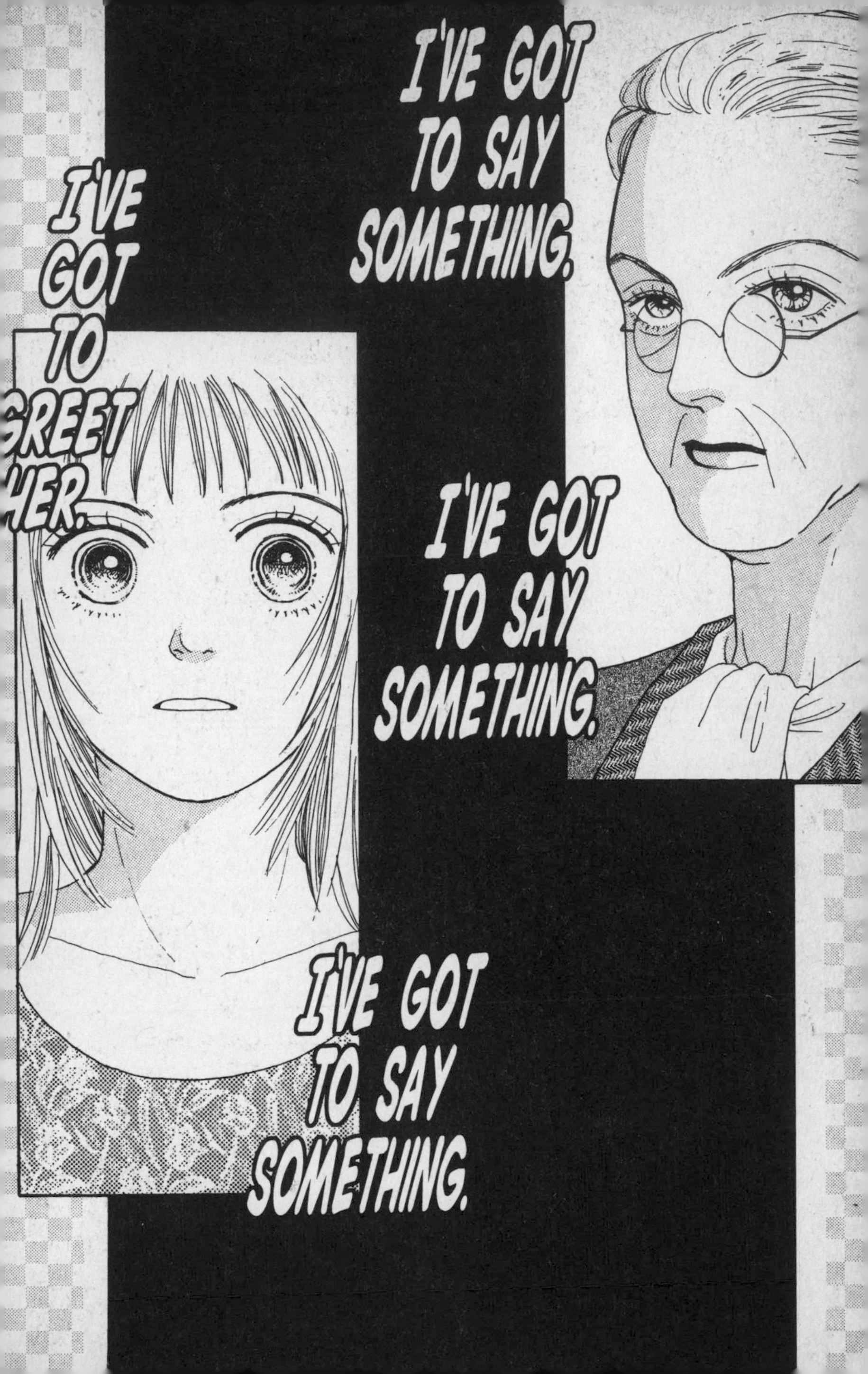
I'VE GOT TO SAY SOMETHING.
I'VE GOT TO GREET HER.
I'VE GOT TO SAY SOMETHING.
I'VE GOT TO SAY SOMETHING.

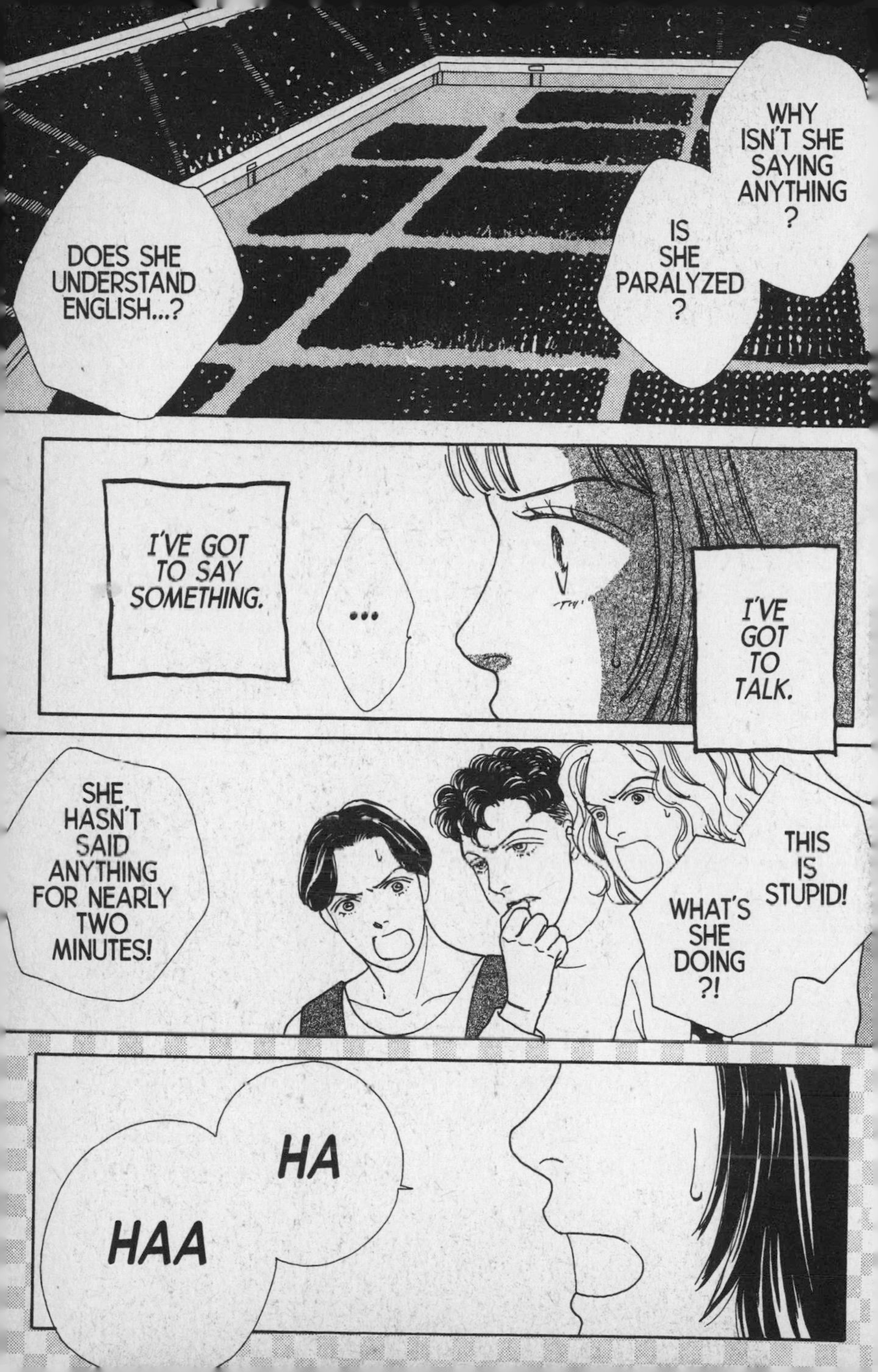
WHY ISN'T SHE SAYING ANYTHING?
IS SHE PARALYZED?
DOES SHE UNDERSTAND ENGLISH...?
I'VE GOT TO TALK.
...
I'VE GOT TO SAY SOMETHING.
THIS IS STUPID!
WHAT'S SHE DOING?!
SHE HASN'T SAID ANYTHING FOR NEARLY TWO MINUTES!
HA
HAA

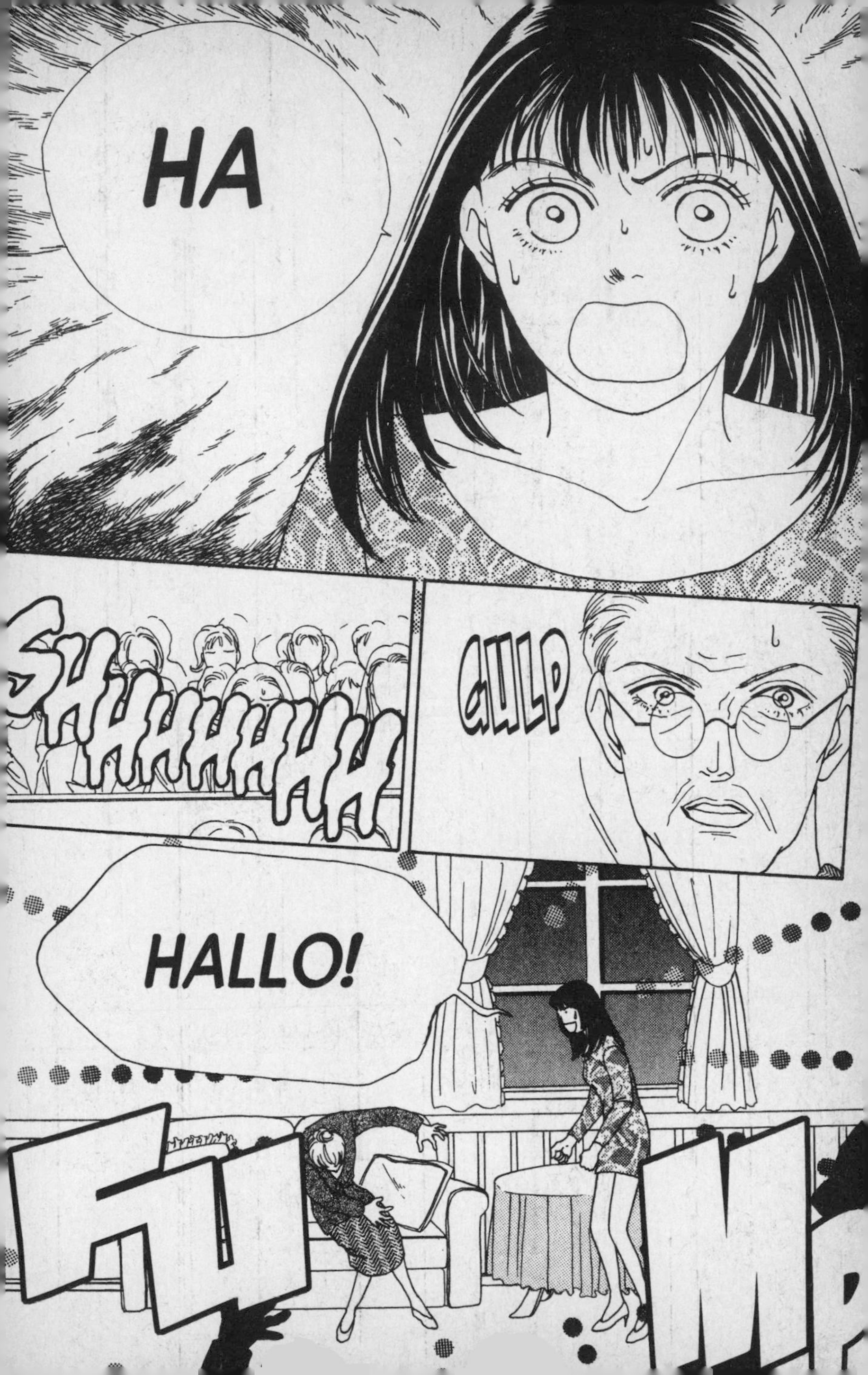
HA
GULP
SHHHHHHH
HALLO!

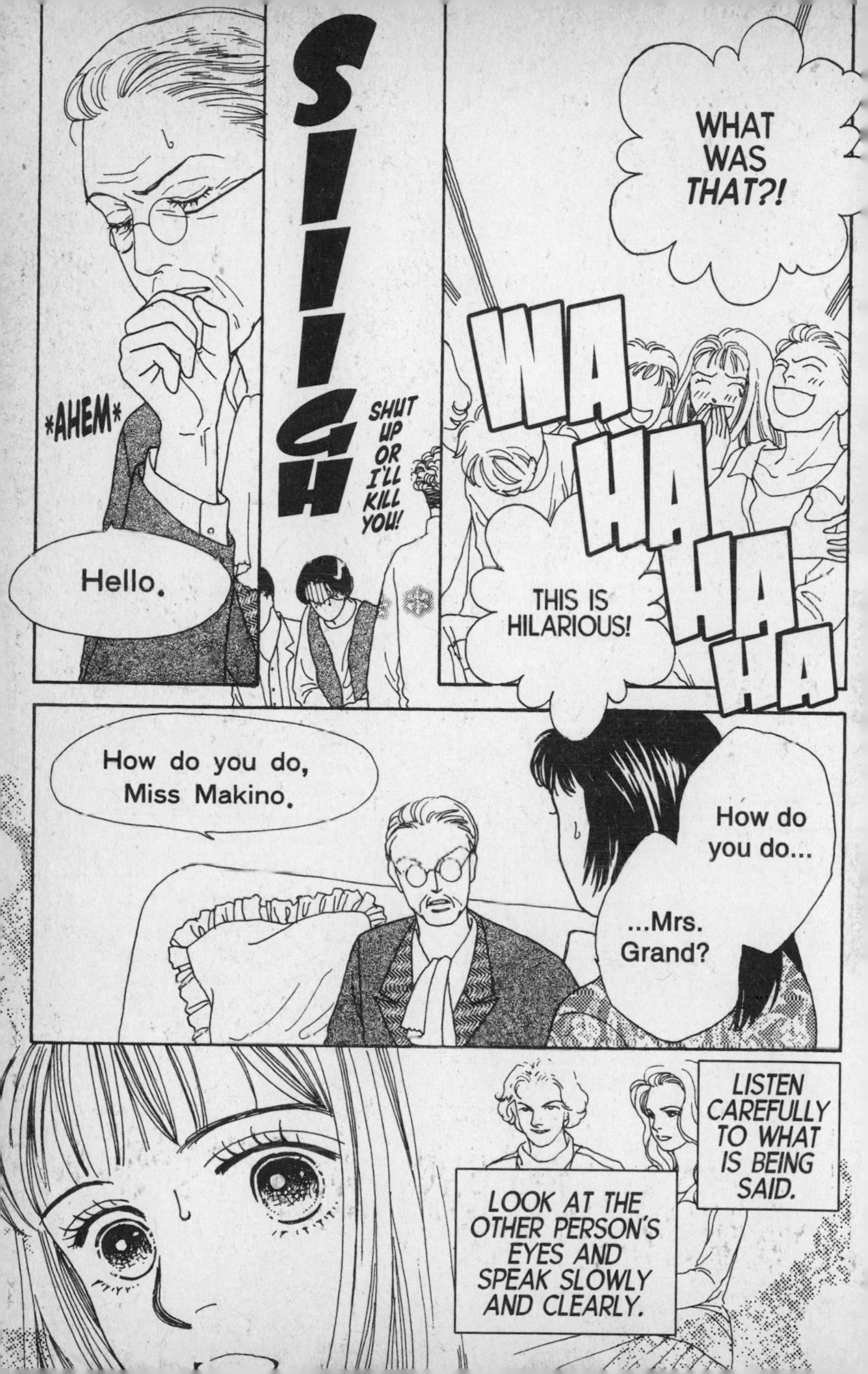
WHAT WAS THAT?!
WA HA HA HA HA
THIS IS HILARIOUS!
SIIIGH
SHUT UP OR I'LL KILL YOU!
AHEM
Hello.
How do you do, Miss Makino.
How do you do...
...Mrs. Grand?
LISTEN CAREFULLY TO WHAT IS BEING SAID.
LOOK AT THE OTHER PERSON'S EYES AND SPEAK SLOWLY AND CLEARLY.

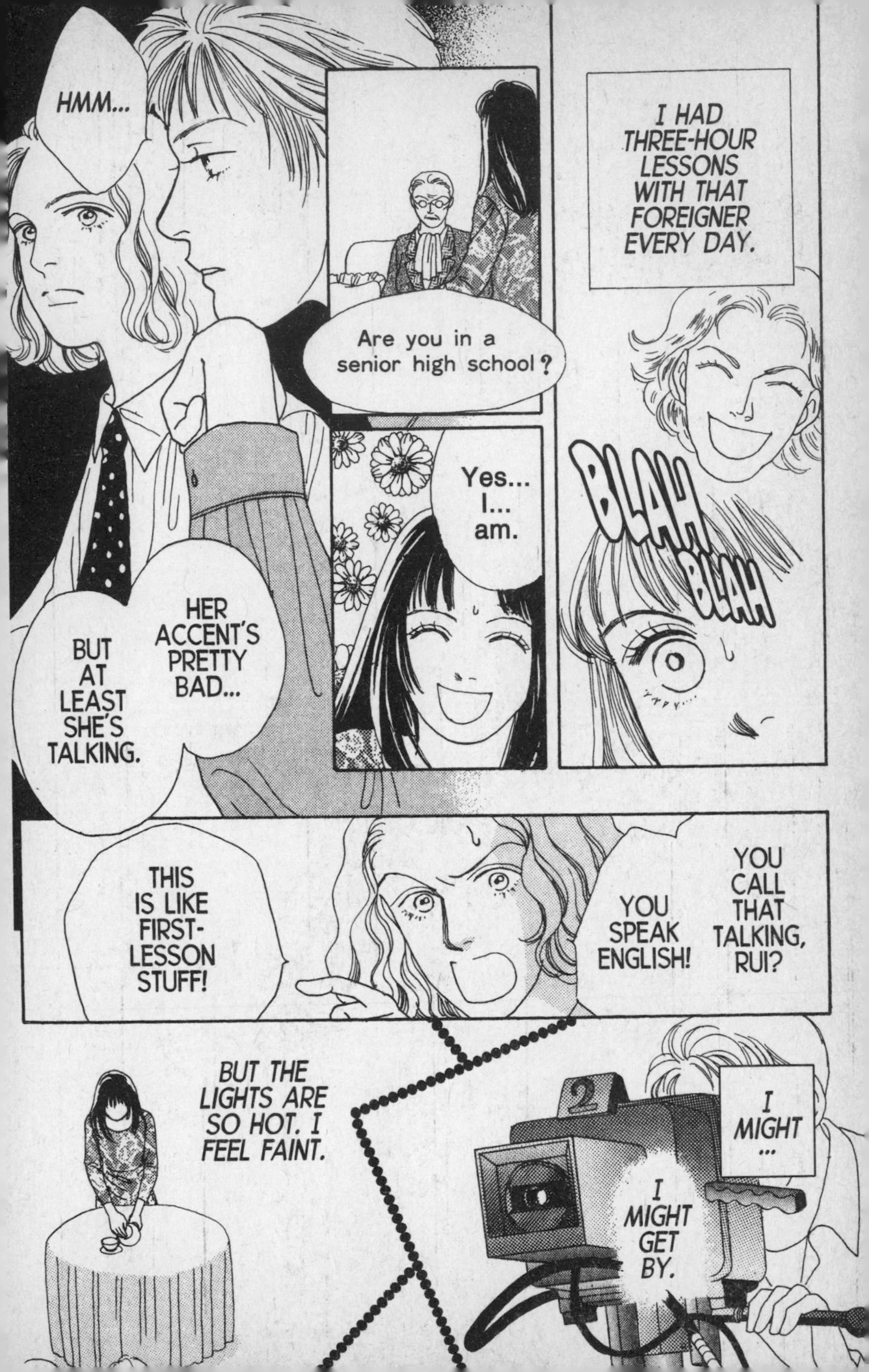
I HAD THREE-HOUR LESSONS WITH THAT FOREIGNER EVERY DAY.
BLAH BLAH
Are you in a senior high school?
Yes... I... am.
HMM...
HER ACCENT'S PRETTY BAD...
BUT AT LEAST SHE'S TALKING.
YOU CALL THAT TALKING, RUI?
YOU SPEAK ENGLISH!
THIS IS LIKE FIRST-LESSON STUFF!
I MIGHT ...
I MIGHT GET BY.
BUT THE LIGHTS ARE SO HOT. I FEEL FAINT.

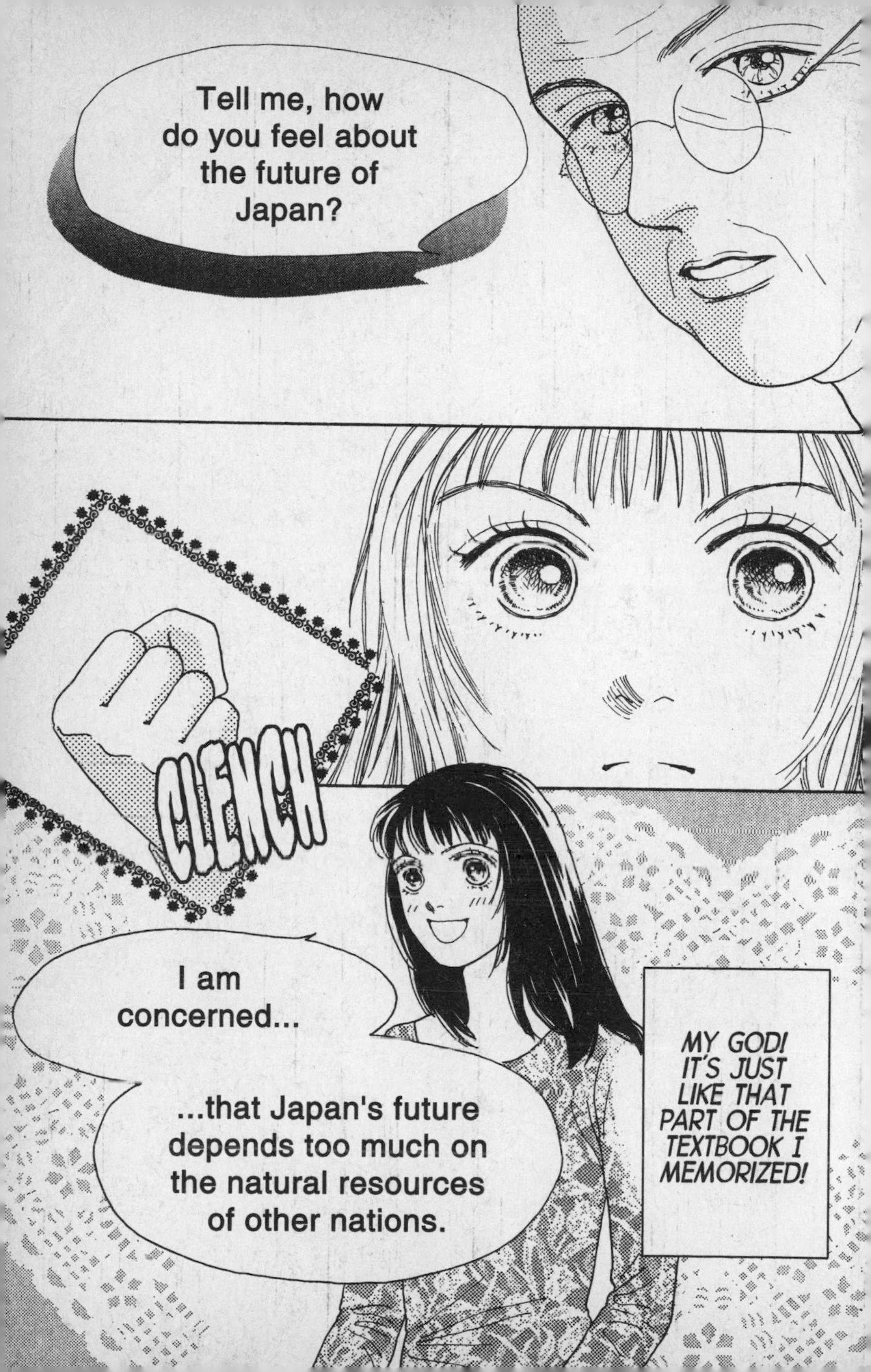
Tell me, how do you feel about the future of Japan?
CLENCH
MY GOD! IT'S JUST LIKE THAT PART OF THE TEXTBOOK I MEMORIZED!
I am concerned...
...that Japan's future depends too much on the natural resources of other nations.

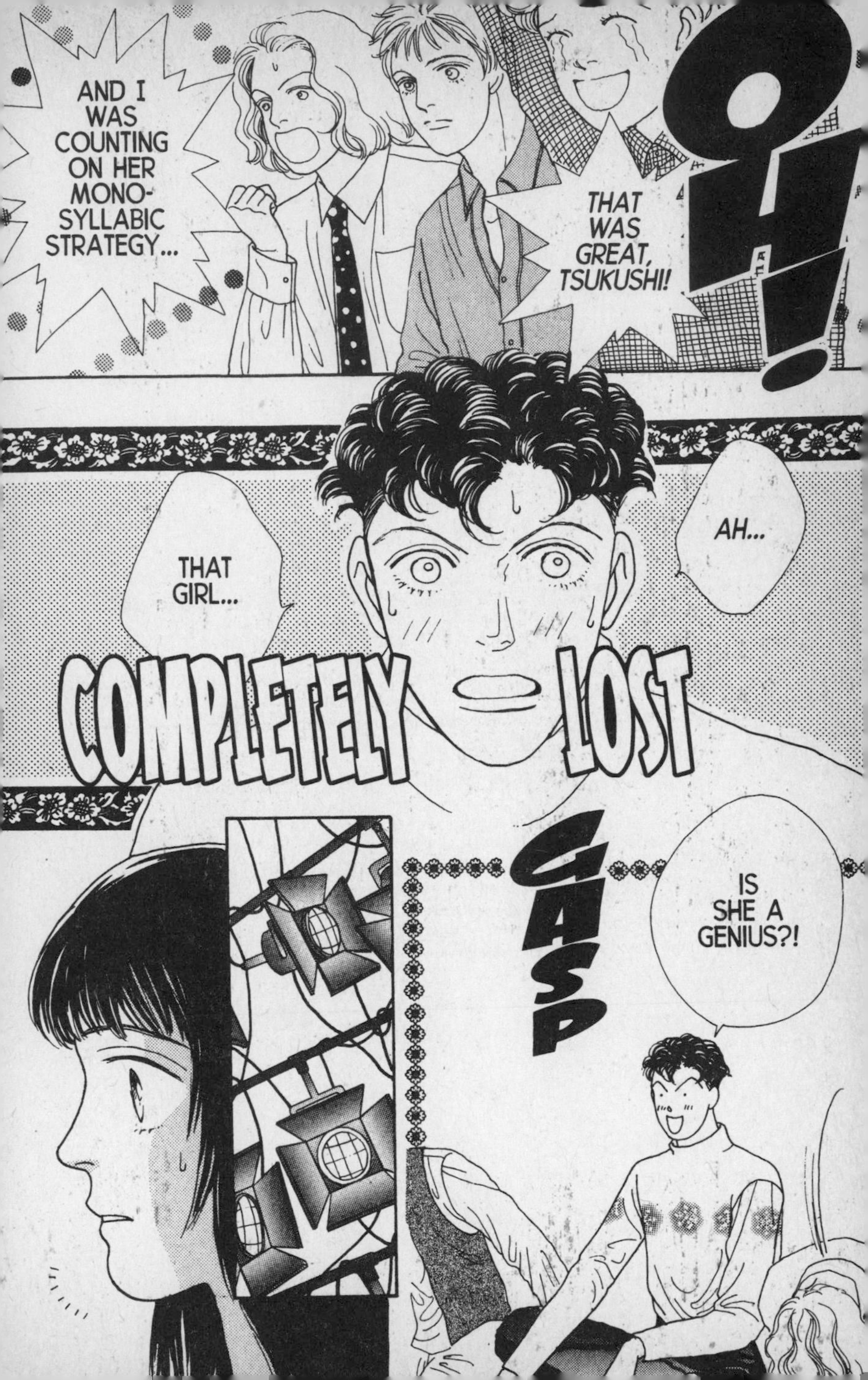
OH!!
THAT WAS GREAT, TSUKUSHI!
AND I WAS COUNTING ON HER MONO-SYLLABIC STRATEGY...
AH...
THAT GIRL...
COMPLETELY LOST
IS SHE A GENIUS?!
GASP

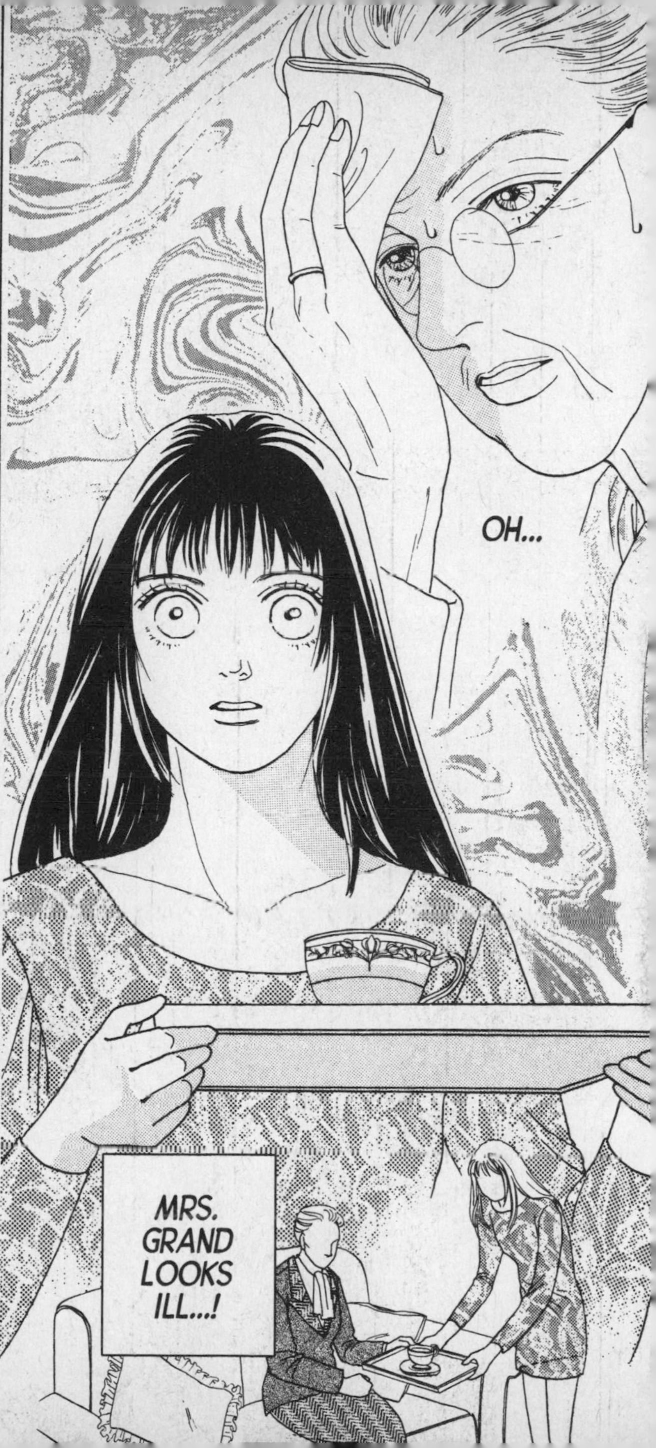
OH...
MRS. GRAND LOOKS ILL...!

GREETINGS

This is the last of my notes to you for this volume!!

Thank you for all the letters and gifts you keep sending me! I'm sorry I'm not able to answer you.

I hope your days are filled with joy!

Good-bye for now.

Yoko Kamio

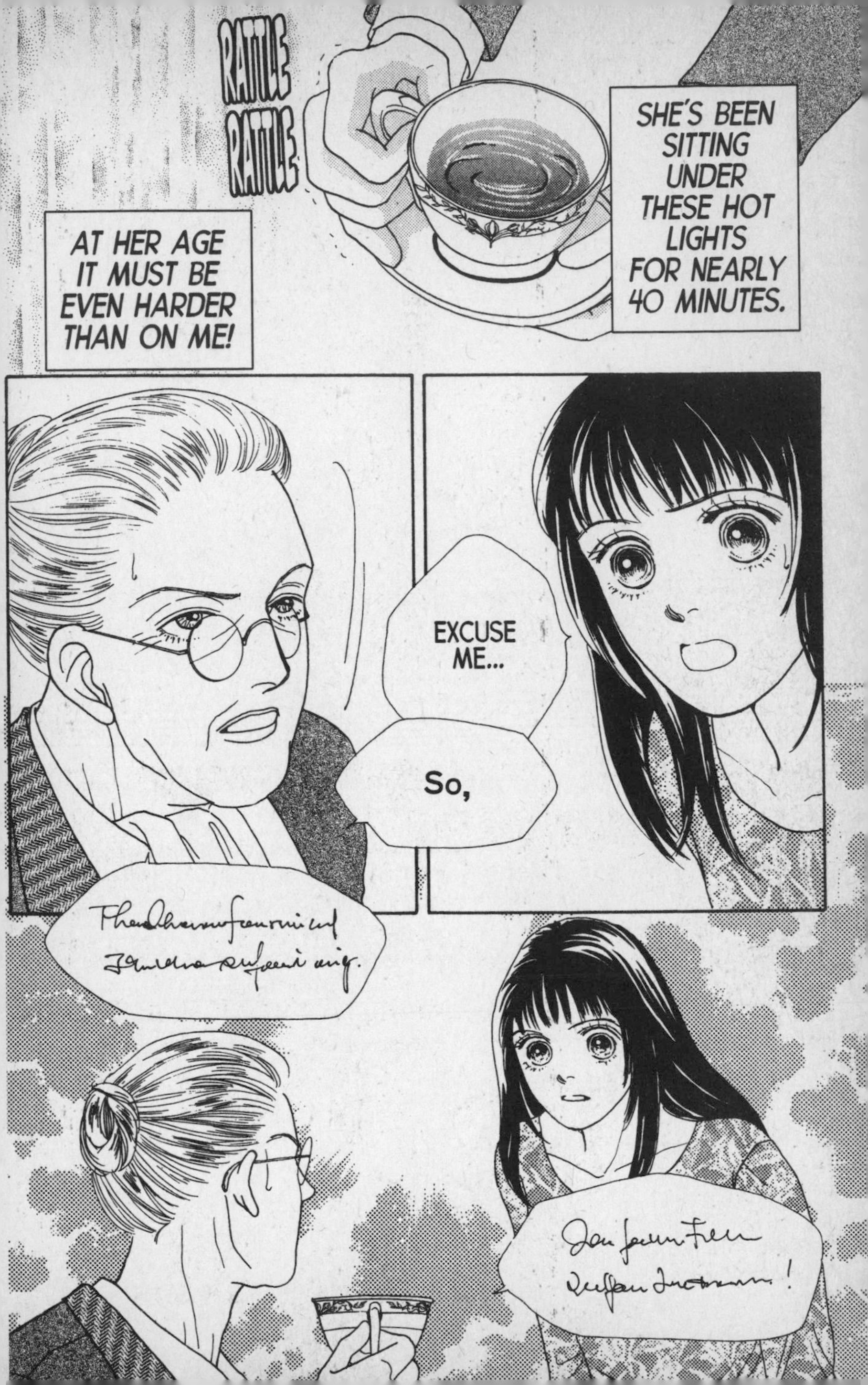
RATTLE RATTLE
SHE'S BEEN SITTING UNDER THESE HOT LIGHTS FOR NEARLY 40 MINUTES.
AT HER AGE IT MUST BE EVEN HARDER THAN ON ME!
EXCUSE ME...
So,

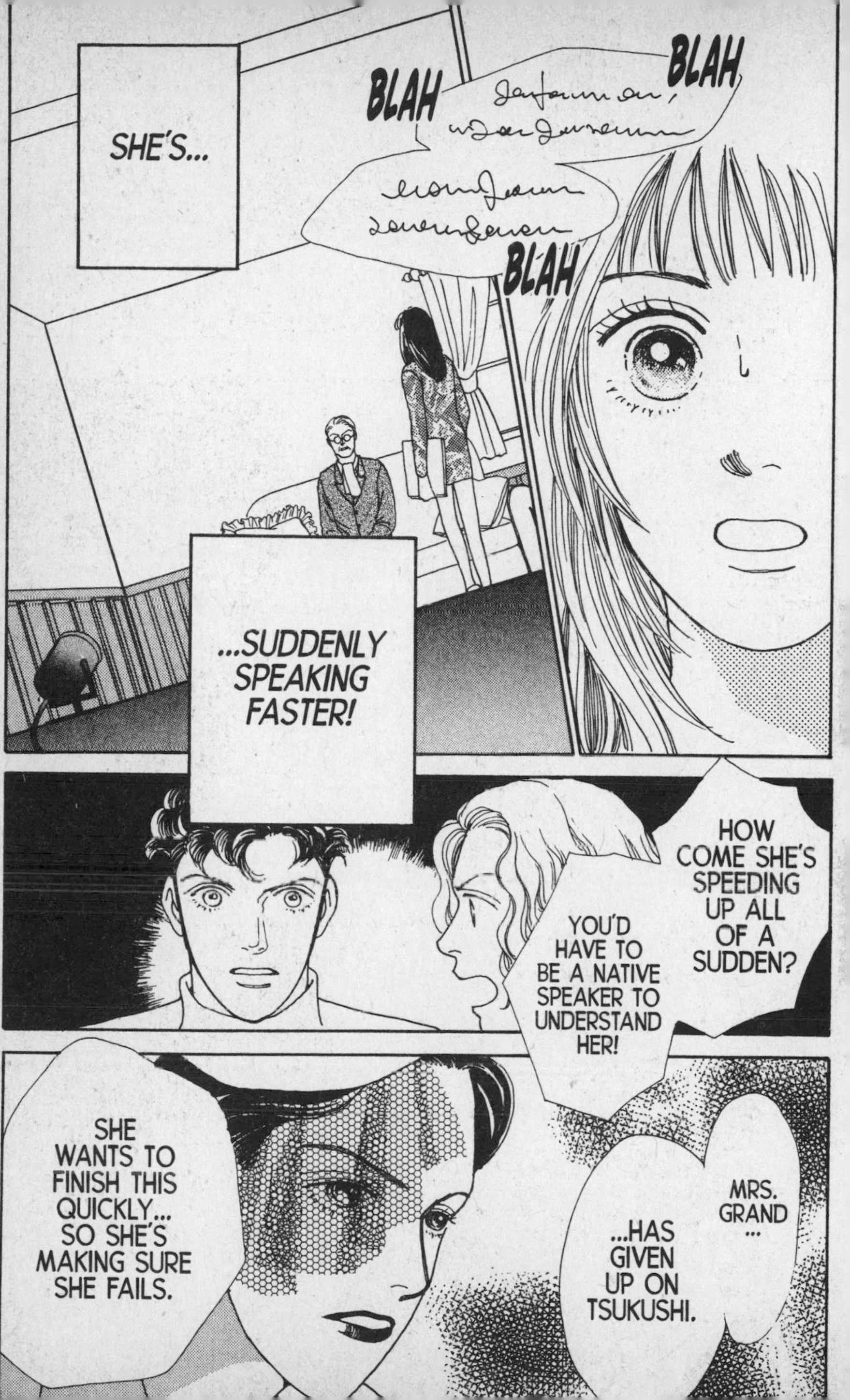
BLAH
BLAH
SHE'S...
BLAH
...SUDDENLY SPEAKING FASTER!
HOW COME SHE'S SPEEDING UP ALL OF A SUDDEN?
YOU'D HAVE TO BE A NATIVE SPEAKER TO UNDERSTAND HER!
MRS. GRAND...
...HAS GIVEN UP ON TSUKUSHI.
SHE WANTS TO FINISH THIS QUICKLY... SO SHE'S MAKING SURE SHE FAILS.

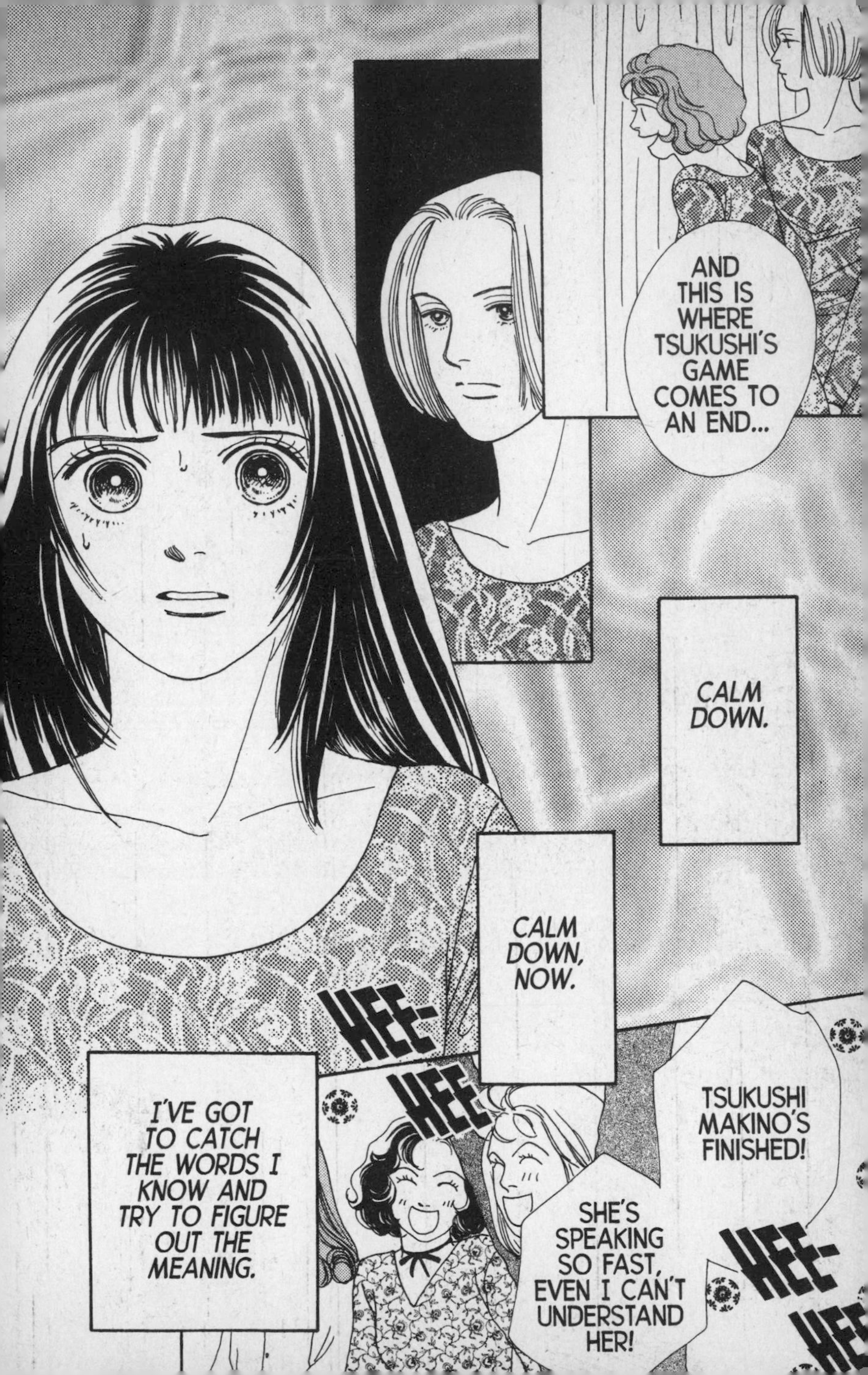

AND THIS IS WHERE TSUKUSHI'S GAME COMES TO AN END...
CALM DOWN.
CALM DOWN, NOW.
TSUKUSHI MAKINO'S FINISHED!
HEE-HEE
SHE'S SPEAKING SO FAST, EVEN I CAN'T UNDERSTAND HER!
HEE-HEE
I'VE GOT TO CATCH THE WORDS I KNOW AND TRY TO FIGURE OUT THE MEANING.

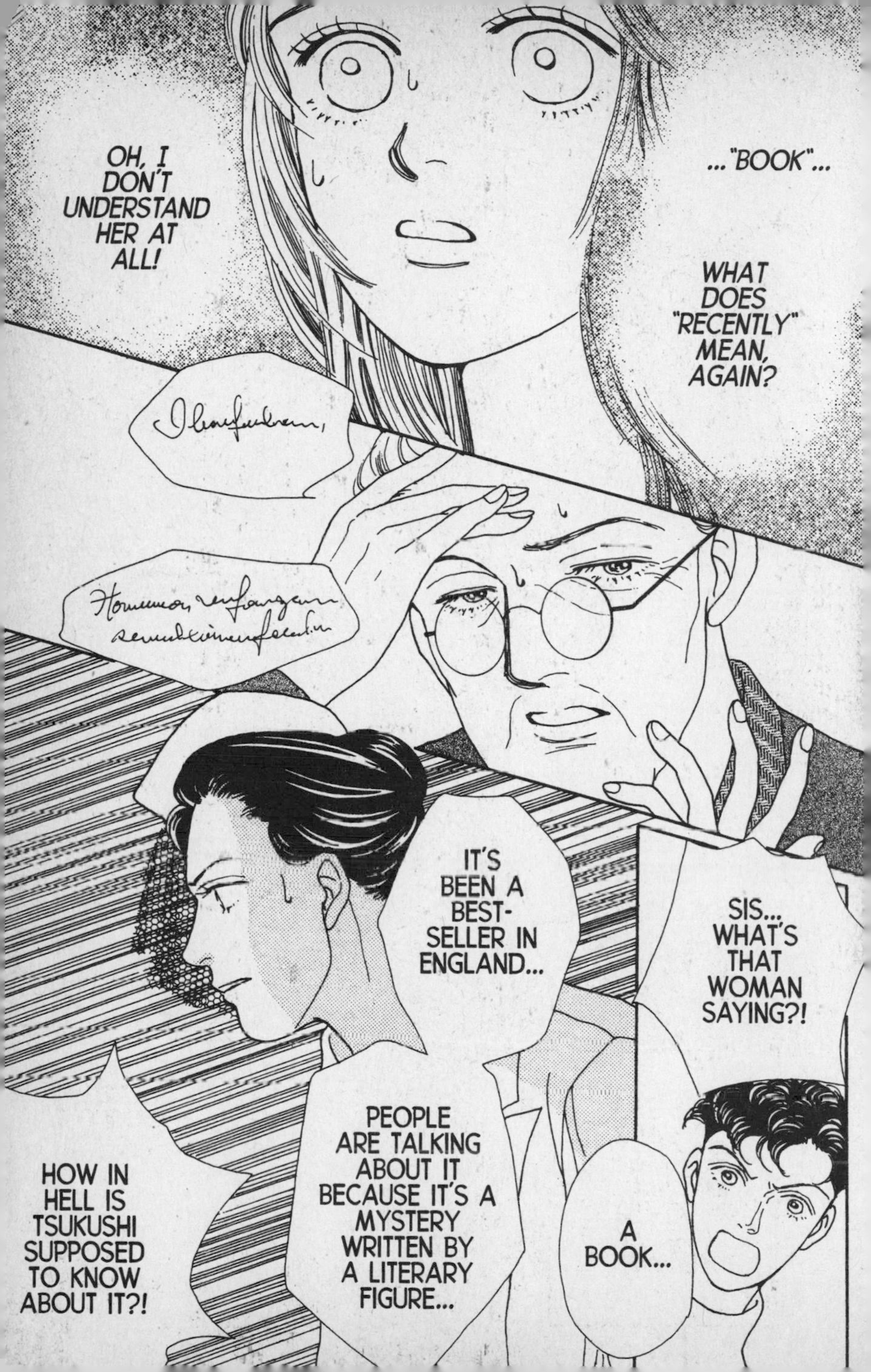
..."BOOK"...
WHAT DOES "RECENTLY" MEAN, AGAIN?
OH, I DON'T UNDERSTAND HER AT ALL!
SIS... WHAT'S THAT WOMAN SAYING?!
A BOOK...
IT'S BEEN A BEST-SELLER IN ENGLAND...
PEOPLE ARE TALKING ABOUT IT BECAUSE IT'S A MYSTERY WRITTEN BY A LITERARY FIGURE...
HOW IN HELL IS TSUKUSHI SUPPOSED TO KNOW ABOUT IT?!

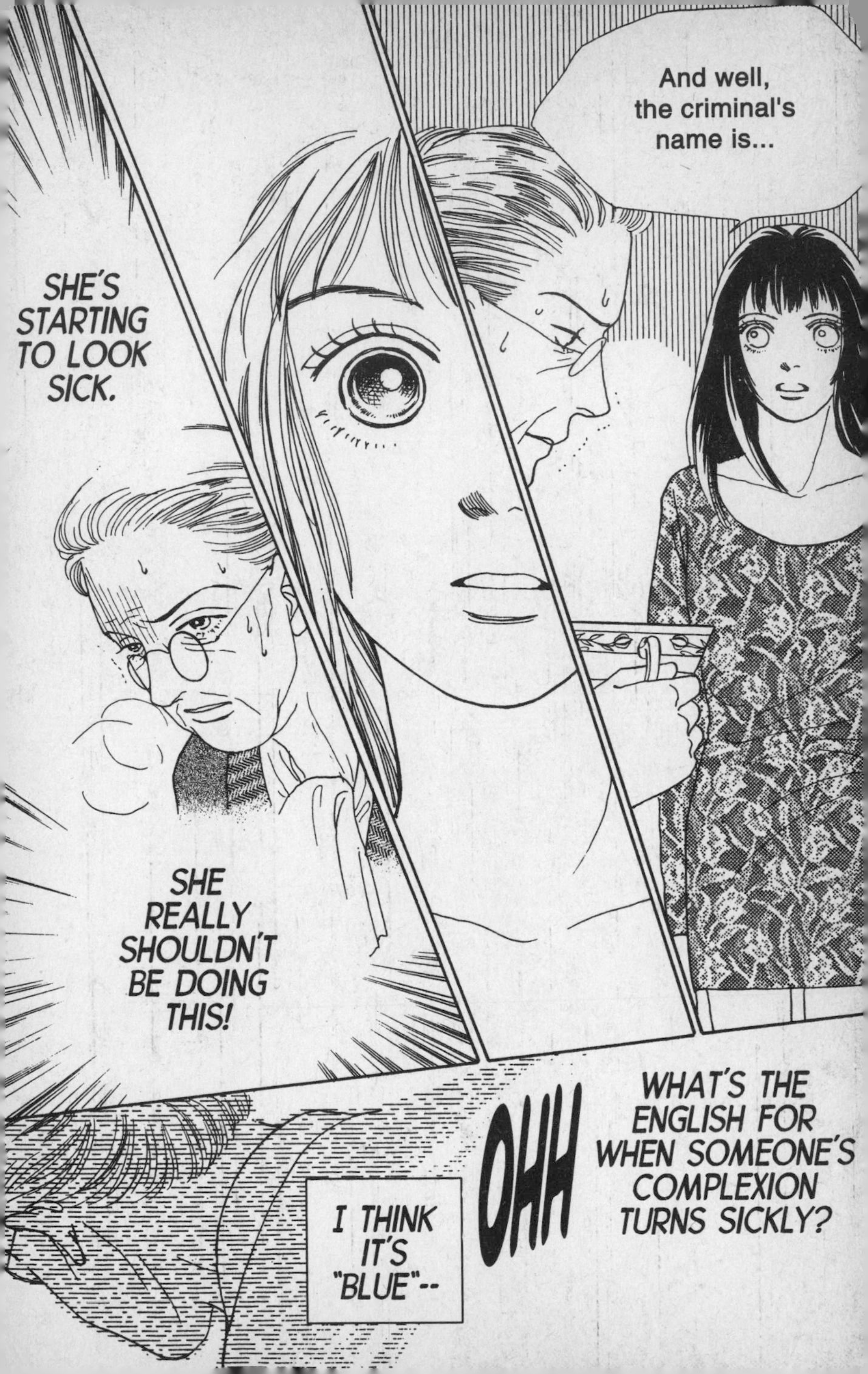
And well, the criminal's name is...
SHE'S STARTING TO LOOK SICK.
SHE REALLY SHOULDN'T BE DOING THIS!
WHAT'S THE ENGLISH FOR WHEN SOMEONE'S COMPLEXION TURNS SICKLY?
OHH
I THINK IT'S "BLUE"--

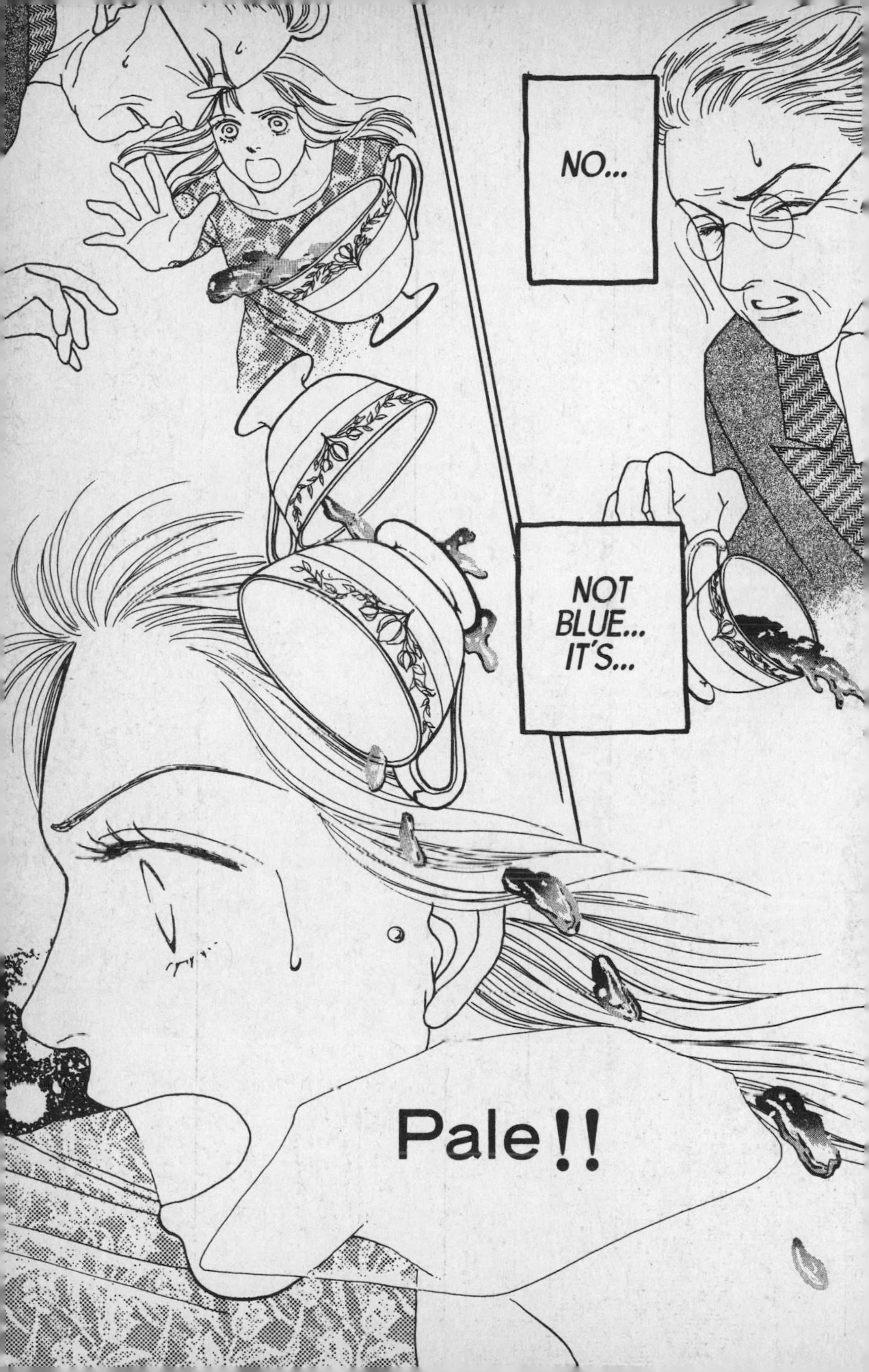
NO...
NOT BLUE... IT'S...
Pale!!

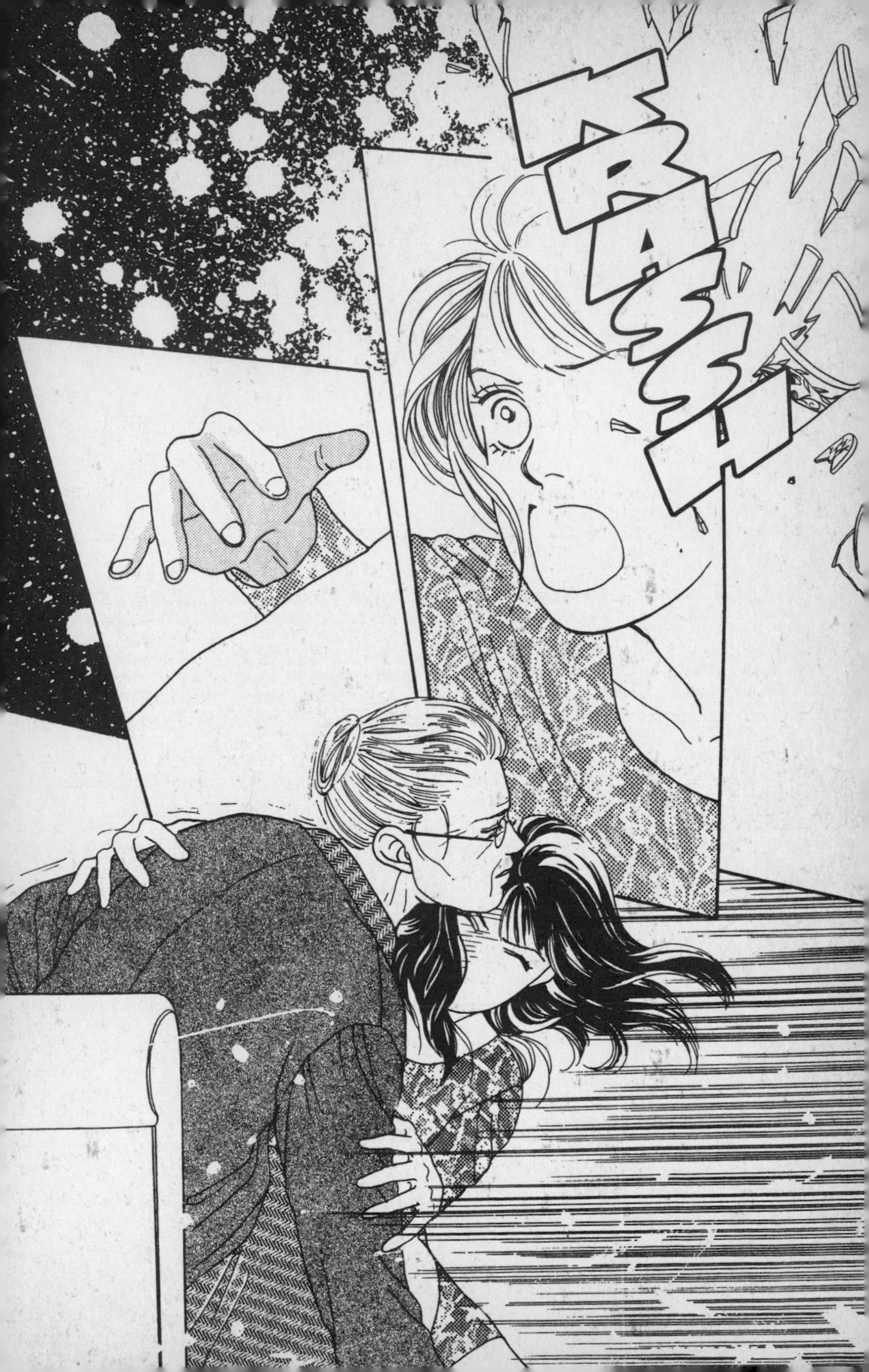
KRASSH

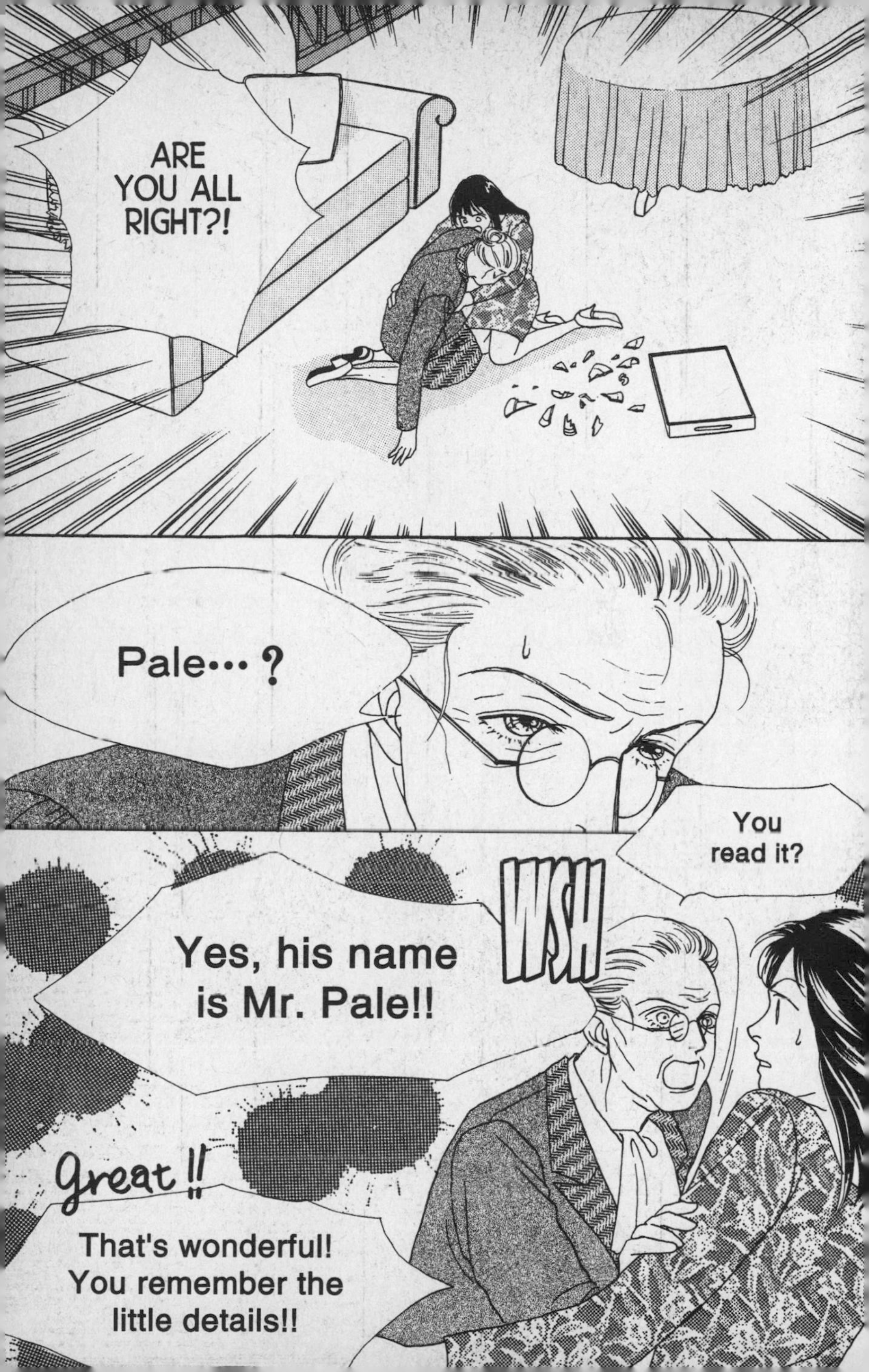
ARE YOU ALL RIGHT?!
Pale···?
You read it?
WSH
Yes, his name is Mr. Pale!!
Great!!
That's wonderful! You remember the little details!!

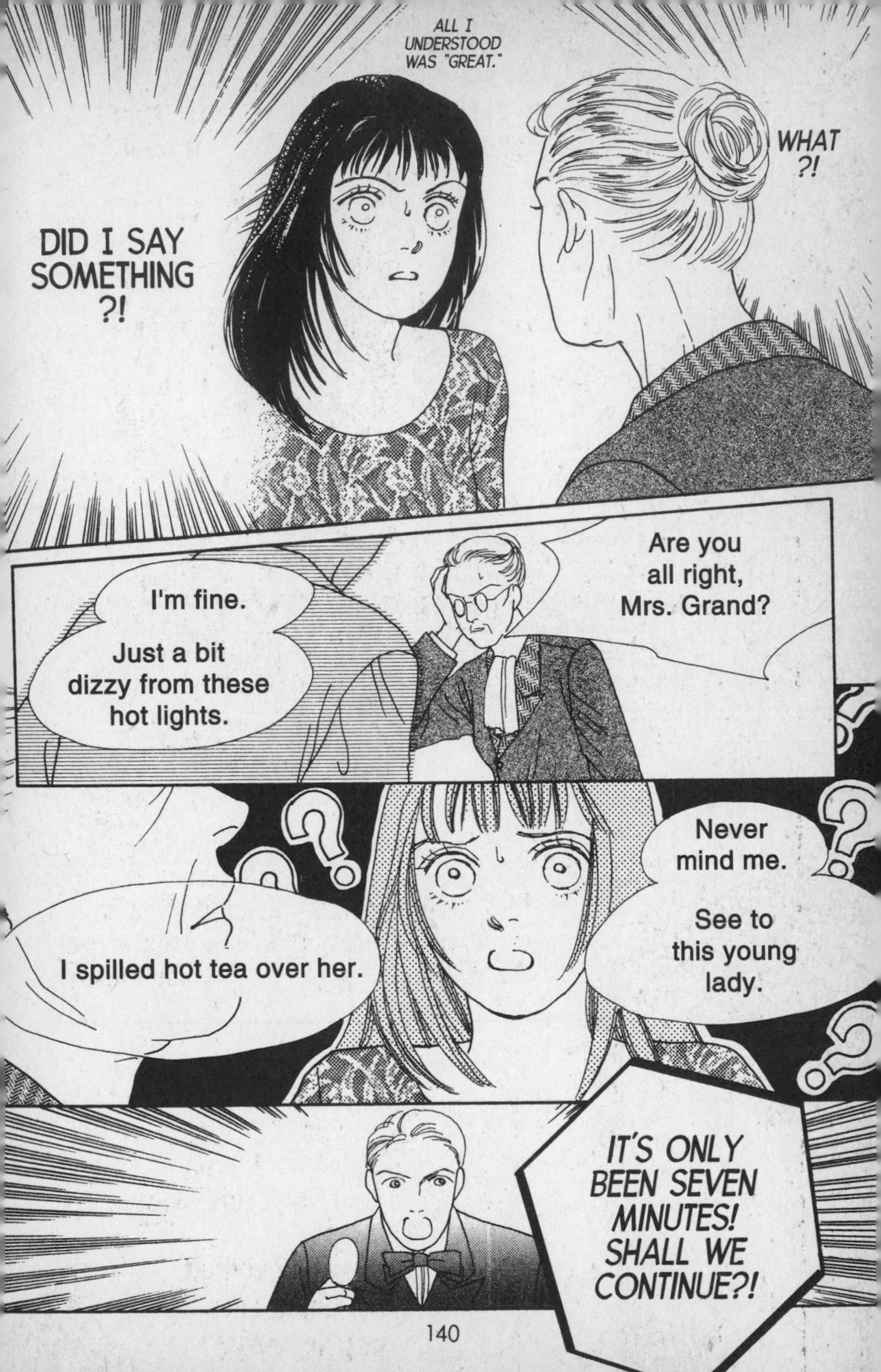
ALL I UNDERSTOOD WAS "GREAT."
WHAT ?!
DID I SAY SOMETHING ?!
Are you all right, Mrs. Grand?
I'm fine.
Just a bit dizzy from these hot lights.
Never mind me.
See to this young lady.
I spilled hot tea over her.
IT'S ONLY BEEN SEVEN MINUTES! SHALL WE CONTINUE?!

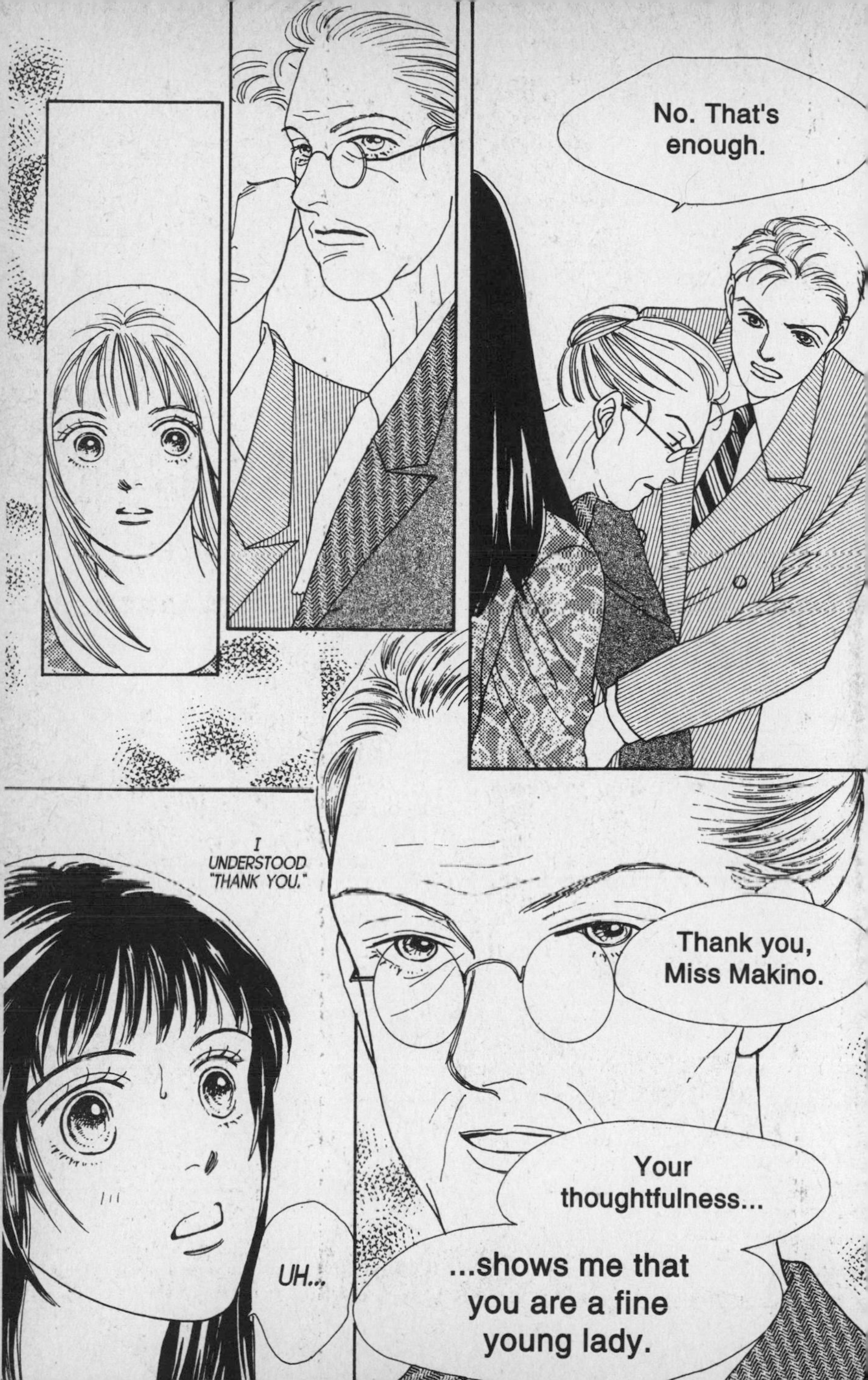
No. That's enough.
Thank you, Miss Makino.
Your thoughtfulness...
...shows me that you are a fine young lady.
I UNDERSTOOD "THANK YOU."
UH...

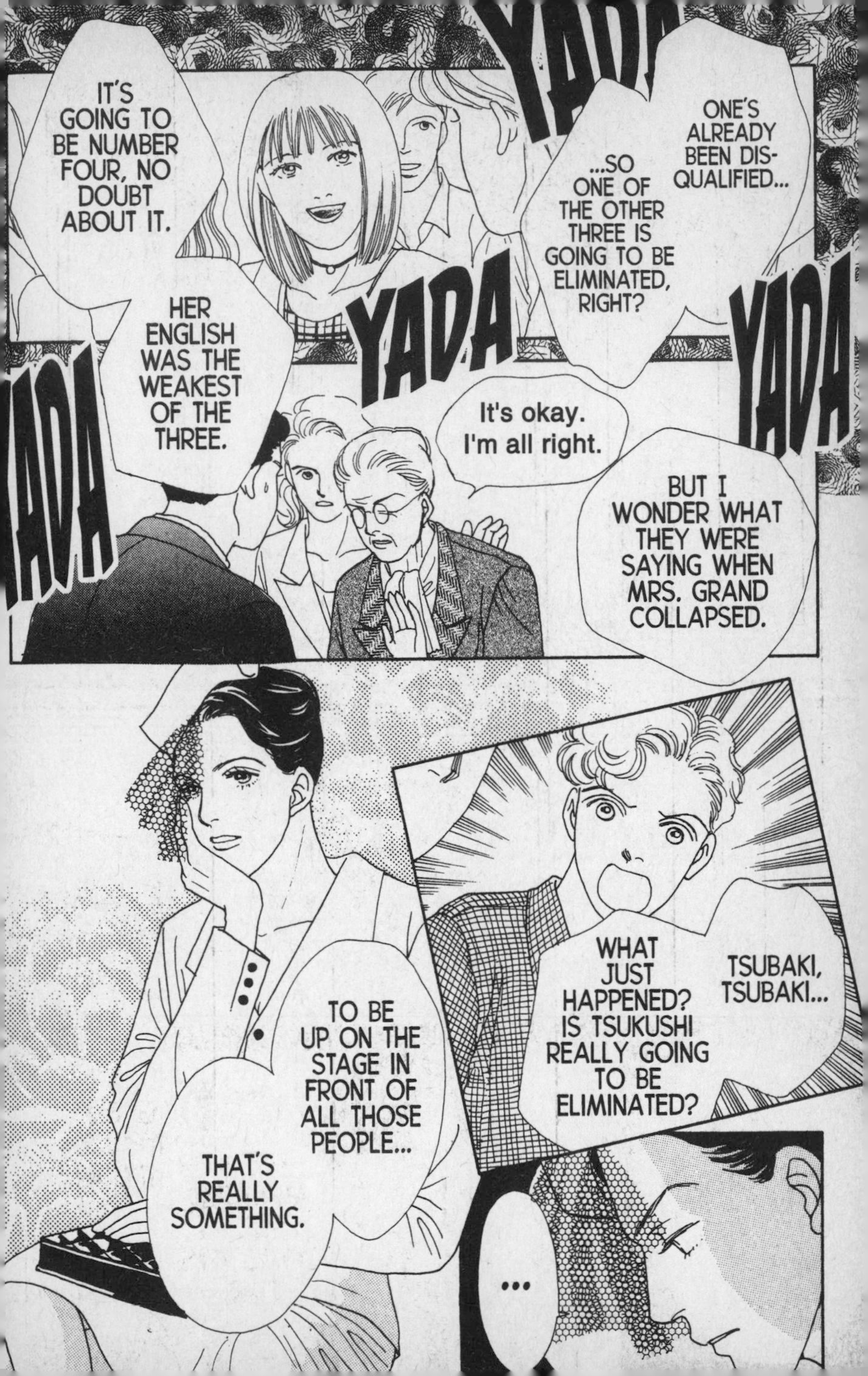
YADA
ONE'S ALREADY BEEN DIS-QUALIFIED...
...SO ONE OF THE OTHER THREE IS GOING TO BE ELIMINATED, RIGHT?
IT'S GOING TO BE NUMBER FOUR, NO DOUBT ABOUT IT.
YADA
YADA
YADA
BUT I WONDER WHAT THEY WERE SAYING WHEN MRS. GRAND COLLAPSED.
It's okay. I'm all right.
HER ENGLISH WAS THE WEAKEST OF THE THREE.
TSUBAKI, TSUBAKI...
WHAT JUST HAPPENED? IS TSUKUSHI REALLY GOING TO BE ELIMINATED?
...
TO BE UP ON THE STAGE IN FRONT OF ALL THOSE PEOPLE...
THAT'S REALLY SOMETHING.

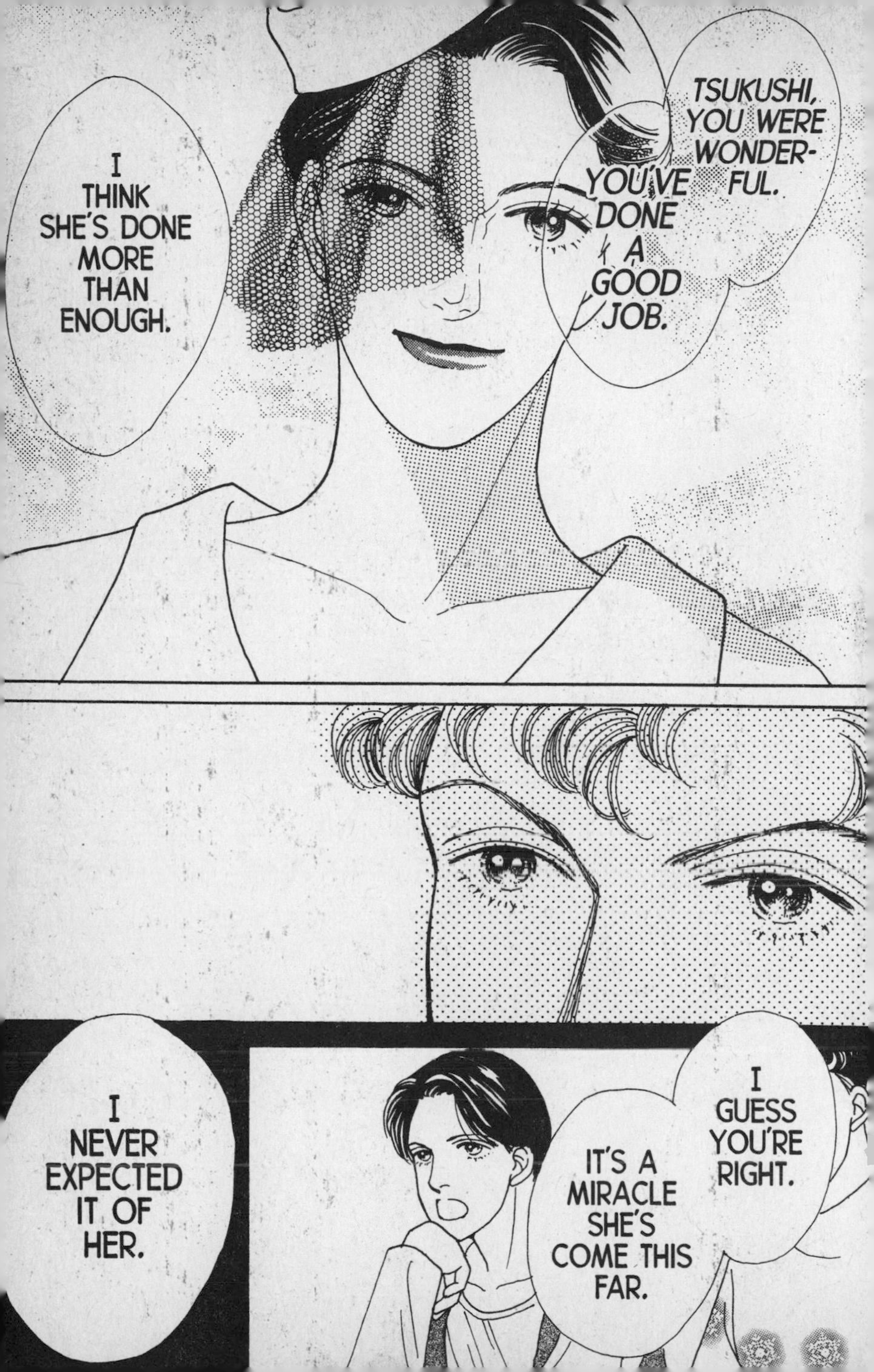
TSUKUSHI, YOU WERE WONDER-FUL.
YOU'VE DONE A GOOD JOB.
I THINK SHE'S DONE MORE THAN ENOUGH.
I GUESS YOU'RE RIGHT.
IT'S A MIRACLE SHE'S COME THIS FAR.
I NEVER EXPECTED IT OF HER.

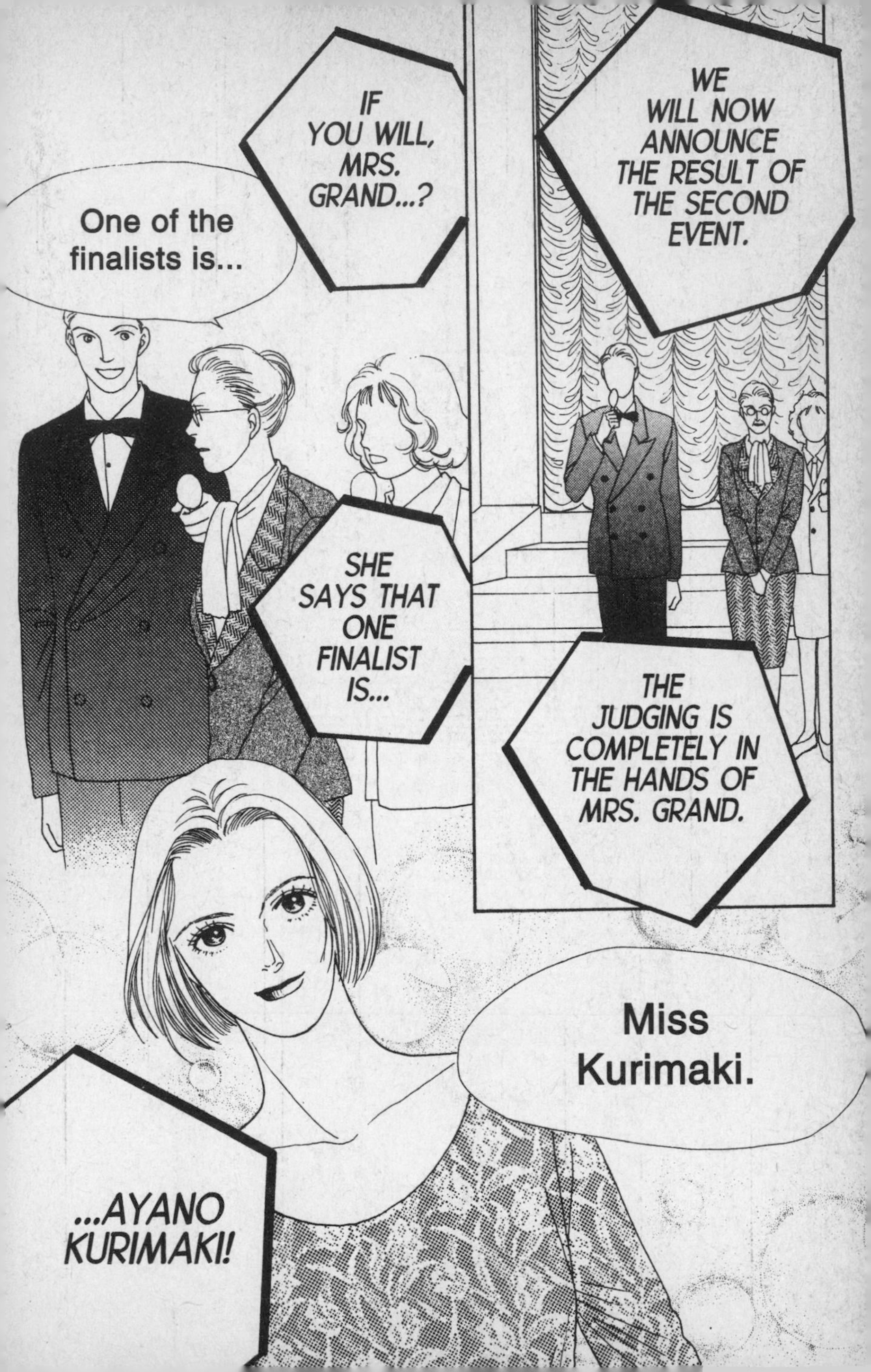
WE WILL NOW ANNOUNCE THE RESULT OF THE SECOND EVENT.
THE JUDGING IS COMPLETELY IN THE HANDS OF MRS. GRAND.
IF YOU WILL, MRS. GRAND...?
One of the finalists is...
SHE SAYS THAT ONE FINALIST IS...
Miss Kurimaki.
...AYANO KURIMAKI!

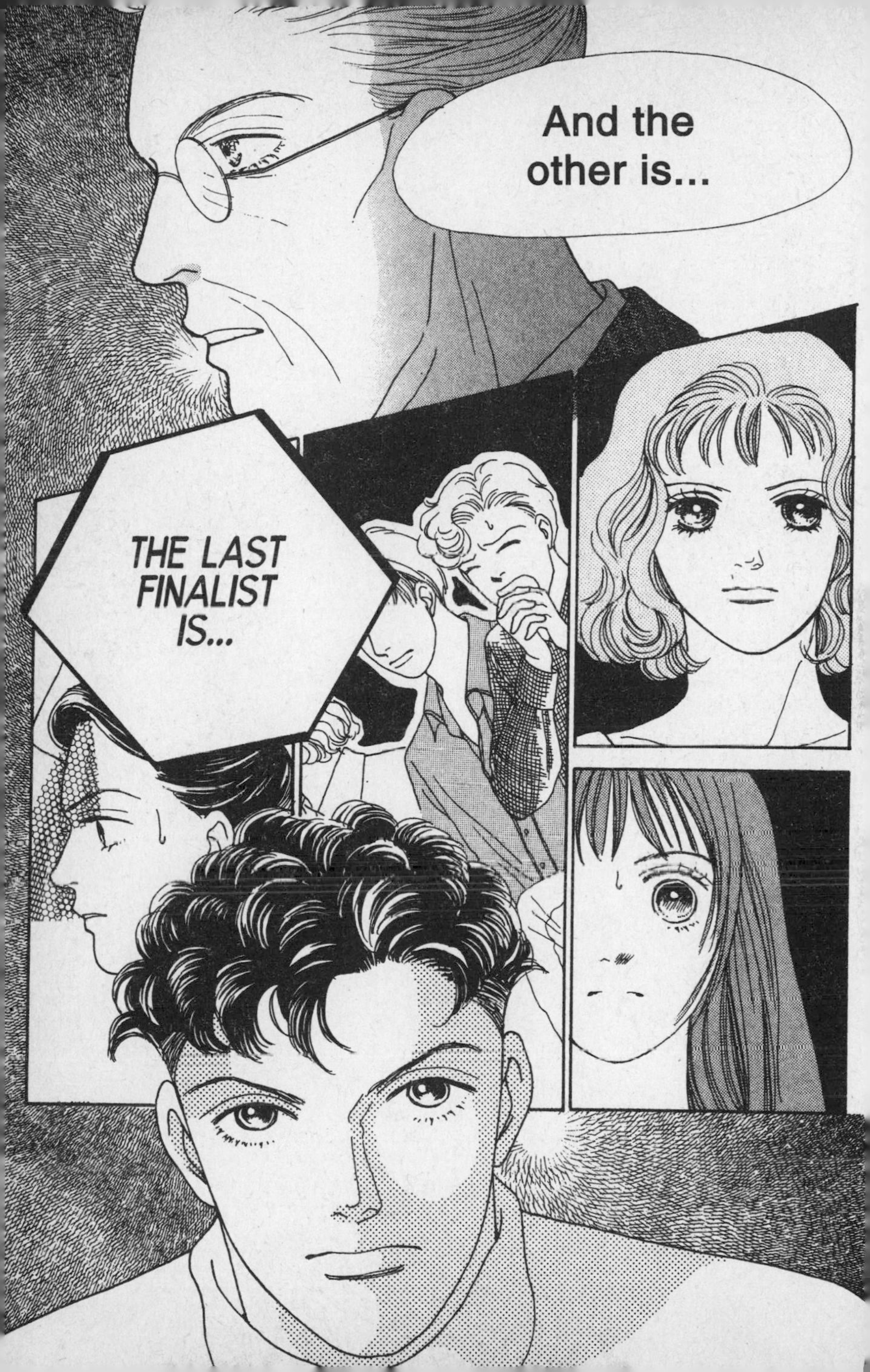
And the other is...
THE LAST FINALIST IS...

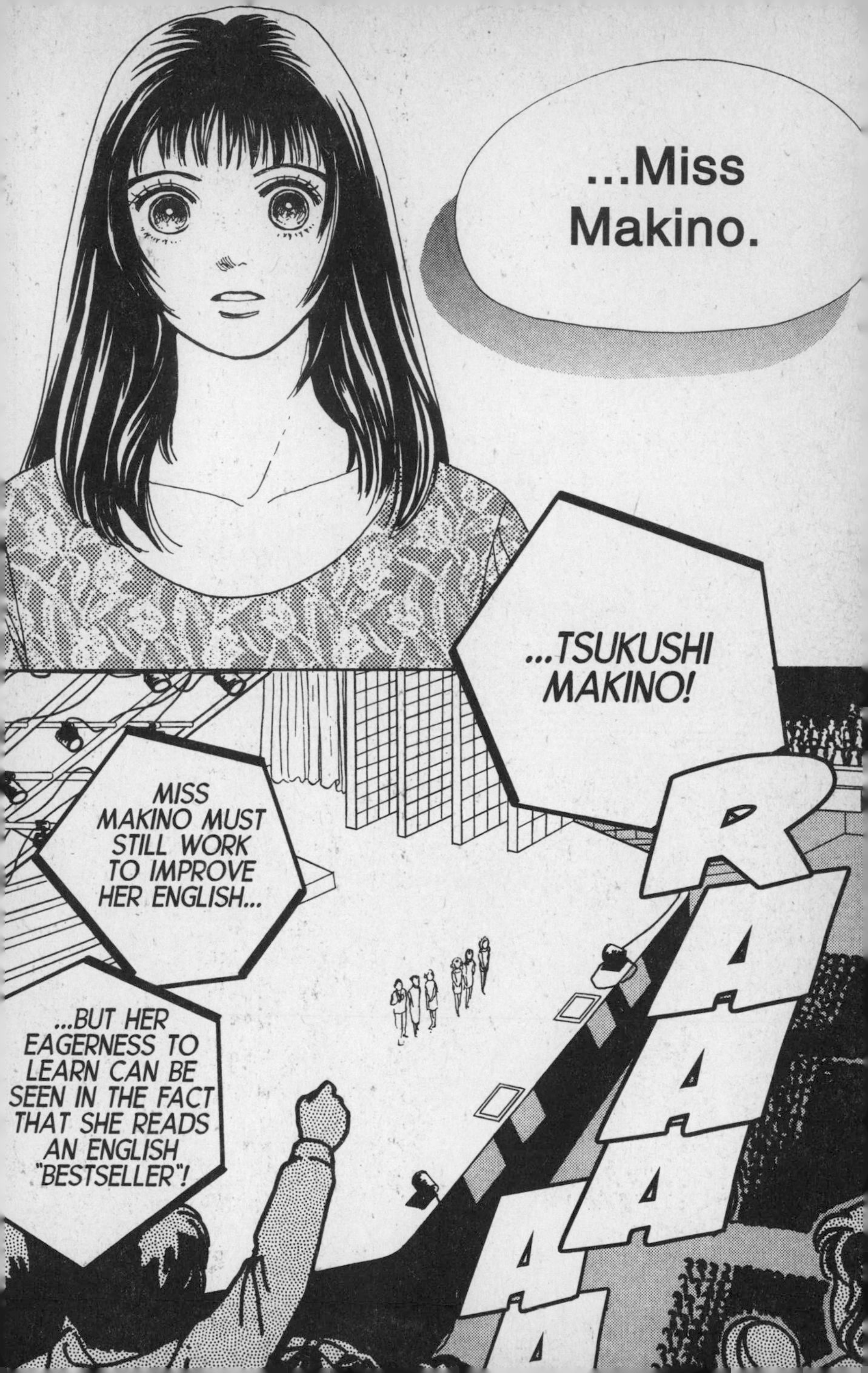
...Miss Makino.
...TSUKUSHI MAKINO!
RAAAAA
MISS MAKINO MUST STILL WORK TO IMPROVE HER ENGLISH...
...BUT HER EAGERNESS TO LEARN CAN BE SEEN IN THE FACT THAT SHE READS AN ENGLISH "BESTSELLER"!

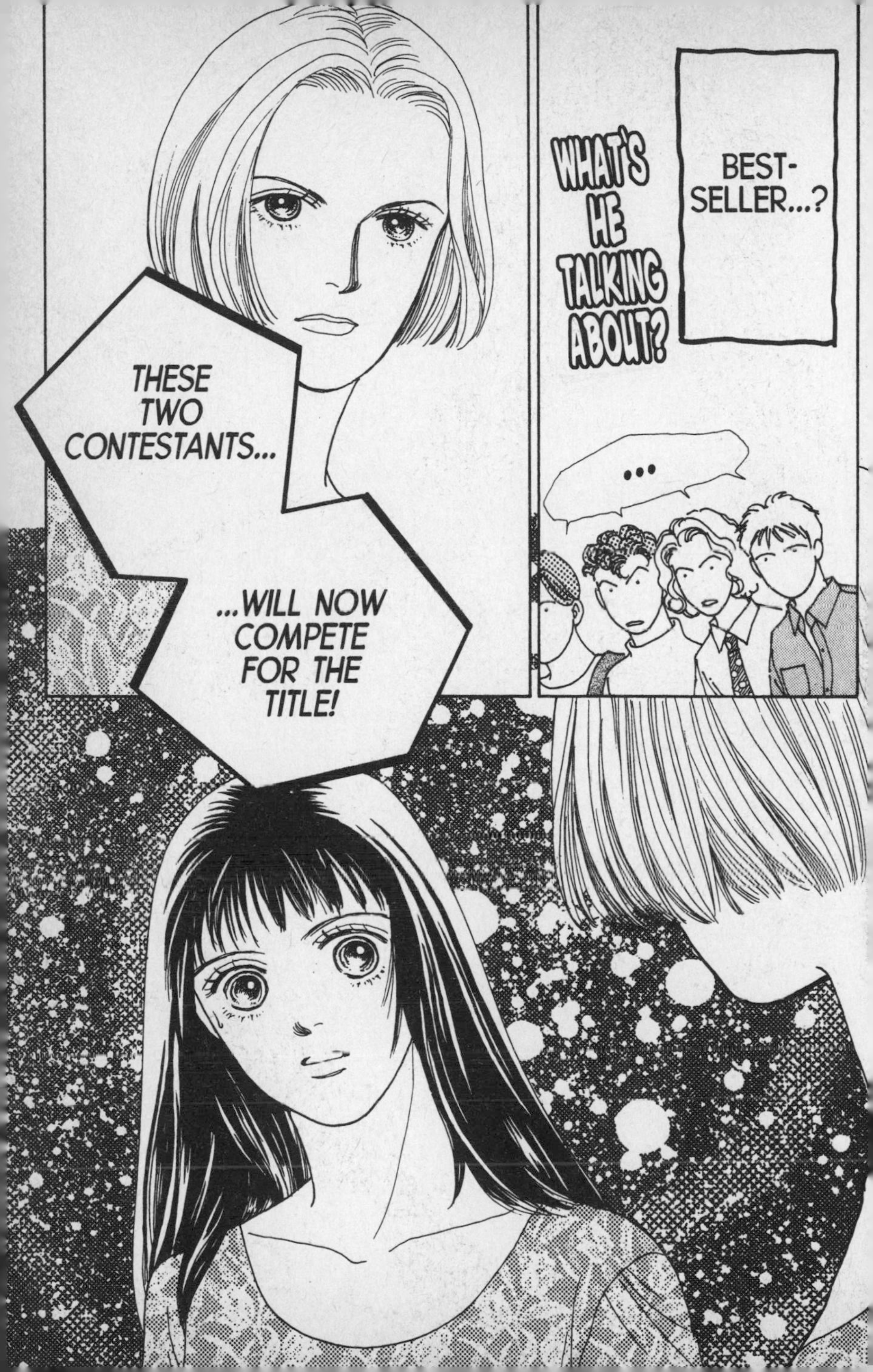

BEST-SELLER...?
WHAT'S HE TALKING ABOUT?
...
THESE TWO CONTESTANTS...
...WILL NOW COMPETE FOR THE TITLE!

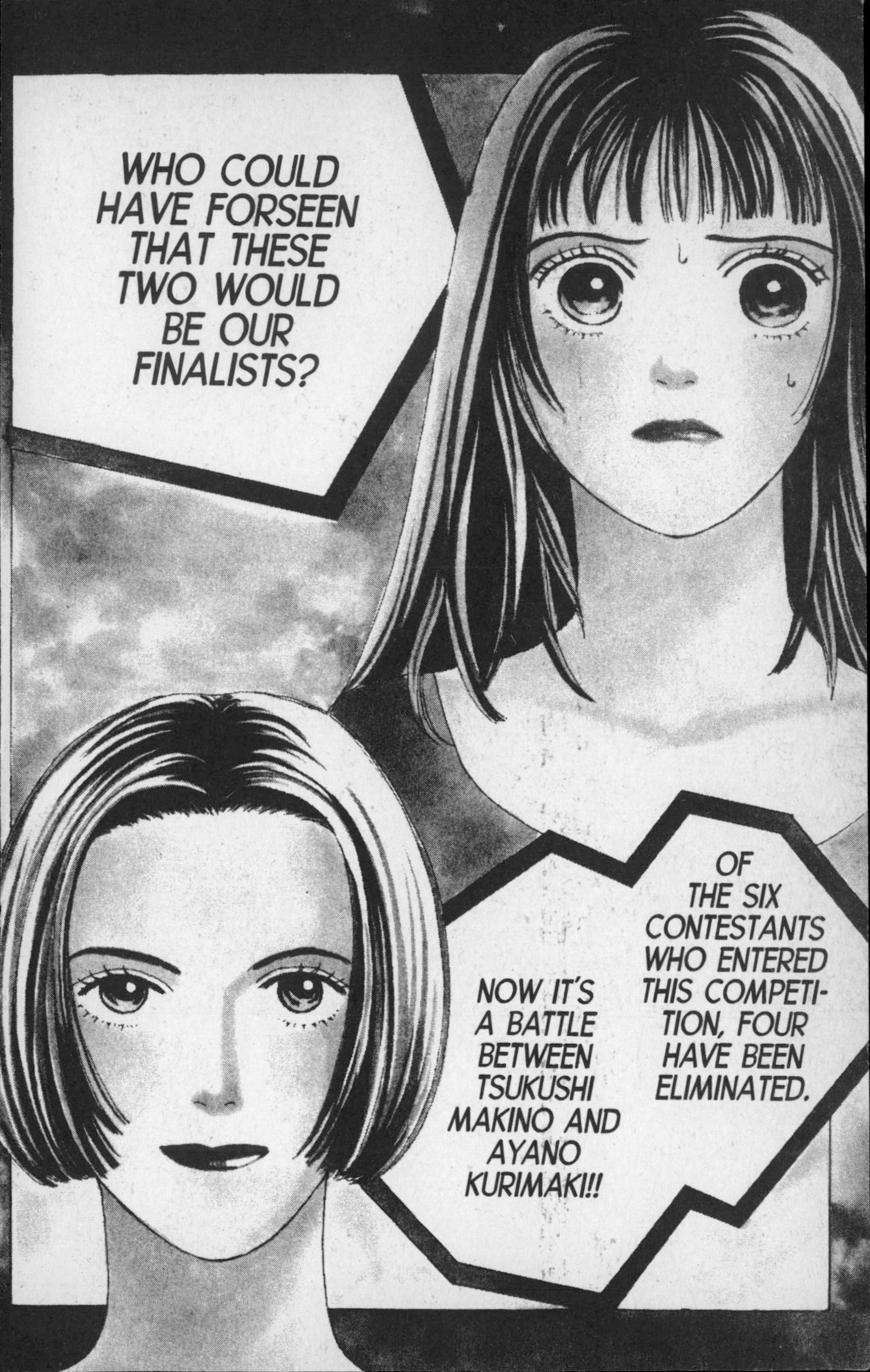
WHO COULD HAVE FORSEEN THAT THESE TWO WOULD BE OUR FINALISTS?
OF THE SIX CONTESTANTS WHO ENTERED THIS COMPETI- TION, FOUR HAVE BEEN ELIMINATED.
NOW IT'S A BATTLE BETWEEN TSUKUSHI MAKINO AND AYANO KURIMAKI!!

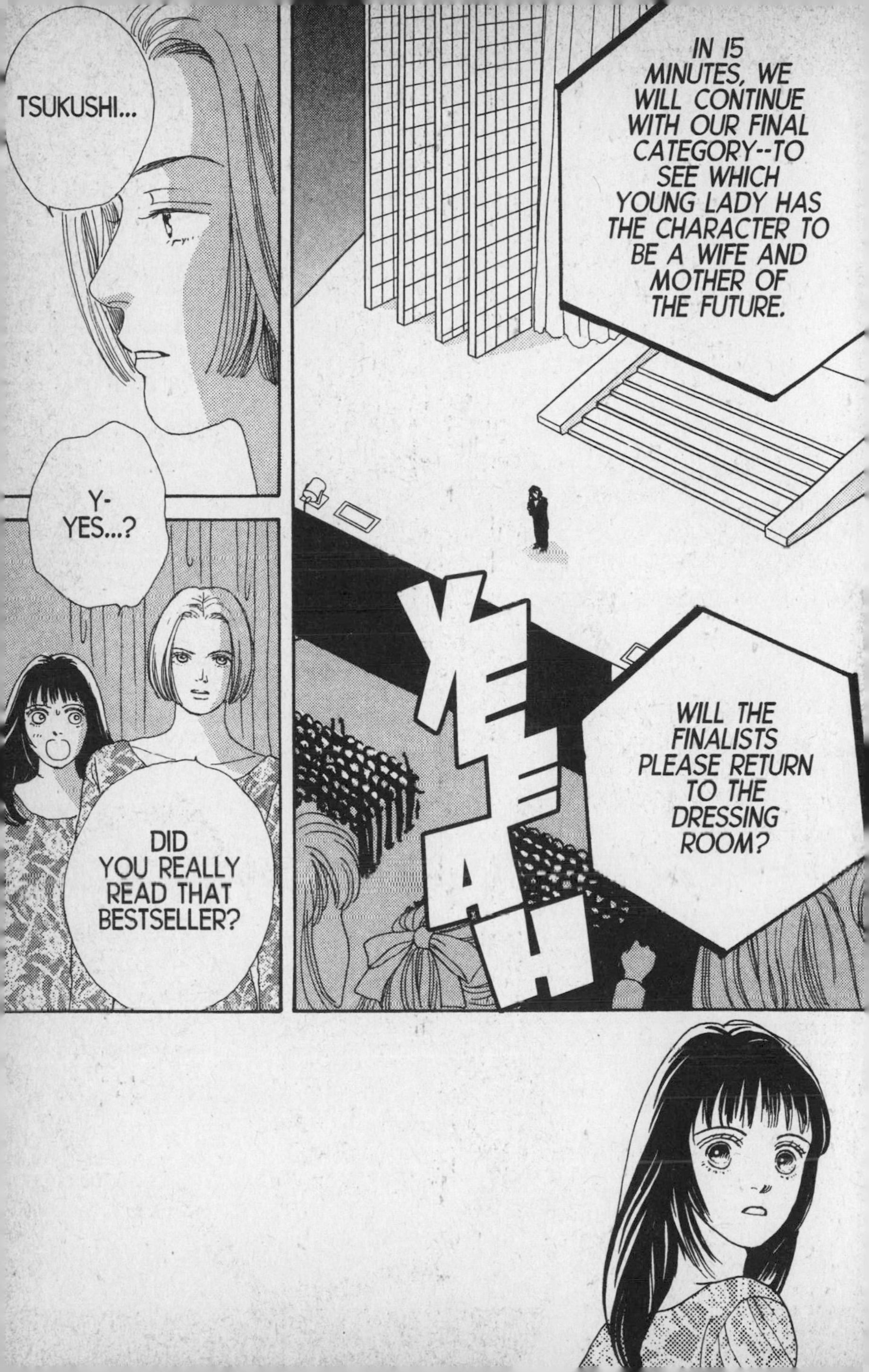
IN 15 MINUTES, WE WILL CONTINUE WITH OUR FINAL CATEGORY--TO SEE WHICH YOUNG LADY HAS THE CHARACTER TO BE A WIFE AND MOTHER OF THE FUTURE.
YEEAH
WILL THE FINALISTS PLEASE RETURN TO THE DRESSING ROOM?
TSUKUSHI...
Y- YES...?
DID YOU REALLY READ THAT BESTSELLER?

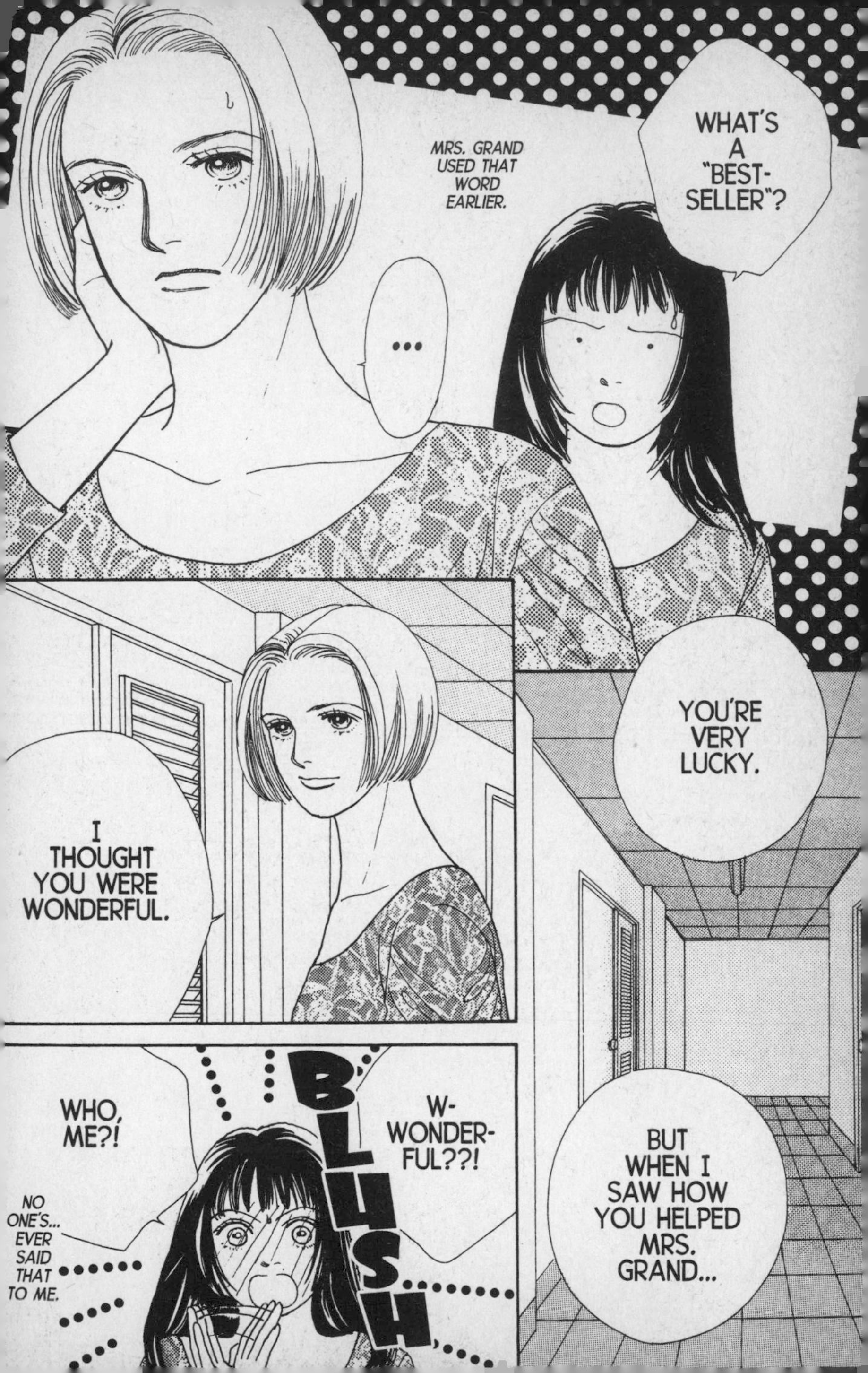
WHAT'S A "BEST-SELLER"?
MRS. GRAND USED THAT WORD EARLIER.
...
YOU'RE VERY LUCKY.
BUT WHEN I SAW HOW YOU HELPED MRS. GRAND...
I THOUGHT YOU WERE WONDERFUL.
W-WONDERFUL??!
BLUSH
WHO, ME?!
NO ONE'S... EVER SAID THAT TO ME.

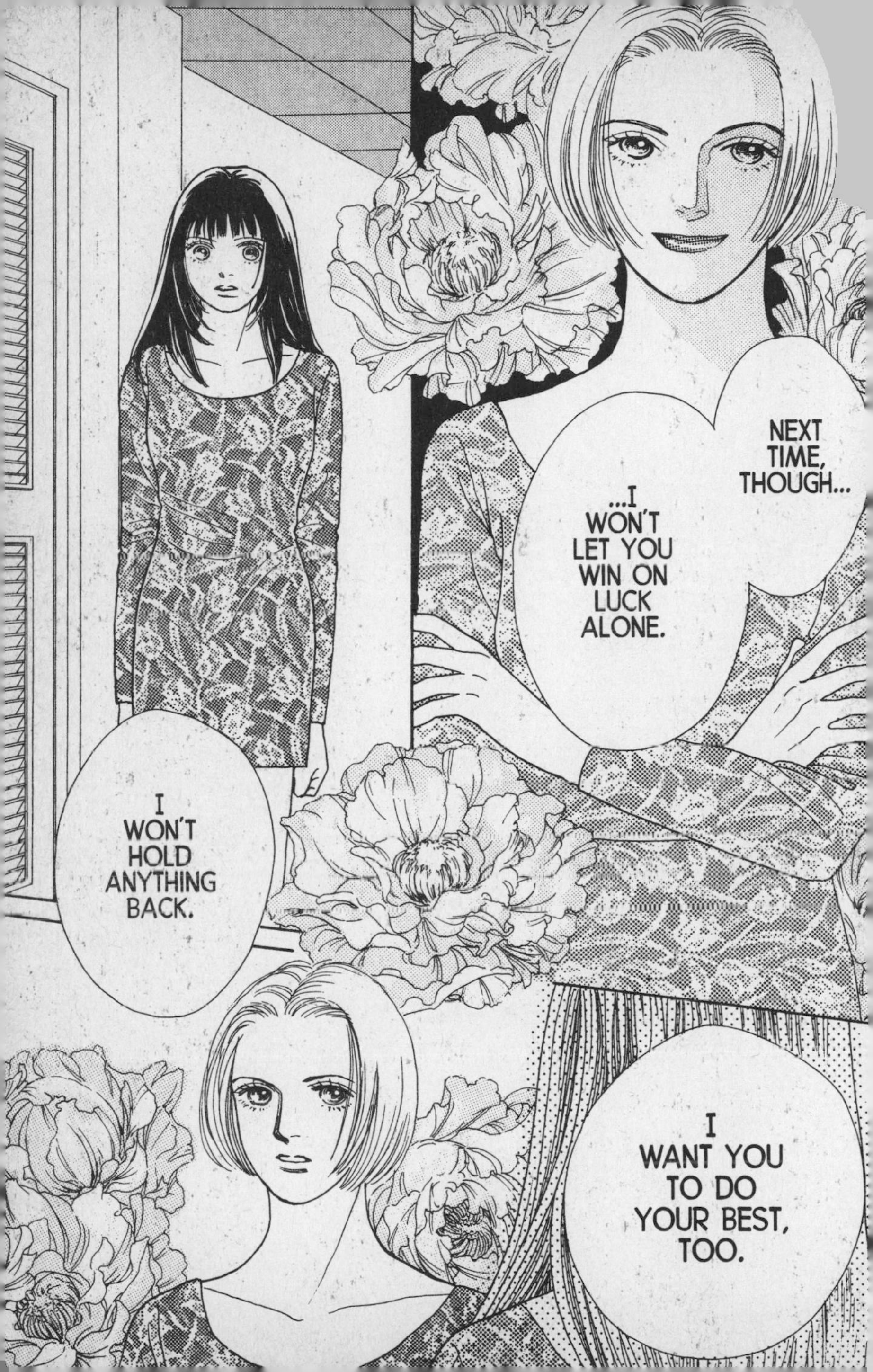
NEXT TIME, THOUGH...
...I WON'T LET YOU WIN ON LUCK ALONE.
I WON'T HOLD ANYTHING BACK.
I WANT YOU TO DO YOUR BEST, TOO.

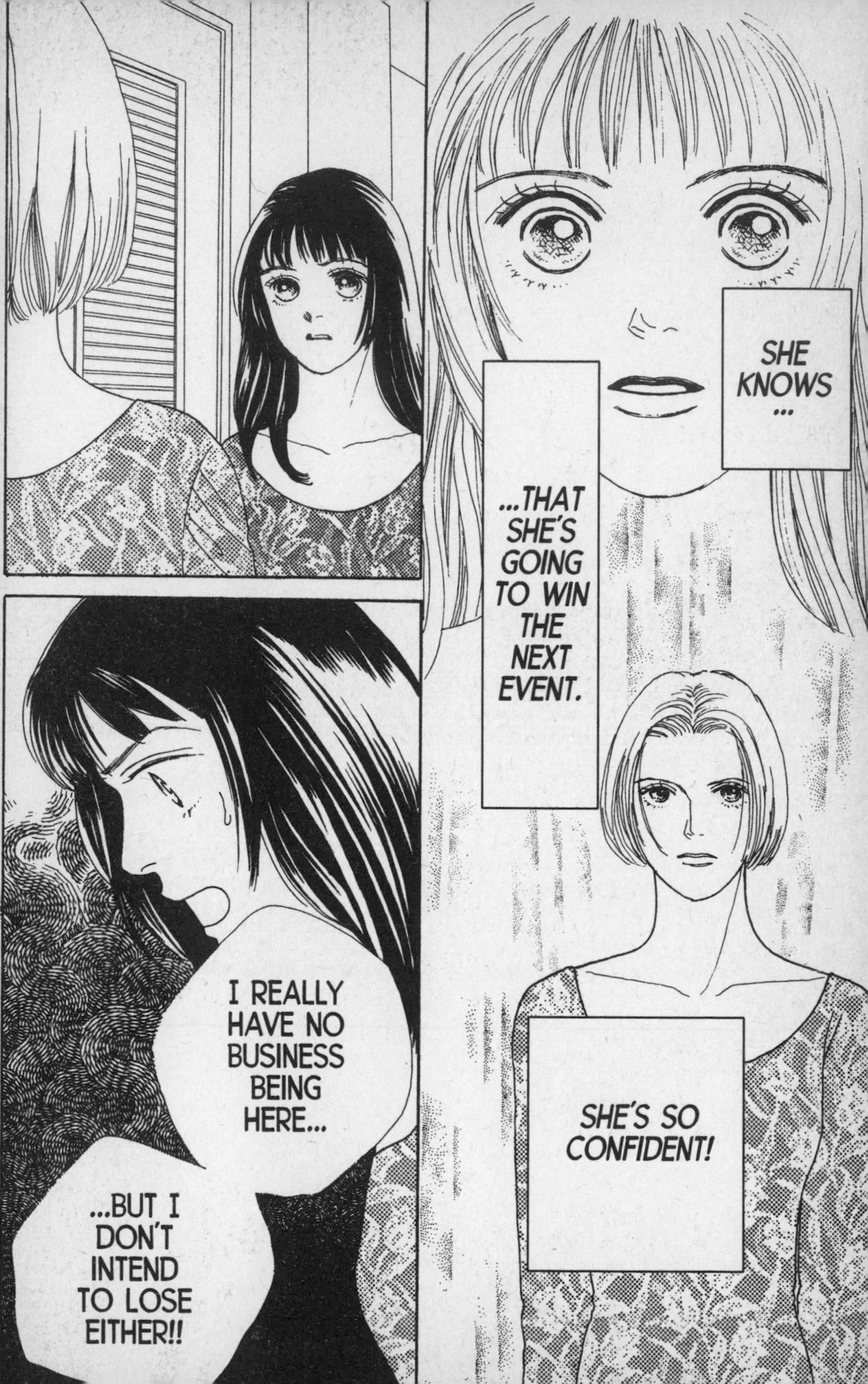
SHE KNOWS ...
...THAT SHE'S GOING TO WIN THE NEXT EVENT.
SHE'S SO CONFIDENT!
I REALLY HAVE NO BUSINESS BEING HERE...
...BUT I DON'T INTEND TO LOSE EITHER!!

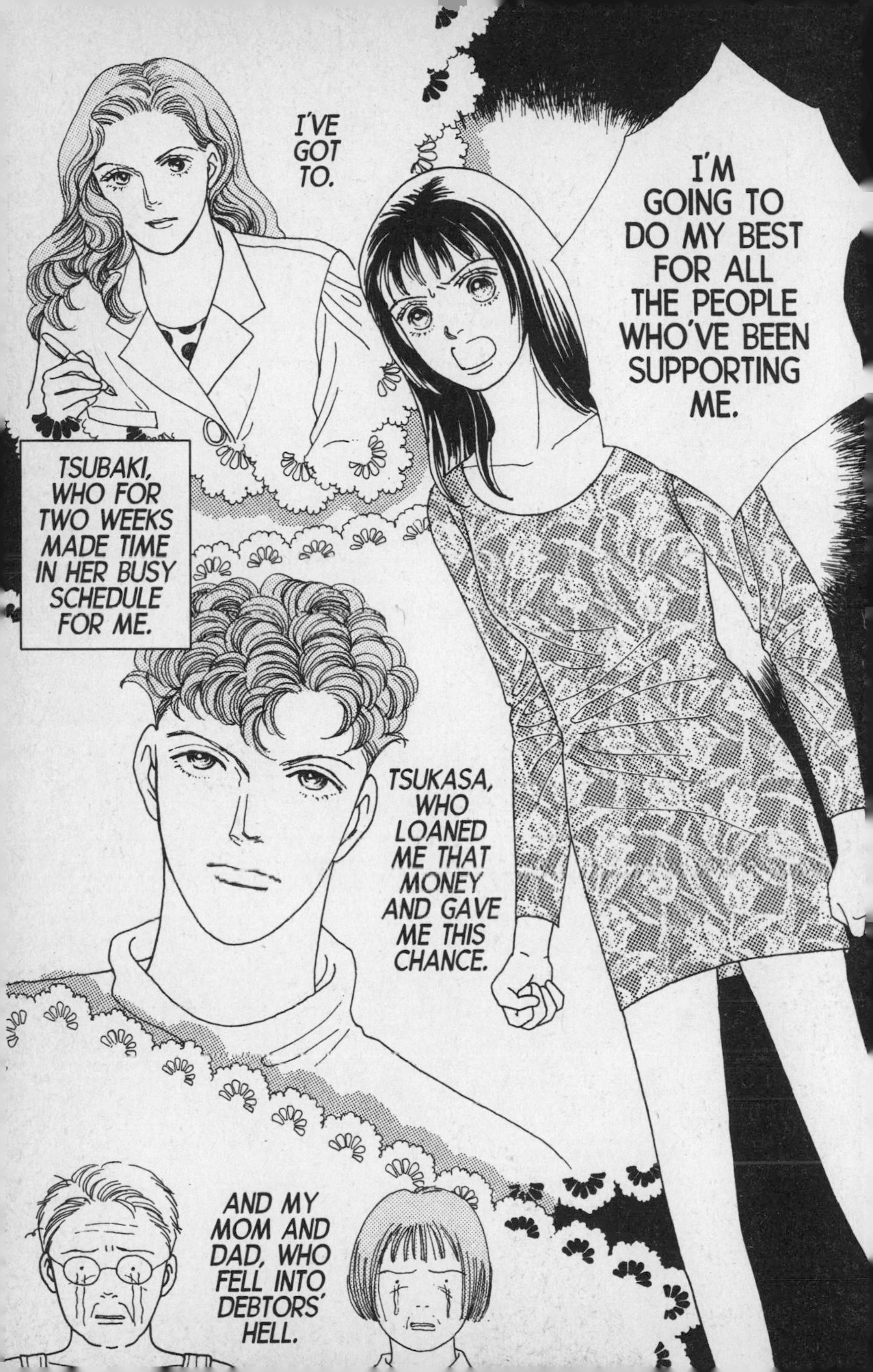
I'M GOING TO DO MY BEST FOR ALL THE PEOPLE WHO'VE BEEN SUPPORTING ME.
I'VE GOT TO.
TSUBAKI, WHO FOR TWO WEEKS MADE TIME IN HER BUSY SCHEDULE FOR ME.
TSUKASA, WHO LOANED ME THAT MONEY AND GAVE ME THIS CHANCE.
AND MY MOM AND DAD, WHO FELL INTO DEBTORS' HELL.

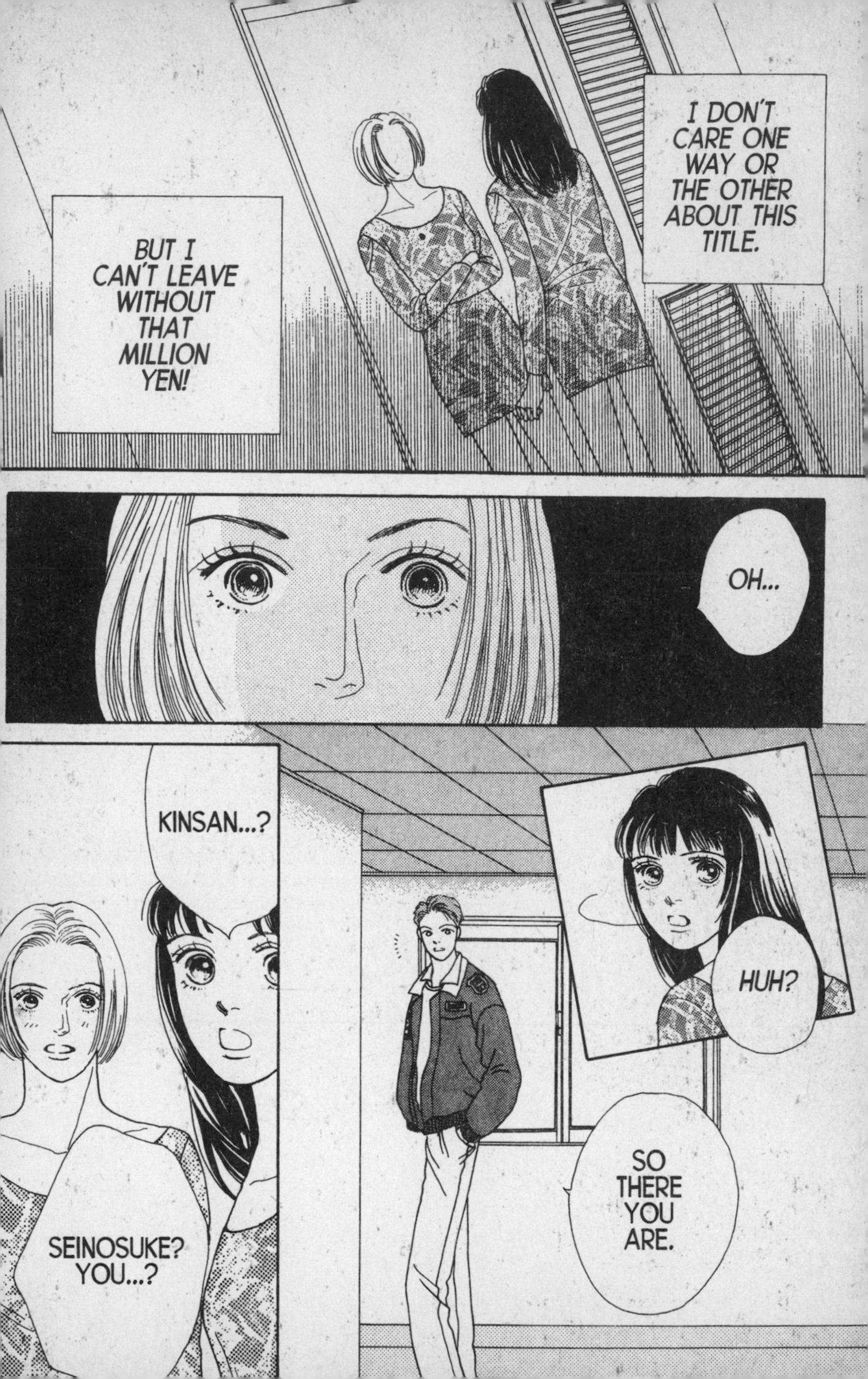
I DON'T CARE ONE WAY OR THE OTHER ABOUT THIS TITLE.
BUT I CAN'T LEAVE WITHOUT THAT MILLION YEN!
OH...
HUH?
SO THERE YOU ARE.
KINSAN...?
SEINOSUKE? YOU...?

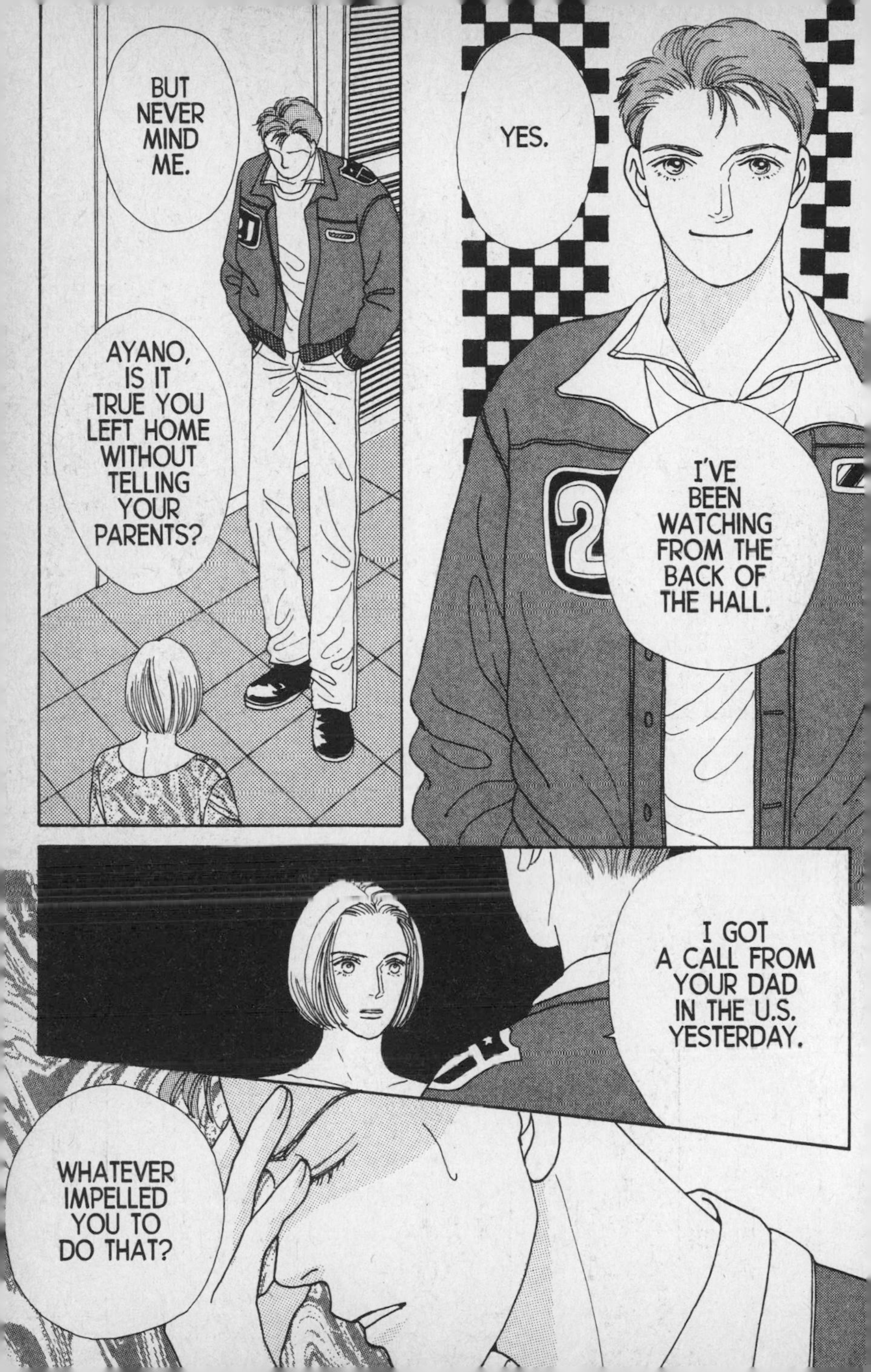
YES.
I'VE BEEN WATCHING FROM THE BACK OF THE HALL.
BUT NEVER MIND ME.
AYANO, IS IT TRUE YOU LEFT HOME WITHOUT TELLING YOUR PARENTS?
I GOT A CALL FROM YOUR DAD IN THE U.S. YESTERDAY.
WHATEVER IMPELLED YOU TO DO THAT?

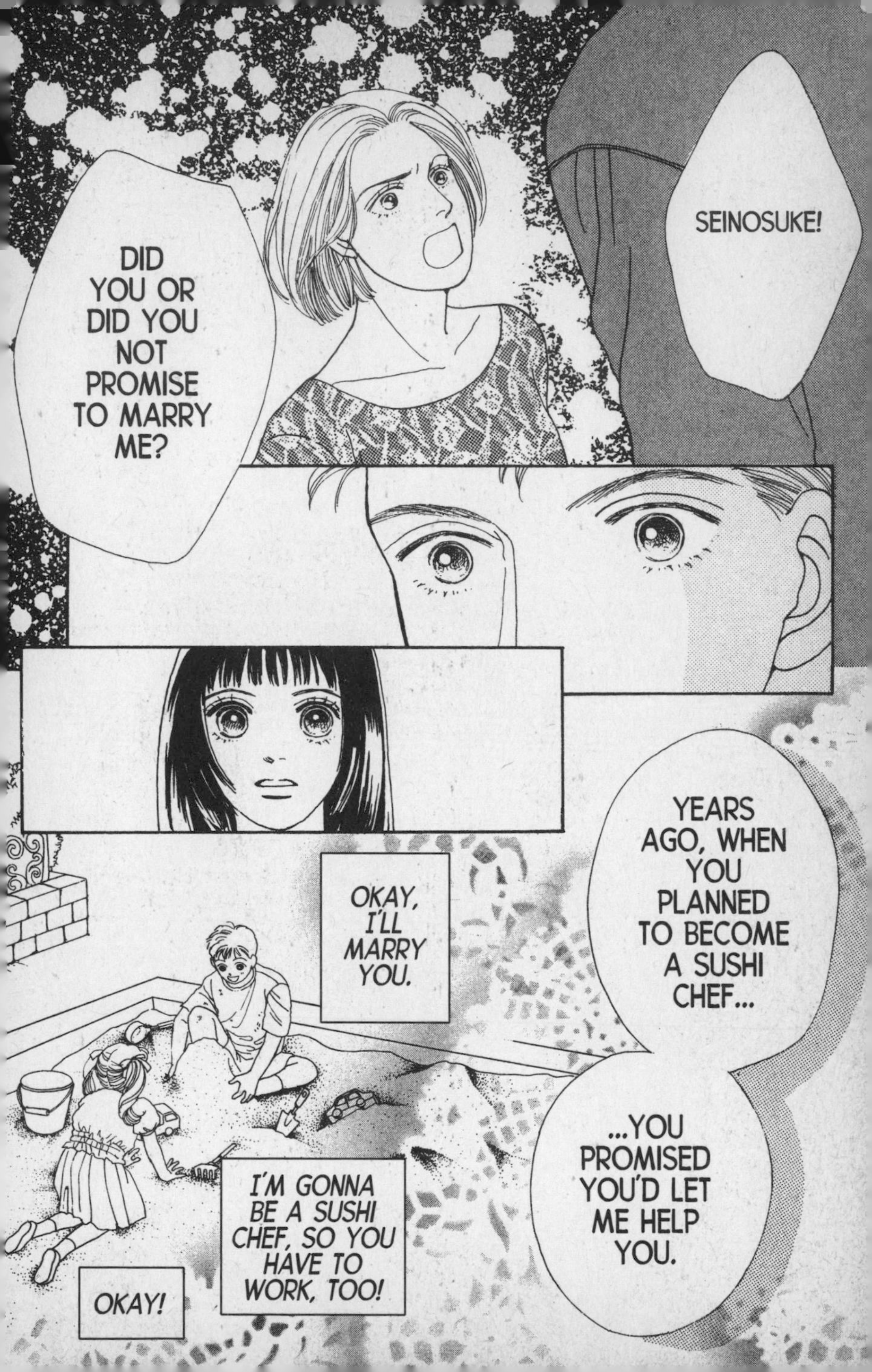
SEINOSUKE!
DID YOU OR DID YOU NOT PROMISE TO MARRY ME?
YEARS AGO, WHEN YOU PLANNED TO BECOME A SUSHI CHEF...
...YOU PROMISED YOU'D LET ME HELP YOU.
OKAY, I'LL MARRY YOU.
I'M GONNA BE A SUSHI CHEF, SO YOU HAVE TO WORK, TOO!
OKAY!

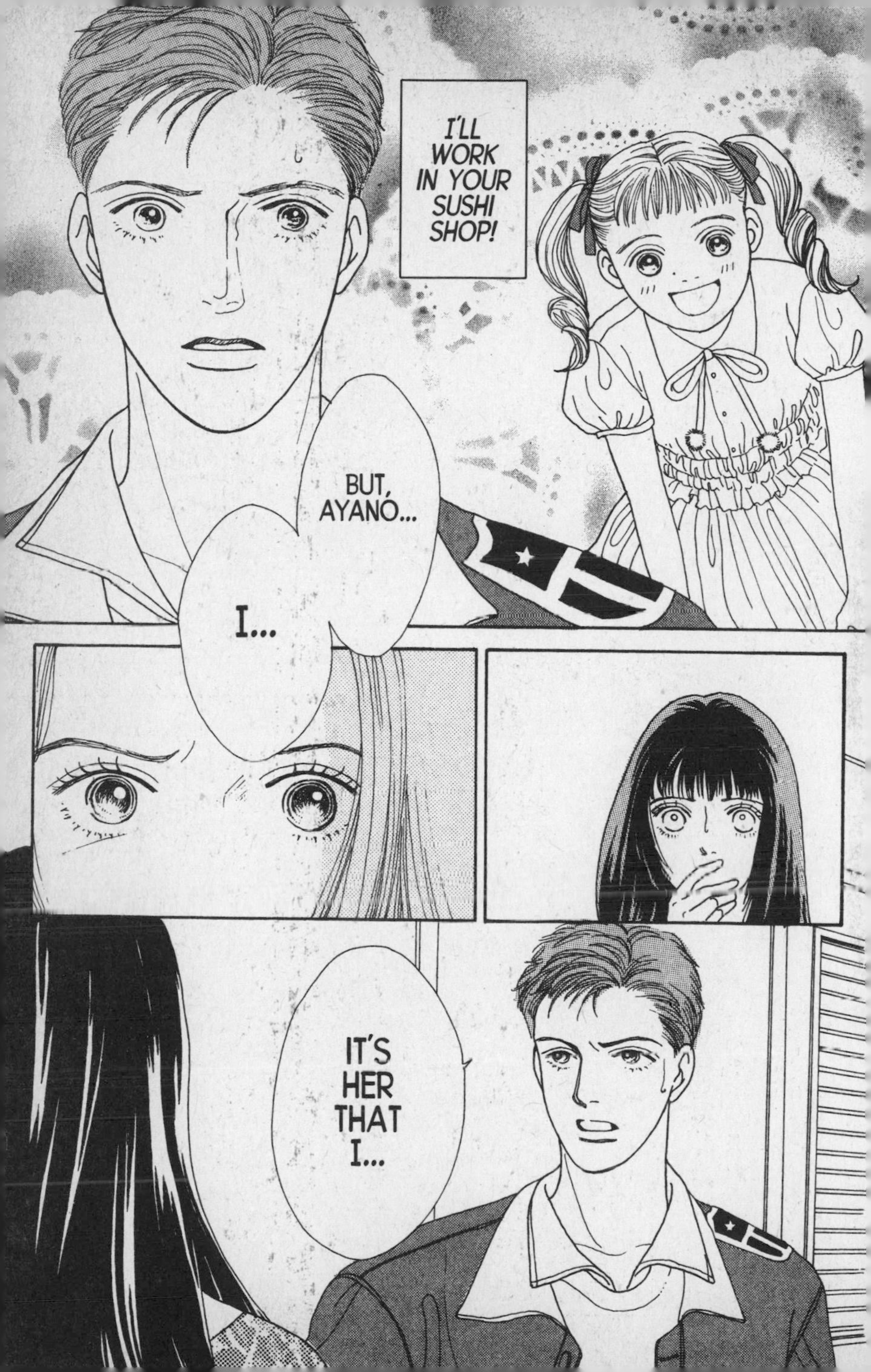
I'LL WORK IN YOUR SUSHI SHOP!
BUT, AYANO...
I...
IT'S HER THAT I...

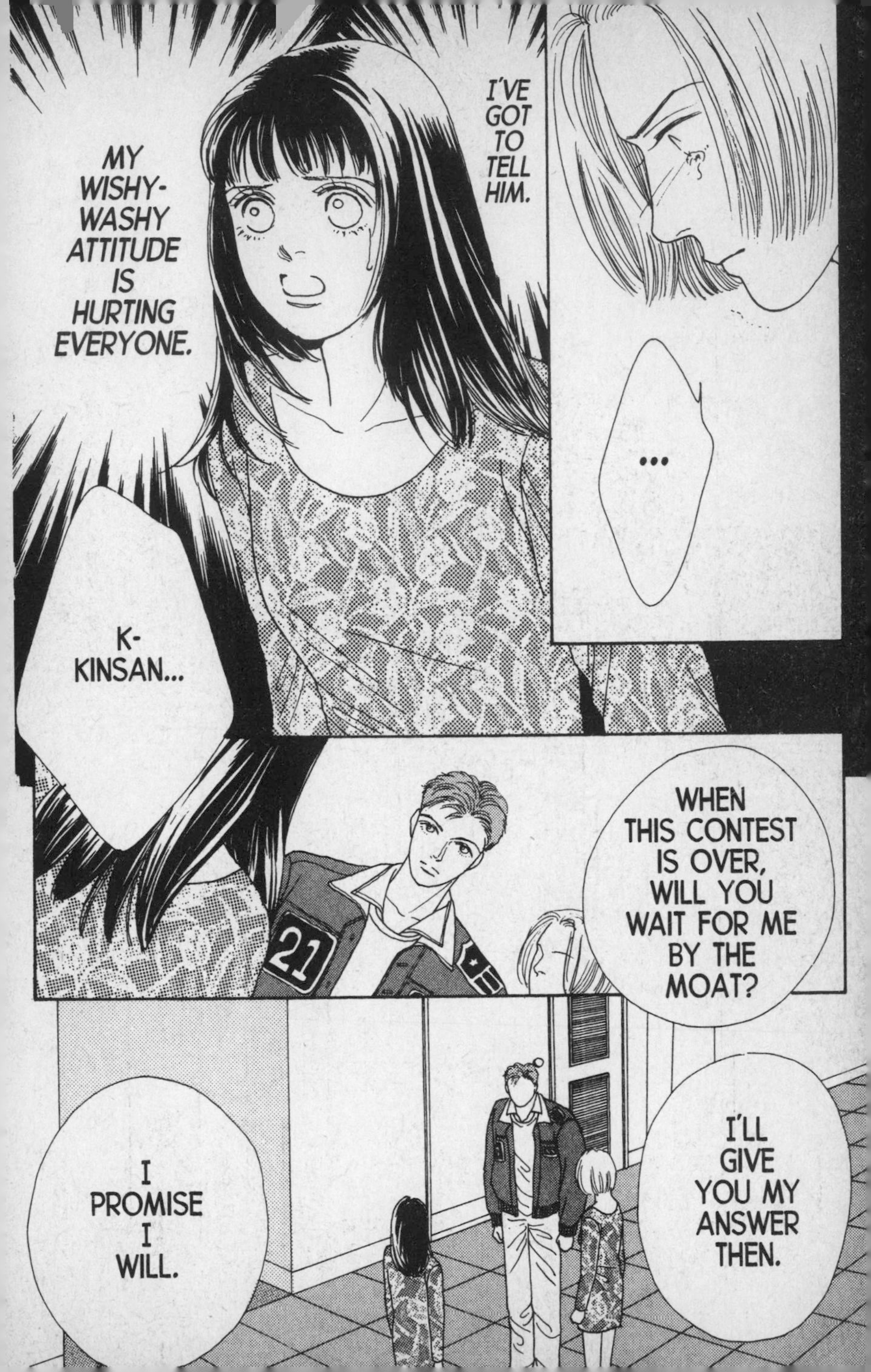
...
I'VE GOT TO TELL HIM.
MY WISHY-WASHY ATTITUDE IS HURTING EVERYONE.
K-KINSAN...
WHEN THIS CONTEST IS OVER, WILL YOU WAIT FOR ME BY THE MOAT?
I'LL GIVE YOU MY ANSWER THEN.
I PROMISE I WILL.

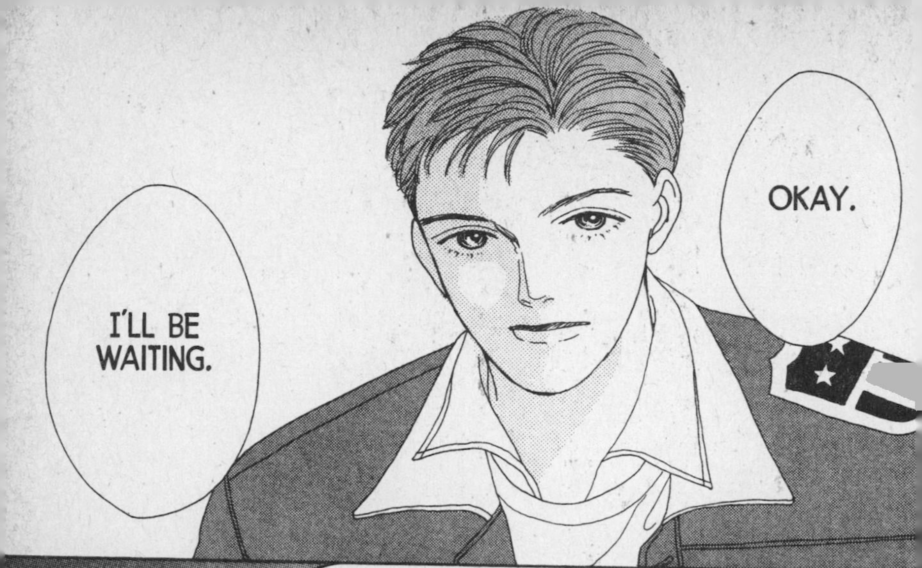
OKAY.
I'LL BE WAITING.

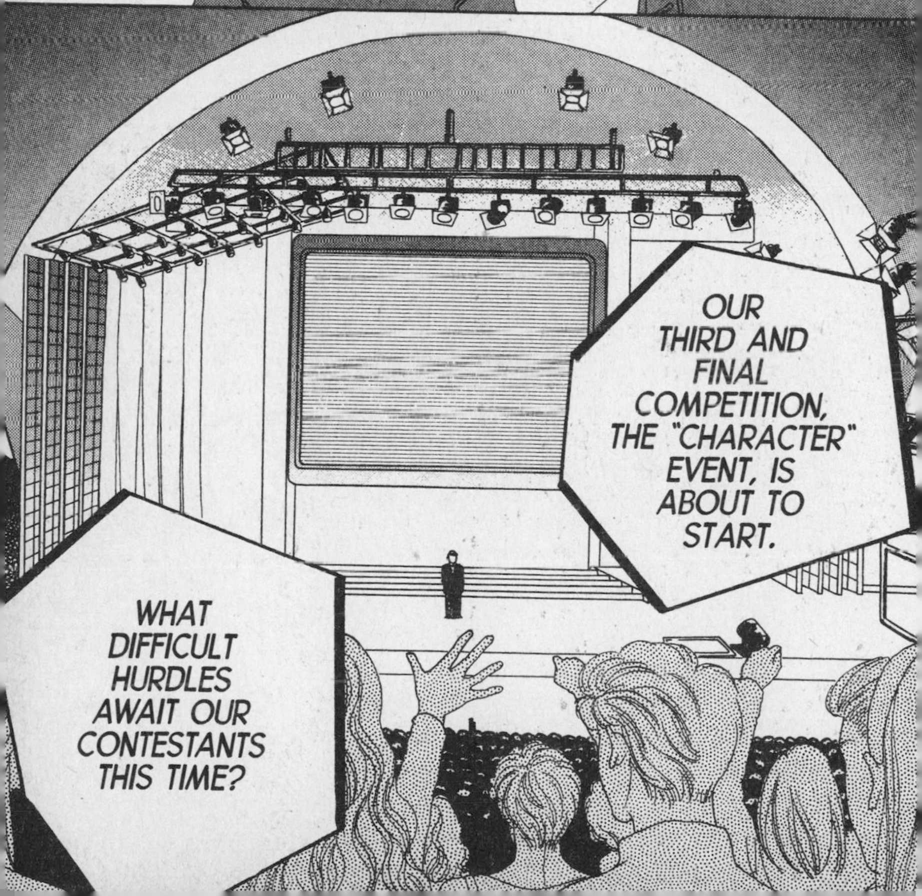
OUR THIRD AND FINAL COMPETITION, THE "CHARACTER" EVENT, IS ABOUT TO START.
WHAT DIFFICULT HURDLES AWAIT OUR CONTESTANTS THIS TIME?

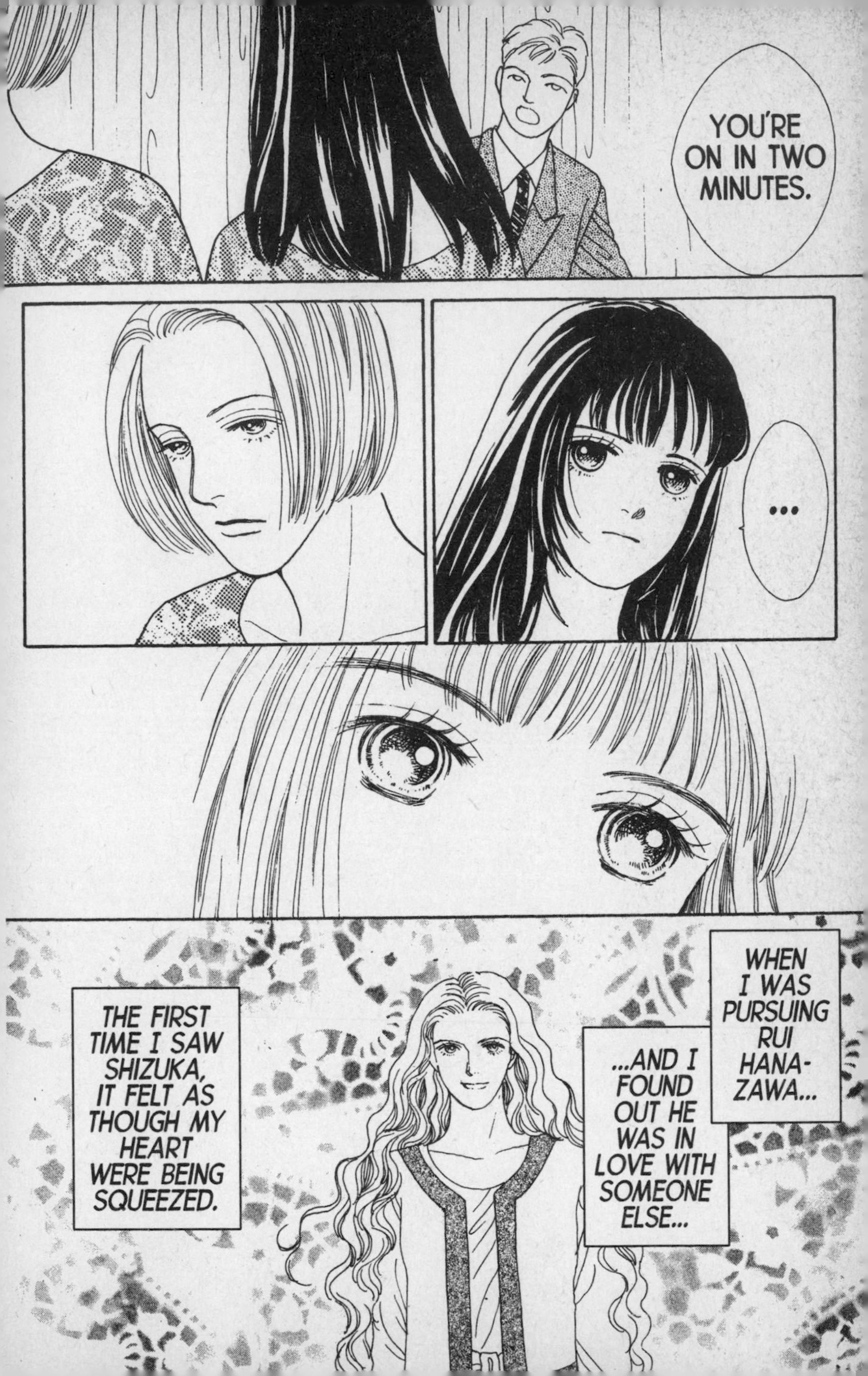
YOU'RE ON IN TWO MINUTES.
...
WHEN I WAS PURSUING RUI HANA-ZAWA...
...AND I FOUND OUT HE WAS IN LOVE WITH SOMEONE ELSE...
THE FIRST TIME I SAW SHIZUKA, IT FELT AS THOUGH MY HEART WERE BEING SQUEEZED.

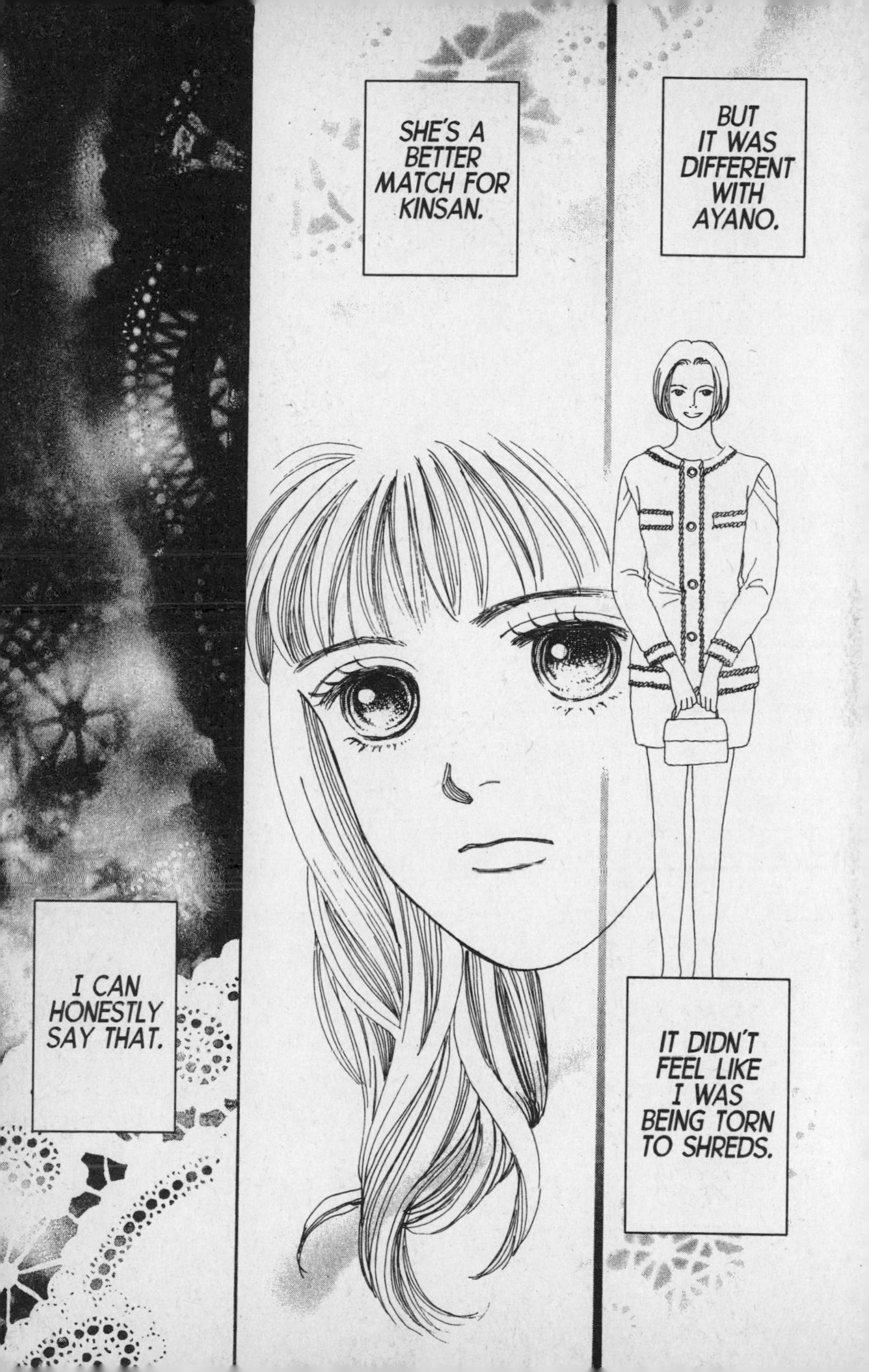
BUT IT WAS DIFFERENT WITH AYANO.
IT DIDN'T FEEL LIKE I WAS BEING TORN TO SHREDS.
SHE'S A BETTER MATCH FOR KINSAN.
I CAN HONESTLY SAY THAT.

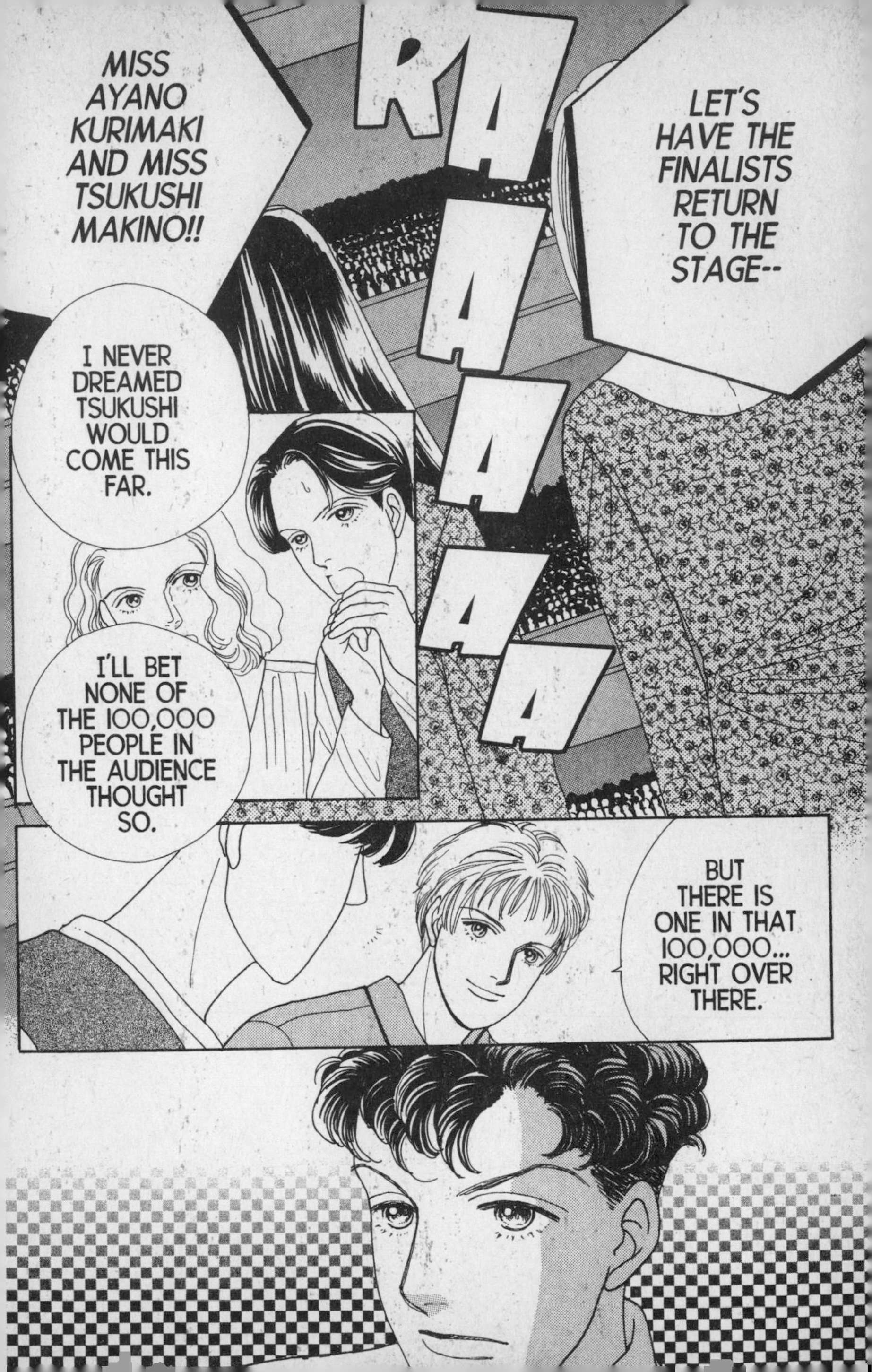
LET'S HAVE THE FINALISTS RETURN TO THE STAGE--
MISS AYANO KURIMAKI AND MISS TSUKUSHI MAKINO!!
RAAAAAA
I NEVER DREAMED TSUKUSHI WOULD COME THIS FAR.
I'LL BET NONE OF THE 100,000 PEOPLE IN THE AUDIENCE THOUGHT SO.
BUT THERE IS ONE IN THAT 100,000... RIGHT OVER THERE.

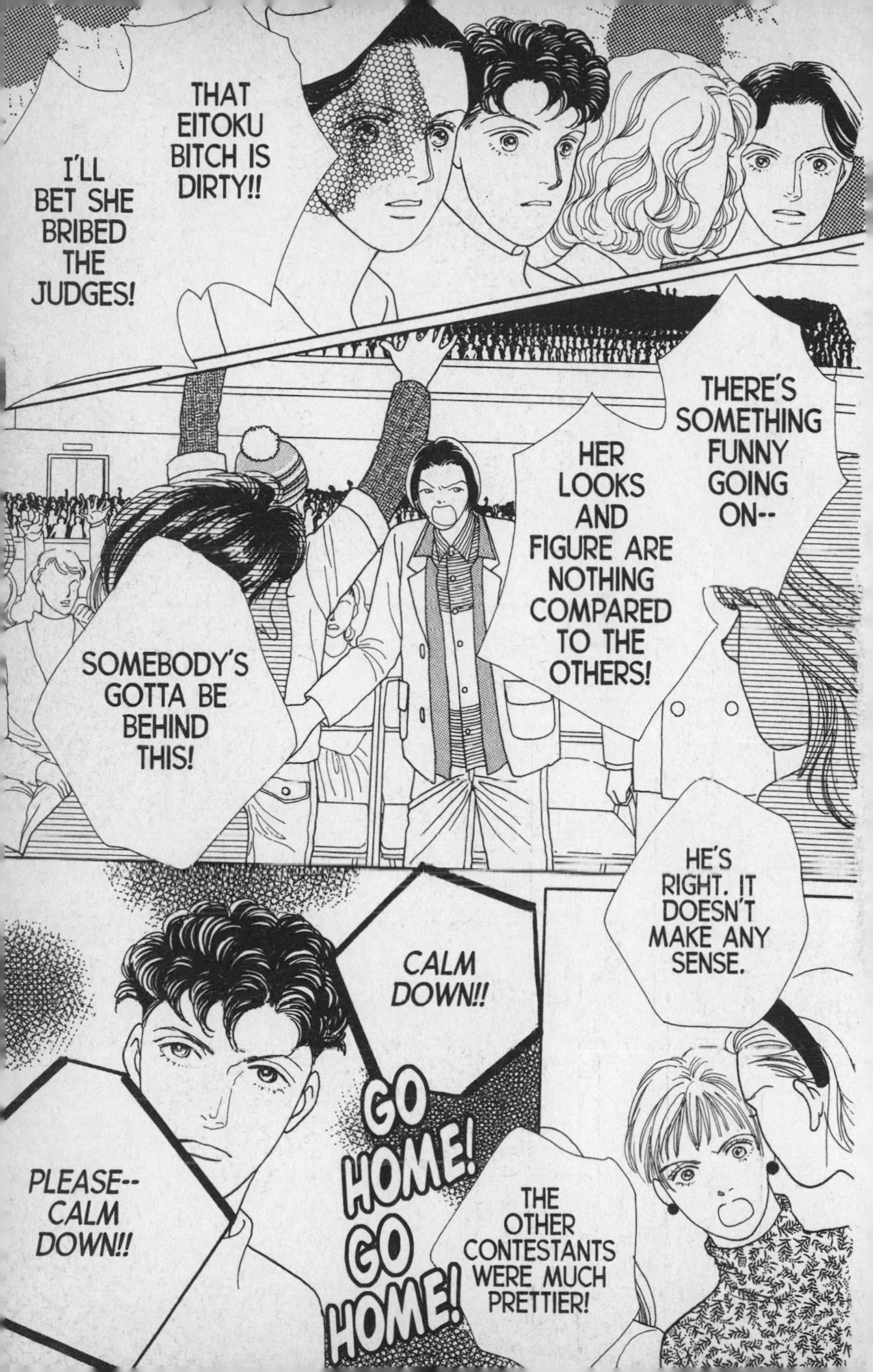
THAT EITOKU BITCH IS DIRTY!!
I'LL BET SHE BRIBED THE JUDGES!
THERE'S SOMETHING FUNNY GOING ON--
HER LOOKS AND FIGURE ARE NOTHING COMPARED TO THE OTHERS!
SOMEBODY'S GOTTA BE BEHIND THIS!
HE'S RIGHT. IT DOESN'T MAKE ANY SENSE.
THE OTHER CONTESTANTS WERE MUCH PRETTIER!
GO HOME! GO HOME!
CALM DOWN!!
PLEASE-- CALM DOWN!!

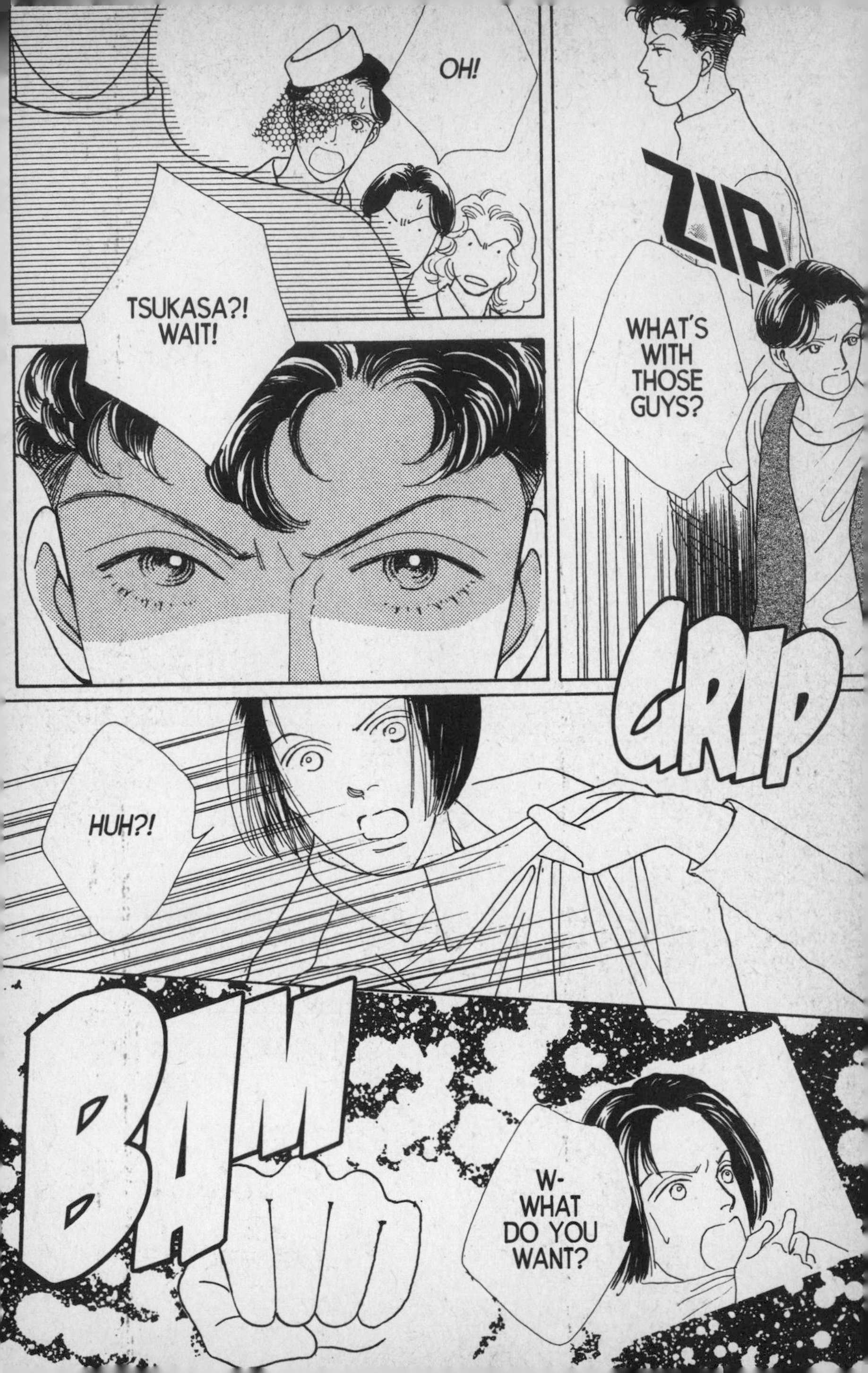
ZIP
WHAT'S WITH THOSE GUYS?
OH!
TSUKASA?! WAIT!
GRIP
HUH?!
W- WHAT DO YOU WANT?
BAM

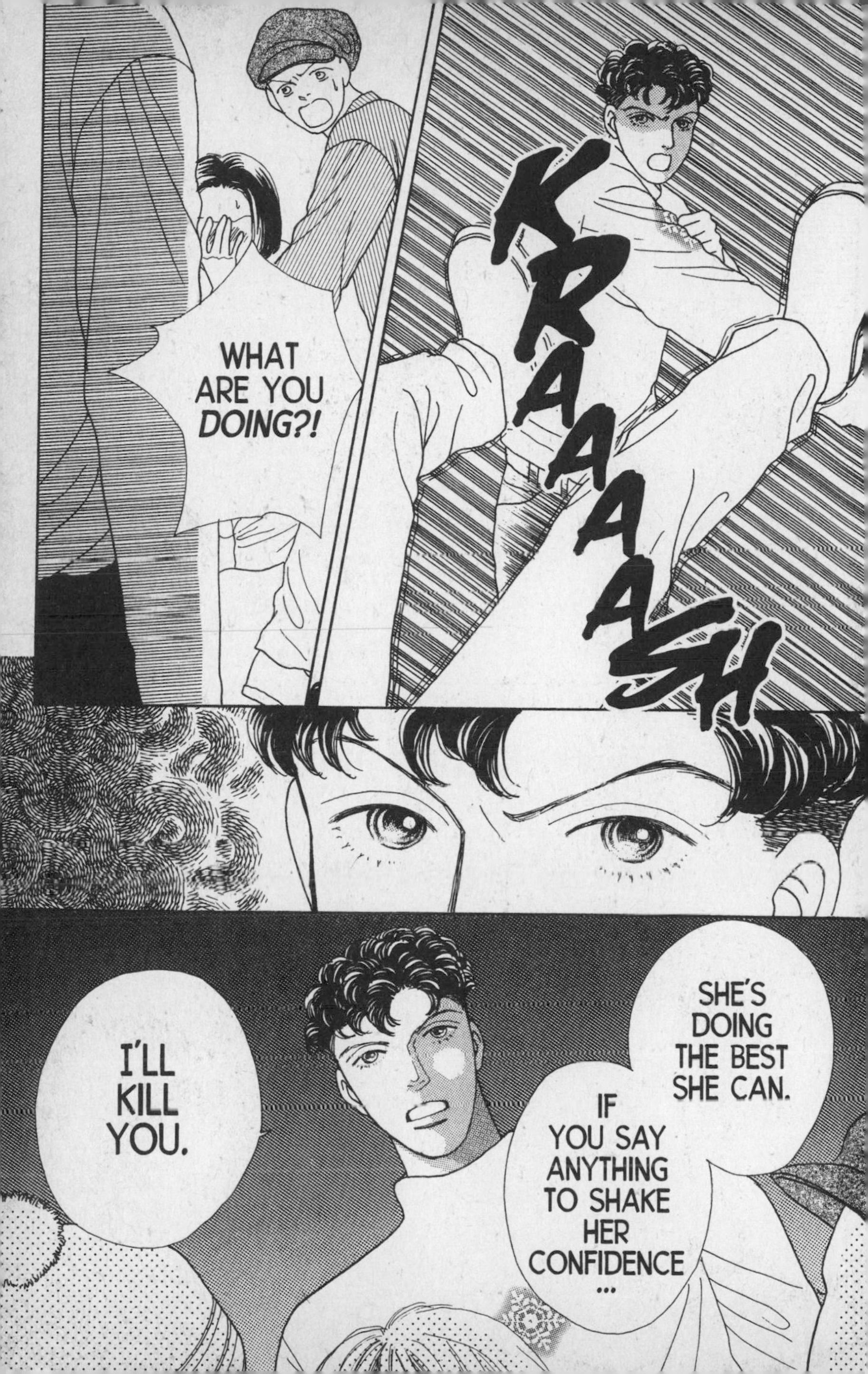
KRAAAASH
WHAT ARE YOU *DOING?!*
SHE'S DOING THE BEST SHE CAN.
IF YOU SAY ANYTHING TO SHAKE HER CONFIDENCE ...
I'LL KILL YOU.

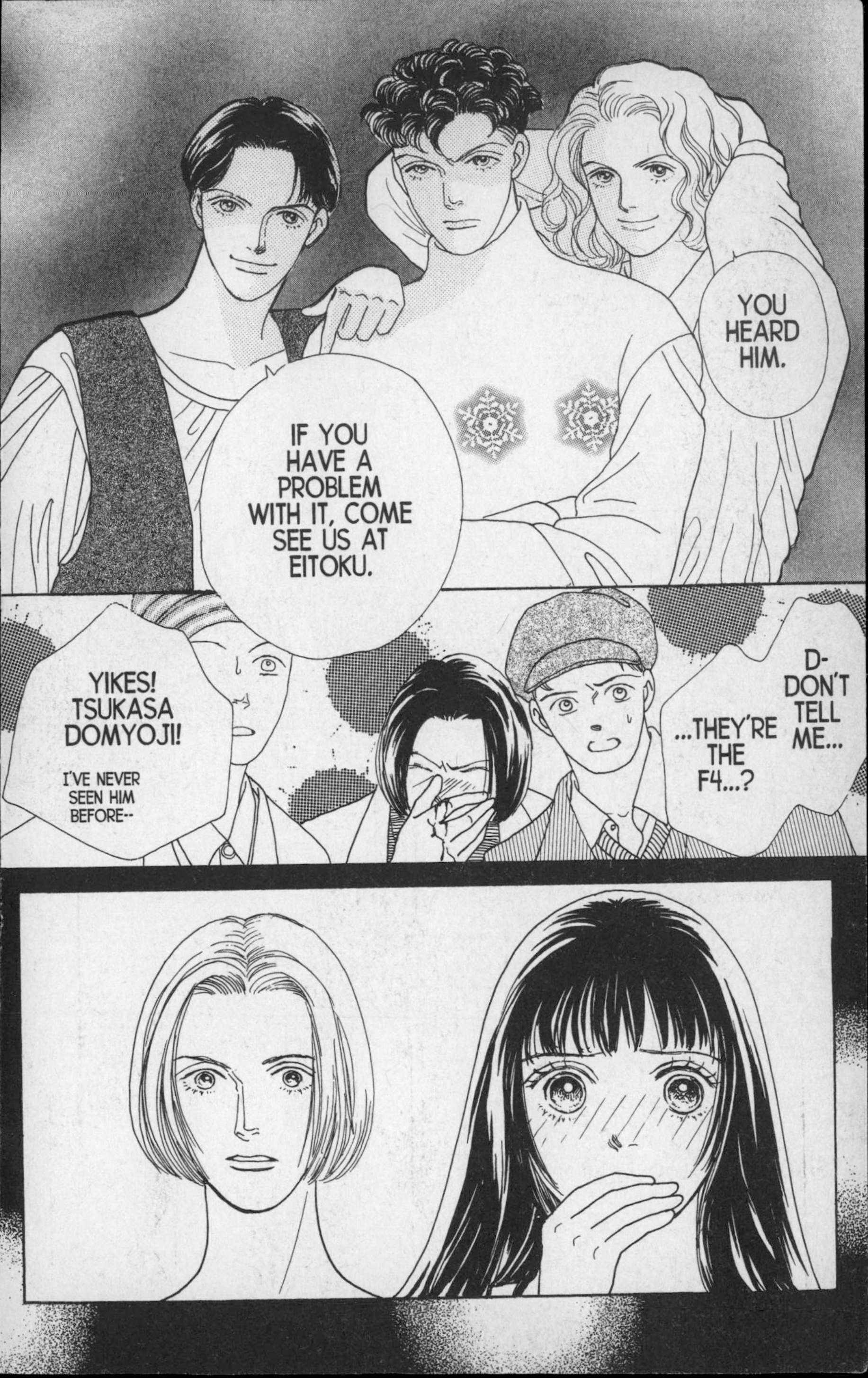
YOU HEARD HIM.
IF YOU HAVE A PROBLEM WITH IT, COME SEE US AT EITOKU.
D-DON'T TELL ME...
...THEY'RE THE F4...?
YIKES! TSUKASA DOMYOJI!
I'VE NEVER SEEN HIM BEFORE--

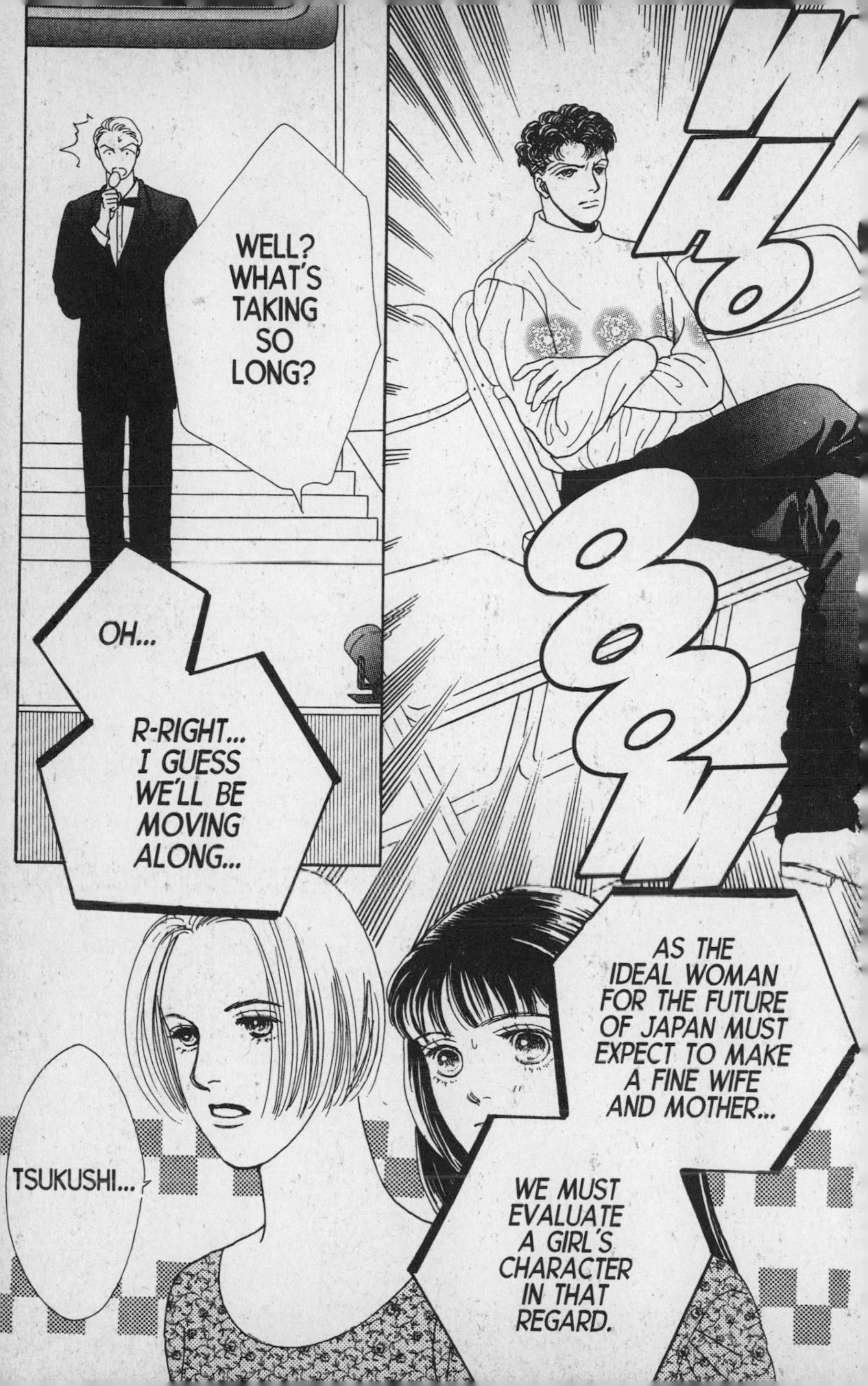
WHOOOOM
WELL? WHAT'S TAKING SO LONG?
OH...
R-RIGHT... I GUESS WE'LL BE MOVING ALONG...
AS THE IDEAL WOMAN FOR THE FUTURE OF JAPAN MUST EXPECT TO MAKE A FINE WIFE AND MOTHER...
WE MUST EVALUATE A GIRL'S CHARACTER IN THAT REGARD.
TSUKUSHI...

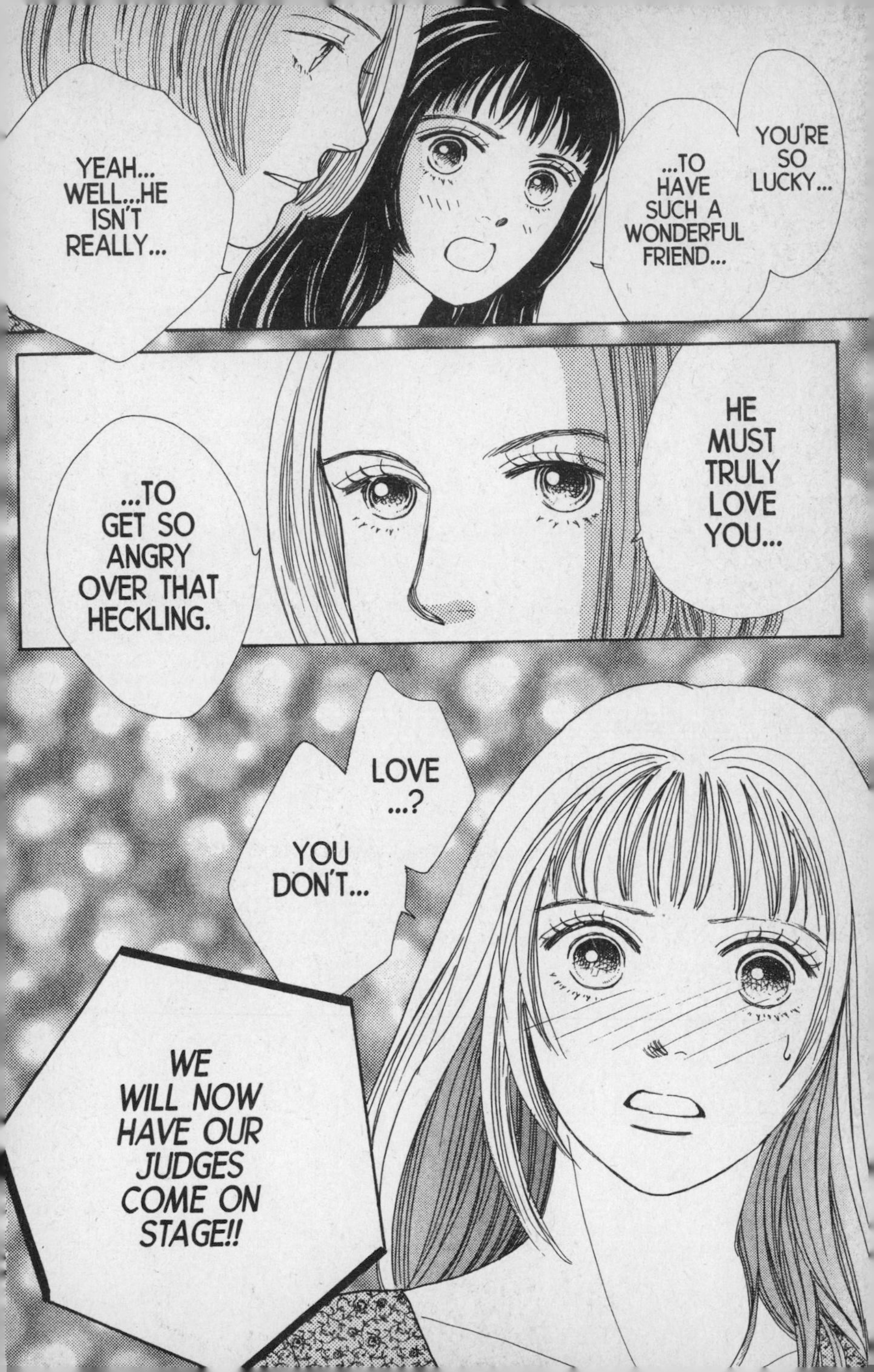
YOU'RE SO LUCKY...
...TO HAVE SUCH A WONDERFUL FRIEND...
YEAH... WELL...HE ISN'T REALLY...
HE MUST TRULY LOVE YOU...
...TO GET SO ANGRY OVER THAT HECKLING.
LOVE ...?
YOU DON'T...
WE WILL NOW HAVE OUR JUDGES COME ON STAGE!!

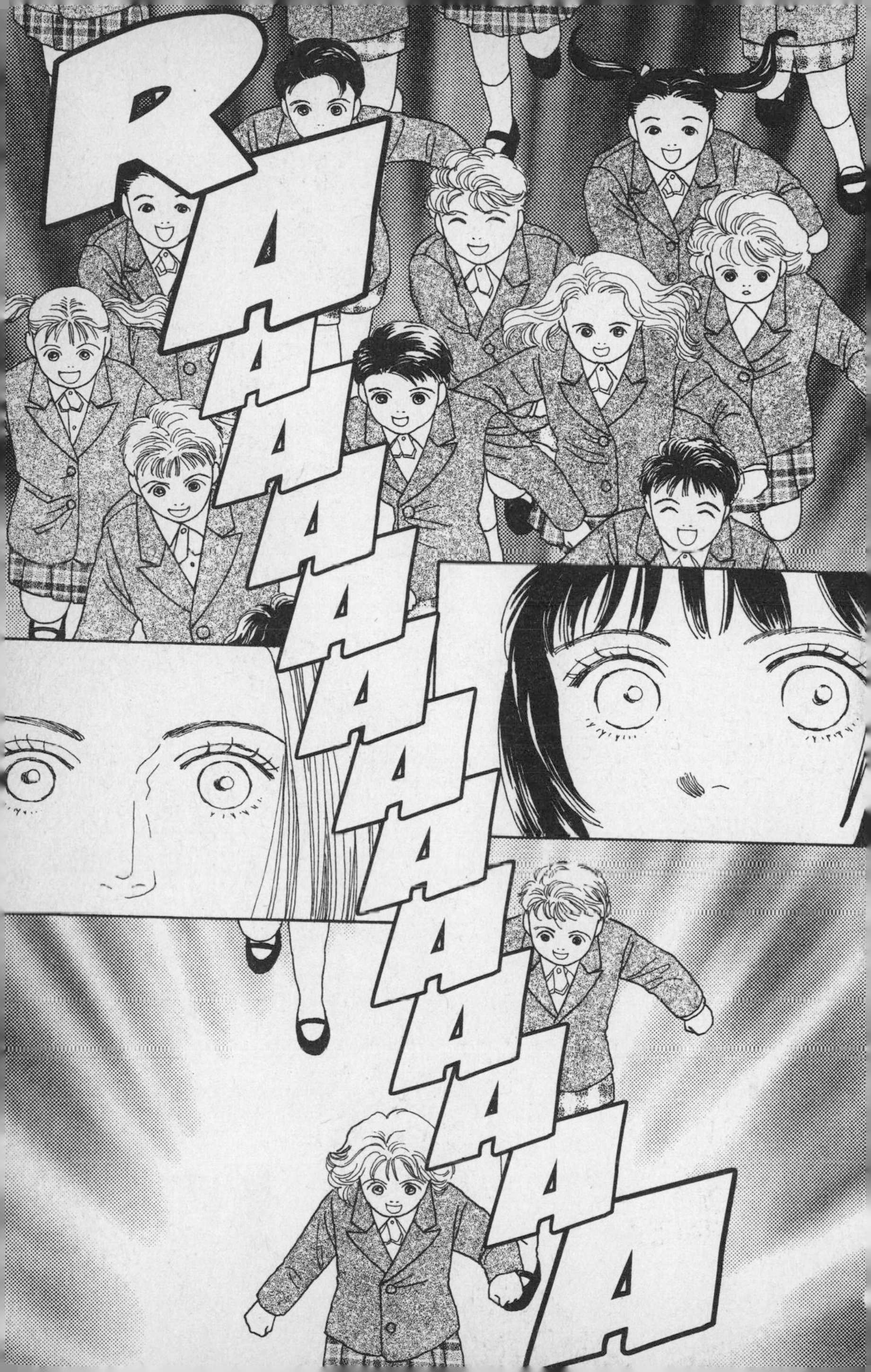
RAAAAAAAAAAAAA

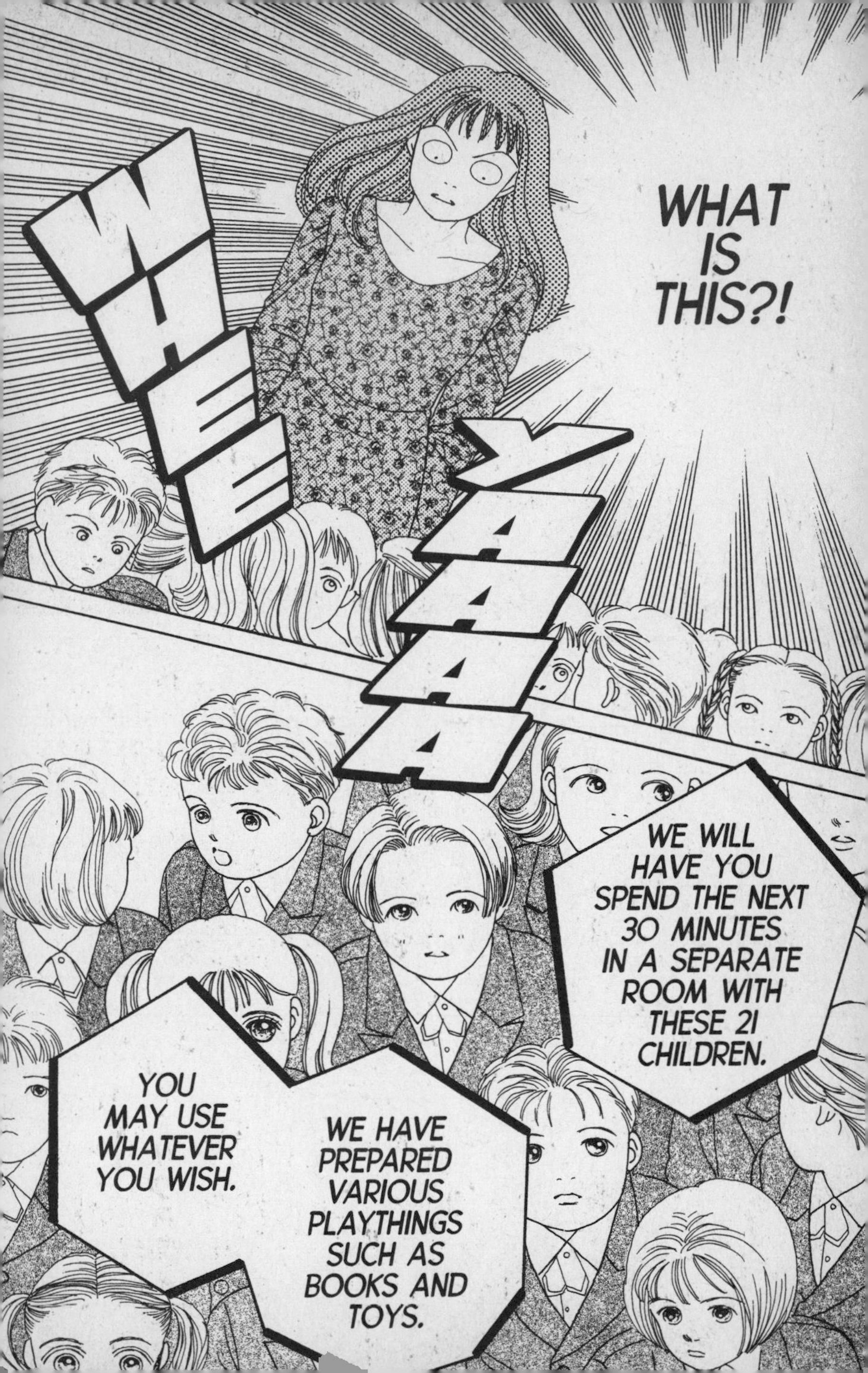
WHAT IS THIS?!
WHEEYAAAA
WE WILL HAVE YOU SPEND THE NEXT 30 MINUTES IN A SEPARATE ROOM WITH THESE 21 CHILDREN.
WE HAVE PREPARED VARIOUS PLAYTHINGS SUCH AS BOOKS AND TOYS.
YOU MAY USE WHATEVER YOU WISH.

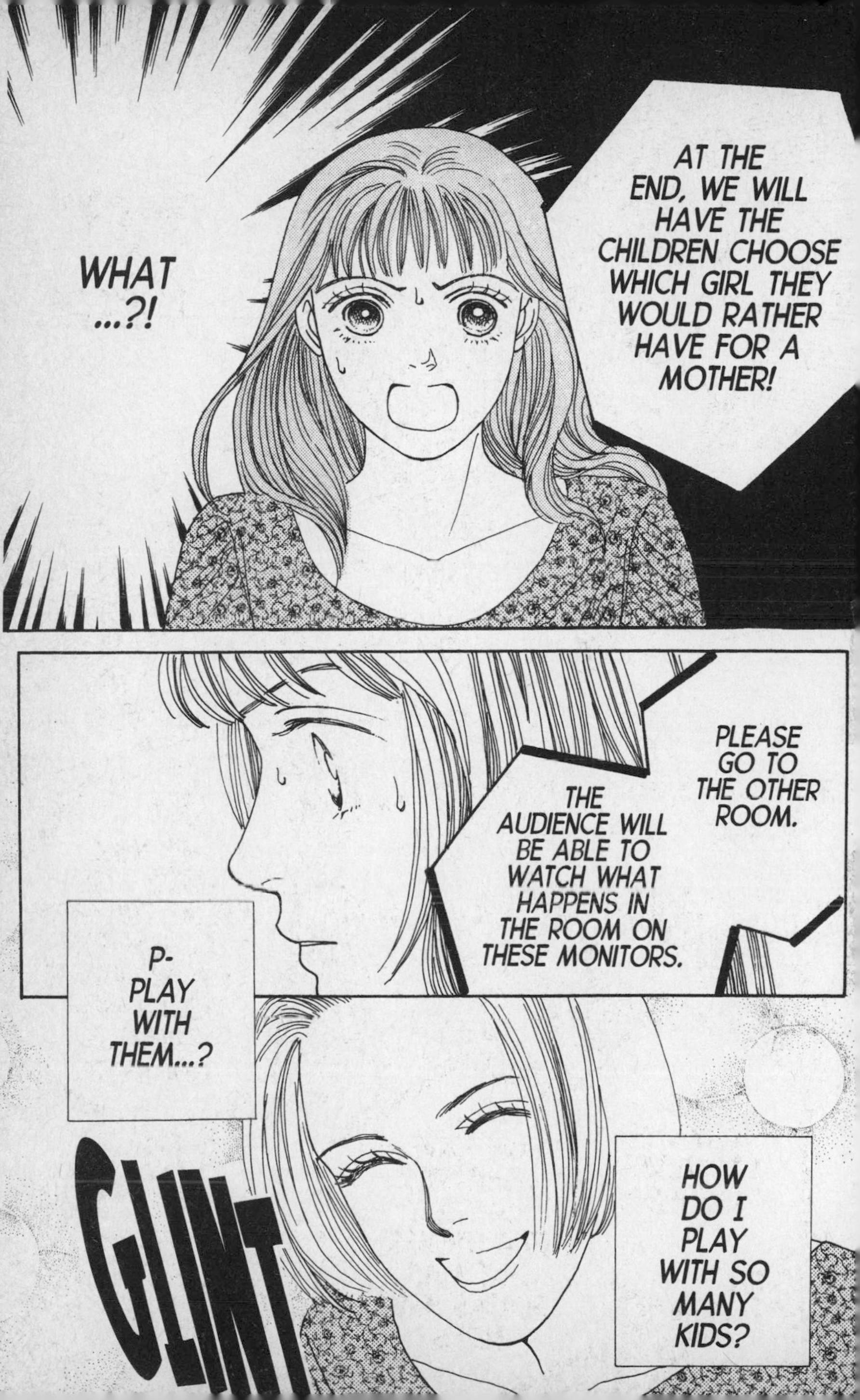
AT THE END, WE WILL HAVE THE CHILDREN CHOOSE WHICH GIRL THEY WOULD RATHER HAVE FOR A MOTHER!
WHAT ...?!
PLEASE GO TO THE OTHER ROOM.
THE AUDIENCE WILL BE ABLE TO WATCH WHAT HAPPENS IN THE ROOM ON THESE MONITORS.
P-PLAY WITH THEM...?
HOW DO I PLAY WITH SO MANY KIDS?
GLINT

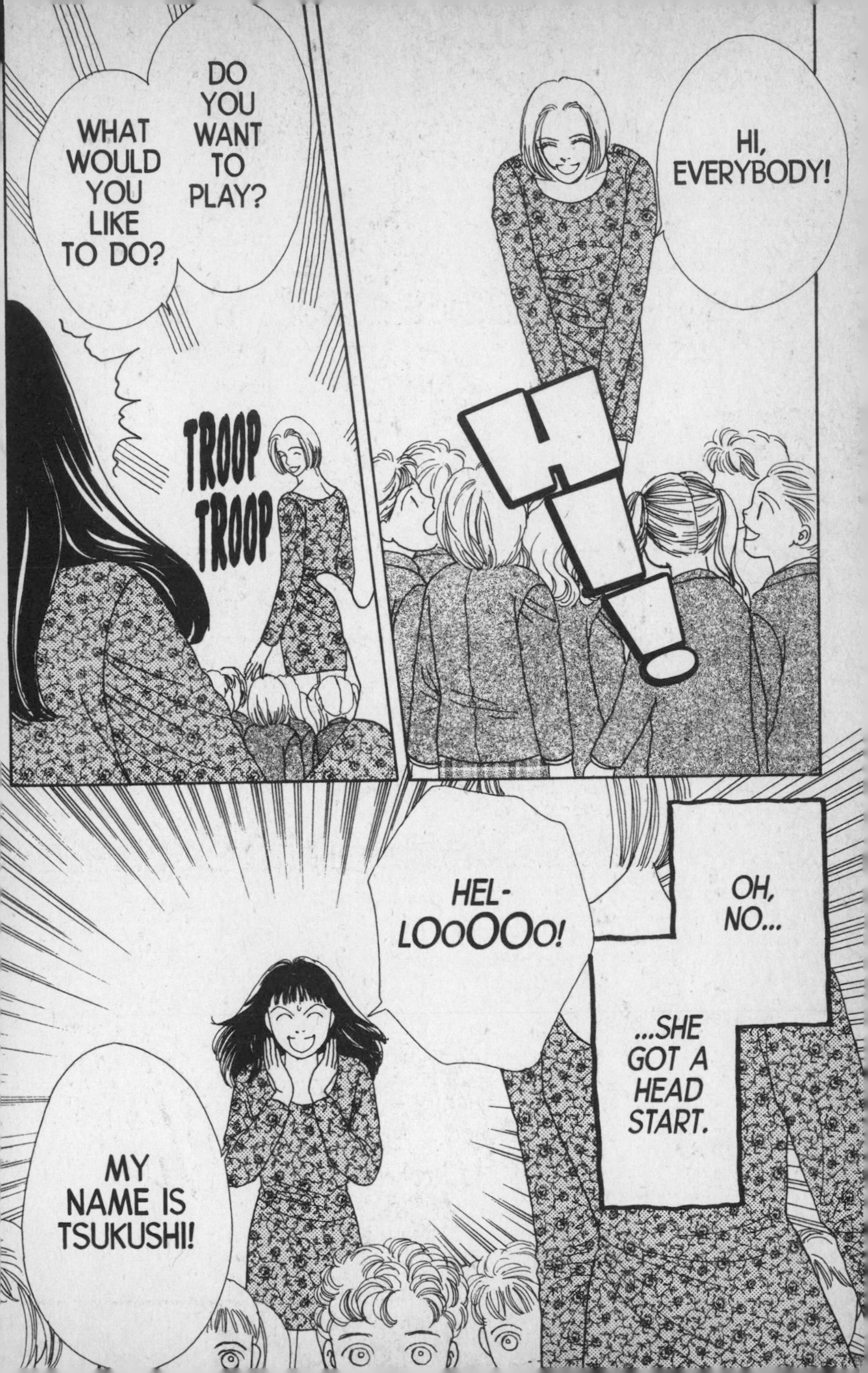
HI, EVERYBODY!
HI!
WHAT WOULD YOU LIKE TO DO?
DO YOU WANT TO PLAY?
TROOP TROOP
OH, NO...
...SHE GOT A HEAD START.
HEL-LOOOOO!
MY NAME IS TSUKUSHI!

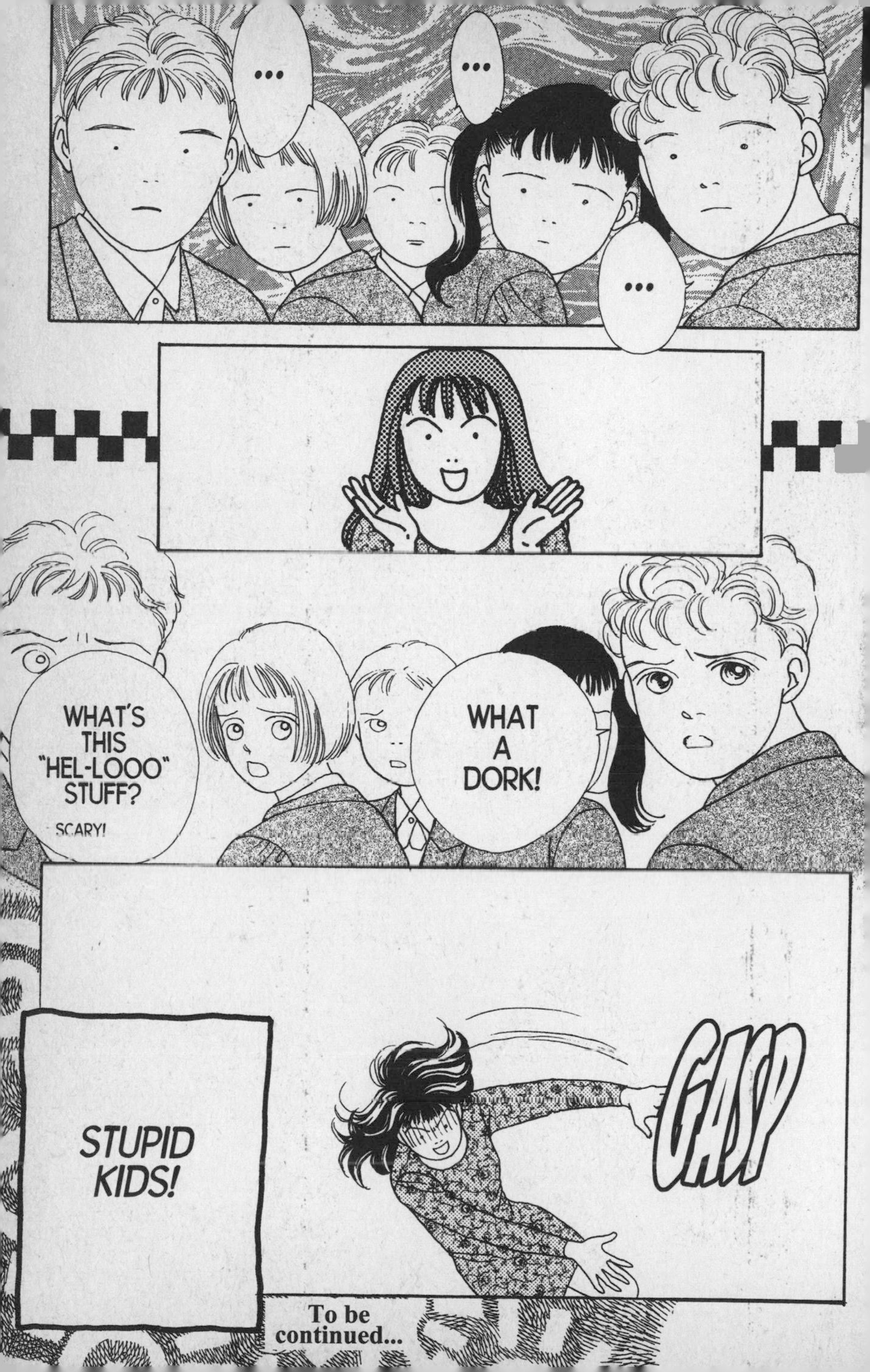
...
...
...
WHAT A DORK!
WHAT'S THIS "HEL-LOOO" STUFF?
SCARY!
GASP
STUPID KIDS!
To be continued...

If you enjoyed this volume of

BOYS over FLOWERS ™
Hana Yori Dango

then here's some more manga you might be interested in.

©1991 Yumi Tamura/ Shogakukan, Inc.

BASARA

Yumi Tamura's *BASARA* is a post-apocalyptic fantasy/adventure series that was one of the most popular shôjo manga of the '90s in Japan. *BASARA* takes place in a very different setting than *BOYS OVER FLOWERS*, but it is similar at its core. They both feature a strong female fighting against an oppressive group. This is the story of how a young girl becomes "the child of destiny," seeking revenge for her dead twin brother. *BASARA* is heavier on the action and lighter on the humor than *BOYS OVER FLOWERS*.

©1992 Yuu Watase/ Shogakukan, Inc.

FUSHIGI YÛGI

In Yû Watase's *FUSHIGI YÛGI* we follow the young girl, Miaka Yuki, as she gets pulled into the world of the book, The Universe of the Four Gods. Within this book is a fictional, ancient Chinese world. In this world she becomes the priestess of the god Suzaku and must find all seven of her Celestial-Warrior protectors. This story is filled with romance and action, with a dash of humor.

©1997 Yuu Watase/ Shogakukan, Inc.

CERES: CELESTIAL LEGEND

Also by Yû Watase, *CERES: CELESTIAL LEGEND* is somewhat darker than *FUSHIGI YÛGI*. Sixteen-year-old Aya Mikage's body houses a legendary power, and her family is determined to kill her in order to suppress it.

COMPLETE OUR SURVEY AND LET US KNOW WHAT YOU THINK!

☐ Please do NOT send me information about VIZ products, news and events, special offers, or other information.

☐ Please do NOT send me information from VIZ's trusted business partners.

Name: _____

Address: _____

City: _____ State: _____ Zip: _____

E-mail: _____

☐ Male ☐ Female Date of Birth (mm/dd/yyyy): ___ / ___ / ___ (Under 13? Parental consent required)

What race/ethnicity do you consider yourself? (please check one)

☐ Asian/Pacific Islander   ☐ Black/African American   ☐ Hispanic/Latino

☐ Native American/Alaskan Native ☐ White/Caucasian   ☐ Other: _____

What VIZ product did you purchase? (check all that apply and indicate title purchased)

☐ DVD/VHS _____

☐ Graphic Novel _____

☐ Magazines _____

☐ Merchandise _____

Reason for purchase: (check all that apply)

☐ Special offer   ☐ Favorite title   ☐ Gift

☐ Recommendation   ☐ Other _____

Where did you make your purchase? (please check one)

☐ Comic store   ☐ Bookstore   ☐ Mass/Grocery Store

☐ Newsstand   ☐ Video/Video Game Store   ☐ Other: _____

☐ Online (site: _____)

What other VIZ properties have you purchased/own? _____

_____

How many anime and/or manga titles have [you purchased in the last year? How many were] **VIZ titles?** (please check one from each column)

ANIME

☐ None

☐ 1-4

☐ 5-10

☐ 11+

MANGA

☐ None

☐ 1-4

☐

☐

☐ 1-4

I find the pricing of VIZ pro[ducts to be:]

☐ Cheap

☐

What genre of manga and a[nime would you like to see more of?]

☐ Adventure

☐ Horror

☐ Romance

☐ Fantasy

☐ Sports

What do you think of VIZ's new look?

☐ Love It   ☐ It's OK   ☐ Hate It   ☐ Didn't Notice   ☐ No Opinion

Which do you prefer? (please check one)

☐ Reading right-to-left

☐ Reading left-to-right

Which do you prefer? (please check one)

☐ Sound effects in English

☐ Sound effects in Japanese with English captions

☐ Sound effects in Japanese only with a glossary at the back

THANK YOU! Please send the completed form to:

NJW Research
42 Catharine St.
Poughkeepsie, NY 12601

All information provided will be used for internal purposes only. We promise not to sell or otherwise divulge your information.